Shakespeare's Double Plays

*Dramatic Economy on the Early
Modern Stage*

Brett Gamboa

Dartmouth College, New Hampshire

CAMBRIDGE
UNIVERSITY PRESS

University Printing House, Cambridge CB2 8BS, United Kingdom

One Liberty Plaza, 20th Floor, New York, NY 10006, USA

477 Williamstown Road, Port Melbourne, VIC 3207, Australia

314–321, 3rd Floor, Plot 3, Splendor Forum, Jasola District Centre,
New Delhi – 110025, India

79 Anson Road, #06-04/06, Singapore 079906

Cambridge University Press is part of the University of Cambridge.

It furthers the University's mission by disseminating knowledge in the pursuit of
education, learning, and research at the highest international levels of excellence.

www.cambridge.org
Information on this title: www.cambridge.org/9781108417433
DOI: 10.1017/9781108277624

© Brett Gamboa 2018

First published 2018

Printed in the United Kingdom by Clays, St Ives plc

A catalogue record for this publication is available from the British Library.

Library of Congress Cataloging-in-Publication Data
Names: Gamboa, Brett, author.
Title: Shakespeare's double plays: dramatic economy on
the Early Modern stage / Brett Gamboa.
Description: Cambridge; New York, NY: Cambridge University Press, 2018. |
Includes bibliographical references and index.
Identifiers: LCCN 2017057297 | ISBN 9781108417433 (hardback)
Subjects: LCSH: Shakespeare, William, 1564–1616 – Stage history. |
Shakespeare, William, 1564–1616 – Dramatic production. |
BISAC: LITERARY CRITICISM / European / English, Irish, Scottish, Welsh.
Classification: LCC PR3091.G36 2018 | DDC 792.9/5–dc23
LC record available at https://lccn.loc.gov/2017057297

ISBN 978-1-108-41743-3 Hardback

Contents

List of Figures   *page* vi
List of Tables   vii
Acknowledgements   viii

Introduction   1

1   'Improbable Fictions': Shakespeare's Plays *without* the Plays   21

2   Versatility and Verisimilitude on Sixteenth-Century Stages   48

3   Doubling in *The Winter's Tale*   85

4   Dramaturgical Directives and Shakespeare's Cast Size   104

5   Doubling in *A Midsummer Night's Dream* and *Romeo and Juliet*   136

6   'What, are they children?': Reconsidering Shakespeare's 'Boy' Actors   156

7   Doubling in *Twelfth Night* and *Othello*   199

Epilogue: Ragozine and Shakespearean Substitution   219

Appendix: Doubling Roles in Shakespeare's Plays   234

Bibliography   272
Index   284

Figures

I.1 Alec Guinness in *Kind Hearts and Coronets* (1949)   *page* 10

2.1 Title page and doubling plan for Ulpian Fulwell's *Like Will to Like* (1587)   68

2.2 Title page and doubling plan for Thomas Preston's *Cambyses* (1569)   73

2.3 Doubling plan for *The Fair Maid of the Exchange* (1607)   76

6.1 Mark Rylance as Cleopatra at Shakespeare's Globe (1999)   161

6.2 'The Names of the Principall Actors in all these Playes', First Folio (1623)   170

6.3 Scene from John Madden's *Shakespeare in Love* (1998)   176

6.4 Panel from the frontispiece to William Alabaster's *Roxana* (1632)   194

Tables

2.1   Plays with casting information, 1560–1610   *page* 59

3.1   Hypothetical doubling plan for Shakespeare's *The Winter's Tale* (c. 1610)   92

4.1   Number of actors necessary to perform Shakespeare's plays (c. 1592–1610)   108

5.1   Hypothetical doubling plan for Shakespeare's *A Midsummer Night's Dream* (c. 1595)   139

5.2   Hypothetical doubling plan for Shakespeare's *Romeo and Juliet* (c. 1595)   146

7.1   Hypothetical doubling plan for Shakespeare's *Twelfth Night* (c. 1601)   201

7.2   Hypothetical doubling plan for Shakespeare's *Othello* (c. 1604)   212

E.1   Hypothetical doubling plan for Shakespeare's *Measure for Measure* (c. 1603)   228

Acknowledgements

This book has been so long in the making that thanking those who inspired or improved it – or just survived it – will take some doing. I am grateful to my editors at Cambridge University Press, both Sarah Stanton (who initially championed the project and embraced its controversial aspects), and Emily Hockley (whose wisdom and patience have been crucial in bringing it to light). Meanwhile, Dawn Preston, Gail Welsh, and other unknown angels are responsible for the text and tables coming out far better than they went in. I am grateful to them, to Sarah Lambert and Tim Mason, and to all who assisted in the publication process. I am also grateful to the most insightful and sacrificial pair of unofficial editors imaginable, Darlene Farabee and Emma Firestone, whose contributions may be fearfully close to eclipsing my own.

My colleagues at Dartmouth – most notably Jonathan Crewe, Alexandra Halasz, and Andrew McCann – offered encouragement and advice that impacted me and the project deeply. I am grateful to each of them, as well as to Adrian Randolph, Barbara Will, and Mike Mastanduno, Dartmouth College deans who ensured that I had sufficient time and financial support. Meanwhile, Laura Neill, Benjamin Riley, and Yi He were smart and dedicated research assistants at Dartmouth who amassed valuable data about the plays and potential performance choices.

I am indebted to colleagues at other institutions, too, who shared comments after reading some or all of the manuscript, or whose willingness to discuss its ideas and their implications influenced the result. These include Tiffany Stern, Lars Engle, Russ McDonald, Lawrence Switzky, Brandon Tilley, Ralph Alan Cohen, James Marino, and Peter Saval. I am also in debt to actors, theatre companies, and directors too numerous to list, for their daring, ingenuity, and insight. I thank, especially, those who have collaborated on Shakespeare productions with me, who taught me much of what informs this book while playing as many as eight roles a night.

This project began as my doctoral thesis at Harvard, where I was fortunate to find advisers whose interest helped to validate the work in my eyes, and whose guidance made it seem possible and even pleasant to work on. Their examples of curiosity and selfless attention continue to influence me every day. Their names are Marjorie Garber, Stephen Greenblatt, and Elaine Scarry.

Those familiar with the topic of doubling roles may anticipate my debt to Stephen Booth. That debt is inexpressible. My undergraduate mentor and a dear friend, Stephen taught me about art and artifice by teaching me to care more about the truth. I was fortunate that he liked my undergraduate thesis; I was at least as fortunate that he thought it was a mess.

My wife deserved better while I was writing this book. But she never let on that she knew it. While not performing eye surgery or rearing up daughters, she doubled as a costumer, set builder, and the graphic designer who made the charts in the Appendix. Her name is Gladys Lee. '... only I have left to say, / More is thy due than more than all can pay' (*Macbeth*, 1.4.20–1).

Last are my daughters, Bayan and Parisa, to whom this book is dedicated, and whose roles in inspiring (and protracting) its delivery are more significant than they will ever know.

> ... and our daughter,
> In honour of whose birth these triumphs are,
> Sits here like beauty's child, whom nature gat
> For men to see and, seeing, wonder at.
> (*Pericles*, 2.2.4–7)

Introduction

ॐ℃४
Methinks I see these things with parted eye,
When everything seems double.
~Hermia, *A Midsummer Night's Dream*, 4.1.187–8[1]
ॐ℃४

Shakespeare is well known for attempting to enhance his audience's experience by recourse to what Samuel Johnson called 'quibbles' and what we commonly call puns. Puns occur when language reaches points of poly-signification, when the minds of audiences following a distinct strand of information find themselves simultaneously settled into two or more concurrent realms of coherence. Puns permit audiences to follow one road to two cities, to equate polarities, to hear with parted ears.

A central concern of this book is how Shakespeare puns with his *actors*. Like words, actors often carry two or more simultaneously pertinent associations or identities, allowing spectators to perform the logically impossible act of perceiving two entirely separable actions as one. For instance, they see David Tennant working at his job as an actor in the same moment that they see Hamlet coping with his situation in Elsinore. Such theatrical conventions as disguise, cross-dressing, impersonation, and plays within plays all manifest the fundamental pun or paradox of the actor: that actors plainly are not the characters they present, and they are those characters too. But nothing enlivens this paradox like doubling, wherein actors take on more than one role in the same play.[2]

---

[1] Except where otherwise indicated, citations are from *The Norton Shakespeare*, 3rd ed., ed. Stephen Greenblatt, Walter Cohen, Jean E. Howard, and Katharine Eisaman Maus (New York: W.W. Norton, 2016). All citations from *King Lear*, however, are drawn from the conflated text in the Norton's 2nd edition (2008).

[2] By 'doubling' I mean multiple employments for actors (tripling, quadrupling, etc.) that allow spectators to recognize the actor through the persona. Not every spectator will recognize every actor playing a secondary role, of course. But just as audiences of *Measure for Measure* recognize the Duke in the friar's habit, though other characters do not, so actors that double in

My book's central premise is that Shakespeare's plays were designed to be more engaging, more pleasurable, sometimes even more credible for audiences when played by ten or 12 actors than they can be when played by 20. I suggest that just as Shakespeare transformed extant plots and stories into masterworks, so he adopted and improved upon the theatrical convention of doubling, orchestrating possibilities for thematic patterning and resonance between or among characters through the unifying agent of a single actor who doubles in those roles. So, if a production of *Hamlet* redeploys the actor who played Polonius as First Gravedigger, then the philosophical and comic exchanges between the 'antically disposed' Hamlet and a comparatively sober Polonius are revived and reversed by the graveside conversation between Hamlet and the Polonius *actor*, the latter having taken Hamlet's former comic literalism as his own, in his new role of Gravedigger. Doubling fosters replications and patterns within the plays, but does so by relying on the audience's ongoing experience of reality alongside its attention to fiction. Because it triggers mainsprings of theatrical attraction by layering the actor-character's core duality, and makes urgently present the potential for theatrical collapse, doubling should be understood as an integral part of Shakespeare's theatrical vision. Indeed, the centrality of doubling to Shakespeare's art has never been fully explored, either on stage or in the academy.

One of my fundamental assumptions in writing this book is that audiences are attracted to actors because they act. Though that idea may seem obvious or redundant, we sometimes overestimate the degree to which our interest in theatre depends on our commitments to *fiction*; that is, to the characters, to their aims and obstacles, to their role in advancing a plot, to the ideas they express. I maintain, though, that the chief contribution actors make to the theatre is the simple, subtle, continuous assertion that they are people that they are not. This essential duplicity allows audiences to experience pun-like pleasure in tracking separable identities and independent realms of coherence at one point of perception, each vying for primacy, each implicitly questioning and threatening the other, even while combining to perpetuate an illusion that is more valuable for the resulting instability. The ever-present *reminder* of the actor – a reminder that the narrative and its characters are illusory and ephemeral, constantly imperiled by the actors themselves – along with the audience's inability to avoid intrusions of the 'real' world (over which the fictional one maintains an ever-tenuous provenance), accounts for a major share of theatrical

---

secondary roles will often be recognized in those roles. I discuss below the critical divide created by what Alan Armstrong has called 'candid doubling'. See 'Doubling in *The Comedy of Errors*', in *Shaping Shakespeare for Performance: The Bear Stage*, ed. Catherine Loomis and Sid Ray (Lanham: Fairleigh Dickinson University Press, 2016), pp. 189–202. The phrase 'candid doubling' first appears on p. 189.

attraction. As J.B. Priestley explains in *The Art of the Dramatist*: 'Everybody and everything on the stage have double character; they are seen in the strange light and shadow of belief and disbelief; they belong to a heightened reality that we know to be unreal.'[3] Every spectator receives every actor with Hermia's 'parted eye, / When everything seems double' (4.1.187–8), since the actor exists in the real world as a fellow human being, while simultaneously participating in an alternate, imaginary realm.

The actor's duplicity and the theatre's unreality are essential to all theatrical experience, but no plays exploit them so extensively and so variously as Shakespeare's do. Among the most famous examples is the character of Rosalind in *As You Like It*, originally performed by a male. Rosalind, already merging reality and unreality, man and woman, dresses as Ganymede, an ambiguously gendered page, who then 'pretends' to be Rosalind (while in men's clothing) for Rosalind's lover Orlando. The audience may see Rosalind as less authentic than the actor portraying her, yet more authentic, in the context of the fiction, than Ganymede, since Ganymede is Rosalind's façade. However, Ganymede enacts *another* 'Rosalind' who is, it follows, more *and* less deceptive than Ganymede him/herself. Ganymede thus resides inside and outside Rosalind, and the audience sees all in one, all at once. The thickly layered effect is analogous to watching a child assemble Russian nesting dolls, building multiplicity and dimension into a single point of perception.

Furthermore, as Marjorie Garber and others have pointed out, Ganymede is more than the sum of its parts, since it conjoins maleness and femaleness, while versions of the dramatis personae it encompasses subscribe to a single gender.[4] Ganymede thus more aptly, perhaps more authentically, represents the (male) actor-as-Rosalind than either Rosalind herself, or the actor alone. The spectator watches *As You Like It* 'with parted eye', since the transvestite; the actor; Rosalind; and Rosalind-twice-removed are joined in a single face. Shakespeare here seizes upon the prime animator of all theatricality – the duality of the actor – and confers upon it a third and fourth dimension. Dr. Johnson famously deplored the 'malignant power' that puns held over Shakespeare's mind: how 'A quibble was to him the fatal *Cleopatra* for which he lost the world, and was content to lose it.'[5] If Rosalind may be admitted among the other puns, this was not a bad bargain.

---

[3] J.B. Priestley, *The Art of the Dramatist* (London: Heinemann, 1957), p. 178.

[4] Marjorie Garber, *Vested Interests: Cross-Dressing and Cultural Anxiety* (New York: Routledge, 1992), pp. 72-8.

[5] Samuel Johnson, *The Yale Edition of the Works of Samuel Johnson. Volume VII. Johnson on Shakespeare*, ed. Arthur Sherbo (New Haven and London: Yale University Press, 1968), p. 74. In *Quotation Marks*, Garber dedicates a chapter to 'Fatal Cleopatra', describing the protean

Doubling roles allowed Shakespeare to achieve Rosalind-like effects from most of his actors and in nearly every moment of his plays. In performance, doubling enables audiences to experience contradictions and inconsistencies that paradoxically affirm the authenticity of characters, allowing heroes to re-emerge as villains, men to become women, and fools to become wise. Frequently, such transitions and oscillations complement, intensify, and/or counteract developments in the plots themselves. Doubling roles can also create analogues outside the fictional frame for plots and characters otherwise animated by inconsistencies. For example, the plot of *Macbeth* prescribes audiences the generic duty to welcome the fall of a usurping tyrant and the rise of a rightful king, though it endows Macbeth with kingly attributes while granting Malcolm all the majesty of wallpaper.[6] Though morally repulsive, Macbeth attracts; though victimized and full of virtues, Malcolm repels. Shakespeare thus puns with his characters, thrusting spectators into a realm where contradictory possibilities cohere. Similar tensions arising from simultaneous attraction and repulsion can be manifested if the actor playing old Hamlet's Ghost returns as Claudius; if Othello's white wife returns as a whore named Bianca; if Angelo is really exchanged for Claudio by having one actor portray both. As a result of such choices, the stage personae in Shakespeare's plays grow more life-like in their complexity, alternately (even simultaneously) cruel and kind, innocent and guilty, masculine and feminine. This heightened experience of 'realism', though, is brought about by more aggressive assertions of artifice.

Establishing Realism and Credibility through Artifice

In *Performing Remains*, Rebecca Schneider suggests that theatricality, the admission of artifice in the artefact, brings us closer to the way things really are than realism does, providing a sense of the real that everyday 'reality' cannot, since reality is always already a citation of something else:

[A]ny enactment might be recognized as re-enactment – recognized as a matter of againness – through the manipulation of give-away signs of theatricality. Here a wiggle of a hand or a wink of an eye are theatrical gestures that give a scene away, prompting the recognition that seemingly discrete acts are never temporally singular nor straightforward but double, triple, or done 'a million times before'.[7]

---

nature of Cleopatra, and of many other characters. She suggests that for Shakespeare 'character' is a kind of paradox with 'two equal and opposite connotations' (New York: Routledge, 2002), pp. 211–30.

[6] Stephen Booth raises the Macbeth/Malcolm problem in 'The Shakespearean Actor as Kamikaze Pilot', *Shakespeare Quarterly* 36 (1985), pp. 553–70.

[7] Rebecca Schneider, *Performing Remains: Art and War in Times of Theatrical Reenactment* (London: Routledge, 2011), p. 32.

For Schneider, performance and theatricality illuminate a limitless cycle of duplications, wherein everything reaches back to some original that itself reaches back to some other. Because it shows awareness of its own manufacture, performance can seem more real than reality, which is comparatively blind to its own 'againness'. Thus artifice that acknowledges itself as such – that preserves and accentuates its inconsistencies – may present audiences with a more potent means to access the 'real' than naturalism or emotional truth.

Shakespeare seems to have intuited that the audience is the locus of reality in the theatre, and that its experience of the real is synonymous with its experience of the instability of his fictional worlds. If, as Bill Worthen has argued, 'the site of drama is the site of acting', the 'drama' initiated by actors may be one of ever-present or impending exposures of artifice – essentially their unavoidable failures at convincing acts of mimesis intensify an experience fundamentally charged by the audience's doubts about whether events will continue or fall apart in the present performance.[8] During a 2008 performance of *King Lear* in New York City's Battery Park, for instance, the actress playing Goneril sprinted off-stage, rounded a magnolia tree, tripped, and fell face-first on the concrete walk. The exit was the last one scripted for her character, just moments before her death offstage. This Goneril actor drew most of the audience's attention away from Edmund's confession as she limped away in the care of Gloucester (already deceased), and she did not return for the bows. The absence of that injured actor haunted the close of the performance even more than the death of Cordelia. Moments like this one are neither easily contrived, nor, strictly, desirable. Yet all productions of all plays are animated by similar potentials.

Our awareness of the theatre's potential to fail, constantly advertised by the slippage inherent in acts of representation and intensified by Shakespeare's recurrent efforts to undermine his illusions, makes us cling to them more fiercely, as if involved in personal dramas wherein our continued access to the fiction is at stake. The more the illusion flirts with its ruin, the more engaged in it the audience grows. This paradox in spectatorship operates not merely because of the theatre's unreality, but because each audience's flirtations with that unreality bring out a sense of the real, and a performance of the real, in that audience. In this context, an actor may thrive in each role he performs precisely insofar as he can be perceived as fractured or imperfect. Marc Robinson hints at this when he argues that the most interesting modern plays 'fail at "effacing the medium", a failure that directs spectators to the drama of "disclosing" as much as to anything disclosed'.[9] A 'drama of

---

[8] W.B. Worthen, *The Idea of the Actor: Drama and the Ethics of Performance* (Princeton: Princeton University Press, 1984), p. 3.
[9] Marc Robinson, *The American Play 1787–2000* (New Haven: Yale University Press, 2009), p. 117; the quoted phrase is Worthen's.

disclosing' is one in which the audience participates as a protagonist; at stake is the question of how, indeed whether, the production will succeed at all.

The ongoing potential for drama at and beyond the margins of fiction, and the vital role that the fractured identities of stage figures plays in our experience of realism, indicate that directors and actors might do well to resist logical impulses to impose sense and consistency on characters whose inconsistencies are part of their attraction. Furthermore, artists might improve their productions by exploiting what Schneider calls 'give-away signs of theatricality'. Some opportunities loudly assert themselves (e.g. Hermione's statue, Dover's cliff, even Crab the dog), but most appear in the natural course of portraying characters, since so many contradict the emotional templates they initially, or most forcefully, suggest. In his essay on character and subjectivity in *Faultlines*, Alan Sinfield suggests that Shakespeare's characters often cannot be understood 'as essential unities'; rather, for Shakespeare, 'character is a strategy ... one that will be abandoned when it interferes with other desiderata'.[10] Sinfield cites Desdemona as an example of a character that encompasses a 'disjointed sequence of positions', each in conflict with the last, arguing that such characters resist being received as psychologically whole or unified.

Doubling can complement and extend the dimensionality of characters as well as actors, routinely multiplying the contrarieties of character that Sinfield describes. Actors doubling roles can create implicit comparisons between characters; reconcile opposing voices, interests, or loyalties; offer *self*-reflections about *other* characters in the fiction; and introduce the density of structural patterning usually witnessed at the level of line, scene, or plot to (and across) characters. Doubling thus allows for thematic and theatrical enhancement, while making the illusion both more engaging and more credible by announcing its ephemerality. Moreover, doubling roles allows actors to seem to divide themselves *as actors*, in a manner similar to the central fracture that produces the actor-as-character. Since actors participate in the 'real' world of the audience, their double employment resembles but *is not* the double employment (acting or cross-dressing) of the actor-as-character. Nor does it quite parallel the adoption of roles by characters within fictions. The double-cast actor, such as one playing Ghost/Claudius, gains dimension inside the fiction (because the first character he portrays is implicitly linked and compared to the second) and outside of it (because his portrayal of the first – technique, voice, bearing, etc. – is intimately related

---

[10] Alan Sinfield, *Faultlines* (Berkeley: University of California Press, 1992), p. 78. Tiffany Stern makes a related argument, suggesting that Shakespeare's characters were generic types in service to the plot rather than individualized personas, noting the frequency with which speech prefixes distinguish characters by such titles as 'King, Queen, Bastard, Fool', etc. See *Making Shakespeare: From Stage to Play* (London: Routledge, 2004), pp. 61–7.

to and yet often different from that of the second), thus rendering two discrete but unified versions of the actor-as-character. Analogous to Ganymede, who wears Rosalind within and without, the actor playing multiple roles in one play has divided duties in and out of the fiction, and the spectator sees three or more in one.

Doubling from Medieval to Modern Times

Hans-Georg Gadamer argues that the Holy Trinity is something of a high-water mark in western culture for thinking about the unthinkable – another way of describing the superordinary feats of mind that figures like Rosalind, or actors doubling Claudius/Ghost or Desdemona/Bianca, make possible for spectators.[11] The idea that the 'son of man' can simultaneously be the 'son of God', as well as a spirit that connects the two and pervades the universe, is markedly like the idea that opposites such as Claudius and old Hamlet – a pair, the play informs us, distinguishable by looks, moral behaviour, and ontological status – can be unified by a common actor, yet a third identity.[12] Setting aside its theological or metaphysical implications, it may be that the historical fascination with the trinity owes something to the simple desire of those who entertain it to resolve a riddle: to experience (repeatedly) their own capacities to harmonize multiple and contradictory personas at a single point of perception or understanding. Spectators who see actors doubling roles also see three faces in one, a lone figure that asserts two supplementary metaphysical realities. Like religious believers, spectators undertake a temporary exercise in faith by accepting a logical fallacy animated by its riddle-like interest and ongoing instability, and that interest grows when actors play additional roles.

It is not surprising that English theatre owes much to liturgical precedents like the *Quem Queritis*, whose crowning moment comforts and delights audiences by assuring them that Christ is present *because* he is absent from the tomb. If manifesting the divine was good theatre, manifesting a divine presence through an absence may have been better, particularly for audiences

---

[11] In Hans-Georg Gadamer, *The Relevance of the Beautiful and Other Essays* (Cambridge: Cambridge University Press, 1986).

[12] Several critics have thought about Elizabethan theatricality and its engagement with Catholic theology and devotional practice. Anthony Dawson writes on how the statue scene in *The Winter's Tale* engages spectators in a dialectic of faith and disbelief, describing audience engagement as analogous to Eucharistic participation; see *The Culture of Playgoing in Shakespeare's England* (Cambridge: Cambridge University Press, 2005), pp. 11–37. Gail M. Gibson originated the phrase 'incarnational aesthetic' in *The Theatre of Devotion* (Chicago: University of Chicago Press, 1989), while Sarah Beckwith suggests that Shakespeare's theatre 'represents … the resistance of (religion's) historical concerns in the incarnation of performance', in 'Stephen Greenblatt's *Hamlet* and the Forms of Oblivion', *Journal of Medieval and Early Modern Studies*, 33 (2003), 261–80, p. 275.

weaned on such riddling ideas as letting the (living) 'dead bury their dead' (Luke 9:60). Christian paradoxes helped early playwrights intuit, as priests and pastors had before them, how engagement could be enhanced when one physical body simultaneously indicates two or more metaphysical realities. Just as the Dionysian theatre took shape when two actors emerged from the chorus and created a three-part conflict from a unified source, and just as Jesus was thought to inhere valences of man, God, *and* Holy Spirit in one face, so too – as early playwrights came to understand – if two identities were good for actors, then three (or more) were better.

Though doubling roles has not received the critical attention it warrants, it has always been a prominent consideration in the theatre. For the ancient Greeks, masks allowed actors to take on multiple characters, foregrounding the illusion in the act of its construction. The fixed countenances of masks allowed spectators to piece out performances with their thoughts, the masks serving as blank slates upon which spectators could mentally inscribe expressions momentarily suited to the speaker, without losing sight of the generic position, or disposition, of the character. But while masks may have facilitated voice projection and presented larger (and more visible) features, they also let the best actors do more acting. Noh drama, *Commedia*, and early Mystery plays sometimes used masks for similar ends. These lead the way for Bunraku and puppet theatres, the latter further complicating the actor/character by dividing the actor's voice from the site of representation (the puppet).[13]

Medieval drama thrived in England because of a belief that nearly anything could be represented on a small wagon or scaffold.[14] Its comfort with an openly artificial style of representation influenced Tudor and Elizabethan playwrights, giving rise to a fascination with disguise plays and those featuring actors, scenes, and plays – *within* scenes and plays.[15] This fascination was greater as a result of England's single-gendered theatre, which added dimension to the actor/character on another axis. All-male casts built hierarchies of truth within frameworks of falsehood, allowing audiences to harmonize stage figures with the metaphysical realities they represented, while remaining aware that the gap between actors and characters was wider for those playing female roles than it generally was for those playing males. Doubling roles became conventional for practical reasons – the pool of qualified actors was limited, and adding

---

[13] Heinrich von Kleist, 'On the Puppet Theater', in *Selected Writings*, ed. and trans. David Constantine (Indianapolis: Hackett Publishing, 2004), pp. 411–16.

[14] See Peter Travis, *Dramatic Design in the Chester Cycle* (Chicago: University of Chicago Press, 1982).

[15] For a discussion of the prevalence of disguise and its theatrical effects, see Peter Hyland, *Disguise on the Early Modern English Stage* (Farnham: Ashgate, 2011).

actors to a troupe meant sharing profits with them – but it created opportunities for playwrights to complicate the actor's paradox still further, exposing the reality of the actor while increasing his range and capacity to signify, and creating tacit links between characters that could potentially support a play's thematic ends.

As a modern theatrical practice, of course, doubling is hardly 'fringe'. It has proven consistently popular with audiences and a rich source of theatrical power for companies producing Shakespeare's plays. Peter Brook's 1970 production of *A Midsummer Night's Dream*, in which the Lords and Ladies of Athens doubled their counterparts in the faerie world, is among the most admired and influential in history.[16] Most contemporary companies double roles, at least as an expedient, and some have explored doubling's potential to inform and comment on the play in question, including Cheek by Jowl, the American Shakespeare Center, Propeller, and Shakespeare's Globe.[17] Likewise, modern films suggest a continuing desire to see actors play multiple roles. Bollywood, the prolific film industry of Mumbai, has produced a huge number of films that cast single actors as pairs of twin brothers or sisters, a ghost of a princess and a living princess-to-be, a father and his son, many of these resembling Shakespeare's plots in their efforts to exploit dualities of situation, setting, character, and actor.[18] These films are so numerous as to make up a genre, and it is considered something of a rite of passage for Bollywood actors to star opposite themselves, such as when Priyanka Chopra played each of 12 eligible women in *What's Your Raashee?* (2009).[19]

Major stars such as Amitabh Bachchan and Hema Malini have played multiple roles, arguing for the appeal of seeing the best actors do more acting, as well as for seeing fictions flaunt their own fictionality through double-casting. Significantly, Bollywood films are known for routinely interrupting their plots

---

[16] See Jeremy Lopez, 'Dream: The Performance History', in *A Midsummer Night's Dream: A Critical Guide*, ed. Regina Buccola (London: Continuum, 2010), pp. 44–73.

[17] Declan Donnelan and Nick Ormerod formed Cheek by Jowl in 1981. The company has been influential in using prominent casting choices (e.g. Adrian Lester as Rosalind) to highlight artifice, and to complement or undercut the thematic import of the plays. Ralph Cohen and Jim Warren founded Shenandoah Shakespeare Express (later the American Shakespeare Center) in 1988, a touring troupe that typically used casts of 12 actors. Edward Hall began Propeller Theatre Company in 1997, using small, all-male casts and frequent doubling. Shakespeare's Globe opened in 1997 with Mark Rylance as artistic director and lead actor. Under Rylance, the Globe made experiments with 'original practices', some using all-male or all-female casts. Though Rylance tended to employ larger casts than the others, he occasionally doubled major roles like Posthumus and Cloten in *Cymbeline* (2001).

[18] *Encyclopaedia of Hindi Cinema*, ed. Govind Nihalani Gulzar and Saibal Chatterjee (Mumbai: Popular Prakashan, 2003), Introduction.

[19] Ibid., p. 189.

Figure I.1 In *Kind Hearts and Coronets* (1949), Alec Guinness stars as all eight members of the D'Ascoyne family, including Lady Agatha.

with spontaneous (yet highly choreographed) songs and dances, another intrusion of artifice that can contribute to engagement. English-language films have also frequently featured actors playing multiple roles, including *Kind Hearts and Coronets* (Alec Guinness plays nine roles, including 'Lady Agatha'), *Coming to America* (a young Eddie Murphy plays four, including an old, white, Jewish man), and *Cloud Atlas* (Tom Hanks, Halle Berry, and most of the other cast members play more than one role).[20] Indeed, a wide array of popular films – *Tootsie* (1982), *Victor Victoria* (1982), *Joe versus the Volcano* (1990), *Mrs. Doubtfire* (1993), *Face/Off* (1997), *Cockpit* (2012), and *Dallas Buyer's Club* (2012) among others – double roles or otherwise exploit the actor's

---

[20] Among contemporary examples, the science-fiction series *Orphan Black* (2013–17) has the lead character play several identical figures, achieving similar effects to doubling despite the premise of cloning explaining the actor's reappearance. *Westworld* (2016–) reverses the trope, creating a fictional world populated by androids who can be substituted for one another in the same fictional roles. Meanwhile, many popular YouTube channels use technology to allow one actor to alternate between characters or appear as more than one character simultaneously.

duplicity to generate dramatic energy. Sketch comedy and comic impersonations present variations on this theme. All attest to the continued attraction of the practice for writers and producers, as well as for audiences, who seem to experience a qualitative difference watching one actor perform multiple roles in the same fiction, as opposed to watching a production that assigns each role to a different actor.

Shakespeare's Double Plays

Throughout his career Shakespeare experimented with intensifying the energies inherent in live theatre by adding dimensions to the actor-character, and by imperilling his theatrical illusions by advertising their artifice. Doubling allowed him to achieve both ends simultaneously, thereby amplifying the fundamental tension between the world of the play and that of the playhouse. Many critics have noticed the attractions created by instability and ambiguity in Shakespeare's language, and how his plays exploit the inherent paradox of acting. Yet this book, more forcefully and thoroughly than any study published to date, asserts how absolutely integral the logic of theatrical doubling is to Shakespeare's unique sense of the dramatic.

My first chapter begins by describing the peculiar position of the Polonius actor, whose role in 2.1 seems designed to destabilize the play: 'And then, sir, does 'a this: 'a does – / What was I about to say? By the mass, I was about to say something—where did I leave?' (2.1.48–50). The lines invite the character to behave like a stage actor who has suddenly gone out of his part, an instance which exemplifies a theory of theatrical attraction – implicit throughout Shakespeare's plays – that disturbing the integrity of illusions leads audiences to engage with them more intensely. Intuiting that audiences are energized by uncertainties associated with the actor's ontological status, Shakespeare appears to have sought to blend the real and the imaginary through such means as having characters forget their parts; suspending resolution concerning 'dead' characters like Desdemona and Cordelia; or creating ambiguities about the symbolic function of the stage, as when the blinded Gloucester visits Dover.

Since theatre is an art energized by constantly staving off its own disintegration, doubling roles provides an unparalleled means of enhancing its fundamental attractions. The recitation of verse speeches – openly artificial compositions – attests to both the coherence of the character and the hypocrisy of the speaker, just as doubling roles destabilizes the illusion while asserting the comparative truth of the eclipsed character. Doubling admits the fiction of the fiction while implicitly arguing for the primal 'reality' of the character being cancelled. For instance, if the actors playing Theseus and Hippolyta emerge as Oberon and Titania, their new identities both advertise the fictionality of Theseus and Hippolyta *and* insist that the two actors are 'really' Theseus and Hippolyta – as opposed to Oberon and Titania. Essentially, the audience credits the fiction as a result of it becoming more incredible. Doubling, then, allowed Shakespeare a means to indicate the artificiality of the theatre at each moment, haunting spectators with their awareness that the illusion is only an illusion and might be disrupted or dispelled as easily as *The Murder of Gonzago* is by Claudius's call for lights. Yet the haunted illusions that result gain a greater pretension to something like truth because of the hierarchies established within them. Chapter 1 concludes with a discussion of *Hamlet*, first as a dramatic vehicle enlivened by seemingly gratuitous disruptions of the theatrical frame, and second as a well-known text that features inviting prospects for doubling roles throughout its dramatis personae.

Having argued the potential for doubling to intensify and proliferate attractions fundamental to acting and theatre, and having also presented doubling as a device particularly germane to Shakespeare's plays, the book pivots in the second chapter towards a consideration of the historical case for doubling in Shakespeare's time. In the wake of David Bevington's work on medieval and Tudor dramaturgy, the chapter considers how sixteenth-century plays called on actors to double with increasing intricacy, economy, and daring. In the first half of the century, plays average two or three roles per actor. The morality play *Mundus et Infans* (1522), for instance, uses two actors for five roles. By the time Shakespeare could have attended plays as a child, actors were far more versatile. The average ratio rises to four roles per man in the 1560s, and Thomas Lupton's *All for Money* (1577) divides 20 roles among just four actors. Hence, as plays grew in length and companies grew in size, the stipulated ratio of dramatis personae to cast size in published plays increases considerably. Drawing on the dramaturgical evidence of printed plays offered 'for acting', as well as extant promptbooks and plots; actor lists and charters for the Lord Chamberlain's/King's Men; first-hand accounts from early modern playgoers; the economics of commercial playing companies; and textual and dramaturgical evidence in plays popular during Shakespeare's formative years as a playwright; alongside my reassessment of the evidence regarding roles allotted to boys, hired men, and sharers, I argue that frequent, ingenious, and economical doubling deserves greater consideration as a fundamental part of Shakespeare's playmaking. Along the way, I examine evidence suggesting dramaturgical and casting practices that run counter to conventional theatre-historical narratives: showing, for instance, that lead actors and sharers often were expected to play multiple roles; that actors took male and female roles in the same play; that adult men sometimes played women; that early Elizabethan playwrights seem to have pursued more striking displays of versatility by the actors and bolder admissions of artifice in the plays than their predecessors.

Chapter 2 also considers the logistics of doubling – how costume changes were effected and how long they took – and shows how early plots seem to facilitate the practice of showcasing lead actors. It includes a section that takes up the aesthetic potential for doubling in *Mankinde* (c. 1471) and the Wakefield *Second Shepherd's Play* (c. 1500), leading to an argument that artistic doubling, far from the 'vulgar necessity' that W.J. Lawrence deplored, emerges early on English stages and was so integral to dramatic construction that it cannot but have influenced Shakespeare.[21] I also describe the influence of other medieval dramaturgical phenomena on Shakespeare's plays, cataloguing staging conventions that were reliable sources of theatrical energy and easy to hand. The third chapter is a case study that aims to show how casting and dramaturgical precedents are reflected in Shakespeare's plays. The chapter focuses on doubling in *The Winter's Tale*, a play that provides efficient and aesthetically dazzling casting options and – because it was written late in his career – argues for the continuing attraction that doubling roles held for Shakespeare.

Chapter 4 focuses on recurring dramaturgical strategies and key internal evidence indicating that Shakespeare's plays were designed to be performed by small casts, that they anticipate company shareholders doubling frequently and potentially filling all speaking roles. Evidence for speculating on play construction and role distribution includes, for instance, the unlikely death of Romeo's mother. In *Romeo and Juliet*'s final scene, Montague learns of Romeo's death and responds with news of another misfortune: 'Alas, my liege, my wife is dead tonight; / Grief of my son's exile has stopped her breath' (5.3.210–11). Romeo's mother appears to die of theatrical necessity. Since no more than 12 speakers appear on stage together in *Romeo and Juliet*, a desire to play with 12 (or to allow the possibility of playing with 12 when touring or otherwise pressed for resources) may explain her absence. Doubling roles would also make sense of the Nurse's profound weeping over Tybalt's death, or the ostentatiously announced, otherwise gratuitous kinship of Paris, Mercutio, and the Prince. Through such examples, the chapter suggests that doubling these roles can provide a foundation outside the fiction for seeming incongruences within it.

A related example is the 'line of kings' that will come to reign in Scotland. The last member of an eight-man line holds a mirror that shows Macbeth 'many more'. Why a parade of eight kings? Why not seven, or nine, or the host of hired men reputed to be acting for the company? To demonstrate that

---

[21] W.J. Lawrence, *Pre-Restoration Stage Studies* (Cambridge, MA: Harvard University Press, 1927), pp. 43–78.

no Shakespeare play requires more than 12 players, my argument examines Banquo's line of kings and other 'limiting scenes' – those scenes that set minimum casting requirements because they feature the greatest number of speakers appearing simultaneously in a given play.[22] The chapter challenges traditional assumptions about cast size and the allotment of roles that have come down to us from critics who, partly due to biases towards verisimilitude, have limited our understanding of the possibilities for doubling on Shakespeare's historical stages. I endeavour to show that the material record (both historical and dramaturgical) indicates that doubling was a mainstay of Shakespeare's theatrical sensibility and practice. Chapter 5 then explores the possibilities for doubling roles embedded in the structures of two plays: *A Midsummer Night's Dream* and *Romeo and Juliet*.

Shakespeare's internal references to bodies and physiognomy figure in the discussion of doubling. He frequently describes boys on the verge of manhood, and his female characters sometimes seem to be oversized boys or even adult men in women's clothing. Malvolio observes that Cesario is 'in standing water between boy and man'; Cesario calls Maria a 'giant'; Tamora and Hippolyta – warriors both – may really be giants; and the Princess of France, Costard notes, is 'the thickest here'.[23] During the Restoration, Edward Kynaston was admired for playing adult roles of both genders, and Thomas Jordan wrote a prologue to *Othello* wherein he exposed the barbaric practices of times gone by: 'For, to speak truth, men act that are between / Forty and fifty wenches of fifteen / With bone so large and never so incompliant, / When you call Desdemona, enter Giant'.[24] Such examples are discussed in Chapter 6, which focuses on Shakespeare's 'boy' actors. The chapter draws upon evidence from illustrations and woodcuts; Puritan tracts; first-hand accounts; studies of voice change and hair growth; apprenticeship articles and more, to argue the high probability that teenaged boys may not have appeared as frequently and numerously on Shakespeare's stages as is commonly supposed. The historical record suggests that the argument for teenaged actors owes its currency to evidence drawn chiefly from non-Shakespearean plays performed well after the playwright's death, as well as to modern assumptions about the importance of verisimilitude for early modern audiences. The evidence indicates, rather, that many males who played female roles for Shakespeare's company would also have been capable of playing (and doubling as) adult men. I argue that young lords such as Claudio, whom Benedick calls 'Lord Lackbeard', emerge as the

---

[22] David Bradley uses the term in *From Text to Performance in the Elizabethan Theatre: Preparing the Play for the Stage* (Cambridge: Cambridge University Press, 1992).

[23] *Twelfth Night*, 1.5.141–2, 180; *Love's Labour's Lost*, 4.1.51.

[24] Thomas Jordan, 'A Prologue, to introduce the first Woman that came to act on the Stage in the Tragedy call'd The Moor of Venice', in *A Royal Arbor of Loyal Poesie, Consisting of Poems and Songs* (London: Printed by R.W. for Eliz. Andrews, 1663), pp. 24–5.

likeliest candidates for such roles as Desdemona, Hermione, and Cleopatra. The chapter also addresses some notorious casting problems in Shakespeare, such as the need for five boys to play *Love's Labour's Lost*. Since most scholars have supposed the King's Men had no more than two suitably trained boys for large roles at one time, and since few boys were apprenticed to company members before the 1600s, the requirements of *Love's Labour's Lost* (and several others) would pose peculiar difficulties if the company had insisted upon a stark dichotomy when casting boys and men.

The last two parts of the book analyse the structures of *Twelfth Night*, *Othello*, and *Measure for Measure*, producing full-cast doubling plans for each. As with the plays explored earlier in the book, each discussion is preceded by a speculative chart that demonstrates the play's dramaturgical structure and shows available opportunities to double roles based on cast sizes established by the limiting scenes. While discussing the opportunities outlined on the charts, I present options for pairing characters and compare the thematic and theatrical virtues of different options. The section on *Measure for Measure* includes speculations on actor substitution, which both its structure and plot seem to invite.

The doubling discussions throughout the book, treating seven plays in detail and touching on most others, trace a developmental arc representing the Shakespearean canon from 1594 to 1610, a period of remarkable stability for the company. Along with presenting innovative doubling speculations that make a difference in production, I review past critical opinions about doubling roles and discuss the effects of proposed pairings on audiences while drawing on examples from productions that – whether by design or accident – work to rich and pleasurable ends. An appendix provides detailed information about staging requirements for *Hamlet*, the first play for which doubling is discussed in the text, as well as speculative casting charts for all Shakespeare's plays written between 1594 and 1610, the years during which he was a resident playwright with the Lord Chamberlain's/King's Men. These collectively demonstrate that the plays all accommodate the use of just 12 speakers (or fewer), without cutting or adaptation, and argue for how small casts can help companies take better advantage of energies latent in the play structures.

Doubling Criticism and Speculation

Actors have doubled roles in performance for centuries, but it was not until Alois Brandl and Wilfred Perrett proposed that one boy actor could have gone to France as Cordelia and returned as Lear's Fool that doubling gained critical attention.[25] Perrett noted thematic links and verbal cues that

---

[25] See Alois Brandl, *Shakspere* (Berlin: E. Hofmann & Co., 1894); and Wilfred Perrett, *The Story of King Lear* (Berlin: Mayer and Müller, 1904).

pertain to both characters, typified by the line 'And my poor fool is hanged', which Lear speaks with the freshly 'hanged' Cordelia in his arms (*King Lear*, 5.3.281). Several critics who followed have attended to similar possibilities in other plays, or to casting patterns that can be traced in the play structures.

Other critics have followed Alwin Thaler, who argued against the possibility that doubling of major roles could have occurred historically, mainly on grounds of taste. W.J. Lawrence, for instance, rejected pairings like Cordelia and the Fool, arguing that sharers would have resented extra work and dramatists would have respected them too much to ask. In reviewing cast lists and plays offered 'for acting' in the sixteenth century, Lawrence concludes that plays such as *Hamlet* would have required doubling, since 'no Elizabethan company rejoiced in the possession of as many as 29 players'.[26] Yet his intuitions about the elite status and prerogatives of the sharers lead him to argue that the 'obvious "doubles" in *Hamlet* [i.e. Claudius/Ghost, Polonius/First Gravedigger] were precisely the ones which were carefully avoided'.[27] For Lawrence, using doubling to establish or underscore thematic correspondences between characters, like self-reflexive references to the theatre, lacked decorum and so would have been ignored.

David Bevington's *From Mankind to Marlowe* has been the most influential study of early modern doubling. Taking a starkly different view from Lawrence, Bevington notes the increasing intricacy of plots and employments of actors during the late medieval and Tudor periods and concludes that 'popular tradition found doubling to be an indispensable, inevitable and congenial technique of dramatic construction'.[28] Bevington rejects notions that suggest the practice was arbitrarily limited (such as T.W. Baldwin's theory of 'acting lines') since the plays seem to demand versatility above all else. He shows that several supposedly illusion-marring devices – doubling major roles, having adult males portray female characters, asking actors to alternate between roles or make quick changes – were not unknown, nor even particularly rare, in the Tudor period. While his survey ends with Marlowe, Bevington's work has major implications for the plotting and casting practices of Shakespeare and his company, who, I argue, demanded still more versatility from actors than their predecessors.

Relying on production histories and his experience as a playgoer, A.C. Sprague organizes potential doubles into three categories: 'deficiency', 'emergency', and 'virtuoso' doubling, accepting or rejecting possibilities based on

---

[26] Lawrence, *Pre-Restoration Stage Studies*, p. 70.

[27] Ibid., p. 71.

[28] David M. Bevington, *From Mankind to Marlowe: Growth of Structure in the Popular Drama of Tudor England* (Cambridge, MA: Harvard University Press, 1962), p. 73.

taste and whether they fit with his ideas about historical practice.[29] His categories roughly coincide with how critics tend to think about doubling, the former
two chiefly concerned with economics, the latter aesthetics. For Sprague, 'virtuoso' doubling pleases audiences more for its potential to show the actor's
range than for any thematic import. His favourite double is Poins/Shallow in
2 Henry IV, while Fool/Cordelia is 'very implausible' because 'Armin would
not have stood for it'.[30]

William Ringler Jr. considers the number and nature of the actors available to Shakespeare and argues for possible pairings that the play structures
seem to anticipate.[31] He attributes doubling to 'convenience' rather than a
desire to display virtuosity or enhance aspects of character or plot. Ringler
was the first critic to offer possibilities that run counter to conventional ideas
about early modern staging – suggesting, for instance, that sharers could
have doubled, and that an actor playing female roles could have returned
as an adult male character in the same play. As Bevington did regarding
late medieval drama, Ringler describes how Shakespeare phases in and
out small groups of characters, such as the faeries and the mechanicals in
A Midsummer Night's Dream, raising the possibility that men may have
played roles that most have assumed were played by boys. Nevertheless, he
largely rejects the possibility of doubling major roles based on the amount
of memorization required.

Others such as Stephen Booth and John C. Meagher have focused on
opportunities for doubling that Shakespeare and his company might have
exploited to thematic or theatrical advantage, each making bold speculations about casting major roles.[32] Booth explains how doubling can 'inform,
comment on, and, perhaps, augment the events enacted' while enabling the
best actors to do more acting.[33] He attends frequently to language that may
indicate and sanction potential pairings, noting how rhyme-like relationships between the Lords and Ladies of *A Midsummer Night's Dream*, Henry
V and the Dauphin, and Antigonus and Autolycus mark them out as inviting candidates for double-casting. Meagher also focuses on choices with
significant thematic implications, and he follows Bevington in examining

[29] A.C. Sprague, *The Doubling of Parts in Shakespeare's Plays* (London: Society for Theatre
Research, 1966).

[30] Ibid., p. 32.

[31] William A. Ringler Jr., 'The Number of Actors in Shakespeare's Early Plays', in *The
Seventeenth-Century Stage*, ed. G.E. Bentley (Chicago: University of Chicago Press, 1968),
pp. 110–34.

[32] Stephen Booth, 'Speculations on Doubling', in *King Lear, Macbeth, Indefinition and Tragedy*
(New Haven: Yale University Press, 1983), pp. 129–55; John C. Meagher, 'Economy and
Recognition: Thirteen Shakespearean Puzzles', *Shakespeare Quarterly* 35.1 (1984), pp. 7–21.

[33] Booth, 'Speculations on Doubling', p. 134.

dramaturgical structure to help determine casting requirements. He describes how possibilities consistent with Shakespeare's structures can comple- ment or undercut a play's salient concerns, noticing, for example, how the Brabantio actor's return as Lodovico seems to allow the former character to witness the ruin he envisioned for Desdemona. Booth and Meagher have inspired others like Tom Berger, Ralph Berry, and Alan Armstrong, who also explore how doubling can augment or complicate established themes.[34]

In *Casting Shakespeare's Plays*, T.J. King presents doubling charts for all Shakespeare's plays.[35] King was the first critic since Baldwin to distribute parts across whole casts, and his study is appealing for its attention to minor roles. However, King often assigns roles haphazardly, largely ignoring aesthetic or theatrical implications of his choices. He attaches a few specific roles to com- pany members – such as when 'Kempe' appears as a speech prefix for the role of 'Peter' in *Romeo and Juliet*) – but assigns secondary roles to major actors only where there is clear documentary evidence. Otherwise, he assumes that sharers and key hired men focused on one role in each play, and that the com- pany deployed a large group of hired men for small speaking roles and mutes. Like some of the critics before Booth and Meagher, King bars any possibility of an actor exiting a scene as one character and returning to it as another, a rule that undercuts the potential for doubling in many plays.

In their study of the Queen's Men, Scott McMillin and Sally-Beth MacLean detail the organization, repertory, economics, and extensive touring of the lead- ing English theatre company of the 1580s, the period just before the Admiral's Men and the Lord Chamberlain's Men came to prominence.[36] Combining his- torical and economic arguments about the troupe with acute attention to the dramaturgical structures of plays in their repertory, McMillin and MacLean project minimum cast sizes and create hypothetical doubling plans, drawing attention to the consistency of the structures and analysing the implications for the company's dramatic economy. They attend to the aesthetic potential of particular casting choices, some of the most interesting of these concerning minor roles, which critics have seldom considered.

---

[34] See Thomas Berger, 'Casting Henry V', *Shakespeare Studies* 20 (1988), pp. 89–104; Ralph Berry's discussion of doubles for *Hamlet* and *Julius Caesar* in *Shakespeare in Performance: Castings and Metamorphoses* (New York: St. Martin's Press, 1993); and Alan Armstrong, '"What is Become of Bushy? Where is Green?": Metadramatic Reference to Doubling Actors in *Richard II*', in *Inside Shakespeare: Essays on the Blackfriars Stage*, ed. Paul Menzer (Selinsgrove: Susquehanna University Press, 2006), pp. 149–55.

[35] T.J. King, *Casting Shakespeare's Plays: London Actors and Their Roles, 1590–1642* (Cambridge: Cambridge University Press, 1992).

[36] Scott McMillin and Sally-Beth MacLean, *The Queen's Men and Their Plays* (Cambridge: Cambridge University Press, 1998).

All the foregoing critics and studies have informed and inspired this book. Like Bevington, I review and analyse Tudor precedents and conventions, exploring how Shakespeare may have adopted and refined them. Like Sprague, I attend to contemporary theatre practice and propose doubles that can impact productions. Like King, I work with whole plays and produce casting charts that include all speaking roles and identified mutes. Like Booth and Meagher, I analyse the thematic links between characters, arguing for how doubling roles can help achieve generic and aesthetic ends otherwise unavailable to productions. And like McMillin and MacLean, I examine Shakespeare's play structures to propose precise casting requirements, attending to the thematic and theatrical potential of realizing these onstage. In brief, by establishing a more thorough historical, dramaturgical, and aesthetic basis for doubling than has thus far been attempted, I hope to present a comprehensive and more compelling assessment of the extent to which doubling was prefigured by Shakespeare, and to suggest how exploiting the casting patterns embedded in his play structures can add to the theatrical vitality of his plays for every company or generation.

By reconsidering the historical record and some common suppositions about Shakespeare's plotting and historical practice, the book entertains the likelihood that Shakespeare improved upon the dramaturgy of his predecessors, punning with his actors through theatrically enlivening doubles, from well-known options like Claudius/Ghost and Perdita/Mamillius to largely unexplored examples like Hermione/Dorcas, Tybalt/Nurse, and the literal fulfilment (via casting) of the Duke's exchange: 'An Angelo for Claudio' (*Measure for Measure*, 5.1.412). The historical narrative I construct and the consistency and range of attractive aesthetic possibilities suggested by Shakespeare's dramaturgy argues that critics should reconsider several widely held assumptions about casting and staging in Shakespeare's time, allowing for the probability that elaborate, highly efficient double-casting, and the ingenious deployment of small and versatile casts was anticipated by the playwright, is facilitated by his play structures, and, in addition to presenting a rich basis for designing contemporary productions, should more directly inform our theories and conceptions of historical practice.

Though I expect that Shakespeare's historical company regularly put on plays with nine to 12 actors speaking all or most of the lines, I cannot prove it. That confession made, the book revisits the documentary record, the company's economics and personnel, the play structures, and much more, assessing the capability of Shakespeare's own company to have realized the plays' inherent and strikingly consistent potential for doubling. Regardless of intent or original practice, Shakespeare engineered plays particularly suited to small companies whose need to play multiple roles would inevitably enhance other paradoxes, contradictions, and replications found throughout the plays. In the end, I argue for the multitude of theatrical energies *available* to the Lord Chamberlain's/King's Men – and available to every contemporary director and company staging Shakespeare's plays – regardless of the degree to which Shakespeare's company exploited these energies near the turn of the seventeenth century.

1   'Improbable Fictions'
Shakespeare's Plays without *the Plays*

ಲಿಊ
> ... and on this stage,
> Where we offenders now appear, soul-vexed ...
> *~The Winter's Tale*, 5.1.58–9

ಲಿಊ

In June of 2008 I attended a performance of *Hamlet* in New York's Central Park. The production limped out of the gate, and by the time Sam Waterston opened Act Two with Polonius's treatise on espionage it was difficult not to envy Francisco, Marcellus, and Barnardo, whose nightly watches were already complete. But then came a point at which Shakespeare invites actors to step to the edge of a cliff. Most flinch, but Waterston stepped to the edge. Then he jumped.

In the midst of teaching Reynaldo how best to slander Laertes in Paris, Polonius momentarily loses his train of thought,

> And then, sir, does 'a this: 'a does—
> What was I about to say? By the mass, I was about to say something—where did I leave?   (2.1.48–50)

In context, the repetition and ellipsis in the first line seem to prompt actors to pause a moment or two while grasping for the right words. Waterston paused that moment or two after 'does 'a this', then took the play to the brink of ruin by hesitating about 30 seconds after ''a does', before resuming the speech and allowing the audience once again to practice respiration.

The effect of half a minute's silence in a production of *Hamlet* is not easily imagined. The pause didn't feel like 30 seconds. It was 30 seconds. It felt like forever. Polonius first seemed powerless to remember the topic of conversation, before blending with and then apparently giving way to Waterston's efforts – as an actor – to find a way back into the role and save the play from collapse. Most interesting was that the shift from character to actor was never complete. The pause was too long for the performance to have been progressing as intended, yet Waterston's refusal to break character or call for a line prevented the audience from wholly giving up on Polonius. The vacant eyes and mounting distress suited character and actor alike, forcing the audience to wait in suspense for a resolution that kept not coming.

Oskar Eustis, the production's director, heightened the sense of uncertainty by adding two attendants alongside Reynaldo, the trio seeming at least as confused about how to proceed as the wax figure playing Polonius. Reynaldo urged his colleague forward in impromptu sign language, apparently as anxious as the audience about whether the show would go on. Electrified by its doubts about what was unfolding, or failing to unfold, the spectators watched as fiction implicated reality as a primary subject, as the calm veneer of artifice was ruptured by unnerving truth. They held their breath through it all like Wilde's Gwendolyn Fairfax, 'This suspense is terrible. I hope it will last.'

Waterston's panicked gaze eventually yielded to a look of desperate resolve, and he demanded of Reynaldo, 'What was I about to say?' The question initially felt like progress, a sorely needed return to a plot whose continuance was in doubt. But as sound gave way to sense, it was clear that the line meant things were as bleak as they had seemed – the play was stalling due to a malfunctioning player. Waterston then seemed more vulnerable for having been on the verge of recovery only to go further adrift. The lines that followed, 'By the mass, I was about to say something—' (2.1.49–50), prolonged the effect. The audience knew he intended to say something; he obviously didn't know what it was. At last, Waterston again asked where he had left off, and Reynaldo recovered sufficiently to respond, 'At "closes in the consequence"' (2.1.51). Suddenly, Polonius – indeed, Polonius again – continued the dialogue as though nothing had been amiss.

Directors don't usually allow Polonius to ask, 'What was I about to say?' as though the actor may be ignorant of the answer. Most avoid confusion by cutting the lines, while those who preserve them tend to have the actor play supreme self-assurance or comic forgetfulness, either way indicating that Polonius and not the actor has lost his way. It seems reasonable to avoid blurring reality and fiction here, but directors who do avoid it may overlook the scene's potential to exploit indeterminacy and fear as primary tools of engagement. They preserve comfort and clarity for their audiences, though at the expense of complexity, doubt, and disorientation – the stuff terror is made on.

Edmund Burke suggests that fear plays an essential role in experiences of the sublime, contributing to 'a state of the soul, in which all its motions are suspended, with some degree of horror. In this case the mind is so entirely filled with its object, that it cannot entertain any other.'[1] For the spectators,

---

[1] *A Philosophical Enquiry into the Origin of our Ideas of the Beautiful and the Sublime*, ed. J.T. Bolton (Notre Dame: University of Notre Dame Press, 1968), p. 58.

Waterston's performance created this fear – a fear that was empathic but also *personal*. On one hand, they empathized with an actor risking public shame because he could not speak; on the other, they faced the no less disturbing possibility that they could no longer go on as spectators.[2] I have seen 29 other actors play Polonius, but none evoked so much anxiety about the status of the performance, or momentarily convinced the audience that 2.1 of *Hamlet* was the most electrifying scene in Shakespeare.

Waterston was not, however, the first to deepen engagement by stretching out the stops. Harriet Walter was among those awed by Michael Bryant, who played Polonius in Richard Eyre's 1989 production:

> I will never forget Michael Bryant as Polonius ... suddenly stopping his own pedantic flow with, 'What was I about to say?' Then the most daringly stretched-out pause I have ever witnessed, during which all our hearts seemed to stop. Had he dried? What was going on? Then 'By the mass, I was about to say something!' Great ad-lib, we thought ... if it is one ... and then, 'Where did I leave?' It was so startlingly natural that I had to look it up when I got home. It was all Shakespeare and Michael Bryant had played it to the hilt.[3]

Several critics described Bryant's pause as 'agonizing' or 'heart-stopping'; Catherine Loomis thought it felt as long as 'one might take to tell a hundred ... thousand'; while Michael Billington considered it the 'single most moving moment in the whole evening'.[4] The reactions suggest that invoking the actor's potential to forget or dry up posed a threat to *Hamlet* that increased the audience's investment in the play's continuance. It involved spectators in a secondary drama, what we might call a play *without* the play, focused on their ability to maintain access to the fiction. Meanwhile, it cast doubt on the boundaries of the theatrical object which, paradoxically, deepened the spectators' engagement with it.

Walter's narrative captures the uncertainty that performances can create about a playtext, even for audiences already intimately familiar with it. Significantly, she traces the actor's power and courage to instabilities rooted in

---

[2] Ben Brantley described the scene as 'breathtakingly poignant', and the silence as 'deeply uncomfortable' in his review for the *New York Times* (18 June 2008). He interpreted the event as an aging courtier's 'senior moment', though the attempt to determine a cause may represent an unconscious desire to manage the discomfort the scene created through its ambiguity and prolonged irresolution.

[3] Harriet Walter, *Other People's Shoes: Thoughts on Acting* (London: Nick Hern Books Ltd., 2003), p. 208.

[4] In 'The Readiness Was All: Ian Charleson and Richard Eyre's Hamlet', Richard Allan Davison cites several reviews (including Billington's) that lauded Bryant and his choice. In *Shakespeare, Text and Theater: Essays in Honor of Jay L. Halio*, ed. Lois Potter and Arthur F. Kinney (Newark: University of Delaware Press, 1999), p. 180. Loomis's paper, 'Must Give us Pause', was delivered at the 2009 Blackfriars Conference in Staunton, VA.

the lines she later revisits at home. Bryant did not invent or add to the play but played what was before him – 'It was' after all, she says, 'all Shakespeare'. Despite being cut or explained away in many productions, these pauses are Shakespeare's. The passage's first wayward line, 'And then, sir, does 'a this: 'a does—' (2.1.49) suggests a memory lapse, but the choice to prescribe vocal falters and leave a metrical void immediately before forcing the scene's featured actor to ask, 'What was I about to say?' – probably the line least likely to be mistaken for verse in *Hamlet* – feels like sabotage. It is as though the playwright not only wants the actor to stumble over his lines and initiate stretches of silent ambiguity, but also for the audience to notice that the actor is struggling to play the part.[5]

Since his interest in the play's reception gainsays attempts at sabotage, we may wonder why Shakespeare did not take care to preserve the coherence of the illusion. Surely, Polonius could show his age or garrulousness without risking our ability to tell fact from fiction. But the plays suggest a playwright who sought to deepen engagement by all available means, one eager to frustrate or alienate audiences if it meant increasing their interest. Shakespeare recognized and exploited the fact that spectators fluently participate in two concurrent worlds of coherence, seduced by the tensions their overlaps occasion, so he sowed doubt about the boundaries of reality and fiction to amplify those tensions. The result intensifies the dramatic situation of the *spectators* and exploits their doubts about whether the performance will attain completion in a unique recital. As a result, spectators consciously tracking the protagonist on stage are simultaneously thrust into protagonists' roles of their own, uncertain about not only which path the play will take to its conclusion but also whether the elected path can arrive there at all.

Drama at and after the Margins

Polonius's bout of aphasia is just one example that helps to reveal an implicit theory of theatrical attraction evident in Shakespeare's plays: namely, that theatre is energized by its impending disintegration, its power of attraction often proportional to the frequency, imminence, and severity of the threat. By offering to undermine or even dissolve his plots, Shakespeare forces us to cling to them more tenaciously, and by creating opportunities for reality – or illusions

---

[5] Editors have handled the elusive metrics of the passage in various ways. The Norton editors follow A.R. Braunmuller's Pelican text in printing two ellipses in a tetrameter line (here a colon and an em dash), then rendering the remainder of the passage in prose. G. Blakemore Evans' Riverside prints the first line as a fourteener, the second as a pentameter line, and lets the final question trail off as a dimeter line. The Hinman facsimile of the 1623 Folio ends a trimeter line at 'a this', and follows it with tetrameter and hexameter lines.

of reality – to intrude upon fiction he multiplies and enriches the fundamental dualities of drama.

Theatre's chief attraction is acting, the phenomenon wherein the people in the playbills participate simultaneously, and signify alternate identities, in two distinct and distinctly coherent realms – that of the play and that of the play-house. Bernard Beckerman describes how theatre presents an audience with 'two overlapping circles of experience, that of the fiction and that of its own reality',[6] suggesting a sort of Venn diagram wherein actors occupy the overlap-ping area, forging a tenuous harmony between two worlds by pertaining simul-taneously to both. Audiences are aware that actors cannot sustain an action by asserting or lapsing into authenticity – they are, like Viola, not that they play. Recitation, then, partitions the actor-character, providing a crucial means by which the actor establishes the duality upon which our interest depends. It instigates and makes legible the duplicity of actors, whose every line attests to the existence and coherence of the characters they personate, and of the fic-tional world in which they participate, despite our continuous and countering awareness of their ongoing work as actors in a play. Paradoxically, to generate interest in a performance, one must convincingly imitate the intended action or character while conspicuously falling short in the attempt. It sounds impos-sible, but it is precisely what actors do. Many of the most admired – Maggie Smith, Mark Rylance, Meryl Streep, or Denzel Washington – manage to seem convincing in the roles they play while never allowing the audience to forget that *they* are playing them.

This counter-awareness, brought on by the inevitable slippage between actor and character, is a prime mover of theatrical attraction. Michael Goldman speaks to this point when observing how the actor's body 'works against the abstract-ness of his art', noting that the ongoing friction between body and character is 'not a flaw in drama but its essence'.[7] In other words, drama exists because the actor's body supports yet simultaneously – and inevitably – undermines the characters he portrays. As a result, all performances are always in the process of failing, and theatre depends on that (at least partial) failure for its animus and energy, something Shakespeare seems to have understood and looked to exploit when he embedded a series of landmines in Polonius's script. Nicholas Ridout argues something similar when noting that performances affect audi-ences most powerfully when the 'machinery' they employ for representation appears to break down, that the theatre's 'failure … is not anomalous, but

[6] Bernard Beckerman, *Dynamics of Drama: Theory, Method and Analysis* (New York: Alfred A. Knopf, 1970), p. 133.
[7] Michael Goldman, *Shakespeare and the Energies of Drama* (Princeton: Princeton University Press, 1972), p. 6.

somehow, perhaps, constitutive'.[8] Through Polonius, Shakespeare makes the latent tension associated with recitation a primary dramatic subject, leaving audiences more insecure – and more interested – by amplifying the risks associated with forgetting. He intuits that audiences respond to actors much as they do to tightrope walkers, and he introduces potential wobbles that can increase appreciation for the performer's ongoing peril.

Before seeing Waterston's performance I thought that in *Poetics, VI* Aristotle overstated the roles that pity and terror play in the experience of drama. He may have been correct, though, about the role these emotions can play, while failing to note that *actors* surpass the capacity of *actions* to excite them. However interested in narrative resolutions, we may be more affected by the uncertain status of an incomplete performance. Memory lapses are frustrating to everyone, but when the absentminded person is performing a role onstage the result can be terror, both for the actor and for an audience suddenly more empathetic than it knew it could be – possibly more empathetic than it wants to be.[9] The audience has consented to watch the tragedy of *Hamlet*, but not the relatively authentic tragedy of the tragedian. The stakes of this actor-centred drama surpassed those even of *Hamlet* because the seemingly unplanned chaos centred on an actor who was, unlike Polonius, one of us. *Hamlet*'s events momentarily paled in importance before the actor's situation, because the play's completion depended upon his recovery and return to it.

Still, though Polonius's lines initiate what seemed a 'real' tragedy of the actor alongside the suddenly more comfortable tragedy of *Hamlet*, the play was not ultimately suspended in favour of reality. The play was 'the thing' all along, and the 'reality' to which the audience momentarily subscribed proves illusory.[10] Shakespeare thus enables *Hamlet* to operate like actors do: manifesting authenticity and artificiality at the same place and time. Hamlet's line praising human understanding, 'In apprehension, how like a God', rarely seems so apt a description of his audience, as when the fiction reaches a precipice from which the audience experiences the sensation of leaping, only to learn that the fictional frame was flexible enough to accommodate the jump into reality. The jump, like Gloucester's from the cliffs of Dover, was the illusion, here a more convincing illusion than theatre ordinarily makes possible.

---

[8] In *Stage Fright, Animals and Other Theatrical Problems* (Cambridge: Cambridge University Press, 2006). Ridout discusses acting failure – and the simulation of failure by modern companies in Chapter 4 (pp. 129–60). The quoted description appears on p. 3.

[9] Dominic Gray describes the pauses in Bryant's performance as being 'drawn into stories of their own'. Cited by Davison, 'The Readiness Was All', p. 180.

[10] Readers may recall that memory is an insistent – though largely non-signifying – theme throughout *Hamlet*. Among other examples are the Ghost's admonition, 'Remember me' (1.5.91), his return to 'whet (Hamlet's) almost blunted purpose' (3.4.101), and Hamlet's use of 'tables' to set down information (1.5.107–8).

Situations that introduce the potential for acting failure at the point of recitation are common in Shakespeare's plays. Orlando twice cannot fill metrical breaks allotted to his responses (*As You Like It* 1.2.214–27), and Beatrice must prompt Claudio when the news of his engagement stupefies him: 'Speak, Count. 'Tis your cue' (*Much Ado* 2.1.269). Leontes notes the 'hums' and 'ha's' that stand in for articulate speech but, while finding fault in others, loses his own way: 'these petty brands / That calumny doth use – O, I am out! – / That mercy does …' (2.1.72–4). And Hamlet makes his own false start when attempting to recall a speech for the troupe of players:

> If it live in your memory, begin at this line – let me see, let me see,
> 'The rugged Pyrrhus, like th' Hyrcanian beast –'
> 'Tis not so, it begins with Pyrrhus –
> 'The rugged Pyrrhus, he whose sable arms …'   (2.2.370–4)[11]

Meanwhile, Hotspur, Cleopatra, and Coriolanus – forgetters all – help argue the playwright's abiding interest in facilitating engagement with fiction by destabilizing the materials of its construction.[12] After all, Shakespeare adds each of these lapses to the source material.

By this point readers may have begun to think about *metadrama*, of the kinds that James Calderwood and Richard Hornby have outlined.[13] The term is supple enough to include some phenomena explored here, but Polonius will not sit comfortably in a category with things commonly considered metadramatic. Overt reference to actors and the stage by actors on stage, direct addresses, choruses and epilogues, plays within plays, and other self-reflexive statements about theatre and scene-making offer similar, but comparatively diluted, effects. When Fabian, delighted by Maria's plotting, says 'If this were played upon a stage now, I could condemn it as an improbable fiction' (3.4.115–16), his audience may note that Fabian's line describes his own situation – he too is an actor in a play full of improbabilities – as aptly as the scene he mocks. The audience can take pleasure in its conscious awareness that the play has proposed a credible hierarchy of falsities, despite everything on stage remaining equally, and admittedly, fictional.

Through metadrama, the audience witnesses the play reaching beyond its bounds to invite *conscious* comparisons of art to life or other forms of artifice. Through Polonius, however, Shakespeare injects reality into fiction without explanation, and without easing tensions provoked by the actor's intrusion.

---

[11] As in the example from *Hamlet* 2.1, metrics and self-reflexive commentary underwrite the pause.

[12] See *1 Henry IV*, 1.3.240–6; *Antony and Cleopatra*, 1.3.87–92; and *Coriolanus*, 1.9.88–90.

[13] James L. Calderwood, *Shakespearean Metadrama* (Minneapolis: University of Minnesota Press, 1971); Richard Hornby, *Drama, Metadrama, and Perception* (Lewisburg: Bucknell University Press, 1986).

The audience is left at the mercy of the play to resolve something that seems outside its bounds. When Rosalind, Puck, or the King of France admit themselves mere shadows or beggar-actors at their plays' ends, the concessions do as much to release as to augment tension, since our perception shifts between poles of character and (character-as-) actor.[14] They ask and attain acceptance as actors who have voluntarily set aside the roles allotted to them by the playwright, whereas Polonius thrusts the actor upon the audience without its consent, and apparently without his own.

Conventions, Casting, and Cutting against the Natural

Like Polonius's scene with Reynaldo, other staged memory lapses offer sites of potential disruption that can strengthen doubts about and attachments to the plot's progress. But it is important to note that a performance such as Waterston's merely amplifies energy that is always present in the theatre. Recitation is much like representation in that it is an artificial convention on which a play's progress depends, and the re-emergence of the actor can interrupt both the convention and the play at any time. Audiences aware that actors are reciting artificial speeches are likewise aware that those actors may lose their way, as routine comments from inexperienced playgoers about the actors' capacities to memorize and recite lines on cue make evident. The Polonius example suggests that Shakespeare understood and wished to intensify the energy present in the mere (yet always virtuosic) act of recitation. Both recitation and representation, he recognized, rely on an ever-present sense of slippage, an impending threat that accounts for a major share of the attraction. Both conventions are foundational and both create ongoing dramatic interest that is essentially unrelated to plot, were it not for the fact that the plot's progress and completion depends unequivocally on the conventions being maintained. And it is this conventionality – the fact that we are so thoroughly familiar with stage figures seeming to be what they are not, and speaking what they do not think – that may explain why audiences are so susceptible to efforts to exploit both as sources of extra-dramatic suspense and conflict. Shakespeare's plays expand the arena of conflict to include actors and audiences, exploring ways to replicate the tensions within the play for the 'real' people in the theatre, both onstage and off.

Facilitating audience engagement by destabilizing the plot and its components was neither haphazard nor occasional for Shakespeare. It was central to his theatrical vision. This chapter aims to show the playwright experimenting with ways to involve audiences in dramatic situations outside the bounds of the

---

[14] See epilogues for *As You Like It*, *A Midsummer Night's Dream*, and *All's Well That Ends Well*.

dramatic narrative, principally by undermining (or at least threatening) the conventions on which plays and audiences customarily rely. In light of the intrinsic prospect of failure that animates the related conventions of representation and recitation, we might profitably reconsider another widespread convention of early modern theatre: the practice of doubling roles. Like the other conventions, doubling casually and consistently betrays the artifice of the enterprise and implicitly undermines the performer's mimetic efforts, making the artificiality of the performance legible in ways that can increase the audience's investment in the plot and its characters. And, like them, its very conventionality helps make audiences more susceptible to the disruptions it creates.

Actors from the Elizabethan era to the present day have engaged audiences despite what many have supposed a comparative lack of emotional truth in acting, and even despite anatomical or other challenges to their attempts at realistic characterization. The 30-something, pale-skinned Richard Burbage appears to have succeeded both as an octogenarian and a Moorish general. Norma Shearer received an Academy Award nomination at 36 for her portrayal of Juliet. More recently, Simon Russell Beale played a short, squat Hamlet at 40 that was widely admired, before taking on Benedick opposite Zoe Wanamaker when she was 58 years old, making up a couple that Quentin Letts felt caught 'the magic of Beatrice and Benedick'.[15] Meanwhile, all-male (or all-female) casts, deployed by such companies as Propeller, Cheek by Jowl, and Shakespeare's Globe, appear not to have diminished their audiences' enjoyment of Shakespeare's plays. On the contrary, examples such as Mark Rylance's Olivia and Vanessa Redgrave's Prospero, both at the Globe, or Adrian Lester's Rosalind for Cheek by Jowl, are among the more celebrated Shakespearean performances of the past 30 years.[16] It may be that cross-gendered casting helps to enhance the audience's awareness of the performance *as* a performance: an awareness that is arguably critical to engagement. Michael Goldman makes this point in *The Actor's Freedom*, suggesting that 'whatever his stylization, whatever his distance from the part, the actor passes into a mode of being that draws strength from a confrontation with the fearful, from the assumption of qualities that cut against the "natural"'.[17]

Sarah Bernhardt faced significant anatomical obstacles in her celebrated portrayal of Hamlet, one that Elizabeth Robbins thought definitive. Robbins' review is curious for what it suggests about the role of realism in the production

---

[15] *Daily Mail*, 19 December 2007. Web.

[16] Rylance played Olivia in Tim Carroll's 2002 *Twelfth Night* at Shakespeare's Globe (remounted in 2012); Redgrave's Prospero was for Lena Udovicki's 2000 Globe production; and Lester's Rosalind came in Declan Donnelan's 1991 production for Cheek by Jowl.

[17] Michael Goldman, *The Actor's Freedom: Toward a Theory of Drama* (New York: Viking Press, 1975), p. 11.

and about the obstacle presented by Bernhardt's gender, which seems to have been evident to all:

> For a woman to play at being a man is, surely, a tremendous handicap in the attempt to produce a stage illusion. There may be room for difference of opinion about her success in simulating the passions, but there is no real difference of opinion about her successes in pretending that she is a man. However well she does it (and I do not believe it could be better done than in the instance under consideration), there is no moment in the drama when the spectator is not fully and calmly conscious that the hero is a woman masquerading, or is jarred into sharp realization of the fact by her doing something that is very like a man. It is a case where every approach to success is merely another insistence on failure.[18]

Robbins's comments, I think, speak to the success of most actors in most roles. Though she considers Bernhardt's performance a *'tour de force'*, she seems as enthused about the *failure* of Bernhardt to perform masculinity as she does by her success at playing Hamlet. The acting was as realistic as Robbins could wish, but Bernhardt's continual failure to be convincing as a man appears to have increased Robbins' admiration for the performance. In an absolute sense, the gap between Bernhardt and Hamlet is not altogether different from the gap between any male actor and the same character. The cross-gendered casting merely provides a local habitation and a name for the inexact matching of actor and character that occurs in all performances.

Robbins's implicit interest in Bernhardt's failure seems to validate the attractions Goldman and Ridout ascribe to it, demonstrating that performances can affect us more powerfully when their tools for representation appear to fall short or break down. Alice Rayner similarly notes how acting considered emotionally realistic in the twentieth century cannot be realistic in any absolute sense: 'With or without the sense of mimesis, representation is a kind of repetition that generates the phantom of a double … The act of representing, regardless of technique, generates questions about … something both there, present, and not there.'[19] One implication of Rayner's argument is that techniques that aim to diminish the complexity of the act of acting, or to make its reception simpler or more comfortable, are not merely self-defeating but actually counterproductive. Not only might audiences better appreciate the skill of actors as the gaps widen between them and the characters they represent; productions that push against naturalistic representation, in foregrounding quotidian reality, might bring about a deeper sense of the 'real'.[20]

---

[18] Elizabeth Robbins, 'On Seeing Madame Bernhardt's Hamlet', *North American Review* 171 (December 1900), p. 908.

[19] Alice Rayner, 'Rude Mechanicals and the Specters of Marx', *Theatre Journal* 54.4 (2002), p. 535.

[20] Lois Potter also explores the power associated with slippage between what she calls 'acting-as-mimesis' and 'acting-as-skill' in the context of the actor's memory. See ' "Nobody's

The benefits of preserving, even widening, the gaps between actors and characters are not necessarily at odds with the naturalism celebrated in western performance. But the attraction of naturalistic behaviour on stage may owe more to its capacity to accentuate, rather than disguise, artifice. Consider Rupert Goold's 2007 production of *Macbeth*, in which Patrick Stewart made himself a sandwich onstage while interviewing the murderers in 3.1, a moment that Ben Brantley found 'unforgettable', and which Charles Spencer described as 'one of the scariest things you've ever seen'.[21] Few onstage actions can be considered more indisputably naturalistic than eating a sandwich. Indeed, eating is an act that renders mimesis irrelevant; any actor who does not choke has accomplished his task perfectly. In the scene, Stewart's matter-of-fact persistence in preparing and consuming his meal elicited titters of laughter and an unusually heightened sense of expectation, bespeaking tension that derived both from the impertinence of Macbeth's actions to the issue at hand and, more decisively, from their contrast with the overt artifice of the play. Audiences appeared to wait for Stewart (rather than Macbeth) to notice that the highly naturalistic act he was performing was somehow unnatural. The attraction of this act lay in its inappropriateness within the context both of the plot of *Macbeth* and of the dramatic event itself – engendering the sense of wonder and fear that critics like Brantley and Spencer appear to have experienced.

Any dog that plays 'Crab' in *The Two Gentlemen of Verona* is likewise freed from the responsibility to simulate anything. Whatever the dog does is real, and whatever the dog does is right. But Crab's power over the audience depends largely on the audience's knowledge that what the dog does might well diverge from his director's wishes. In *The American Play*, Marc Robinson makes a related point about other elements of the theatre, noting how

on any realist stage, objects and figures slip the yoke of narrative and even *mise-en-scène*. They elude a playwright's or director's attempt to control our access to them as they radiate magnetic power unharnessed by dramatic structure.[22]

Crab is merely an extreme example of what Robinson suggests occurs on all sides, since a director cannot limit the audience's awareness that the bodies and objects on stage have an existence independent from their function in the current performance. Neither can the theatre prevent audiences from noticing where it proves inadequate in its ability to represent.

Perfect": Actor's Memories and Shakespeare's Plays of the 1590s', *Shakespeare Survey* 1 (1990), pp. 85–97.

[21] Ben Brantley, 'Something Wicked This Way Comes; Review of *Macbeth*', *New York Times*, 15 February 2008. Charles Spencer, 'The Best Macbeth I Have Seen; Review of *Macbeth*', *Telegraph*, 27 September 2007.

[22] Robinson, *The American Play*, p. 112.

Doubling roles provided Shakespeare a means to create ongoing sources of rupture and near-constant advertisements of the gaps between performers and characters, revealing and enriching the sense of slippage and paradox at the sites of representation and recitation by raising the actor's profile in the spectator's consciousness, and by involving tertiary personas (those beyond the actor and initial character) to complicate reception. Rather than receiving separable existences of actor and character at one point of perception, those watching an actor play multiple roles apprehend further contrasts and contradictions between the roles themselves. Subsequent chapters will re-examine the historical evidence for doubling roles in Shakespeare's plays, describe the patterns embedded into his dramas that suggest its centrality to his playwriting, and explore the ramifications of doubling for staging and reception. Doubling roles, I shall argue, was an essential part of Shakespeare's theatrical logic.

Here, however, I hope to show that the kinds of effects that doubling makes possible are intimately related to what the plays seem otherwise committed to achieving. If sparking audience engagement by destabilizing the plot and its components was central to Shakespeare's theatrical vision, then doubling would have provided an implicit yet ever-present means to do it. If Shakespeare's plays place spectators in dramatic situations by threatening to undermine core conventions of theatre-making, doubling would have intensified those dramas by complicating the ontological status of the stage figures. If aesthetically productive instigations of failure at the site of the performer are essential and widespread in Shakespeare's plays, we might better understand and appreciate them in light of doubling's potential to complicate and even dramatize the position of the actor.

Metadrama 2.0

The most prominent examples of Shakespeare's fascination with destabilizing plays to enhance their dramatic potential are the plays within plays, none of which go uninterrupted. These are conventionally metadramatic moments but are perhaps less interesting for their capacity to create frames within the frame than they are for showing how easily the membranes separating fact and fiction can be ruptured or obliterated. The mechanicals' performance of 'Pyramus and Thisbe' in *A Midsummer Night's Dream* and the 'Pageant of the Nine Worthies' in *Love's Labour's Lost* are repeatedly delayed, altered, interpreted, and eventually disintegrated by their onstage audiences. *The Murder of Gonzago* is also interrupted by Hamlet, who undermines the players' efforts, and the play, by revealing what is still to come. When spectators watch onstage 'audiences' as the plays before them are delayed or dissolved their experience is charged by a latent awareness that the play they have come to see is likewise under threat.

The ways in which 'actors' in the plays within plays are exposed as actors, and thus placed in uncomfortable positions that force offstage spectators to share in their anxieties, is still more powerful. As I have argued concerning real audiences, the onstage audiences are preoccupied with (and appear to derive significant pleasure from) the fact that the people performing are not who they pretend to be. These characters often voice awareness of stage artifice in ways that question and unsettle the actor's ontological position in the eyes of the spectators. The onstage audience at the pageant of the 'Nine Worthies', for instance, sweeps aside the performers' attempts at representation and pushes them into unforeseen, presumably undesirable dramatic situations, much like that of the Polonius actor. The pageant opens with Costard in the role of Pompey:

Enter [Costard *the clown* as] Pompey

COSTARD [*as Pompey*]	'I Pompey am –'
BIRON	You lie: you are not he.
COSTARD [*as Pompey*]	'I Pompey am –'
BOYET	With leopard's head on knee. (5.2.543–5)

The pageant is so miscast and clumsily staged that audiences can laugh along as Biron, Dumaine, and Boyet join forces to mock it. But while the farcical performance suits the play and echoes the lords' prior failures to fool one another and then impersonate Muscovites, audiences tend to be uncomfortable with the extended abuse of amateur actors, particularly as directed at Holofernes when he enters as Judas Maccabeus. His parting line – 'This is not generous, not gentle, not humble' (5.2.623) – can leave audiences, both onstage and off, in guilty silence, as a fragile human voice erupts from what had seemed a stock character in a patently artificial play. Such was the case in Dominic Dromgoole's 2007 production at the Globe, when Holofernes' exit left spectators silent, stunned by the arrogance and condescension of Biron, his fellows – and themselves. In the right hands the moment can be among the most moving in Shakespeare. I suggest that this stems from the audience's sympathy for the failing actor's situation (albeit a fictional actor) and for its own loss of part of the play (albeit a play-within-a-play). The broken contract between the onstage audiences and those performing for them cannot but foreground the tenuousness of our own relationship to the play before us.

The experience of comedy here is quite like that experienced watching the bitter reception given to Starveling (as Moonshine) by the newly married men of *A Midsummer Night's Dream*, or the entertainments practised on Malvolio in *Twelfth Night*. However the scenes are played, Shakespeare's onstage audiences tend to enjoy watching these characters squirm more than we do, even though we may nervously titter along at the mean-spirited jokes.[23] Each situation forces the offstage audience to share in the anxiety of a stage figure unwillingly revealed as an actor. These characters achieve, as characters, the effects available to the Polonius actor: cast out of plays within plays and seemingly ostracized from the narratives themselves. The offstage audience enters its own drama – one made complex by conflicting desires: we want the play within the play to continue, yet we hope that the players in *the play* will stop what they are doing.[24]

Love's Labour's Lost is a play deeply concerned with deception, and with acting's failure to effect it. Prior to the pageant of the worthies, Moth is interrupted and then scuttles a prepared speech in praise of the Princess and her retinue: 'They do not mark me, and that brings me out!' (5.2.173). His failed effort was intended to introduce Navarre's scholars in the habits of Muscovites, themselves victims to a deception by masked female counterparts who impersonate one another. The effect achieved by having the actor go out of his part is like that available to Polonius, but through different means. While Polonius seems to be obscured by the emergence of the actor, Moth lapses into his primary fictional identity while on a stage full of characters disguised as other people. His admission that he cannot recite a speech or maintain a persona creates a hierarchy of legitimacy among equally false stage figures. The failed recital thus leaves Moth comparatively ill-suited to duplicity, so that while he is no more authentic as Moth than the scholars are as Muscovites or the women are as one another, he momentarily seems so as a result of a failure at representation.

Something similar occurs in *Twelfth Night*, when a speech that Viola has 'taken great pains to con' is cut short and she admits her inability to address what is 'out of [her] part' (1.5.161–6). These comments may pass as Fabian's reference to the stage does, but Olivia challenges her further, 'Are you a comedian?'

---

[23] Holofernes endures 33 lines' worth of abuse, while Starveling undergoes nearly as much torment in *A Midsummer Night's Dream*, 5.1.231–51. Both examples feel protracted and do little to advance the plot. Malvolio plays roles arranged for him by Maria, Toby, Fabian, and Feste, but, though he picks up the right cues, his scenes continually reveal him as an actor ready for a play other than the one in which he is cast. The generic call of *Twelfth Night* pits the audience against him, but his treatment is clearly unjust (see esp. 3.4.16–113 and 4.2).

[24] Compare the trial scene in *The Merchant of Venice*, where Shylock is punished beyond what feels just to most spectators, another example of a play that contrasts the audience's sense of justice with that of the characters onstage. In keeping with its genre, the play ends happily but spectators typically feel haunted throughout Act Five by Shylock's fate, a feeling exacerbated because the other characters seem to have forgotten him entirely. See my essay, 'Letting Unpleasantness Lie: Counter-intuition and Character in *The Merchant of Venice*', in *Shakespeare's Sense of Character: On the Page and From the Stage*, ed. Yu Jin Ko and Michael Shurgot (Aldershot: Ashgate, 2012).

(1.5.169). Of course, she is a comedian. The actor of Cesario – that is, Viola – and the *actor* playing Viola are both comedians. Viola first denies imposture, yet soon after betrays herself by confessing, 'I am not that I play', to which Olivia responds that Viola is now 'out of [her] text' (1.5.171, 214). The scene works to reveal a fictitious persona within a fictitious persona, each complicating Viola's ontological status.[25] By acknowledging the veneer that is Cesario, Shakespeare allows Viola a stronger claim to authenticity. Characters such as Viola, Leontes, and Moth illustrate Shakespeare's interest in splitting seams that bind actor and character, thereby increasing our susceptibility to the fiction. When actors double roles, the secondary or tertiary characters likewise undermine and advertise the artifice of their primary roles, while drawing awareness to those roles as primary or original, and thus somehow more legitimate in a hierarchy of artifice, despite everything in that hierarchy being equally fictitious.

Onstage Graveyards and Embodied Ghosts

Good places to see Shakespeare create effects analogous to those thus far described are his onstage graveyards, among the dead and (not entirely) gone. Consider the generous attention we pay to the diaphragms of 'deceased' stage figures. Our attendance on the stage-dead parallels the simultaneous tracking of actors and characters that we perform (almost) unconsciously. Virtually no audience member can resist a quick check to reassure him- or herself that Romeo's abdomen continues to rise and fall even after he drinks off his quick drugs, or that soldier #2 appeared to make himself portable when it was time for his dragging offstage. At such moments, the play cannot entirely control the elements that manifest it, and the audience cannot resist the temptation of watching the actor fail in his attempt to perform what is scripted. The continued animacy of the stage-dead brings the actor, as actor, into the fiction, proving with each breath his unfitness for the part. Bill Worthen argues for the actor's capacity to participate *alongside* the character he enacts, by noting that 'the site of drama is the site of acting' and that 'acting and drama share the politics of duplicity'.[26] I would add that the site of acting becomes a dramatic site, or at least a richer one, because of its potential to host acting failures. Stage death, in its essence, underscores the actor's inescapable failure to deceive absolutely. In Shakespeare's hands, 'death' becomes a crux: an opportunity for the actor to imperil the fiction, the threat of which can likewise be magnified for the audience's sake.

---

[25] Many characters similarly question their identities. See Iago's 'I am not what I am' (1.1.63), or Hamlet's inversion of the same idea in his phrase 'I know not "seems"' (1.2.76).
[26] Worthen, *The Idea of the Actor*, p. 3.

Among the best-known examples, Lear and Othello hover over 'dead' bodies, repeatedly voicing doubt about the legitimacy and finality of the deaths, and enabling the audience's awareness of the living actor to intensify the energies of fiction.[27] The effect begins in *Othello* when Othello's first attempt to smother Desdemona proves unsuccessful:

> EMILIA   My lord! My lord! What, ho, my lord! My lord!
> OTHELLO What noise is this? – Not dead? Not yet quite dead?
>   I, that am cruel, am yet merciful:
>   I would not have thee linger in thy pain.
>   So. So.   (5.2.84–8)

Othello's effort at suffocation will always leave the actor breathing – and the spectators watching her breathe – while giving us cause to believe that the character has died. Spectators fluently harmonize the actor's life and the character's death. But when Othello finds her living, we learn that the reality we perceived (of a living actor) was, in fact, a component of the fiction. So, in the moment at which Othello finds life – 'Not dead? Not yet quite dead?' – we learn that we have more misjudged the state of the drama than he, while mistaking our own capacity to keep fiction separate from truth. Shakespeare anticipates how spectators will perceive and process stage deaths, then uses our understanding against us. We trust convention by setting truth aside for a fictional reality, only to learn that truth was necessary for correctly interpreting fictional events.

Predictably, Shakespeare lingers over the effect. At 'So. So', Othello confirms the death of Desdemona. She had been near death; now she is gone; and the spectators readopt their former understanding – she has died while her enactor lives. But then Othello continues:

> Yes. – 'Tis Emilia. [*Calling*] – By and by! – She's dead.
> 'Tis like she comes to speak of Cassio's death:
> The noise was high. – Ha, no more moving?
> Still as the grave. Shall she come in? Were't good?
> I think she stirs again! No. What's best to do?
> If she come in, she'll sure speak to my wife.
> My wife! My wife! What wife? I ha' no wife!   (5.2.90–6)

This is a riveting theatrical moment. Othello has killed Desdemona, found her 'yet not dead', then smothered her again. Emilia's imminent arrival adds urgency to his attempt to complete the murder. He delays her long enough to confirm death ('By and by! – She's dead'), questions the death immediately after confirming it ('no more moving?'); then responds to his own question with a full stop ('Still as the grave'). Both question and answer independently affirm

---

[27] T.W. Craik discusses both deaths in 'I know when one is dead and when one lives' (British Academy Shakespeare Lecture, 1979, in the Academy's *Proceedings*, vol. lxv).

and deny what the audience knows to be true about the figure in question. Convinced that she is 'still', Othello then notices Desdemona *stirring*, before assuring himself that she cannot stir: 'I think she stirs again! No.' (5.2.94). Convinced of his wife's death, he then imagines her alive again and speaking with Emilia, before finally declaring that he has 'no wife' at all. Every true statement about the character rings false about the actor whose identity as actor conspicuously invades the scene. Conversely, each sign of life in Desdemona is true concerning the actor yet (we must assume) false about the character.

Emilia arrives with news of the unfinished murder of Cassio, whereupon Desdemona's murder proves likewise unfinished when she cries out: 'O, falsely, falsely murdered!' (5.2.115). Again, our attention to the actor's barely perceptible movements provided a truer account of Desdemona's health than the narrative frame allowed. Reality and illusion once more cannot be held apart; each asserts primacy in the delivery and interpretation of the plot. Desdemona's line, 'falsely murdered', augments the effect, providing evidence of life while conveying news of its absence. At the character's death, she simply bristles with life. The actor has become the chief site of duplicity and drama—*within* the fiction.

The closing scene of *King Lear* operates by similar means and to similar ends. Lear enters with Cordelia limp in his arms and declares her dead, while claiming a peculiar expertise in distinguishing the dead from the living:

> Howl, howl, howl, howl! O, you are men of stones:
> Had I your tongues and eyes, I'd use them so
> That heaven's vault should crack. She's gone forever.
> I know when one is dead and when one lives;
> She's dead as earth.   (5.3.256–60)

In these lines Cordelia's death is affirmed, and the play's tragic end becomes certain.[28] Yet, in the next breath Lear asks for a 'looking-glass' to make assurance double sure: 'If that her breath will mist or stain the stone, / Why then she lives' (5.3.261–2). At this point, the actor enters the fiction. Cordelia's breath *will* mist the stone. Shakespeare advertises the presence and aliveness of the actor just when spectators most desire to see life signs in Cordelia, adding weight to tragedy by delaying its confirmation.

Othello repeatedly affirms the death of a character that clings to life; Lear continually finds life in a character dead and gone. Shakespeare has Lear gauge Cordelia's death in ways that draw acute attention to the live actor: 'This feather stirs; she lives. If it be so, / It is a chance which does redeem all sorrows' (5.3.264–5). Lear's feather test forces the audience to process, with Edgar and

---

[28] Three pertinent critical discussions here are Craik's Academy lecture; Marvin Rosenberg's *The Masks of King Lear* (Berkeley: University of California Press, 1972), esp. pp. 313–16; and Booth's *King Lear, Macbeth, Indefinition and Tragedy*, esp. pp. 27–40.

Kent, the idea that the feather *does not* actually stir, despite our awareness that the actor's breath will move it. The life we desire to see extended is perceptible, but in the world of truth, not fiction.

The ambiguous suspension between death and life lingers over Cordelia as it does over Desdemona. Lear states plainly, for the second time, that Cordelia has died: 'now she's gone for ever' (5.3.272). Perhaps there was some faint breath to mist the stone and stir the feather, but now it is gone. But then, immediately, Lear appears to hear the dead figure speak:

> Cordelia, Cordelia, stay a little. Ha,
> What is't thou say'st? Her voice was ever soft,
> Gentle and low, an excellent thing in woman.   (5.3.270–2)

Actors can temper ambiguity by playing Lear as merely delusional here, but the play leans towards enabling actor and audience to revive faint hopes for Cordelia's survival: first through Lear's divinations, now through her supposed *speaking*, much as Desdemona spoke even after her (second) suffocation.[29] To the verge of his own death, Lear persists in descrying signs of life in Cordelia:

> Pray you, undo this button. Thank you, sir.
> Do you see this? Look on her. Look, her lips,
> Look there, look there.
>   *He dies.*   (5.3.308–10)

We might expect that a playwright would wish to avoid enlisting audiences in scrutiny of the 'dead' character's lips. But Shakespeare flaunts the fact that she lives and breathes, forcing us to overlook truth in favor of fiction, only to undermine that fiction by frequent attentions to the truth we're trying to overlook. Tension and discomfort builds and further engages spectators as the logic of the representational conventions seems to break down.

Shakespeare's plays offer many examples wherein heightened awareness of the actor can complicate reception of the character: Othello's epilepsy, Macbeth's encounters with the supernatural, Hermione or Thaisa's retrieval from death, and Lady Macbeth's sleepwalking are among those widely known. While these examples provoke conventionally metadramatic interest, each also potentially blurs boundaries between actor and character, setting and bare stage, commonplace object and theatrical prop. Human beings, when pretending to be ghosts, dual-gendered witches, Polonius, Holofernes, 'actors', or someone 'still as the grave' might be more interesting than even real ghosts or witches or dead people could be, at least more interesting than convincing representations

---

[29] Compare, too, Kent's situation. Lear thinks Kent's adopted persona, Caius, is 'dead and rotten' before encountering Caius in the person of Kent. Kent's resurrection in Caius, and Caius's in Kent, create context for the potential resurrection of Cordelia that is persistently imminent but never realized.

of such things, precisely because of their deficiencies in representation. It may be, too, that placing human beings in intensely vulnerable positions due to representational failures or intrusions of reality creates anxiety and empathy that cannot be rivalled by any conceivable fictional situation. I suggest that one never fears for Desdemona so much as one fears for the actor being suffocated with a pillow, nor worries about Mercutio when Romeo enters the fray so much as one does for the actor playing young Arthur in *King John*, if he climbs over the balcony unprotected, looks down, and leaps.

Though the deaths and near-deaths in *Othello* and *King Lear* present brief dramas of an emerging actor, the plays find other occasions to destabilize their narratives. One of the best known is the leap from Dover Cliff, which always stands out as confusing, even ridiculous, to the audience of *King Lear*. Try as they might, directors will not convince us that Gloucester is climbing 'that same hill' or that he leaps from Dover's chalky cliffs. They certainly will not convince us that Gloucester *thinks* he has fallen from a cliff. Jan Kott considered the moment an occasion where Shakespeare 'shows the paradox of pure theatre', as the limitations of the stage become prominent in the fiction when Edgar relies upon them to deceive his father.[30] Shakespeare does offer a paradox of theatre, but its chief interest may be the audience-centred drama it initiates by providing us with inadequate tools for interpreting what the stage momentarily represents. Our awareness of theatrical convention is pitted against us, as the play offers explicit fakery without initially signalling that the cliff *is* fake. The dutiful, theatrically literate audience to the scene, that is, will at first assume that its responsibility is to *imagine* a 'real' cliff. Then, when Gloucester leaps to his death – a death we will not credit in any case – we learn that the imagined cliff was imaginary. There was no cliff in the fiction, just as there is no cliff on the stage. Again, the reality that leaked into the fiction was party to it, a truer guide to the play's events than those events.

There is no air-drawn dagger either. And there is no blood on the hands of Macbeth or his Lady. The vigorous washing that the husband imagines and the wife performs *will* wash their hands clean. Shakespeare's effort to draw attention to the blood of Duncan, and to its capacity to weather all storms and seas, raises a kind of resistance in an audience that knows better.[31] In these moments

---

[30] Jan Kott, *Shakespeare Our Contemporary* (Garden City: Doubleday, 1964), p. 146. On the flat 'cliff' at Dover in *King Lear*, 4.6, also see William Matchett, 'Some Dramatic Techniques in *King Lear*', in *Shakespeare and the Theatrical Dimension*, ed. Philip C. McGuire and David A. Samuelson (New York: AMS Press, 1979), pp. 185–208; and Alan C. Dessen, 'Two Falls and a Trap', *English Literary Renaissance* 5 (1975), pp. 291–307. Derek Peat traces the origin and history of the discussion in '"And that's true too": *King Lear* and the Tension of Uncertainty', in *Aspects of King Lear*, ed. Kenneth Muir and Stanley Wells (Cambridge: Cambridge University Press, 1982), pp. 43–54.

[31] Cf. examples of gore in *Titus Andronicus*, or the conspirators' interest in bathing their hands in Caesar's blood.

we attend to a gap between truth and fiction so transparent as to be tiresome, as if we felt compelled to admit that yonder cloud, so clearly in the shape of a camel, really were backed like a weasel. Put another way, if Shakespeare wishes to focus his audience on the story of *Macbeth*, he ought not to linger over blood that is not there, and he certainly shouldn't ask Lady Macbeth to sleepwalk. The sleepwalking scene, again, cannot but advertise that the actor is not quite up to the part. Yet, even when they get poor reviews, Lady Macbeths are regularly lauded for their performances in the sleepwalking scene – just as Ophelias tend to draw compliments on their mad scenes, however much the critics think they fall short when playing sanity. I think much of these scenes' power to attract owes to our awareness that Lady Macbeth *is not* sleeping, and that Ophelia is no madder than we. At such moments we watch the actor acting. That sounds ridiculous, since we always watch actors act, but appreciating elements of performance in support of a character and watching a drama that concerns whether that character's actions are supportable are of two houses.

From the bear-suited actor who pursues Antigonus to Hermione's attempt to present inanimacy; from Lavinia's doubtful lack of hands and tongue to Titus's home-cooking; from the physical presence of Macbeth's trunkless head to that of Cloten's 'headless' trunk, we repeatedly see Shakespeare asking actors to represent what they cannot convincingly represent, initiating actor-centred dramas that put the fiction under pressure. Often, these alternate dramatic journeys are energized because audiences do not want to be on them, even if their power to engage may surpass that of the narratives. Watching Cloten hide his head down a trap door, or behind a makeshift hillock, we are aware of nothing so much as the fact that he is not *really* headless, so our interest gravitates towards how the actors achieve (or fail to achieve) the playing of the play. Such moments are analogous to recitation in stimulating dramatic interest, since they offer the playing company and its audience potential sites of rupture and risk.

In short, I suggest that Shakespeare anticipated critics like Goldman and Ridout in understanding that destabilizing the fiction by exploiting the actor's dramatic position could deepen engagement. This proposed, we might reconsider the practice of theatrical doubling in Shakespeare's artistry. It is widely acknowledged that Shakespeare's company doubled roles, but scholars may have underestimated the degree to which his plays are prefigured for doubling; the extent of doubling practised on historical stages; and how integral the logic of theatrical doubling was for Shakespeare and his fellow sharers.

Shakespeare's interest in twins, double plots, puns, and other forms of replication is well known. Doubling roles would have provided him means to achieve two theatrical objectives he pursued throughout his career: complicating the fundamental duality of the actor, and imperilling theatrical illusions by advertising their artifice. Like the examples discussed in this chapter, the practice of doubling roles disrupts the fiction and may be seen to mar the surface of the illusion. In fact, actors playing multiple parts embody the impending eradication of illusion like nothing else, since in their secondary or tertiary roles they make a constant, oblique admission to the fiction of the fiction. Yet, through doubling Shakespeare opens up artistic possibilities for his actors and audiences that are wholly unavailable without it. Just as the live actor playing the dead Cordelia intensifies tragedy by prolonging uncertainty, so the actor who trips to France as Cordelia and returns as Lear's Fool intensifies Lear's regret, reminding him and his audience in every moment that he 'did her wrong' (1.5.22).

Embodied Ghosts and Doubling in *Hamlet*

Returning to *Hamlet*, we can see how doubling lends coherence to the play's world, even as it highlights the artifice that brings that world about. Note the complications that arise when the actor of the King's ghost also takes on the role of the usurping Claudius – two figures whose differences *and* likenesses the play takes all occasions to insist upon. Such an actor watches, with the eyes of Claudius, a dumb show in which a (false) false king murders a (false) real one before an audience that sees both false and real king in him. He is false for having obtained the throne through murder, yet he is also the rightful king, both because he has been crowned and because the actor playing him alternates as Hamlet's father. A production of *Hamlet* employing the double enriches its audience's experience significantly. In addition to augmenting the actor's duplicity, Hamlet's hesitancy, Gertrude's incest, and Claudius's guilt all gain interest and make more improbable and interesting the dividedly loyal position of audiences. Meanwhile, as I have noted already, if the production doubles Polonius and First Gravedigger, then the philosophical and comic exchanges between the antically disposed Hamlet and the comparatively sober Polonius are revisited in the graveside conversation between Hamlet and the Polonius *actor*, the actor taking Hamlet's antics and penchant for literalism as his own in his new role of Gravedigger.

Such choices further the play's ability to achieve its thematic and theatrical ends. After all, few plays work to compromise the illusion like *Hamlet*. Polonius's memory loss may be its bravest moment, but *Hamlet* takes every chance to advertise artifice, repeatedly demonstrating an obsession with play-acting and a desire to build comparative levels of truth into fiction. The play begins with a changing of the watch, at which Horatio plays sceptic to news of a ghost sighting:

> MARCELLUS What, has this thing appeared again tonight?
> BARNARDO I have seen nothing.
> MARCELLUS Horatio says 'tis but our fantasy

> And will not let belief take hold of him
> Touching this dreaded sight twice seen of us.   (1.1.20–4)

Hamlet begins with a ghost story, an improbable fiction the validity of which is much in question. Yet the play soon renders this secondary fiction 'real' when the ghost appears and interrupts his own biography: 'Peace, break thee off – look where it comes again!' (1.1.39). The audience to *Hamlet* sets out on its journey by watching stage figures 'watch' for the appearance of a protagonist in a fantastical narrative. In other words, it watches a version of itself. These characters, too, are parties to a story centered upon a figure pertinent in both the physical and metaphysical worlds. The ghost belongs to the 'undiscovered country from whose bourn / No traveler returns' (3.1.78–9), yet it returns at the start of Act One, just as the Polonius actor returns to the living realm of *his* audience near the top of Act Two (through aphasia) and Act Five (through 'death' and double casting). The audience likely shares Horatio's suspicion of the supernatural, and the actor playing the ghost will be seen as less authentic or convincing in that role than those actors playing the comparatively authentic Horatio, Marcellus, and Barnardo are in theirs. So the appearance of old Hamlet's Ghost, through ontological improbability, serves to legitimize the fictional beings who watch him. Horatio, Marcellus, and Barnardo enter as audience to something improbable, and lose something of their own improbability thereby.

When the ghost appears onstage, spectators will always fail to match the awe that the characters feel. Horatio admits that the ghost looks like the king, that it 'harrows [him] with fear and wonder', while Barnardo notices Horatio trembling and asks him, 'Is not this something more than fantasy?' (1.1.43, 53). Audiences will answer *no*. They may experience fear and pity on seeing a performance like Waterston's, but they cannot do so here. They can, however, see something more than fantasy in the *characters* confronting the Ghost, because those characters – just as fictional as the Ghost – are somehow less fantastical. Directors who try to make the supernatural entity seem credible get little for their efforts. Spectators cannot help but concern themselves with the fact that the supernatural being, like the 'bear' that chases Antigonus from the stage, is *acted*. And, as we have seen, this awareness contributes to engagement. *Hamlet*'s incorporation of the metaphysical world adds a dimension to the audience's experience, making the play a middle ground between the real world of the audience and the doubtful one of the ghost. Shakespeare divorces the fictional narrative from its dichotomous relationship with reality, making it a bridge between truth and artifice, as actors are by definition.

Shakespeare then uses the Ghost to compromise the theatrical frame and unsettle the audience, while commanding deeper engagement. The Ghost's role in asserting comparative truth in a fictional Denmark is one means, but

Shakespeare variously threatens the ghost's ontological status – his 'ghostliness' – thereby threatening our ability to accept that the characters can credit something the fiction deems credit-worthy. In 1.1, the ghost begins to depart after the cock crows:

HORATIO	… Stay and speak! Stop it, Marcellus.
MARCELLUS	Shall I strike at it with my partisan?
HORATIO	Do, if it will not stand.
BARNARDO	'Tis here.
HORATIO	'Tis here.
MARCELLUS	'Tis gone.

> We do it wrong, being so majestical,
> To offer it the show of violence,
> For it is as the air, invulnerable,
> And our vain blows malicious mockery. (1.1.138–45)

It is, of course, impossible to mock this 'ghost' with blows, since the actor's body – the audience may be sure – is vulnerable. In fact, the actor's vulnerability is highlighted not only by his physical body, but also by the armour he wears to protect it. Stephen Greenblatt notes the distinction drawn between the fantastic and the phantasmal nature of the Ghost and how the descriptions of Horatio and the others point to its immateriality.[32] Interestingly, the lines establishing that immateriality also compromise the figure's ghostliness, a paradox alluded to by Marvin Rosenberg, who concludes that the vanishing Ghost and the attempts to hold it by force make up a 'theatrical coup that mystifies and delights audiences'.[33] The play thus takes pains to highlight the mortal limitations of the one actor tasked with playing immortality. It would be easier on his play for Shakespeare not to have his characters strike something solid and then attempt to make fools of the audience by pretending to have struck at air. But here the fiction aggressively questions the validity of its components. The triptych phrase "'Tis here. 'Tis here. 'Tis gone' works to similar ends. It describes the ghost flitting about and suddenly vanishing, which will prove noticeably impossible for the mere mortal undertaking the role.[34] Even the most elegant trapdoor effect will put the reality at odds with the fiction, a problem Shakespeare goes out of his way to create.

---

[32] Stephen Greenblatt, *Hamlet in Purgatory* (Princeton: Princeton University Press, 2001), p. 212.

[33] Marvin Rosenberg, *The Masks of Hamlet* (Cranbury: Associated University Presses, 1992), p. 32.

[34] Alan Dessen notes the difficulty of staging scenes like this one, along with the ghost of Caesar, the witches in *Macbeth*, and others, according to stage directions that call for figures to 'vanish' in *Recovering Shakespeare's Theatrical Vocabulary* (Cambridge: Cambridge University Press, 1995), pp. 196–215. David G. Brailow considers how stage directions might help describe, if not its original performance, at least options and difficulties for performing the scene in '"'Tis here. 'Tis gone." The Ghost in the Text', in *Stage Directions in Hamlet: New*

Having an actor's body represent Hamlet's Ghost – more so than any ghost of our imagination, or the spectral projections or disembodied voices that directors sometimes deploy on stage – enhances a play obsessed with acting, seeming, performing, and putting on dispositions. It enhances a play that casts Reynaldo, Ophelia, and Hamlet as actors within the fiction, and one in which a troupe of actors receives direction from someone who repeatedly intrudes on their performance and ultimately gives away the ending. Hamlet's disruptions, Claudius's call for light, and Polonius's earlier interjection ('this is too long'), which derails the actor approaching the climax of his story about Priam's death, are all augmented by a Ghost whose attempt at representation is undermined by the need to flit about and seem ethereal in the face of blows.

In the case of the Ghost, *Hamlet* makes the audience mindful of the actor's inability to fulfil the demands of the character, and to present what the other characters claim they have seen. We see something similar in the witches of *Macbeth*, who straddle genders, as well as the natural and supernatural worlds,[35] and whose disappearance makes Banquo and Macbeth wonder:

> BANQUO   The earth hath bubbles as the water has,
>   And these are of them. Whither are they vanished?
> MACBETH Into the air. And what seem'd corporal
>   Melted as breath into the wind.   (1.3.80–3)

Both plays expose the limitations of actors to do what characters onstage claim to see them do, forcing spectators to credit what is obviously incredible for the sake of the narrative's endurance. The spectators witness reality's intrusion into fiction – in this case, the limitations that mortality imposes (since flesh and bone cannot melt 'like breath into the wind') – and accept statements about the situation that they know to be untrue, in part because the speakers seem more 'real' than the ontologically dubious witches. All this, despite every figure onstage being indisputably false *and* as real as the spectators themselves.

Detailing *Hamlet*'s obsession with artifice would make up a volume, but Hamlet's situation deserves elaboration. He is often thought a remarkably 'human' character, one that advocates holding 'the mirror up to nature' to reveal something of ourselves therein (3.2.20). But however authentic

---

Essays and New Directions, ed. Hardin L. Aasand (Cranbury: Associated University Presses, 2003), pp. 101–14.

[35] The 'weird sisters', Banquo observes, 'should be women, / And yet your beards forbid me to interpret/ That you are so' (1.3.46–8). They resist both masculinity and femininity by straddling the two, much as they mingle supernatural traits with worldly bodies and behaviours.

Hamlet appears, Shakespeare relentlessly exposes him as an illusion, giving the actor long, conspicuously metaphorical verse speeches, and having him spend much of the play actively deceiving other characters with his 'antic disposition'. Yet when not feigning madness, he alternately seems to experience 'real' fits (the nunnery scene) or attests to a legitimate madness that is highly dubious (e.g. explaining before the 5.2 duel that his wrongs to Laertes resulted from 'madness'). Meanwhile, he evaluates acting; discusses London's theatre scene; gives acting lessons to a group of actors pretending to be actors; and helps compose and orchestrate a play within the play. The scene in which *The Murder of Gonzago* is staged calls for an actor to play a false king before Claudius, a king both false and true, though the performance is intended *not* to deceive the audience so much as to mirror forth for Gertrude and Claudius truths about their (fictional) lives from within the fiction. And Hamlet's play requires the actor playing the false king to murder the actor playing the true king in front of the Claudius actor, who represents a false king who has murdered a true one, and who may be playing both.

Having come again to the doubling of Claudius and the Ghost, we may notice that the Ghost, despite being as different from Claudius as 'Hyperion to a Satyr', hardly convinces us of the fact (1.2.140). Conspicuously, for instance, he tells Hamlet that he is 'for the day confined to fast in fires / Till the crimes done in my days of nature / Are burnt and purged away' (1.5.11–13). Yet surely we should have expected *Claudius* to suffer for his crimes. Such confession and daily suffering for one's sins matches our expectations for the usurper, but not for Hamlet's father. To that end, we see Claudius soon after in prayer, seeking redemption. While assuring us that the two brothers could not be more different, the play pushes their similarities and even seems to confuse their aspects and attributes, lending support and substance to the proposed double – which merely extends this agenda into a further dimension. Furthermore, the play is greatly concerned with rightful succession; yet Claudius, when doubled with King Hamlet, in one true sense *is* a rightful king. So the more the play insists that Hamlet, or Laertes, or Fortinbras is fittest to rule, and ought to displace Claudius on the throne, the more the audience will hesitate before assuming the role dictated to it by the narrative – perhaps experiencing a version of what makes Hamlet hesitate at the prospect of killing a version of his father by killing his father's murderer. Related complex effects are achieved if the Polonius actor returns as the Gravedigger; if Ophelia returns to further suffer Hamlet's affected lunacies as Osric; if Rosencrantz and Guildenstern reprise prior turns as Marcellus and Barnardo, and Cornelius and Voltemand; if the Laertes actor goes again to France as Reynaldo to spy on himself, then returns to Elsinore as one of the tragedians; perhaps even if

Horatio and Ophelia are linked still more closely to Hamlet because they are portrayed by a single actor.[36]

Throughout the play within the play, Hamlet offers commentary (Ophelia says he is 'as good as a chorus' [3.2.227]), solicits feedback, and interprets events for his onstage audience, detracting from the coherence of his illusion in the moments of its unfolding. Finally he wrecks the play by spoiling its climax – 'You shall see anon how the murderer gets the love of Gonzago's wife' (3.2.244–5) – causing Claudius to obliterate the leavings of the illusion by rising and calling for 'light'. Hamlet also exposes artifice in others: how the player 'in a fiction... / Could force his soul so to his own conceit' (2.2.471–2); how the king is a thing 'Of nothing' (3.5.29); how women 'paint an inch thick' (5.1.174); and, from his earliest lines, he contrasts the reality of his feelings with shows and 'actions that a man might play' (1.2.84). Even this brief overview shows Shakespeare repeatedly pushing the artifice of the illusion to the fore, threatening the credibility of the fiction. When we contextualize Hamlet's behaviour in light of the play's persistent scene-making (e.g. the deployments of Ophelia, Gertrude, and Reynaldo as conscious actors; the eavesdropping performed by Hamlet, Polonius, and Claudius) alongside language that complements themes of action, performance, and deception (e.g. the gravedigger's ornate distinctions about Ophelia's suicide: 'an act hath three branches – it is to act, to do, and to perform' (5.1.11–12), any claims *Hamlet* might make to privileged truth or authenticity must seem suspect.

Yet exposing artifice at every turn is precisely what creates the sense of authenticity surrounding *Hamlet* – not to mention around Hamlet, a character whom generations of critics and theatre-goers have received as compellingly, even uniquely credible. This ability to perpetuate and enhance an illusion's viability, even in the moments of its undermining, helps make Shakespeare's art so special. And while this paradoxical result is achieved through all the foregoing means, the practice of doubling roles gave Shakespeare a way to constantly and implicitly make and mar the illusion, and to complement every other strategy by so doing. Like Hamlet himself, Shakespeare has been praised for accurately depicting human beings and the human condition, for placing 'the mirror up to nature'. We may see him that way, however, because he is the poet most comfortable with letting art co-opt and change nature, the very case that Polixenes makes to Perdita in *The Winter's Tale* (4.4.88–97). For Shakespeare the means to greater truth in art is to offer, Polonius-like, less matter with more art, repeatedly indicating that the art pretending to truth is only pretending,

---

[36] The dramaturgical structure of *Hamlet* enables only nine actors to play 33 roles. Charts that document the structure, and propose possibilities for performance with nine actors, are included in the Appendix.

and is better for it. Since doubling roles intimately coheres with Shakespeare's implicit theory of theatrical engagement, the practice deserves greater consideration as a central concern of his artistry. We might therefore profitably review the historical case and probability of doubling roles, alongside its ability to further the actor's paradox and the ongoing instability of the theatre, aspects that Shakespeare repeatedly seized on and exploited when writing plays.

2　Versatility and Verisimilitude on Sixteenth-Century Stages

ଈଓଔ

CLOWN　　　Give me the lie, do, and try whether I am not now a gentleman born.
AUTOLYCUS　I know you are now, sir, a gentleman born.
CLOWN　　　Ay, and have been so any time these four hours.

~The Winter's Tale, 5.2.124–7

ଈଓଔ

The Winter's Tale winds towards its close with a scene (5.2) between the newly genteel Clown, his father the Shepherd, and the rogue Autolycus, who had impersonated a nobleman and wheedled the two rustics out of much of their money just two scenes prior. The Clown's naive conviction that a swift change in social status has overwritten the facts of his birth highlights one of the great comic scenes in Shakespeare, likewise made entertaining by the reversal of fortunes of the two young men: the Clown here making amateur attempts at playing a nobleman; the scoundrel (who previously posed as a courtier) now humble before the newly made man. This scene, as I argue in the next chapter, generates the kind of theatrical energy that may most have inspired and fascinated Shakespeare. Yet my immediate interest is not in what the 'gentleman born' sequence tells us about Shakespeare's theatre or dramaturgy, but in what it recalls about his own life.

Like the Clown, Shakespeare was not born a gentleman. His father, John Shakespeare, was a farmer's son who married well and rose to prominence in Stratford-upon-Avon, becoming an alderman and, in 1568, mayor. But the elder Shakespeare's bid to receive a coat of arms was rejected, and he retired quietly from public life, having fallen on hard times financially and into some disrepute for illegal trading in wool.[1] Thus lay the scene in 1596, when his son William offered the College of Heralds some 30 pounds and a new application, coming

---

[1] Given his father's early retirement – and records indicating that he was in debt and had been prosecuted for illegal activities – scholars have traditionally concluded that William departed for London without substantial means and with a responsibility to help support his family. Recently, however, David Fallow has argued that John Shakespeare stayed active (and quietly prospered) in a thriving wool trade, and that William may have initially gone to London to promote his father's business interests. See 'His Father John Shakespeare', in *The Shakespeare*

48

away with a family crest and the news that he, and his father after him, was at last a gentleman … born. The Clown delights in recounting the preposterous details of his newfound lineage: 'I was a gentleman born before my father' (5.2.129–30), and Shakespeare may have taken pleasure writing lines that realized his experience, charmed by the paradoxical notion that gentility – denoting an inborn condition of blood – could be acquired,[2] that society could admit a fundamental change in a person's identity and rights of birth because of a superficial change of title, circumstance, even garment.[3] In *The Winter's Tale*, Autolycus passes as a courtier because 'his garments are rich' (4.4.733–4); the Clown expects new clothes will actually ennoble him: 'See you these clothes? Say you see them not and think me still no gentleman born' (5.2.122–3); and Perdita is a 'real' princess unconsciously masquerading as a 'lowborn lass' (4.4.156), together demonstrating Shakespeare's attraction to paradoxes wherein the clothes make the (wo-)man.

Multiple and diverse conventions of Tudor-period drama alerted playwrights and playgoers to theatre's potential to threaten what had seemed unassailable binaries. Costume and stage impersonation blurred distinctions between male and female; noble and common; rich and poor; spirit and flesh. Critics in the period worried that fluid changes of status accomplished onstage would corrupt audiences, or debase the authority of those who owed their livings to the hierarchies that theatre so adroitly subverted. If changing clothes was sufficient to make one Prince or Friar, then true Princes and Friars might become indistinguishable from false ones. Queen Elizabeth reaffirmed English 'sumptuary' laws during the 1570s, in part because the rise of an English middle class allowed people to buy clothes that made it difficult to tell commoners from gentlemen, and even men from women.[4] Elizabeth exempted troupes of players from these laws, but Puritans saw the compromise of core societal binaries following hard upon their daily breakdowns on Elizabethan stages.[5]

Circle, ed. Paul Edmonson and Stanley Wells (Cambridge: Cambridge University Press, 2015), pp. 26–39. Still, John Shakespeare appears in town records (1592) on a list of those who avoided church for fear of being arrested for debt, for which his brother Henry was twice arrested in the early 1590s, so the family likely was not very prosperous at the time. See Robert Bearman, 'John Shakespeare: A Papist or Just Penniless', *Shakespeare Quarterly* 56.4 (2005), pp. 411–33, esp. 429–32; and Bearman's *Shakespeare's Money* (Oxford: Oxford University Press, 2016), esp. pp. 10–23.

[2] See Henry V's proclamation that the soldiers fighting by his side at Agincourt will become blood brothers, that 'Be he ne'er so vile, / This day shall gentle his condition' (4.3.62–3).

[3] Among other parallels, the Clown's father, the 'Shepherd', by definition trades in wool, and the play's fourth act is set at a sheep-shearing feast. For a thorough discussion of Shakespeare's biography in relation to the theatre see Lois Potter, *The Life of William Shakespeare* (Chichester: Wiley-Blackwell, 2012).

[4] Especially the 'Statute Issued at Greenwich', 15 June 1574, by order of Elizabeth I.

[5] In *Plays Confuted in Five Actions* (1582) Stephen Gosson argues, 'In Stage Plays for a boy to put on the attire, the gesture, the passions of a woman; for a mean person to take upon him the

Critics like Laura Levine and Jean Howard have pointed out how stage transvestism was both a way to explore transgressive behaviour and a site of significant cultural anxiety.[6] Many objected to cross-dressing on moral grounds,
but some critiques were surprisingly perceptive about the sources of its power.
William Prynne's *Histrio-Mastix, the Player's Scourge*, for instance, argues
that stage players 'unman, unchristian, uncreate themselves ... to make themselves, as it were, neither men nor women, but monsters'.[7] The term 'monster'
is surprisingly apt, and it is the very term Viola uses self-referentially when her
disguise makes her legible as a man (*Twelfth Night*, 2.2.33). When the male
actor plays a female role, it is not quite correct to say 'look at the woman' or
'look at the man'. Something similar may be true of actors playing roles consistent with their genders, but cross-dressing makes the conflation of actor and
character more conspicuous. Prynne seems attuned to the disquieting though
enlivening multiplicity of stage figures capable of taking on any identity the
author assigns. He thus anticipates critics like Michael Goldman, whose more
flattering analysis suggests that the player presents 'a particularly interesting
and energetic human being, who is not simply the actor, and not properly the
character, but the actor-as-character, whom we relate to in a special way'.[8]

If Prynne saw *Twelfth Night*, he watched a male actor impersonate a woman
(Viola) and then disguise 'herself' as a man (Cesario). A second male actor,
also impersonating a woman (Olivia), pursues the first. Two figures play out
three distinct sexual attractions: the fictional attraction of Olivia to Cesario;
the likewise fictional and unconsciously same-sex attraction of Olivia to
Viola; and the same-sex but meta-fictional attraction of one male actor to the
other. The effect is monstrously complex, and makes a perceptive critic of
Viola when she notes that disguise is 'a wickedness / Wherein the pregnant
enemy does much' (2.2.26–7). Potential for such complexity helps explain
why doubling has (and had) such appeal. Since an actor onstage is at once
a human being with a clear and consistent identity *and* a palimpsest that can

title of a Prince with counterfeit port, and train, is by outward signs to show themselves otherwise than they are, and so within the compass of a lie'. Cited from *English Professional Theatre,
1530–1660*, ed. Glynne Wickham, Herbert Berry, and William Ingram (Cambridge: Cambridge
University Press, 2000), p. 165. See also Deuteronomy, 22:5, which states that 'A man's
item shall not be on a woman, and a man shall not wear a woman's garment; whoever does
such a thing is an abhorrence unto Adonai'. See also Phillip Stubbes's *Anatomie of Abuses*
(London: Richard Jones, 1583).

[6] Laura L. Levine, *Men in Women's Clothing: Anti-theatricality and Effeminization, 1579–
1642* (Cambridge: Cambridge University Press, 1994); Jean Howard, *The Stage and Social
Struggle in Early Modern England* (New York: Routledge, 1994). Also see Stephen Orgel,
Impersonations: The Performance of Gender in Shakespeare's England (Cambridge: Cambridge
University Press, 1996).

[7] *Histrio-Mastix, The Player's Scourge* (1633), cited from *Shakespeare's Theater*, ed. Tanya
Pollard (Oxford: Blackwell, 2004), p. 291.

[8] Goldman, *The Actor's Freedom*, p. 6.

accommodate new impressions without entirely erasing the old, and since the actor-character's duality is a prime mover of audience attraction, playwrights can exploit the stage figure's potential to fascinate through cross-dressing, disguise, impersonation, or doubling roles.

In *The Winter's Tale*, Shakespeare employs all these devices: his all-male troupe was deployed for seven female roles, a man-eating bear, the winged abstraction 'Time', a dozen dancing satyrs, a child, and a statue. Within the fiction, Autolycus beguiles the Clown three times in three disguises (none of which fools the audience), changing habits and personas both onstage and off. Meanwhile, Florizel disguises himself as a rustic to match Perdita, who (having been abandoned in Bohemia and raised by shepherds) is likewise disguised without knowing it. The long scene in Bohemia (4.4) generates interest by featuring so many concealed characters, most of which perceive the true identities of some, but not all, of the others. For example, Polixenes and Camillo put on disguises to attend the shearing feast, where they see through Florizel's façade, but not Perdita's. Only the audience sees things as they are, while maintaining awareness of the diverse but limited perspectives of all those onstage. Every disguised character announces and enriches itself as a site of representation and rupture, enabling spectators to witness stage illusions repeatedly (sometimes simultaneously) established, compromised, and destroyed. Autolycus's costume changes are especially vitalizing, since he is a genuine (though fallen) courtier, a genuine scoundrel, and so adept at playing both that spectators cannot but admire his deceptions and delight in not falling victim to them, as the Clown does repeatedly. But when the Clown and Shepherd are promoted to genuine nobility, their changes in dress without corresponding changes in disposition are unconvincing. Autolycus's imposture and the Clown's transformation are both theatrical fictions, but audiences apprehend and admire two extraordinarily layered performances: one, by (a man playing) a rustic who plays a nobleman as if he were a commoner; the other, by (a man playing) a courtier-turned-scoundrel who plays the commoner like a nobleman. Complicating the effects further, spectators are typically more convinced by the more explicitly theatrical impersonation (Autolycus's) than by the 'real' one (the Clown's), even while the Clown's failure at portraying a courtier helps to 'convince' us that he is really a Clown (which of course he is not).

All these disguises and impersonations, recognitions and misrecognitions, can be complicated further if the shepherds have begun life – within the play – as 'real' courtiers. The Clown, the Shepherd, and Autolycus (like Florizel and Perdita) do not appear onstage until Act Three. Common sense suggests that they would have already been tapped to portray noblemen in Sicilia. Antigonus, Archidamus, and others give significant speeches before leaving the stage for good, and characters such as Cleomenes and Dion don't return until Act Five, leaving those actors free to double as Bohemians. The Clown's patently absurd notion of being a 'gentleman born' would have carried a strong valence of truth for playgoers who had already seen him in fine clothes.

'Put money in thy purse'

But while doubling roles would have had significant aesthetic implications for Shakespeare's company, it was an economic imperative. Shakespeare did not stumble upon faerie gold with which to gentle his condition; he made his living in the theatre business, one founded on the premise that any common man can turn King. And Shakespeare excelled at the business of theatre. William Ingram notes that when Shakespeare arrived in London most hired players earned little or nothing above the subsistence level (£8–10 per year).[9] Playwriting was not very lucrative either.[10] Yet by 1594 Shakespeare, likely having left Stratford without substantial means, purchased a share in the Lord Chamberlain's Men at a cost of what may have been four or five years' wages for a hired actor.[11] Once established as a company sharer and playwright, Shakespeare was so successful that within three years he secured his position among the gentry and the second-largest house in Stratford.[12] This success was achieved despite

[9] According to Ingram, statutes regulated the 'London journeyman's annual wage'. In 1585, the fixed wage was £8 per year for such professions as goldsmiths and painter-stainers, half if meat and drink were provided. He estimates that to 'succeed' economically – i.e. earn more than what was required for sustenance – a player would have to earn in excess of £10 per year. See William Ingram, 'The Economics of Playing', in *A Companion to Shakespeare*, ed. David Scott Kastan (Oxford: Blackwell, 1999), p. 315. Bearman notes that Shakespeare may have earned less than 6s. per week as a hired player (*Shakespeare's Money*, p. 38).

[10] Andrew Gurr argues that the 1580s and early 1590s presented 'a buyer's market for plays' and that its writers endured a form of 'economic servitude' to playing companies. He cites a contract for Richard Brome, which paid 15s. per week, though this was for an established author in 1635, suggesting that a little-known playwright 40 years earlier may have contracted for two or three plays a year at a wage near that of the hired players. See Gurr, *The Shakespearean Stage, 1574–1642* (Cambridge: Cambridge University Press, 2009), p. 21. Ingram notes that the average play sold for about £6 in the early 1600s, which given the inflation in the period should be considerably more than what was paid 10–15 years earlier. Ingram, 'Economics', p. 320.

[11] The cost Shakespeare paid for his share is unknown. In 1594, the same year the Lord Chamberlain's Men formed, Philip Henslowe records a loan to his nephew of £15 as a first payment 'for his share to the Quenes players'. A year later he loans him £9 more to help pay off the total owed. See *Henslowe's Diary*, ed. R.A. Foakes and R.T. Rickert (Cambridge: Cambridge University Press, 1961), 7. According to Ingram, Edward Alleyn sold his share in the Admiral's Men for £50 in 1597. We can surmise, then, that Shakespeare's share might have cost between £25 and £50. After capital expenses, sharers also were responsible for rent, costumes, properties, wages, etc., so Shakespeare must have thrived as a player and writer, able to generate far more money than most of his fellow players and playwrights, even during his early years in London. See Ingram, 'Economics', p. 321.

[12] James Forse reviews Shakespeare's large expenditures during the 1590s in *Art Imitates Business: Commercial and Political Influences in Elizabethan Theatre* (Bowling Green: Bowling Green State University Press, 1993). Though his father was sued twice for debt in 1589 and 1590, in the decade that followed Shakespeare bought not only his share in the company and the family's coat-of-arms, but also a large farm near Stratford, the large

two years of plague that frequently closed the theatres,[13] and the instability of a relatively new and mistrusted profession under siege from many sides.[14] David Fallow has argued that John Shakespeare's renewed success in the wool trade – and William's hand in representing his interests in London – may help explain the son's ability to become a sharer in the company and purchase property.[15] Nevertheless, theatre clearly became his focus and source of income sometime in the early 1590s, and he made theatre pay like no other actor or playwright in the period.

Andrew Gurr describes Shakespeare as 'an exceptionally good business-man', while Ingram warns against underestimating the importance of profit and the fear of insolvency for Shakespeare and his company, since 'a proper concern for making money [through stage playing] was part of the texture of their lives'.[16] Even for men of considerable talent, professional theatre in Shakespeare's time was an extremely risky commercial enterprise. Changing laws; licensure; plagues; want of skilled actors or good plays; weather; royal favour; and public taste, together combined to ruin many companies. While Shakespeare bequeathed to his friends more than £300 in cash at his death, Ben Jonson admitted that he did not earn £300 for all his plays combined, and he died nearly penniless.[17] Shakespeare's success probably owed something to his company's superior product, but the company was consummately efficient in production.

James Burbage, whose son Richard was the company's lead actor, had pioneered ways to boost profits, most notably by building London's first

house called 'New Place', and his share in the Globe Theatre. While maintaining his family, he would have had to earn about £447 to pay for the Globe share and the properties, a sum he probably could not have raised from writing alone had he written all 37 plays before 1600. Ibid., pp. 52–3. Bearman observes that Shakespeare may have been able to purchase New Place because he was 'creditworthy', but his income still must have been substantial (*Shakespeare's Money*, p. 98).

[13] Plague in London forced the playhouses to close for all of 1593 (1 February to 27 December 1593) and for much of spring 1594. See Andrew Gurr, *The Shakespearean Playing Companies* (Oxford: Oxford University Press, 1996), p. 91.

[14] Players were often viewed as vagrants living on public charity. In 1580, *A Second and Third Blast of Retreat from Public Theatres* appeared anonymously, arguing that players were those 'which cannot live of themselves live at the devotion or alms of other men, passing from country to country ... which is a kind of beggary' (cited in Wickham *et al.*, *English Professional Theatre*, p. 163). Such attacks were often extended to those who went to see plays as well.

[15] Fallow, 'His Father John Shakespeare', pp. 26–39.

[16] William Ingram, *The Business of Playing: The Beginnings of the Adult Professional Theater in Elizabethan London* (Cornell: Cornell University Press, 1992), p. 16.

[17] Forse attributes the wide difference in the fortunes of Shakespeare and Jonson to the fact that Shakespeare was owner, author, and actor, whereas Jonson was only a playwright (*Art Imitates Business*, p. 56).

dedicated playhouse. Ownership of 'The Theatre' eliminated the need to hire performance spaces and reduced the uncertainty and expense associated with touring.[18] Shakespeare's company did without an impresario like Henslowe to keep books (and profits), and no sharer held a special financial prerogative as Edward Alleyn had in the Admiral's Men.[19] Each man held rights as both householder and player, increasing individual earnings that were already greater for going without a manager or landlord. In 1599, when its land lease became troublesome, the company took greater charge over their economic enterprise by dismantling the building, moving the lumber and thatch to the bankside, and erecting 'The Globe'. The sharers showed their entrepreneurial spirit yet again when they established the first artificially lit, indoor venue at Blackfriars in 1608, creating the chance to play in all weathers and to give more performances at higher prices. Each of these steps increased the value of individual shares and the wealth of the sharers.[20]

Considering its unique organization, entrepreneurism, and success, it is unlikely that the company let many chances to maximize profits pass without notice. Prices at outdoor theatres seem to have been fixed, so profits depended largely on keeping costs down.[21] The sharers all played roles onstage, but the joint-stock model dictated that they manage and cover costs for everything their productions required. They had to secure venues, scripts, costumes, and properties; maintain theatre spaces; advertise; pay licensing fees; and more. And they needed to hire gatherers, stage keepers, tiremen, and musicians, who did

---

[18] As Gurr notes, playing companies proliferated in London between 1575 and 1595, before thinning out as the Lord Chamberlain's Men and the Admiral's Men gained prominence. Owners of venues could count on a substantial share of the profits, which James Burbage circumvented by building his own theatre. The Chamberlain's/King's Men thus became the sole 'joint-stock' theatre company in London, eventually owning both the Globe and the Blackfriars. See Gurr, *The Shakespearean Stage*, pp. 27–41.

[19] Henslowe (c. 1550–1616) owned the Rose Theater and later the Fortune, and he managed the Admiral's Men, rivals of Shakespeare's company. His accounts contain a wealth of information about theatre and finance in the period, though – because Shakespeare's company had no manager and could therefore dictate how its business was done – any lessons learned should be applied cautiously to the Lord Chamberlain's/King's Men.

[20] The Lord Chamberlain's men formed in 1594 with six sharers. Though sharers came and went, the number soon moved to eight and then to 12 in 1604 when they became the King's Men. Concerning economics and Shakespeare's company, see also Roslyn Knutson, *Playing Companies and Commerce in Shakespeare's Time* (Cambridge: Cambridge University Press, 2001); Lars Engle, *Shakespearean Pragmatism: Market of His Time* (Chicago: University of Chicago Press, 1993); and Frederick Turner, *Shakespeare's Twenty-First-Century Economics: The Morality of Love and Money* (Oxford: Oxford University Press, 1999).

[21] See Alfred Harbage, *Shakespeare's Audience* (New York: Columbia University Press, 1941), pp. 19–52. Until the boy companies emerged around the turn of the century, the two companies split the bulk of the London audience, about 2,500 people in 1595, and perhaps 3,000 by 1600. Price of admission, one penny to stand, one more to sit, and additional fees for gentlemen's rooms or other amenities, was apparently standard. See also Ingram, 'Economics', pp. 325–6.

what the sharers could not while performances were in progress. The greatest expense of all, though, was the employment of wage-earning actors. Gatherers and stage keepers might be found and trained quickly, but actors, especially those expected to speak and be understood in a large outdoor theatre, required training. Even actors in the smallest roles required some rehearsal (to learn cues, entrances and exits, etc.) and they would need to be compensated for it.

The surest way to limit costs would be for the sharers to duplicate their offstage versatility on the stage itself by doubling roles. Doubling could dramatically reduce the need for hired players – and the distraction and cost of training, rehearsing, and supporting them. Doubling would also make tours or travel to play at alternate venues easier, and since charters fixed the number of players in the companies, each livery coming with substantial expense to the Lord who furnished it, the players had further incentive to keep numbers low.[22] Given the volatility of playing in London, whose Master of the Revels could censor plays or close theatres without warning, touring remained a potential contingency plan even in the best times. Doubling roles may have obviated the need to travel with journeymen, or to contract with bit players at each stop.[23] And if the company planned for such contingencies, doubling had the additional advantage of not forcing the company to change its schedule or reassign duties when hired men were not available. In short, doubling minimized costs, the need for coordination, and uncertainty, without compromising – perhaps even improving – the quality of the product. And it did all this while allowing the sharers to be more responsible for their own success.

The sharers could put still more money in their purses by choosing plays for which the company's material resources were a good match, or if they could

---

[22] According to the 1572 statute against 'rogues and vagabonds' issued by Parliament, troupes of players could only travel in England while under the sponsor of a nobleman or woman. The number of actors in the companies was fixed by licence, most carrying about six to eight sharers. Even well established companies toured frequently, possibly for reputation as well as profit, or while en route to play at court or at the estates of the high-ranking nobles who retained them. See Alan Somerset, ' "How Chances it they Travel?": Provincial Touring, Playing Places, and the King's Men', *Shakespeare Survey* 47 (1994), pp. 45–60; and Sally-Beth MacLean, 'Tour Routes: "Provincial wanderings" or Traditional Circuits?' *Medieval and Renaissance Drama in England* 6 (1993), pp. 1–14.

[23] Playhouse closures may have forced troupes to travel more than they preferred, though G.E. Bentley notes the lack of evidence 'that touring was ever very profitable', as well as the difficult conditions of travel in unseasonable weather. It seems unlikely that companies would have preferred to travel and split the proceeds with surplus personnel. See *The Profession of Player in Shakespeare's Time, 1590–1642* (Princeton: Princeton University Press, 1984), pp. 177–84. McMillin and MacLean document the extensive travels of the Queen's Men after the company's formation in 1583. Interestingly, this relatively large company frequently divided itself so it could tour using several small troupes (requiring more ingenious casting) to multiple places at once, thereby maximizing profits. There is no evidence that the Queen's Men, or other companies of the period, travelled with supernumeraries. See *The Queen's Men*, pp. 41–4.

save the expense and labour of procuring scripts by producing some of their own, engineered to optimize the in-house talent. This would require a resident playwright. If that playwright were a sharer who could act, it would be light upon light. And the Chamberlain's Men had just the man. The author of *Greenes Groatsworth of Wit*[24] dismissively referred to Shakespeare as '*Iohannes fact totum*', a Jack-of-all-trades, but the epithet points out one of Shakespeare's greatest strengths: versatility.[25] Like his fellow sharers, Shakespeare filled multiple roles, onstage and off. Though some scholars assume that he seldom acted, or that his responsibilities as company playwright exempted him from onstage participation, no evidence exists to substantiate this.[26] On the contrary, his profit margin and what circumstantial evidence we have suggest that Shakespeare performed whenever it was financially prudent. One might speculate that having chosen a life in the theatre, Shakespeare enjoyed acting and was good at it; further, that his knowledge of the plays – their structure, dialogue, entrances and exits, props, etc. – coupled with his acting experience, would have made him the actor least likely to be exempted. Bart van Es argues that Shakespeare's early career as an actor may be overstated, but the evidence suggests that he was recognized as a player, one who participated fully in the performances of his plays.[27] After all, when Greene attacks him as a playwright,

---

[24] The tract was published as the work of Robert Greene, though scholarly opinion favours Henry Chettle as the author. See Steve Mentz, 'Forming Greene: Theorising the Early Modern Author in the *Groatsworth of Wit*', in *Writing Robert Greene: Essays on England's First Notorious Professional Writer*, ed. Kirk Melnikoff and Edward Gieskes (Aldershot: Ashgate, 2008), p. 115.

[25] Robert Greene, *Greenes Groatsworth of Wit, Bought with a Million of Repentance* (London: John Haviland, for Henry Bell, 1629 [1592], C3ᵛ). The passage that concerns Shakespeare reads: '[T]here is an upstart Crow, beautified with our feathers, that with his *Tygers hart wrapt in a Players hyde,* supposes he is as well able to bombast out a blanke verse as the best of you: and being an absolute *Johannes fact totum*, is in his owne conceit the onely Shake-scene in a countrey' (84–5).

[26] Scant documentation exists for sharers playing specific roles, but the cast list for *Sejanus* (1603) includes Shakespeare alongside his fellows, and there is no indication that the performance was unusual. As an example of the widespread assumption that Shakespeare was eager to give up acting, Peter Ackroyd suggests that he could have retired by or soon after 1603, probably based on the date in *Sejanus*. Here, ironically, a rare piece of documentary evidence confirming his participation onstage becomes the basis for speculations about his retirement thereafter. See *Shakespeare: The Biography* (New York: Vintage Books, 2006), p. 440.

[27] Van Es argues that Shakespeare's focus was writing and that he may have acted only as a result of joining the Lord Chamberlain's Men. Nevertheless, he concedes that Shakespeare's duties as a sharer would have dictated roughly equal participation onstage, and the reference to him as a 'player' suggests that he had been performing by 1592. See ' "Johannes fac Totum"? Shakespeare's First Contact with the Acting Companies', *Shakespeare Quarterly* 61.4 (2010), pp. 551–77. Lois Potter takes a different view, attending to how Shakespeare's playwriting seems influenced by his experience as an actor (*Life of William Shakespeare*, pp. 99–100).

for 'bombast[ing] out a blanke verse', his objection is not that Shakespeare lacked a university education but that he was *'wrapt in a Players hyde'*.

Some could elect to write for reputation or pleasure while preserving themselves from the supposed drudgery of acting, but, as Ingram observes, Shakespeare's company produced plays to make money. Shakespeare had watched his father go broke. His fellow sharers were professionals, but they had trained as joiners and grocers, leaving those professions behind in hope of higher earnings.[28] Like the Clown, they could appreciate both in life and art the possibilities for changing one's social status. Doing so required attracting paying audiences and retaining as large a share of the proceeds as possible. And doubling roles was the surest means of economizing, fiscally and theatrically.

But while doubling was a convention in which the rising London companies were well versed, and though we can reasonably expect that Shakespeare's company would not hire two actors when one would do, critics have consistently speculated that it used more actors than were necessary, and that the efficiency suggested by printed doubling plots that accompany Tudor and early Elizabethan plays was diminished or neglected by Shakespeare and his fellow sharers.[29] However, based on precedents and the peculiar success of the Lord Chamberlain's Men, I suggest that dramatic economy should more directly inform projections about how the company functioned, particularly when it comes to casting. Since, 'the play' was, Hamlet declares, 'the thing', and actors were, according to the *Henry V* Chorus, 'ciphers to this great accompt', scholarly analysis and speculations should begin with the premise that employing and training excess labour would have been avoided whenever possible.

Doubling in Early English Drama

Though the Lord Chamberlain's Men had remarkable vision and business acumen, doubling roles was hardly a novel concept. G.E. Bentley observes that doubling was 'a normal feature of casting for generations before Shakespeare came to London', and Bevington has demonstrated how the efficiency and

---

[28] John Heminges was a grocer; Robert Armin apprenticed to a goldsmith; James Burbage himself had been a joiner by trade before turning actor. Acting was not a guild-based profession, though the companies may have operated similarly in some respects. Though some actors took apprentices, it is uncertain whether those apprentices were trained as actors or according to the actor's own trade. David Kathman discusses the guilds and Shakespeare's company in 'Grocers, Goldsmiths, and Drapers: Freemen and Apprentices in the Elizabethan Theater', *Shakespeare Quarterly* 55.1 (2004), pp. 1–49. I discuss apprenticeship in Chapter 6.

[29] I discuss cast size in Chapter 4. Although scholars projecting cast sizes have assumed a larger cast than necessary, I show that each of Shakespeare's plays can be performed with nine to 12 actors filling all speaking roles and acknowledged mutes.

potential impact of the practice rose significantly throughout the sixteenth century.[30] According to him, until about 1550 the printed plays 'offered for acting' – those with doubling plots appearing on or after the title page – assign an
average of two or three roles to each actor. The morality play, *Mundus et Infans*
(1522), for instance, requires two actors for five roles (5:2), while Bale's *Three
Laws* (1538) divides 14 roles among five players (14:5).[31] Gradually, the doubling grows more efficient and elaborate, and later plays such as Pickering's
Horestes (1567), 27:6, or Preston's *Cambyses* (1569), 38:8 – which may have
more directly influenced Shakespeare – demand much more from their actors.
Still closer to the start of Shakespeare's career, Thomas Lupton's *All for Money*
(1577) asks just four actors to take on 20 roles, a high point of dramatic efficiency with a ratio of five roles per man. During the sixteenth century the
average play grew in length and the average troupe grew in number, yet despite
increased demands on personnel from longer and more complex texts, and
despite the increased availability of actors, the ratio of characters to actors
widens considerably. The century's dramaturgical arc thus describes a continu-
ously evolving economy wherein the entertainment and complexity grows in
disproportionate measure to the resources necessary to produce it. Lupton's
play was written after professionalism took hold and the first dedicated theatre
was erected in London, suggesting that the trend towards more efficient casting
was still rising at the dawn of the great age of Elizabethan drama.

Ideas about early modern staging often reflect rules for representation that
have been fixed according to critical taste.[32] But, given the origins and history of the English stage, rules about representation are not especially useful
when thinking about early modern casting. The plays popular in Shakespeare's
youth were filled with *Johannes factotums*, whose representational capacity
was limited only by their material. Consistent increases in the lengths of plays
and the number of characters they contained indicate the public's desire for
more elaborate stories. But companies addressed that desire not by expanding

---

[30] Bentley, *Profession of Player*, pp. 228–9. In *From Mankind to Marlowe*, Bevington assesses 26
plays 'offered for acting' between the 1530s and 1570s and demonstrates a continual increase
in the frequency, intricacy, economy, and daring with which actors doubled, an arc continuing
through to Shakespeare's early career.

[31] While late medieval and early Tudor plays call for less efficient casting than those that came
later, it is interesting to note that they tend to assign multiple roles to lead actors, while doubling among the minor characters is less common. Critics have guessed that bit parts were
more frequently double-cast in Shakespeare's, thus allowing featured actors more credible
pretensions to realism, but early companies seem to have asked their most talented actors to do
more acting.

[32] As noted previously, Lawrence thought extant doubling plots from the period could not have
been used by London troupes because they would require players to 'resort to the crudest and
most illusion-marring of expedients' (*Pre-Restoration Stage Studies*, p. 61). The question of
verisimilitude and critical taste is addressed further in Chapters 4 and 6.

Table 2.1 *Plays with casting information, 1560–1610*[a]

Year	Play	# Roles	# Actors
1560	*Impatient Poverty*	10	4
1560	*Lusty Juventus*	10	4
c. 1560	*Misogonus*	18	10
c. 1565	*King Darius*	21	6
c. 1565	*Enough is as Good as a Feast*	18	7
1566	*Patient and Meek Grissell*	23	8
1567	*Horestes*	27+	6
1567	*The Triall of Treasure*	16	5
1567	*The Life and Repentance of Mary Magdalene*	14	4
1568	*Like Will to Like*	16	5
c. 1568	*The Longer thou Livest the more Fool thou Art*	16	4
1569	*Cambyses, King of Persia*	38[b]	8
1573	*New Custom*	11	4
c. 1576	*Common Conditions*	21	6
1576	*Tide Tarrieth No Man*	18	4
c. 1578	*The Most Virtuous and Godly Susanna*	17	8
c. 1578	*All for Money*	20	4
1579	*The Marriage of Wit and Wisdom*	19	6
1581	*The Conflict of Conscience*	18	6
1589	*The Battle of Alcazar*	48?	25?[c]
1598	*Mucedorus*	15	8
1607	*The Fair Maid of the Exchange*	21	11
1610	*Mucedorus (Q3)*	17	10

[a] This table reflects information compiled using information from Bevington and King, as well as from early printings (and facsimiles of early printings) of the plays.

[b] The doubling plan for *Cambyses* distributes only 38 roles among eight actors, though the play contains 40 roles in all. As discussed below, the omissions of Marian and the waiting maid can be accounted for by a cast of eight.

[c] The surviving plot is incomplete, so we cannot determine precisely how the roles were assigned.

their numbers, but by distributing more roles to each man. This argues either that the pool of skilled actors, or their willingness to divide profits, was limited. As a result, plays would have become more valuable as they offered a greater variety of characters and action without a corresponding need for more actors. Table 2.1 includes those Tudor and Elizabethan plays for which we have documented casting information, focusing on plays whose dates of composition and performance roughly overlap with Shakespeare's life and career.

Medieval audiences had learned to take for granted that a makeshift scaffold or wagon could host Jonah and the whale, the crucifixion of Christ, or Noah's flood. The Digby *Mary Magdalene* (c. 1515–1520), perhaps the most ambitious play before the rise of commercial theatre, includes more than 50 speaking roles: kings and queens, angels and vices, tavern keepers, apostles, sailors, even Jesus himself.[33] The play unfolds across at least 19 localities, including scenes in Jerusalem, Marseilles, 'heaven', and before a 'flaming temple' of Mohammed. None of these could have been represented realistically, especially given demands for other scenes set in taverns, castles, forests, deserts, or at sea.

Given *Mary Magdalene*'s ambitious casting and staging requirements, scholars have generally acknowledged that doubling of roles (and scaffolds) would have been necessary for performance.[34] But while most imagine that 20 or more actors and an elaborate, differentiated network of stages was required, it is possible to confine the play's action to a single scaffold, relying on audiences to see heaven and earth as Shakespeare's audience saw Rosalind enter the forest of Arden. If changes of demeanour (and simple cloaks or hats) were sufficient to surround Mary with French kings, then sailors, then St. Peter and his retinue, and so on, then the play requires only 12 actors. The episodic construction facilitates doubling, much like Shakespeare's *Pericles*, or other plays that feature a pastoral world whose inhabitants have little or no interaction with the court (e.g. *A Midsummer Night's Dream*, *As You Like It*, *The Winter's Tale*). Characters can exit each scene in *Mary Magdalene* and enter the next representing whatever is required, since only Mary appears consistently.

Conceptual Casting in Medieval Drama

Though medieval plays routinely facilitate the efficient use of personnel, even very early examples suggest that playwrights understood how to use doubling as a tool to enrich their plays' thematic and theatrical potentials. If plays as far back as *Mankinde* (c. 1471) and the *Second Shepherd's Play* (c. 1500) exploited doubling to aesthetic advantage, and if Tudor period playwrights made

---

[33] EETS *The Late Medieval Religious Plays of Bodleian MSS*, ed. Donald C. Baker, John L. Murphy, and Louis B. Hall, Jr. The manuscript is dated by watermark c. 1515–1520, though the play was probably written in the late fifteenth century.

[34] Bevington, John C. Coldeway, Darryl Grantley, and Glynne Wickham have spoken to the difficulties of staging *Mary Magdalene*. Grantley supposes that the play would require 23 actors, while most propose around a 2:1 ratio of roles to actors. Bevington suggested that the play may have been presented 'in the round', without transferring stages. Others assume that, while individual scaffolds may have been used more than once, the diverse locales would have prevented, for instance, the same platform from successively representing a ship at sea and then Jerusalem. See John C. Coldeway, ed., 'The Digby Mary Magdalene', *Early English Drama: An Anthology* (New York and London: Garland Publishing, 1993); Darryl Grantley, 'Saints' Plays', in *The Cambridge Companion to Medieval English Theatre*, ed. Richard Beadle (Cambridge: Cambridge University Press, 1994), pp. 165–89; and Wickham, *Early English Stages, 1300–1660*, 3 Volumes (London: Routledge and Kegan Paul, 1959–1981).

increasingly ingenious use of double-casting to complicate their play-worlds and facilitate engagement, then the assumption that Elizabethan playwrights like Shakespeare would have diminished or neglected a convention so well-tried, so integral to, and so effective in promoting the ends they pursued, would be strange indeed. It is far more likely, rather, that Shakespeare and his contemporaries took its advantages for granted, then sought ways to make more extensive and more imaginative use of doubling than their predecessors.

Morality plays typically centred on the fall and subsequent redemption of an everyman figure. Dramaturgically, the protagonist often remained on stage while two or three virtues or vices took turns onstage to guide or beguile him. The structures seem designed to facilitate doubling, since the same actors can alternate as both virtues and vices who never meet onstage. But *Mankinde* varies the strategy by allowing one actor to play both Mercy and Titivullus, the play's tempter and redeemer, and its two most demanding roles. While four lesser characters remain onstage almost constantly, these two roles alternate, and their speeches are similar for being longer and more sophisticated than those assigned to the others. The phased casting structure and the similarities in speech suggest that the roles may have been designed for the most persuasive and commanding actor to take both, thence enabling that actor to pull the protagonist in opposite directions.

Doubling Mercy and Titivullus allows the lead actor to do more acting, but its primary effect is to unite the primary sources of attraction and repulsion (for the protagonist, Mankind, and, by extension, the audience) at the same point of focus. Audiences generically disposed to welcome Mankind's redemption see through the temptations of the Vice, but their awareness that the Vice is closely associated (or even conflated) with 'Mercy', through doubling, works to undermine the response dictated by the genre. When one actor plays the roles, whichever character is *not* present onstage still seems to be there: the Vice becomes doubly deceptive (though partly reclaimed), the Virtue always slightly contaminated. Because Mercy begins the play, the actor will gain interest when he returns as Titivullus by seeming to have lapsed, like Mankind, from virtue into vice. The actor then mirrors – outside the fiction – the chiasmic arc that describes Mankind's fall and rise within it, the return of Vice as Virtue (in the performance) complementing the story of Mankind's redemption in the play.

Moreover, Titivullus emerges from the fiction to banter with the audience as an actor, even attempting to collect money for the performance. This behaviour potentially reinforces his role as an actor alternating between roles, even as it suggests Titivullus's primacy as a character. The tensions that accrue because of the liminal status of both actor and character – poised between vice and virtue, reality and fiction – along with the vibrant rhetorical speeches assigned to Titivullus, combine to make him far more attractive than Mercy, his sober counterpart. The result tempts audiences to favour, as Mankind himself does, vice over virtue, and the Vice over the Virtue, thus internally resisting the appropriate generic outcome. But this temptation, and the potential for the play to achieve its thematic ends, is diminished when the roles are played by different actors.

Considering *Mankinde*, it's tempting to look ahead to Shakespeare, who often presents audiences with characters and plots that fulfil generic roles while simultaneously undermining them, forcing us to take sides against ourselves with respect to characters or outcomes. The close of *Measure for Measure*, for instance, generates interest because audiences struggle to accept a generic result the play has long anticipated: a marriage between the attractive bachelor and the ingénue. After the Duke produces Claudio alive, stays Angelo's execution, and enables both of their marriages, there are two ostentatiously eligible parties left on stage. Given the Duke's position, wealth, and (albeit unsavoury) magnanimity, the generic pull towards his marriage with Isabella is great. But audiences are aghast if Isabella takes his arm and goes offstage in triumph, since they have watched him deceive her; use her as a pawn to entrap Angelo; let her believe her brother was dead; and fashion himself a gallant hero who saves the day, when it wouldn't have needed saving if he had stepped forward sooner. Beyond all this, Isabella is a prospective nun, while the Duke has spent most of the play posing as a friar. For Isabella, marrying the Duke is unimaginable, yet generically desirable. The marriage both makes and mars the play. It is hard to imagine how a play in Shakespeare's time could more effectively compromise (yet also energize) its reception than to have the nun marry the Friar. But this effect is analogous to that frequently achieved through doubling roles, a practice that allows actors to seem to unify opposing attitudes, arguments, professions, or genders. Doubling can enable audiences to harmonize what should not be capable of harmonization. *Mankinde*'s audience may not struggle as much as Shakespeare's, but when it assigns its two lead roles to one actor it draws audiences into a more complex relationship with the play, one richer for the resulting ambivalences and contradictions.

Perhaps more than any play of the period, the Wakefield *Second Shepherd's Play* suggests a dramatist excited by the paradoxical and punning nature of drama. Here, the main character, Mak, is a conscious 'actor' like Autolycus. He begins the play by impersonating a King's yeoman so he can cheat three shepherds of their money and food. The shepherds see through his device, but Mak then plays on their sympathy, claiming that his wife Gill 'lyys walteryng, by the roode, by the fyere, lo! / And a howse full of brude' (236–7). Having won them over, Mak pretends to sleep before absconding with a sheep, which he deposits at home before returning to 'awaken', seemingly blameless, among the shepherds. During the night, one shepherd dreams that Mak comes dressed in 'wolf's skin' to steal a sheep, but Mak invents a dream of his own in which his wife gives birth, taking the excuse to depart before the sheep can be found missing. When the shepherds do find out and seek the missing sheep at Mak's house, Gill devises a trick to swaddle it and present it as the baby foretold in Mak's 'dream'. In response, the shepherds apologize and offer gifts, before discovering the plot, tossing Mak in a blanket, and then, at the advice of an Angel, departing to Bethlehem, where the real nativity transpires, the shepherds stepping into the roles of the Magi.

Like *Mankinde*, the play appears to have been designed for five actors – so that the actor playing Mak apotheosizes to the angel heralding the birth of Christ, while his wife Gill, who first masqueraded as the mother of Mak's stolen lamb, morphs into the Virgin Mary, the mother of Jesus, aka 'the lamb of God'.[35] With the roles thus doubled, Mak's false complaints and false dreams gain retroactive valences of truth. He has indeed had tidings of a birth, a birth of both child *and* lamb. Gill and Mak's parody thus transforms into the nativity scene, rather than being displaced by it; and the dramaturgy complements the forgiveness of sin prefigured by the arrival of Christ, at a level outside the fiction, before an audience to a cycle of plays centred on that birth and the redemption of mankind that it enables. Mak and Gill, by playing extremes of impiety and piety in their alternate roles, come closer to the condition of humanity as suggested by Christian doctrine than they can by playing just one role apiece. The Angel and Mary are minor figures in the play, but their roles gain significance if former sinners portray them, heightening the metaphysical implications of the nativity by realizing them in the performance. The shepherds further manifest their duality and spiritual maturation by playing Magi, roles they had already unwittingly acted in the farce at Mak and Gill's 'manger', when they brought gifts to the baby lamb. In performance, that farcical setting can 'double' as the site of the real nativity, and the fake 'lamb' that Mak uses as a prop to fool the shepherds can be transformed into something divine, when the same bundle represents both.

Clearly, the play's disparate parts can become more intensely interrelated, and its themes significantly enhanced, through doubling roles. Even Mak's choice to impersonate a 'King's yeoman', one who carries messages from great men, is echoed when Mak-as-Angel returns on behalf of the King of Heaven with a message that all should make offerings in gratitude for the newborn child. Mak first robbed them of a lamb; later he offers them the Lamb in return. Recreating so many falsehoods as 'truths', through playing, complicates the spectator's experience considerably. But the complexity serves not to confuse but to clarify and reinforce essential themes, making the play more coherent

---

[35] Maynard Mack suggests that the play's architecture suits five actors and the two major doubles I suggest here in '*The Second Shepherd's Play*: A Reconsideration', *PMLA* 93.1 (1978), pp. 78–85. Like some others, Mack attends to structure but does not pursue the aesthetic implications of adapting the cast to the structure.

even as it is made more complicated. A dramatist or playing troupe would be foolish to forgo such opportunities, especially when locating, training, and splitting the takings with two more actors is the price for forgoing them.

Though there is no hard evidence that confirms the Wakefield Poet intended the play for five actors, no analysis can show comparable benefits for letting the actors playing Mak and Gill watch the finale from offstage. The structure, like that of *Mankinde*, enables and anticipates efficient casting, and the play's thematic potential is greater for it. Such aesthetically and economically advantageous casting practices from the medieval stage inspired the Tudor playwrights, as did the protean vision of actors and stages evident in plays like *Mary Magdalene*. As we have seen, the Tudor playwrights improved on the dramatic economy of their predecessors, in turn inspiring writers like Shakespeare, whose plays ask for still braver representational feats and whose play structures suggest radical evolutions in both the efficient use of personnel and the thematic possibilities enabled by that efficiency.

'Four men and a boy'

Regarding the medieval plays, Bevington concludes, 'the impression one receives is that of an imaginative flexibility on the part of the audience, and dauntless versatility on the part of the players'.[36] That modern audiences welcome the premises of *Hamilton* or *Harvey* – the former a musical in which America's 'founding fathers' are portrayed by a conspicuously diverse cast that tells their stories through hip-hop lyrics and dance; the latter a play about a 6ft tall invisible rabbit – suggests that this imaginative flexibility continues, and that testing mimetic conventions still contributes to engagement and pleasure. For playgoers who accepted that a wagon could host Noah's flood, that Mary could 'sail' atop a scaffold to Jerusalem, or that the Vice could return as the Virtue, the choice to have one actor take four or five roles in the same performance could not have been strange; on the contrary, it would have best agreed with the other conventions.[37] The playgoing culture of Shakespeare's time seems to have fetishized acting and all forms of impersonation, so that revealing the gaps between actors and what they attempted to represent was not avoided but encouraged. Based on the theatrical traditions they inherited, neither actors nor audiences would have had reason to believe there was any advantage to assigning only one part to one man.

---

[36] Bevington, *From Mankind to Marlowe*, p. 86.
[37] See Shakespeare's depiction of sailing and sea storms or the participation of spirits and gods in plays like *Pericles* or *The Tempest*, which presume the stage is nearly unlimited in its capacity for representation.

Lawrence notes that troupes generally used a 'four man system' during the first half of the 1500s, an average of five actors in the middle of the century, with larger companies becoming common in the 1570s and 1580s.[38] Until the 1580s, no travelling troupe is known to have had more than ten actors, even though many plays contained 30 or more roles. The actors were male, with some troupes employing boys for women's roles and others using adult men – a practice Shakespeare may have taken up and parodied with the rude mechanicals of *A Midsummer Night's Dream*. Anthony Munday's *Sir Thomas More* (1592), part of which Shakespeare may have written or revised, presents a fictional version of a Tudor acting troupe that may have resembled those that Shakespeare would have seen as a boy.

> MORE   How many are ye?
> PLAYER Four men and a boy, sir.
> MORE   Then I see there's but few women in the play.
> PLAYER Three my Lord: dame Science, Lady Vanity and Wisdom she herself.
> MORE   And one boy play them all? By'r Lady, he's loaden.[39]

The exchange affirms some principles of Tudor drama. Tudor plays typically required between four and eight actors, with an average of five.[40] Doubling is assumed, as is the practice of having the youngest available actor play female roles. The five-actor troupe offers More his choice among four plays in their repertoire, each of which is fitted for five actors.

Once More selects a play and his guests gather for the performance, the troupe's leader announces a delay because the young actor playing 'Good Counsel' has no beard. That actor, we learn, requires a false beard to look old enough to be wise. The play (within the play) pauses over his absence, with More filling in as Good Counsel for a time. The scene thus hints that markers such as false beards could be relied upon to represent shifts in ontology. A false beard will not persuade us that the young actor is an old man, and there is no such pretence on the fictional actor's part. But the troupe waits until the prop can be obtained, suggesting that theatrical illusions depended on audiences interpreting a set of signals. The implicit theory recalls the mechanicals' discussion of how to represent a Wall or the Man in the Moon, or verbal cues used elsewhere to obviate the need for representation, allowing Rosalind, for example, to gaze into the crowd and declare, 'This is the forest of Arden' (2.4.11).

---

[38] See Lawrence, *Pre-Restoration Stage Studies*, p. 50. Four- and five-man companies are in evidence at least into the 1570s, when the intricacy and length of new plays begins to ask for six to eight actors on average.

[39] Cited in Bevington, *From Mankind to Marlowe*, p. 18.

[40] Ibid., p. 5.

The chief player in the fictional troupe depicted in *Sir Thomas More* waits to begin the performance not merely because the actor lacks a beard, but because he has gone away in search of one. With only four actors present he worries that they cannot perform the second act, affirming that this company had no surplus actors. As Simon Palfrey and Tiffany Stern point out, the concept of the 'understudy' originated in the nineteenth century,[41] so sixteenth-century troupes had to answer for an actor's absence by adapting the play or its doubling plan. The play within *Sir Thomas More*, 'The Marriage of Wit and Wisdom', recalls an anonymous Tudor morality play of that name written for *six* actors, though it is actually a modified version of *Lusty Juventus* (c. 1550), which wants only four.[42] The 'players' thus seem to have chosen and/or adapted their source material with their five-member troupe in mind.

'There's time enough for that'

The highly efficient doubling plans and limited casts of the Tudor period raise questions about how long it took to effect changes of persona and how quickly such changes could be achieved. Bevington observes that 'Rapid changes between roles are surprisingly common', counting 38 changes that occur in less than 25 lines' time.[43] On average, playwrights grant more time for changes from male to female roles, presumably more difficult because of dresses and wigs, but they repeatedly count on actors to return in new roles in less than a minute. Peter Hyland notes that 'many disguises necessitate a quick change that would have been very difficult if the actor had to get out of one elaborate costume and into another'.[44] Costume changes, therefore, were typically simple, the actors likewise comfortable with the fact that the outward changes necessary to convince fellow characters need not seem convincing to the spectators. On the contrary, convincing the spectators might diminish their experience of the play, one enhanced by watching onstage audiences be taken in by impersonations and disguises that echo those transacted by every actor onstage before the offstage audience.

---

[41] Simon Palfrey and Tiffany Stern, *Shakespeare in Parts* (Oxford: Oxford University Press, 2007), p. 50.
[42] *The Marriage of Wit and Wisdom*, c. 1570, of uncertain authorship, was considered an old morality play by the time of *Sir Thomas More*. Though the travelling players in *Sir Thomas More* somewhat resemble the characters in *Marriage*, these lines come from *Lusty Juventus*, c. 1540, attributed to Richard Wever. The playwright assigns six actors three or four roles each, and the lead actor also takes the prologue and epilogue. The roles in the *Marriage of Wit and Wisdom* are cast loosely according to relative age and gender, though versatility is anticipated.
[43] Ibid., p. 91.
[44] Peter Hyland, *Disguise on the Early Modern English Stage* (Farnham: Ashgate, 2011), p. 12.

Most of the historical evidence concerning quick changes comes from stage directions or dialogue that explains how actors arranged or layered their costumes in preparation. In Ulpian Fulwell's *Like Will to Like* (1568),[45] for instance, the author notes that 'Lucifer', played by an actor who must play several other roles, should have 'this name ... written on his back and in his breast', allowing the removal of a cloak to advertise his new identity to the audience. Fulwell's notes are a rare gift to historians because they indicate some authorial assumptions about staging and doubling roles. For instance, Fulwell's text advises the actors to retain their 'doublets and hose' while using quickly altered markers like cloaks, hats, and beards to signal changes of character. Again, the author seems to prefer speed and versatility to convincing illusions. Bevington found similar examples elsewhere: *Impatient Poverty* specifies that 'a gown' marks a change from Peace to Prosperity, the rest of the actor's costume remaining unchanged, while stage directions for *In Wisdom Who is Christ* advise the Devil to wear 'gallant's clothes *within*', presumably underneath his devil's cloak or robe.[46]

Using beards, hats, gowns, gestures, and accents to indicate changes of character enabled quicker changes and more efficient doubling. In their study of the Queen's Men, Scott McMillin and Sally-Beth MacLean argue that the period's players developed 'a system of acting by brilliant stereotype', one in which 'the unmistakable sign is crucial ... the gesture no eye can misread, the accent no ear can misunderstand'.[47] It is now common to see Theseus and Hippolyta double as Oberon and Titania, despite the fourth act requiring the actors to end one scene as one couple and begin the next as the other. Brook's production was hugely admired, perhaps never so much as for that particular transition, but the lack of an intermediary scene to facilitate it has led some to conclude that however engaging the choice to double the Lords and Ladies, it could not have been done on Shakespeare's stage. Yet the *Marriage of Wit and Wisdom* (c. 1569–1570), another play popular during Shakespeare's lifetime, is just one example of a play that requires an actor to end a scene as one character and begin the next scene as another, and it requires an additional change to occur in only three lines' time. So, the supposition that the casting choices Brook's production employed could not have happened in Shakespeare's time is not consistent with the material record. However limited the evidence, it again favours versatility, efficiency, and the lack of rules that would limit them. Because

---

[45] Ulpian Fulwell (c. 1545–1586) was a contemporary of Shakespeare's who wrote comments for staging *Like Will to Like*, a play that distributes 16 roles among four or five actors. It contains no female roles, though the plot requires versatility, and one actor alternates as vice and hero.

[46] Bevington, *From Mankind to Marlowe*, p. 94.

[47] McMillin and MacLean, *The Queen's Men*, p. 127.

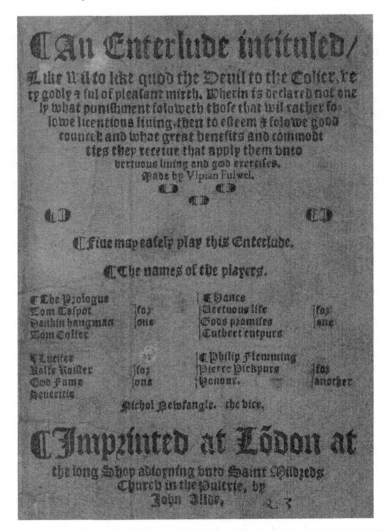

Figure 2.1 Title page and doubling plan for Ulpian Fulwell's *Like Will to Like* (1587). Folger STC 11473.2. Used by permission of the Folger Shakespeare Library under a Creative Commons Attribution-ShareAlike 4.0 International License.

actors could change accessories, accent, and posture while leaving their basic dress intact, nearly instantaneous changes of persona were possible, and they should have been as enjoyable in Shakespeare's time as they have proven to be on contemporary stages.

Other Precedents and Contemporary Analogues

Two plays popular while Shakespeare was in London confirm the enduring attraction of quick changes. *Mucedorus* (c. 1590), a play that the King's Men brought into their repertory, calls for extensive doubling, and for one actor to exit and return in a new role within eight lines.[48] Meanwhile, George Chapman's *The Blind Beggar of Alexandria* (1596) features a trial scene wherein Cleanthes, the play's lead, cycles through three separate disguises – Leon, Count Hermes, and Irus the 'Blind Beggar' – with as few as three lines in which to perform the changes.[49] Chapman's text includes references to the 'velvet patch' and 'robe' that will signify the Count. Disguise, a kind of doubling by *characters* within the fiction rather than by actors outside of it, speaks to early modern playwrights' continuing interest in exploiting and augmenting the duality of the actor/character, to the ease with which they supposed such changes could be accomplished, and to their seeming indifference to credibility. The explosion of disguise plays in the early 1600s suggests that the trope remained attractive throughout Shakespeare's career.[50]

In addition to the evolving dramatic economy suggested by the ratios of roles to actors, period playwrights refined such devices as suppression and alternation of parts to allow for more complicated plots without increasing cast size. A playwright could free an actor to take a new role by suppressing a character, as Shakespeare seems to do when characters like Mercutio or Caesar are killed in Act Three, or by abandoning characters like Antiochus, Poins or Lear's Fool. Plays containing a large number of characters, or that moved a single character through several locales, could resort to what Bevington calls 'progressive suppression'.[51] As plots grew in complexity and efficiency, playwrights began to suppress characters only to bring them back into the fiction once their secondary (or tertiary) duties were complete. This practice became more refined as playwrights surrounded their protagonists with character groups made up of actors who could retire and return in new roles, then alternating between those roles throughout the play. As allegorical figures were individualized and the psychomachia broadened to involve more players at its centre, the plays evolve further. By the 1560s and 1570s, for example, we begin to see plays with more than one protagonist, such as *Enough is as Good as a Feast* (1560), *Horestes* (1567), and *Cambyses* (1569). In these it is no longer sufficient to have a trio of bad influences exit and return to the protagonist as a trio of friends. This shift,

---

[48] Lawrence, *Pre-Restoration Stage Studies*, p. 58.
[49] Hyland notes that *Blind Beggar* would have called on Edward Alleyn, the lead player for the Admiral's Men, to play four roles and make multiple quick changes. Hyland, *Disguise on the Early Modern English Stage*, pp. 17–18, 91.
[50] E.g. *Look About You, The Blind Beggar of Bethnal Green, The Alchemist, Volpone.*
[51] Bevington, *From Mankind to Marlowe*, p. 144.

though, from allegorical to individual identities can lead to a dubious conclusion: namely, that the move to individualism *in* characters somehow prefigures a move to individual and thus more 'realistic' casting choices, thence to a new operative theory about theatrical representation. On the contrary, the consequence of more realistic characters was to double roles more frequently. In the years just before Shakespeare begins writing plays, the plots grow more complex, with more individual characters becoming the focus of dramatic interest, but this occurs in part because the plays more efficiently enable actors to alternate between the characters required. Shakespeare and his fellow actors grew up watching fledgling troupes perform on makeshift stages, absorbing conventions of efficient and versatile casting and representation, and learning to trust in the audience's mental dexterity. They would have noticed and valued the ways in which the dramatic economy of the time made the plays more playful, and how doubling, like representation itself, was a co-animator of nearly every scene.

Morality traditions and conventions influenced Shakespeare's plots and characters as well as his dramaturgy, and devices from morality plays are common in Shakespeare. From personified abstractions like 'Time', who sweeps aside 16 years in *The Winter's Tale*, to allusions to medieval plays, such as Hamlet's warning lest the actors attempt to 'out-Herod Herod', to subtler representations of the 'Vice' or 'Everyman' figures in the starkly human derivations of Iago and Othello, Shakespeare draws richly on the tropes and traditions of the past. The history of Shakespeare's appropriation of medieval characters and structures is well established, but doubling merits greater consideration as a convention he inherited from his predecessors, then reimagined and refined. The line between Tudor and Elizabethan drama cannot have been clearly drawn for Shakespeare, and more evidence would be necessary to establish that he and his company, simply because of their increased stability and professionalism, made a radical break with conventions they inherited. Since Shakespeare's plays reflect strong medieval and Tudor influences, and since they are engineered so that a cast of nine to 12 actors can perform plots that involve 50 or more roles, we cannot reasonably presume that the practice of doubling roles was a marginal consideration in his playwriting or his company's approach to casting. On the contrary, Shakespeare's plots show a logical extension of the efficiency seen in the earlier plays and doubling plans. His plots were arranged so roles could be doubled at ratios exceeding even that of *Cambyses*. Moreover, Shakespeare was sufficiently mindful of theatrical economy and strategic doubling that the ideas surface as subjects in his plays, such as when Bottom wants to play all the parts in the mechanicals' performance of 'Pyramus and Thisbe' or when four amateur players in *Love's Labour's Lost* undertake among themselves to present a pageant of 'Nine Worthies'.

Since doubling was a matter of course in sixteenth-century plays, troupes could rely on the playwright to determine how many actors were necessary, a number that correlated – for every printed play that includes a doubling chart – to the minimum possible number necessary based on the play's structure. As Bevington notes, the need to minimize costs gave rise to 'an unwritten code among dramatists' not to use more actors than were strictly necessary.[52] Across more than 20 plays, not once does a playwright presume that there will be extra people available to fill small roles. This fact is important because the notion that Shakespeare's company employed more people than were necessary to perform the plays has such currency. But Shakespeare cannot reasonably have desired to hire surplus, presumably less competent, actors to take on work that sharers could do, and that the plays were structured to let them do.

Ambidextrous Actors All

When Shakespeare was a boy, several theatre companies performed in or around Stratford-upon-Avon. Terence Schoone-Jongen notes that 'no fewer than five companies visited Stratford' in 1586–1587, the period during which some have proposed that Shakespeare may have left for London, perhaps in the company of travelling players.[53] One such company was Leicester's Men, who visited Warwickshire at least three times in the 1570s, including a three-week residency at Kenilworth Castle in the summer of 1575, when Shakespeare was 12 years old.[54] Kenilworth was home to the Earl of Leicester, Robert Dudley, and it sits just 12 miles north of Stratford. These visits are intriguing because of the company's membership and repertory. James Burbage was among its principal actors during the 1570s; Will Kempe joined the troupe in the 1580s, while George Bryan and Thomas Pope – like Kempe, future players in the Lord Chamberlain's Men – may have also been members.[55] The company's repertory included Thomas Preston's *Cambyses* (1569), a play mentioned by Falstaff in *1 Henry IV*, and whose Middle Eastern setting was renewed by Shakespeare in plays like *Pericles*. *Cambyses* was also a play that surpassed most others when it came to dramatic economy. While we can determine on a dramaturgical basis that plays

[52] Ibid., p. 101.
[53] Schoone-Jongen compiles a list including The Queen's players (1568–1569); Worcester's Men (1574–1575, 1576–1577, 1580–1581, 1581–1582, 1583–1584); Leicester's Men (1572–1573, 1576–1577); Warwick's Men (1574–1575); Strange's Men (1579); Countess of Essex's players (1579); Berkeley's Men (1580–1581, 1582–1583); Chandos's Men (1582–1583); Oxford's Men (1583–1584); and Essex's Men (1583–1584). See *Shakespeare's Companies* (London: Ashgate, 2008), p. 15.
[54] See F.E. Halliday, *A Shakespeare Companion 1564–1964* (Baltimore: Penguin, 1964), p. 263.
[55] Schoone-Jongen, *Shakespeare's Companies*, p. 174–5. See also Andrew Gurr, *The Shakespeare Company, 1594–1642* (Cambridge: Cambridge University Press, 2004), pp. 217–46.

like *Mankinde* and *The Second Shepherd's Play* were designed with doubling in mind, *Cambyses* was printed with a viable doubling plan that distributes 38 of its 40 roles among just eight actors.[56] According to the plan, each of the eight plays multiple roles, two taking seven roles apiece.

Like the medieval plays already discussed, *Cambyses* also exploits doubling to thematic advantage. The actor playing 'Ambidexter', for instance, doubles one other role, but the playwright further highlights his duality by having him deliver several direct addresses, making the spectators partners in the character's deceptions while legitimizing the stage figure as an authentic persona outside the fiction. During one of these, Ambidexter explains a long absence from the stage:

> Indeed, as ye say, I have been absent a long space.
> But is not my cosin Cutpurse with you in the meane-time?
> To it! to it, cosin, and doo your office fine!
> How like you Sisamnes for using of me?
> He plaid with both hands, but he sped il-favourdly!
> The king himselfe was godly up trained;
> He professed vertue – but I think it was fained.
> He plaies with both hands, good deeds and ill.   (ll. 603–10)

Based on the doubling plan, the character exits so the actor can re-enter as 'Triall', whose business concludes just before Ambidexter's return. The explanation, though, suggests not that Ambidexter left to enable the instance of doubling the spectators have seen but rather one they have overlooked. The speech hints that the actor has remained involved not as Triall but as Ambidexter's 'cosin Cutpurse', a 'character' absent from the dramatis personae. Ambidexter carries out a one-sided conversation with 'Cutpurse', as though the latter were still among the audience, but the language he uses to describe the cousin ('with both hands, good deeds and ill') seems best suited to 'Ambidexter' himself, which he soon admits: 'Mary, when I had doon, to it I durst not stand. / Therby ye may perceive I use to play with eche hand.' The audience knows Ambidexter to be a hypocrite – the play's two-faced (or two-handed) Vice. His role as the play's deceiver is enhanced by an actor straddling the line separating fiction from reality, and by doubling as Triall. But the play here augments his deception, hypocrisy, and 'doubleness' by indicating that he has spent his time offstage depriving playgoers of their purses. As a result, Ambidexter, the character that

---

[56] Martin Wiggins considers the plot 'not workable, because it omits two roles'. However, as Wiggins notes, the seventh actor is available to play Marian. The maid appears only once and can be assigned to an apprentice or journeyman, though the actor playing Ambidexter is free to double the role and keep the cast at eight. See Martin Wiggins in association with Catherine Richardson, *British Drama 1533–1642: A Catalogue. Volume II, 1567–1589* (Oxford: Oxford University Press, 2012), p. 46.

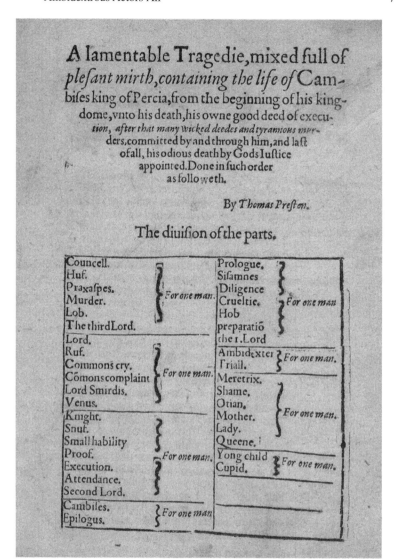

A lamentable Tragedie, mixed full of *plefant mirth, containing the life of* Cambifes king of Percia, from the beginning of his kingdome, vnto his death, his owne good deed of execution, *after that many wicked deedes and tyrannous murders*, committed by and through him, and laft of all, his odious death by Gods Iuftice appointed. Done in fuch order as followeth.

By *Thomas Prefton*.

The diuifion of the parts.

Councell. Huf. Praxafpes. Murder. Lob. The third Lord.	} For one man.	Prologue, Sifamnes Diligence Crueltie. Hob preparatiõ the 1.Lord	} For one man
Lord. Ruf. Commons cry. Cõmons complaint Lord Smirdis. Venus.	} For one man.	Ambidexter Triall.	} For one man.
Knight. Snuf. Small hability Proof. Execution. Attendance. Second Lord.	} For one man.	Meretrix. Shame. Otian. Mother. Lady. Queene.	} For one man.
Cambifes. Epilogus.	} For one man	Yong child Cupid.	} For one man.

Figure 2.2 Title page and doubling plan for Thomas Preston's *Cambyses, King of Persia* (1569), showing the 'division of the partes'. Folger STC 20288.

supposedly doubles least in the fiction, can seem to 'double' three times: first as 'Triall'; then as an actor addressing the audience; then (in the perception of playgoers) as a ubiquitous cutpurse – that is, as a member of the audience.

In his study of Tudor plays, T.W. Craik notes that in the same play an actor 'might expect to play any combination of parts – a good man, a bad man, a rustic, a youth, an old man, even an old woman – and to be in alternate scenes of the same play a devil and an angel'.[57] The printed doubling plan for *Cambyses* reflects this kind of versatility, requiring each actor to play roles that vary greatly in age and temperament. Actors are expected to play both serious and comic roles, and allegorical figures as diverse as 'Counsel' and 'Murder', or 'Diligence' and 'Crueltie', are assigned to the same actor. The plan also assumes that actors were willing and able to be on stage almost constantly, since seven of eight appear in nearly every scene.

The *Cambyses* plan also contains valuable information about gender representation in the period. An all-male cast approaching the play had to account for seven female roles and one child. The plan allows the seventh actor to specialize in female roles (playing four), but he also must portray Otian, the (adult) son of Cambyses, and 'Shame', whose fellow vices are assigned to actors playing adult males. And while 'Mother', 'Lady', and 'Queene' might be imagined as suited to a young male actor, the fourth female role is 'Meretrix', a brash female companion to the soldiers. Whatever the seventh actor's age, he must have been possessed of great range; clearly, though, the playwright anticipated an actor who would be viable in mature roles for both men and women. It is worth noting that theses roles are allotted to 'one man' like the others. While this is hardly proof of anything, it raises the question of whether the division of duties for 'men' and 'boys' in the period may be overdetermined.

The eighth actor does specialize (Young Child and Cupid), possibly indicating that at least one boy actor was desirable. But demands for versatility in gender representation stand out elsewhere in the doubling plan, most notably in the assignment of the goddess 'Venus' to the second actor, who also plays Lord Smirdis and a ruffian solider. The casting of Venus indicates that adult males were at least occasionally tapped to played female roles and that actors played male and female roles in the same play. We must accept either that an adult male played Venus, or that a 'boy' actor played Lord Smirdis. This example could be dismissed as an exception to an imagined rule, but given the scant number of these doubling plans, only about 30 of which survive, no rule can be so well established as to make it reasonable to exclude contradictory evidence.

---

[57] T.W. Craik, *The Tudor Interlude: Stage, Costume, and Acting* (Leicester: Leicester University Press, 1958), p. 41.

The notion that female characters must always have been played by actors considered too young to double adult male roles, despite being contradicted by the evidence, is a prime reason that many critics assume Shakespeare's company used larger casts than his dramatic structures anticipate. But Shakespeare inherited a theatre that relied on spectators to piece out the performance with their thoughts. And, in fact, the example from *Cambyses* is not exceptional. Katie Normington has shown that adult men played female roles on English stages as far back as the Corpus Christi plays.[58] She notes how one such actor played female roles for at least five years consecutively, hinting at a longer career in female impersonation than what is typically imagined for boy players. For the plays that contain female roles, and for which we have casting information, nearly every one asks at least one actor to play both a female role and an adult male role in the same play – a possibility generally rejected outright by those speculating on casting practices in Shakespeare's time.[59] The plans for such plays as *Cambyses* and *The Tide Tarrieth No Man* (1576) require actors to take both adult male and female roles, and some, like *Horestes* (1567), ask as many as four actors to do so. Since no travelling troupe at the time is known to have had more than two boys, and some had none, staged femininity must sometimes have been accomplished using grown men.[60]

Heywood's 'Man-Woman Monster'

Though adult men portrayed women before Shakespeare's time, there is good reason to believe that the practice continued into the seventeenth century. Among the evidence for this is the 1607 Quarto of *The Fair Maid of the Exchange*, often attributed to Thomas Heywood. The play is one of very few produced during Shakespeare's career in London that includes casting information in the form of a printed doubling plan.[61] Given that much of the material evidence for casting in the period pertains to texts and performances produced before 1590 or after 1620, such a document would ordinarily attract significant interest. However, it – and its implications for Elizabethan drama – has been largely ignored, or else dismissed as a product of the printer and not the playwright.

The plan comes under suspicion because it tests rules of representation believed to have governed stage practice in the period. Among these, it calls

---

[58] Katie Normington, *Gender and Medieval Drama* (Cambridge: D.S. Brewer, 2004), p. 64.

[59] Bevington, *From Mankind to Marlowe*, pp. 74–9.

[60] Ibid., pp. 68–89. The subject of boy actors is addressed in Chapter 6.

[61] The play is a city comedy set in contemporary London, which may suggest an early Jacobean date of composition. Wiggins dates the play to 1602, though there is no record of it until its entry into the Stationers' Register in 1607. The play was apparently popular, at least with readers, since it was reprinted in 1616 and 1637.

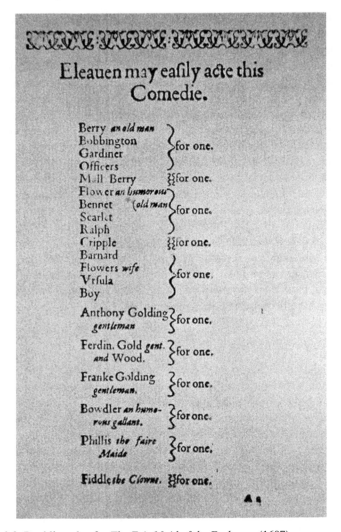

Figure 2.3 Doubling plan for *The Fair Maid of the Exchange* (1607).

for several quick costume changes, for actors to exit as one character and return as another in the same scene, and, critically, for the actor playing Bernard – an eligible bachelor whose engagement is a central concern of the final scene – to double three other roles: a Boy, Ursula, and Mistress Flower. Bernard is referred to in the play as a 'proper little man', but the document's creator clearly assumed that the actor could portray adult male and female characters in the same play.

Lawrence called the plan not only 'inoperative' but 'mendacious', concluding that it must have been designed 'on behalf of strollers or amateurs'.[62] Martin Wiggins affirms that the plan 'is not feasible for staging', noting the aforementioned challenges but ultimately deeming it 'unworkable' because Bernard twice exits and immediately returns to the stage as Mistress Flower, and because, in the final scene, the characters appear to meet onstage, the first of two instances of simultaneous participation.[63] On the surface, these seem reasonable objections. Actors cannot be in two places at once, and credible illusions of femininity, through dress, wigs, and make-up, cannot be achieved instantaneously. Still, what if the obstacles that have led critics to question the plan's feasibility were not seen as insurmountable by the playwright or the original company? What if the evidence and its implications have been neglected based on biases about representation that were not shared by the Elizabethans?

If playing companies insisted upon representing women in ways that required substantial preparation and make-up, without exception, and if they never permitted a character temporarily uninvolved in a scene to absent himself and return in a new role, then we might reasonably assume that the document was not produced by the playwright or playing company. Such rigidity, though, seems at odds with the ingenuity in casting and representation reflected in early English plays, and with the creative solutions to deficiencies in personnel, properties, or scenery that modern playwrights and theatre companies routinely introduce to productions. Notwithstanding this, however, the critics are simply wrong about this doubling plan. Implementing it requires no great imagination or ingenuity, but only a willingness to forgo some received ideas of early modern casting – ideas that redound chiefly to taste. If the plan is feasible, it makes more sense to revisit ideas about early modern casting that conflict with it than to reject the document because it does not suit a prevailing theory.

The plan's first allegedly insoluble problem is its call for quick changes from Bernard to Mistress Flower. Since both changes to Mistress Flower occur between scenes (after 10 and 12) they could be facilitated by music or an interlude. But setting aside that possibility, accepting or rejecting such changes inevitably depends on taste. As we have seen, quick rapid changes were hardly unprecedented, and of the roughly two dozen Elizabethan plays for which we have casting information at least five – *Enough is as Good as a Feast* (c. 1565), *Horestes* (1567), *The Longer thou Livest the more Fool thou Art* (c. 1568), *Cambyses* (1569), and *The Marriage of Wit and Wisdom* (1579) – require an actor to end a scene as one character and begin the next as another.[64] In two of these, *Horestes* and *Cambyses*, actors were called on to play both adult male

---

[62] Lawrence, *Pre-Restoration Stage Studies*, p. 74.
[63] Wiggins, *British Drama 1533–1642, Volume IV*, p. 378.
[64] Bevington, *From Mankind to Marlowe*, p. 97.

and female roles. If the company staging *The Fair Maid of the Exchange* was content to have the actor forgo make-up and accomplish the change through a wig and simple change of dress, there is no impediment to having the Bernard actor perform the roles allotted to him. While some companies in the period used stage make-up to facilitate female representation there is no basis to conclude that this was a non-negotiable practice, and, as we have seen, there are clear precedents suggesting that companies routinely used simple markers to indicate changes of persona and even ontological status.

Moreover, before attributing the doubling plot to someone other than the playwright, we might compare its supposed anomaies of representation with implicit theories of representation evident in the play itself. Since *The Fair Maid of the Exchange* includes disguises and costume changes that occur onstage, attending to these may help justify suspicion for the document or uphold its value. Frank Golding, the play's lead, twice disguises himself – first as a Porter and later as Cripple, another of the play's characters. His brother Ferdinand furnishes the first of these disguises in scene 7:

> FERDINAND Here is a Porter's habit, on with it brother.
> FRANK   Your hand then, brother, for to put it on,
>   So now 'tis well, come brother, what's my task?

Frank asks help donning the disguise, but no syllable is spoken between the request and his expressed satisfaction with the result. If the costume were elaborate, we might expect dialogue to accompany the change. Dead air being generally unwelcome in the theatre, it seems likely that the disguise was expected to be accomplished with easily adopted markers like a cap and jacket. This change is more interesting because Frank disguises himself to deceive Anthony Golding, his other brother. It is hard to imagine any disguise assumed in the gap between two verse lines plausibly deceiving one's own brother. Of course, the audience's recognition of that implausibility contributes to its pleasure, while giving the actor occasion to display his range, likewise welcome to spectators. Frank's second disguise also tests credibility, since his appearance in Cripple's 'crooked habit' deceives Phillis – who is in love with Cripple. The plot repeatedly calls attention to Cripple's posture (he is 'crooked') and use of crutches, but his clothes go unmentioned. While Frank's disguise may include Cripple's outer garment and hat, the crutches and his assumption of a crooked posture seem the primary means of deception. These could be adopted quickly, again highlighting the actor's performance.

In a play that features two improbably successful deceptions by its lead character, each accomplished as the result of costume changes that occur onstage and almost instantaneously, quick changes between Bernard and Mistress Flower would not seem out of place. On the contrary, they would enhance the play's theatricality and contribute to a production's coherence. At the play's climax, Frank (disguised as Cripple) comes to marry Phillis, only for Cripple himself to enter and be mistook for a ghost, at which point Frank reveals himself and wins Phillis's love in his own person. In this context, the obvious 'disguise' of the Bernard actor as Mistress Flower (and vice versa) could make the climax feel like the culmination of a play-long pattern of similar deceptions, these transpiring for the audience offstage as the others do for the characters upon it. Rapid changes from Bernard to Mistress Flower, then, are not only possible, but improving. Whatever we conclude, though, the changes are possible, and Frank's disguises provide a precedent for them in a play for which deception and role-playing are central themes.

The more intractable problem with the doubling plot would seem to be the instances of simultaneous participation in the final scene, first when Bernard and Mistress Flower meet onstage, and then when Berry must appear as an officer despite seeming to be present for the play's end. Each of these problems is manageable, though, and seems to be accounted for by the play's structure and dialogue. The final scene's initial focus is on Frank Golding's plan to persuade both Flower and his wife that his brothers (Ferdinand and Anthony) have given up their respective engagements to Phillis. Each parent has secretly promised her to a different brother, but when Frank delivers letters from his brothers renouncing her (letters that Frank has forged) each privately asks Frank to marry Phillis, allowing for the resolution of the love plot. After this marriage is arranged, though, Mistress Flower goes conspicuously silent for more than 100 lines, during which the focus shifts to settling Bernard's engagement to Mall Berry. Mistress Flower's silence could allow the actor to change costume and speak the lines assigned to the other character. Once Bernard's marriage is settled, he goes mute and unmentioned for the rest of the play, freeing the actor to resume the role of Mistress Flower, who renews her participation amid the confusion brought about when Phillis swoons at news of her engagement. If the costume changes are accomplished quickly, there is nothing to prevent the Bernard actor from playing the roles allotted to him. The other change is likewise accommodated, since Berry, who is tapped in the document to play the speaking Officer who enters near play's end, is the only character who goes entirely mute during the play's last 115 lines. In line with the document, Ferdinand and Anthony withdraw so that Anthony can play Wood, who enters with the officers. If the Berry actor sees the brothers out he can easily return and fulfil the final role allotted to him.[65]

These manageable instances of simultaneous participation and the quick changes likely wouldn't seem insurmountable were it not for the fact that the

---

[65] No stage directions are included for the brothers' exits, so the omission of Berry's is not remarkable, at least not as remarkable as his otherwise inexplicable silence.

document suggests that at least one playwright and company in Shakespeare's time might have found it acceptable, even desirable, to accomplish female representations using adult male actors. Since, according to prevailing ideas, this should not be, then the doubling plan must be a mistake, interpolation or the work of amateurs. Suspicion about this plan's validity has had the natural result of making critics sceptical about all such plans, seeming to sanction the dismissal of evidence that counteracts the prevailing theories. But it may be that the document should lead us rather to suspect those theories, and that at least some of the 'man-woman' monsters Prynne decried were, even into the seventeenth century, not stage boys but adult men.

Evidence and Its Abuses

There are no extant doubling plans for Shakespeare's plays. If not for the Globe fire in 1613 fewer speculations might be needed to explain how the company's casting principles contributed to its success. The limited evidence we do have has occasioned some unfortunate trends in performance scholarship. First, scholars have tended to privilege material evidence from the 1620s and 1630s over that which could have influenced Shakespeare in his formative years as a playwright. Second, some have adopted too clean a distinction between 'Tudor' and 'Elizabethan' drama, essentially doubling down on the value of using the Caroline era records to inform our understanding Elizabethan stage practice. Third, fear of reading too much into internal evidence – which addresses casting, rehearsal, play production, and structure – has caused some to dismiss it entirely. As a result, widespread conclusions about the company's approach to casting have been erected on doubtful foundations.

Caroline records contain limited casting information for the King's Men, most notable among these being the staging plots for Massinger's *The Roman Actor* (1626) and *Believe as You List* (1631). Both plots show that doubling continued to be a major consideration for the company, and both break some supposed 'rules' for casting in the period, such as that sharers did not double multiple roles or that actors did not play characters of both genders in the same play.[66] In these respects, the plays are like Shakespeare's in suggesting a more flexible approach to casting and representation than is commonly held, especially concerning female impersonation. However, the plots also suggest that the company used more actors than was strictly necessary, coming short of the efficiency seen in the Tudor period models (based on printed doubling plans), or those we might derive from Shakespeare's dramaturgical structures.

---

[66] Bentley discusses the two plays extensively in *The Profession of Player*, pp. 229–31, 250–1, 267–9.

If, in this respect, they are an accurate reflection of company practice during Shakespeare's career, there is cause to imagine a break from Tudor casting conventions in the early Elizabethan period, and a growing bias towards verisimilitude in the company's casting practices during Shakespeare's tenure.

But several problems arise for those making projections based on the Massinger plots. First, they concern plays that Shakespeare did not write, and performances in which no sharers active in Shakespeare's lifetime participated. Theatrical taste continually evolves, or at least changes, and it is possible that Massinger (or the company for whom Massinger was writing) had a different vision from Shakespeare. To project Shakespeare's casting considerations from the plots requires that we assume that operating principles current in the late 1620s closely resembled those of 1590s and 1600s, some 20–30 years prior, and that Massinger closely followed Shakespeare's lead, despite writing for a larger, more well-established company that had seen enormous changes across the previous two decades.

By 1596, 30 years before *The Roman Actor*, Shakespeare had written about 15 plays; by 1606, 33 of the 37 plays most commonly ascribed to him were likely complete. The former group would have been directly informed by the theatrical culture in which he came of age, while the latter reflect that culture as well as his hands-on experience while writing and performing in the 1590s. These creative periods are far removed from the Caroline period, between which came the rise and proliferation of competing theatre companies (including those that featured boy actors exclusively); the so-called 'war of the theatres'; a new monarch and a change in company patronage; the Gunpowder plot; the introduction of dedicated indoor playing spaces; the acquisition of Blackfriars; the Globe fire; and the retirement of every sharer for whom Shakespeare wrote. In addition, as Leeds Barroll observes, 'frequent return of the bubonic plague made for an incredibly patchwork series of playing seasons during Shakespeare's last ten years of production'.[67] In fact, the playhouses were almost entirely quiet for two long stretches (from June 1606 to April 1608, and from July 1608 to February 1610).[68] The latter of these appears to coincide with the end of Shakespeare's tenure as the company's principal playwright, while the Globe fire in 1613 may correspond to his permanent retirement. So while we must learn from the company's practices of the 1620s and

[67] Leeds Barroll, *Politics, Plague, and Shakespeare's Theater: The Stuart Years* (Ithaca: Cornell University Press, 1981), p. 172.

[68] Ibid., p. 173. Gurr documents the King's Men's extensive travel schedule during the summer months of 1608–1610, further suggesting significant upheaval during the late years of Shakespeare's tenure. See *The Shakespearean Playing Companies*, p. 390. There were also frequent playhouse closures during Shakespeare's early years in London, which may have taught him to bear the possibility of touring in mind when creating plots and projecting the casts necessary to perform.

1630s, there are numerous and substantial reasons to suspect that major shifts in those practices would have been traceable to the period marked by so many changes. It seems likely that the company's eventual expansion depended on early success brought on by the efficient use of resources, and that monetary success, changes of personnel, playwrights, and taste led to employing more actors onstage in Massinger's time. I will consider the expansion of personnel in more detail hereafter, but for now we must at least admit that Shakespeare cannot have been influenced by what happened after he died.

Regarding the 1590s, we should reasonably assume that, like other playwrights, Shakespeare inherited and refined pre-existing theatrical conventions rather than originating them, just as he seized on and improved existing plots when constructing his plays. Explicit references to Tudor-period drama (e.g. Falstaff offers to impersonate King Henry 'in King Cambyses' vein' [2.4.352]) affirm Shakespeare's familiarity with the existing repertory. Though we may imagine *Cambyses* (1569) seemed old-fashioned to the audience of *1 Henry IV* (1597), the gap in years between these two plays is smaller than that between *1 Henry IV* and the aforementioned Massinger plays (1626, 1631). The conversations in *Hamlet* about changing theatrical tastes in London seem to question and resist the 'late innovation' and rising popularity of boys' companies in favour of the 'tragedians of the city', suggesting that Shakespeare may have gone in for older fashions. Elsewhere, Hamlet alludes to Mystery Cycle plays while giving instructions to the players, 'I would have such a fellow whipped for o'erdoing Termagant – it out-Herods Herod' (3.2.11–12), while many other plays suggest medieval influences, for instance by incorporating vice figures (e.g. Richard; Iago) and personified abstractions (Rumour; Time). Considering Shakespeare's fascination with medieval and Tudor traditions and tropes, it may be beneficial to assume a fluid evolution from Tudor to Elizabethan practice, at least for Shakespeare, and to explore further how he adapted and improved on inherited principles.[69]

We are right to be cautious about internal evidence. But dismissing period accounts of playing troupes, conventions, and discussions of taste, physiognomy or voice, merely because the information occurs in plays, is as limiting as depending on the latter-day King's Men to inform us about the practices of its originators. And while innovations no doubt occurred in the Elizabethan period, no evidence suggests that Shakespeare was aware of the boundary between Tudor and Elizabethan drama that some editors and critics have sensed. Shakespeare not only employed Tudor conventions, but adapted plots, language, and characters from plays he had seen, which were designed

---

[69] A comprehensive recent study advancing this premise is Helen Cooper's *Shakespeare and the Medieval World* (London: Bloomsbury Methuen, 2010).

to double roles with impressive efficiency.[70] Also, as may be obvious, his plays within plays typically feature 'actors' obsessed with representation, cross-gender casting, and doubling roles.

Judging which roles may have been doubled historically forces speculations. But evidence in and out of the plays is deeply suggestive when combined with close and consistent attention to embedded casting patterns. Informed by historical precedent, internal cues and commentary, and a fresh review of the documentary record, we can analyse the play structures and the possibilities they open up for casting, showing not only the benefits of doubling roles for contemporary companies and audiences, but also that it is not rational to assume that Shakespeare and his company avoided or could have been ignorant of possibilities so consistently anticipated by the dramatic structures they produced, and so much in their interest.

Conclusion

Though I have suggested that Shakespeare's company did not embrace verisimilitude to the degree some have supposed, at least where it concerns casting, evidence from the 1620s and thereafter does support the argument that the King's Men grew in number during that decade, and that they used more hired men to play roles, indicating a decrease in the need for doubling. I will discuss the evidence and the roles for hired men presently, but it is clear that casting considerations changed at some point and began to favour actors playing fewer roles in the same play. The emergence of boy companies had a strong influence, training more young actors and helping to change tastes. Later, after the Restoration, women appear on English stages, Aristotelian theories of drama gain attention, and the theatre increasingly shies from attempts to represent what the audience will not credit. But we cannot determine from any of this that Shakespeare participated in the theatre's move towards verisimilitude back in the 1590s or early 1600s, especially when his plays seem so at odds with the concept. With this in mind, the next chapter turns again to *The Winter's Tale* and the possibilities for doubling it makes available. The play also speaks directly to the question of the degree to which Shakespeare valued pretensions to credibility in the theatre. Few plays are as brave or ambitious as *The Winter's Tale*, whose scope resembles something from the Mystery Cycles or the liturgy itself. It resurrects a dead character, and

---

[70] We can only speculate about plays Shakespeare saw as a youth, though direct references to *Cambyses* and *The Spanish Tragedy* demonstrate some familiarity with plays popular during his youth. Common sense suggests that just as the stories Shakespeare grew up reading (of Plutarch, Holinshed, Ovid, etc.) inspired his plots, so the productions and staging conventions he saw informed his dramatic tastes and practice.

makes possible other resurrections, since characters that die in the play's tragic first half might return to the fiction in body, if not spirit, when actors double roles in the second.

Further, Shakespeare wrote *The Winter's Tale* towards the end of his career. If he was retreating from principles of representation and staging to which Restoration-era writers objected, we might expect this late play to show signs of it. What we find, instead, is just the reverse.

3   Doubling in *The Winter's Tale*

ഇ)൫

... they were to be known by garment, not by favor.

~The Winter's Tale, 5.2.46

ഇ)൫

If Shakespeare valued achieving credible stage illusions, it isn't evident from *The Winter's Tale*, a play that asks actors to figure forth 'Time', a flesh-eating bear, dancing satyrs, and an inanimate statue. The play is full of anachronisms (Julio Romano) and mistakes (e.g. the coast of Bohemia) that, along with Paulina's sorcery and Apollo's intervention, combine to strain credibility at every turn. *The Winter's Tale* seems devoted to exposing and promoting its artifice, from Time's jump across 16 years to Polixenes's debate with Perdita about blending art and nature to providing no plausible reason for Leontes's jealousy. As if daring the audience to disbelieve in it, the play advertises itself as unworthy of credit even through its title, and it frequently builds scenes around preposterous stories: from Mamillius's tale 'Of sprites and goblins' (2.1.27), to Autolycus's fantastical ballads, one recounting how a 'usurer's wife was brought to bed of twenty money-bags at a burden', another about a woman who became a fish (4.4.253–70).

   The Winter's Tale also teems with disguise and theatre making, repeatedly highlighting the presence of actors and their roles in constructing illusions otherwise already under threat. Leontes stages the trial; Autolycus directs others and performs in scenes of his own devising; Camillo orders costume changes for Perdita and Florizel, describing how the pair will be 'royally appointed' in Sicilia, 'as if / The scene you play were mine' (4.4.584–5). Some of the play's critical moments are charged and unsettled by metadrama, such as when Leontes reflects about his dead queen in 5.1:

> No more such wives, therefore no wife. One worse
> And better used would make her sainted spirit
> Again possess her corpse, and on this stage,
> Where we offenders now appear, soul-vexed,
> And begin, 'Why to me?'   (5.1.56–60)

Like Hamlet, Puck, and others, Leontes here discloses his status as an actor in a play, and Shakespeare shakes the theatrical frame even when it might be least expected, since Leontes is at the verge of reuniting with Perdita – what audiences ignorant of the greater reunion in store believe to be the play's climax.

The play's most interesting experiment with the status of actors, illusions, and credibility may be the statue of Hermione. The statue is another patently artificial device, though here the artificiality exists because the statue is composed of flesh and not stone. Watching the statue and processing the ontological revisions it undergoes is electrifying. The actor first represents the statue of a dead character, before stirring to life: first as a kind of animate statue – a mute, ghostly version of Hermione – then as the living queen. Hermione's death is well established: she collapses on stage; Paulina reports the death ('I'll say she's dead. I'll swear't' [3.2.200]); Leontes visits her 'grave' daily for 16 years; she appears as a guiding and angelic voice in Antigonus's dream. All this combines to assure audiences of the character's absence from the resolution. History, though, is rewritten in 5.3 when Hermione explains that she has 'preserved' herself until the oracle's condition – that Perdita be found – was fulfilled.

No stage deaths, of course, are real. In the first chapter, I considered how our interest in stage death results partly from the divided attention we bestow, often quite consciously, to dead characters and the live bodies that represent them, as our habitual scrutiny of Juliet's abdomen – after she makes use of her 'happy dagger' – confirms. Stage deaths operate, and carry attractions, quite like the phrase 'The King is dead. Long live the King': riddles that allows for the assertion of extreme opposites without compromising the validity of either.[1] It may be useful to think of the Hermione actor *doubling* as a statue of herself. That is, while the scene creates great anticipation due to the inevitability of any live body showing signs of life, the actor enters 5.3 *playing* an inanimate statue that resembles the dead character. When the actor begins to stir, Paulina must caution Leontes, saying, 'Do not shun her / Until you see her die again, for then / You kill her double' (5.3.105–7). 'Double' is suggestive here, signifying 'a second time' while carrying the connotation of 'replication' or 'copy'. Interest depends on the actor's capacity to exploit dualities, to harmonize the live actor and the statue, the dead character and the living Hermione.

The characters watching Hermione come to life advertise the artificiality that the play has been striving variously to disclose. Paulina prepares them to see 'life as lively mocked as ever / Still sleep mocked death', but when

---

[1] The phrase's attraction is rooted in its illogic. We cannot help understanding something like 'The King is dead. Long live the King ... who is dead'. We comprehend both that one king is dead while a new one lives, and that a single king is both dead and living. The phrase thus presents a riddle whose pleasure cannot be exhausted easily because the syntactic ambiguity is never wholly resolved, much like the riddle-like effects all actors initiate for audiences.

she reveals a 'live' statue, the notion that the inanimate figure is more alive than those living is no longer hyperbolic (5.3.19–20). Leontes confirms that the statue seems more alive than he does, 'as we are mocked with art', asking, 'what fine chisel / Could ever yet cut breath?', an absurd yet apt question in the context (5.3.78–9). The scene blurs truth and art, giving literal expression to Polixenes's argument about the value of grafting flowers to make artificial combinations (4.4.88–97). Meanwhile, the statue creates degrees of truth among things that are patently artificial. Hermione seems (yet is not) more authentic than her 'statue'. The characters watching her play the statue reasonably believe that they live and it does not (and that she does not), yet all are living and all are fictional. The discussions of life and art here, as in the rest of the play, undermine the audience's confidence in being able to determine what the statue represents or might prove capable of.

Hermione's statue, and the reports about how the character has spent the years during which the audience thought her dead, gain additional interest when we consider that the actor, and the other actors, may have spent the interim performing other roles in the play. When Hermione does return at play's end, the play rewrites its history through her announcement that she was not dead after all, but merely in hiding:

> ... for thou shalt hear that I,
> Knowing by Paulina that the oracle
> Gave hope thou wast in being, have preserved
> Myself to see the issue.   (5.3.125–8)

That Paulina has been sneaking food and drink to Hermione for 16 years is as improbable as anything else in the play. But the return of Hermione, and these lines particularly, gain interest and energy if the Hermione actor, who otherwise would sit idle for half the play before appearing as the statue, had been put to use in Bohemia. Her return then represents an intenser paradox, both more surprising and more familiar. The added surprise comes because, by taking a new role, the actor tacitly doubles down on the play's assurances about Hermione's suppression; the familiarity results because her appearance among the Bohemians would have literally 'preserved [her] to see the issue' since her daughter Perdita was abandoned there as a baby. The actor's double-duty in Bohemia thus contributes to the play's coherence, further exploiting her position as actor-character and character-statue.

Whom might she play? The most famous potential double for Hermione in modern performance is Perdita, a choice that seems unlikely historically because the characters meet together onstage in the final scene. Though Judi Dench played both roles to acclaim in Trevor Nunn's 1969 production, the substitution of the Perdita actor, while impressively staged, somewhat diminished the mother's reunion with a daughter who was conspicuously turned away from the audience so as not to be discovered. The Clown is an interesting candidate: he is conspicuously absent from 5.3, and he could then have seen 'the issue' of Hermione as Perdita's elder brother. Yet there are more attractive possibilities, like Mopsa and Dorcas.

Mopsa and Dorcas are marginal figures in 4.4, which features the sheep-shearing feast and is one of the longest and most complicated scenes (in terms of personnel deployed and theatre-making) in Shakespeare. They come to centre briefly, however, to play out a love triangle in which the Clown makes a third. The Clown is 'in love with Mopsa', but while the girls wrestle over his affection, Mopsa accuses Dorcas of bearing the Clown's baby out of wedlock: 'He hath paid you all he hath promised you – maybe he has paid you more, which will shame you to give him again' (4.4.232–3). The revelation closely resembles Leontes's accusation of Hermione. If the Hermione actor returns to the play as Mopsa or Dorcas, the scene can be thrilling. Her reappearance as Mopsa will put the actor in the position of one accusing her friend of a sexual indiscretion with her paramour, creating an inverse echo of the love triangle in which Leontes imagines himself caught. Dorcas is an even more compelling choice. Hermione's return as Dorcas, a woman accused of bearing the child of someone who is not her husband, picks up on and complicates the queen's innocence regarding the same accusation in Act One. Doubling the roles tacitly sanctions the accusation by which Hermione was tried and convicted. It cannot imperil Hermione's character in the eyes of spectators, but the trace of adulterous behaviour that it suggests nevertheless clings to the actor playing her. The association creates artificial, retroactive, yet still potent sanction for Leontes's former conclusions and curses, accenting the play's gravitation towards his pardon for unconscionable crimes, and even allowing his conclusions some validity, albeit in an alternate dimension wherein the actor's identity fights for precedence. Doubling Paulina with Mopsa would complement this choice, for the figure who argued vehemently for the legitimacy of Hermione's child would mock the illegitimacy of Dorcas's: seeming, again, to undo effects achieved in the play's first half, though only after they had been achieved in full.[2]

Doubling roles like these can also complement the play's varied efforts to strain credibility and create hierarchies of artifice among equally artificial things. But Shakespeare's play structure allows far more extensive doubling, and the pairings thus far mentioned grow in interest and power as other roles are doubled. In the last chapter I suggested that Shakespeare, even late in his career, structures plays to create possibilities for doubling that are much in

---

[2] The Emilia actor is also available to play Mopsa. If that choice is made, the waiting woman who cared for Mamillius and helped deliver Perdita accuses Hermione of sins that she was in good position to discover.

line with Medieval and Tudor precedents. In *The Winter's Tale*, a play that revives morality traditions like personification, dramaturgical strategies like suppression and the kind of alternate plotting seen in *Mankinde* are evident. As is typical of Shakespeare's dramaturgy, two distinct worlds emerge, each populated by a separate set (and roughly equal number) of characters, most of which never meet onstage. Just ten actors can play its 21 speaking characters. That is, ten actors can speak every line without adaptation or cutting. In fact, all the play's mutes (including a dance of 'twelve satyrs') can be accounted for by a cast of ten.[3] That the play can be done with ten actors is critical because it comes near the end of Shakespeare's career, when the Blackfriars was in operation and when economic limitations should have been minimal. The theatrical implications of playing the piece with ten are breathtaking, far surpassing what can be accomplished using surplus actors.

The play's two largest roles – Leontes, its tragic lead, and Autolycus, the lead comic – also never meet on stage.[4] About 1,200 lines pass between Leontes's exit in 3.2 and his return in 5.1. And though Autolycus appears in 5.2, he (like the Clown and Shepherd) never arrives in the final scene to see 'the queen's picture', despite his expressed intention to do so. If the Leontes actor does not take on a second role in Bohemia, more than an hour will pass during which the company's lead actor is idle. This would be like seeing The Beatles give a concert in which John Lennon relaxes backstage for nearly half the show. The same can be said about the actor playing Autolycus, a role whose several impersonations already suggest range and versatility. If that actor does not first appear in Sicilia, we must imagine a company willing to enter the fourth act with its most skilful comic actor still in the wings. As may be obvious, though, the Leontes actor is free to double as Autolycus. What is more, the similarity of the roles – each rhetorically complex, each demanding actors with unusual

---

[3] In evaluating cast sizes and possibilities for doubling I typically focus on speaking roles and identified mutes, because it is not clear that dancers or musicians need to be trained actors. The dance of satyrs and like moments might have featured musicians or other attendants who otherwise swelled progresses and made up trains. Adding 'twelve satyrs' to a scene with Florizel, Perdita, the Shepherd, Polixenes, and Camillo, would make 4.4 of *The Winter's Tale* one of the largest scenes in Shakespeare, though there are never more than ten speakers onstage. Still, even the dancing satyrs can be managed by a cast of ten, without using any attendants or musicians, because the dance described comprises four distinct trios: 'three carters, three shepherds, three neatherds, three swineherds' (4.4.317–18). It is therefore possible, and it may improve the comedy, to bring on Autolycus (the former courtier-turned-rogue who has recently deceived the stage audience while disguised as a peddler) along with Mopsa and Dorcas, who joined him earlier in the same scene to sing as a trio. These three actors can then present each wave of satyrs, quickly adopting new props, mannerisms, and dance steps to create the necessary distinctions. Chapter 4 discusses Shakespeare's dramaturgy and the number of actors predicted by his structures, including several such scenes that stretch or transcend seeming limits.

[4] Antony Sher discusses an aborted attempt to play both parts in Greg Doran's production in 'Leontes in *The Winter's Tale* and *Macbeth*', in *Players of Shakespeare 5*, ed. Robert Smallwood (Cambridge: Cambridge University Press, 2003), pp. 91–112.

range, vocal stamina, and pace – suggests that they may have been created with a single actor in mind, a choice that would allow the feature actor to feature, save the company money, and complement the production's other emphases on duplicity. The choice would also produce a genuine 'beggar-king' transformation, a popular trope already approximated in this play through Perdita's anonymous presence in Bohemia.[5] If the lead actor doubles in these roles the play gains interest and coherence in ways it cannot otherwise, for instance, by fulfilling – via the actor though not the character – Camillo's suggestion in 1.1, 'I think this summer the King of Sicilia means to pay Bohemia the visitation which he justly owes him' (1.1.5–6). If the king doubles as Autolycus, that visit is made.

Correspondences between the two characters abound, setting them in a rhyme-like relationship that is enhanced by doubling. Leontes is a king whose jealousy drives his courtiers away, and he ends the third act as a humbled and broken man. Autolycus lives among the rustics after losing his place at court, and he begins his first scene posing as a man who has suffered a beating – dressing in rags and faking injuries to trick the Clown. Leontes deceives himself for three acts, thinking himself 'a very trick, / For them to play at will' (2.1.52–3). Autolycus spends the fourth act making fools of others. Both use similar phrases and metaphors, and both deliver torrents of rhetorical questions for which their further questions are the only allowable answers, with the result that the audience, in Leontes's terms, may 'mannerly distinguishment leave out / Betwixt the prince and beggar' (2.1.87–8). Moreover, both harm those around them only to do unexpected good: Leontes abandons Perdita in Bohemia where she becomes engaged to the heir apparent; Autolycus deceives Perdita's adopted family, but does them 'good against my will' by bringing her royal identity to light, facilitating the marriage that brings the Shepherd and Clown into grace. The two are further linked because Autolycus's artificial rise, through his adopted courtier's clothes, is a necessary step for Leontes's reunion with her. An actor playing both roles falls from grace as Leontes; takes up an analogically fallen role as Autolycus; rises again through his pretence as a courtier; then proceeds to full recovery and redemption in his return as the King. The characters thus participate in a continuum, within the plot, based on their connections outside it. All the while, doubling underscores the similar receptions afforded to the two characters, one a jealous tyrant who doubles in the generic role of hero for a play working to redeem him; the other a rogue,

---

[5] Note references to 'King Cophetua and the Beggar Maid', or the 'beggar and the king' in plays like *Love's Labour's Lost*, *Richard II*, *Othello* and *All's Well that Ends Well*, among several others. The recurring trope operates a bit like the 'gentlemen born' construction discussed previously.

liar, and thief who is ultimately forgiven, the central point of theatrical interest in the comic scenes, much like Leontes in the tragic ones.[6]

Like the Hermione actor, the one playing Leontes will increase energy and interest if he takes another role in Bohemia. This is evident, for example, when Autolycus attends the shearing feast disguised as a peddler. One of the ballads he offers for sale is called 'two maids wooing a man' (4.4.279), which he sings alongside Mopsa and Dorcas, momentarily displacing the Clown as the male figure in the love triangle. As already observed, Hermione can double as Dorcas, reversing the situation wherein two men woo one woman, as Leontes imagines in the first act. But if Leontes is present as Autolycus, then he takes part as a figure torn between two potential lovers, each accusing him of swearing love to them. He thus participates alongside the Hermione actor as she accuses him of straying, deepening the echo of his initial jealousy. The spat between Mopsa and Dorcas is always a brief, interesting digression. If the roles are doubled thus, the brief interlude becomes strangely essential.

The doubling plan in Table 3.1 is mine, modelled on the one for *Cambyses*.[7] It shows how the smallest necessary cast can account for the complete dramatis personae and contribute significantly to the play's theatricality and thematic coherence. We cannot know precisely who doubled what roles on Shakespeare's historical stages, of course, but the chart represents possibilities embedded in the dramaturgical structure, which allows ten actors to play the full text, in line with Tudor precedents and his company's financial interests. These possibilities were available and advantageous to his company, as they continue to be to contemporary practitioners.

The plan is arranged for ten actors, but even if Shakespeare's company arranged it for 11 or 12, there were enough sharers to stage the play without using hired help or apprentices. That is not to say that surpluses of money or

---

[6] The attractions and complexity resident in the language of the two characters is starkly in contrast to the way nearly every other character speaks. Both speak in large swaths and with a seeming momentum that every other character lacks. Both also have unique roles in advancing the plot and helping to attain a fitting generic resolution, and, together, the two represent opposite, yet mutually inextricable, generic poles in the play. Having one actor portray both is to literalize the very idea of tragicomedy, which operates at large in the play.

[7] After *Hamlet*, *King Lear* and *A Midsummer Night's Dream*, *The Winter's Tale* has received the most critical attention with respect to doubling. In addition to Booth's argument about Camillo and Antigonus, Perdita and Mamillius, see Stanley Cavell's 'Reading *The Winter's Tale*', in *Disowning Knowledge: In Seven Plays of Shakespeare* (Cambridge: Cambridge University Press, 2003); and Northrop Frye's 'The Triumph of Time', in *A Natural Perspective* (New York: Columbia University Press, 1965). Critics have typically discussed specific doubles in isolation – e.g. whether it is best for Antigonus to double Camillo or Autolycus – but have neglected opportunities for thematic improvement brought on by doubling smaller roles (e.g. Hermione/Dorcas) across whole casts.

Table 3.1 *Hypothetical doubling plan for Shakespeare's* The Winter's Tale *(c. 1610)*

The Winter's Tale
c. 1610 (F)
❧ The division of the parts ☙

Leontes Autolycus	} For one actor	Archidamus Jailer	}		
		Mariner Servant (4.4) Messenger (5.1)	} For one actor		
Polixenes 2 Servant (2.3) Officer 1 Gentleman	} For one actor				
		Mamillius 1 Servant (2.3) Perdita	} For one actor		
Camillo Antigonus	} For one actor				
		Hermione Dorcas	} For one actor		
Cleomenes / 1 Lord Shepherd 2 Gentleman	} For one actor	Paulina Mopsa	} For one actor		
2 Lady Dion / 2 Lord Clown 3 Gentleman	} For one actor	Emilia / 1 Lady Florizel	} For one actor		

personnel, skilled apprentices, the need for actor training, or other reasons did not persuade them to assign roles to others. But the play appears to have been built for ten. I have noted already the advantage of doubling the Sicilian king and queen in the wilds of Bohemia, and previous critics and directors have also noticed or exploited the advantages of doubling Perdita and Mamillius, which allows the play with an improbably happy ending to achieve a still happier and more improbable end by seeming to resurrect the dead son in the body of the lost daughter.[8] In the opening scene, Archidamus and Camillo discuss the prospects and poise of Mamillius:

> ARCHIDAMUS You have an unspeakable comfort of your young Prince Mamillius. It is a gentleman of the greatest promise that ever came into my note.
> CAMILLO I very much agree with you in the hopes of him. It is a gallant child; one that, indeed, physics the subject, makes old hearts fresh; they that went on crutches ere he was born desire yet their lives to see him a man.   (1.1.29–35)

---

[8] After Booth, Palfrey and Stern note the possibility in *Shakespeare in Parts* (p. 53), as does King (*Casting Shakespeare's Plays*, p. 244).

In the fourth act Camillo and Polixenes exchange similar, superlative-laden descriptions of Perdita:

> POLIXENES This is the prettiest lowborn lass that ever
> Ran on the greensward. Nothing she does or seems
> But smacks of something greater than herself,
> Too noble for this place.
> CAMILLO He tells her something
> That makes her blood look out; good sooth she is
> The queen of curds and cream. (4.4.156–61)

Such exchanges supplement the connection between the siblings, which can be further strengthened by doubling roles suited to a young male actor.

In suggesting that the troupe's relative ages were probably considered in casting, I do not mean to undermine the notion that the playwright and company seem to have taken for granted that actors possessed almost limitless capacities for versatility and representation. On the contrary, I suggest merely that among any group of actors, the strongest will likely play Charles the Wrestler, the plumpest, Falstaff, and the youngest and most beautiful, Juliet. The company could have used bald, bearded men of 40 to play ingénues (companies like Cheek by Jowl have done so) but it seems probable that Shakespeare's company would have chosen one of its youngest and least hirsute options for Juliet. Where possible, I assume that those initially cast in female roles may have typically doubled other female roles, though, on the precedent of the Tudor plays so far considered, they may also have been tapped for young lords. As we have seen, the plots from *Cambyses*, *Mucedorus*, *The Fair Maid of the Exchange*, and others argue that no hard-and-fast rules governed what roles adult male actors were thought capable of playing.

The Mamillius/Perdita pairing is most interesting because of what it enables during the unacknowledged reunion of father and daughter. In 5.1, Leontes welcomes Florizel and Perdita to his court and, ignorant of Perdita's true identity, reflects on his two lost children: 'What might I have been, / Might I a son and daughter now have looked on, / Such goodly things as you!' (5.1.175–7). The lines generate unusual energy because Leontes *is* looking on his daughter, and on his prospective son-in-law, even while asserting their absence. And since Leontes refers to Polixenes as his 'best brother', Florizel is something of an unknown relation, like Perdita, though the two have never met. But a production that doubles Mamillius and Perdita adds the 'real' (dead) son to the scene, enhancing these effects and intensifying the audience's experience of dramatic irony. The lines thus make it possible for Leontes to long for the daughter who stands before him (in the fiction) and the son who stands before him (outside the fiction), even while Florizel vies for status as an unacknowledged son. The result allows the play to lean towards generic possibilities otherwise impossible (the restoration of Perdita *and* Mamillius), and these are just the sort of possibilities it does realize through Hermione's 'resurrection' in the final scene.

Florizel's arrival in Sicilia can also augment the extent of the reunions both in and out of the fiction, depending on what role(s) the Florizel actor played during the first three acts. The Emilia actor is available to play Florizel in Acts Four and Five, and that actor was presumably a relatively young company member who could feasibly double the young lord. Emilia sports with Mamillius as a boy and later helps to deliver Perdita, so her association with Perdita has precedent. The Mamillius actor is also available for Florizel, but the physical characteristics that make him a desirable choice to play a young boy may better suit him for a teenaged girl than Florizel. If he does double Florizel, though, the scene soon animated by expressions of Leontes's incestuous desire for a girl he cannot recognize as his daughter will be enhanced, because the young couple's relationship will also seem haunted by incestuous feelings. In either case, the Mamillius actor's presence is generative, far beyond what is available if the actor is left backstage. But no alternative can equal the value of doubling Mamillius and Perdita, a choice that so well complements the play's miraculous conclusion that *not* employing it seems actively to thwart the play's objectives and to deprive the audience of the full-throated redemption and reunion that the structure and genre facilitate. When this choice is made, the play better achieves its thematic ends, allowing the classic tragedy that occurred in the first three acts to be more completely rescued by the continued live presence of the Mamillius actor.

Almost as improbable, and delightful, as Mamillius's presence in Perdita is Leontes's spontaneous decision to crown the unexpected reunions by contracting a marriage between his notably loyal, notoriously duplicitous servant, Camillo, and Paulina. Nothing in the play hints at this possibility, which may explain the laughter and joy it routinely sparks in audiences, who experience by it something that seems perfectly in tune with other magical transformations that turn the play into a full-blown romance. Yet the moment has troubled some directors enough to cut it, presumably because there is little to motivate Paulina to welcome the news mere seconds after lamenting her husband's death:

> I, an old turtle,
> Will wing me to some withered bough, and there
> My mate, that's never to be found again,
> Lament till I am lost.   (5.3.132–5)

The marriage augments the comic resolution, but the play can create far more interest and excitement by restoring her to the very husband who went missing on the Bohemian coast. Camillo and Antigonus never meet on stage; doubling them subtly sanctions the marriage and makes this (re-)union as fantastical and fitting as the other miracles that mark the play's end, giving Paulina not just a husband but *her* husband, the third in a trio of 'dead' characters thus unexpectedly resurrected through doubling. It also makes Leontes's proposal, in Booth's terms, seem 'less arbitrary, less an act of mere authorial tidiness'.[9] Booth has discussed the effects of doubling the two roles, a choice employed occasionally in performance, though it is worth adding that the parallels between Antigonus and Camillo are also significant *in* the play: each is a chief counsellor to Leontes; each goes to Bohemia to save the life of one Leontes wants dead.[10]

In recounting the effects of doubling roles across Act Five, I have skipped 5.2, a scene I consider the bravest of all in Shakespeare's bravest play. Given the ontological complexity and subversion of the doubling possibilities so far discussed in 5.1 and 5.3, the strange scene of exposition that fills the interim, wherein three 'gentlemen' describe the reunion of the kings, before the Shepherd and Clown enter to flaunt their new gentility, may seem pedestrian. But it is easy to forget that *The Winter's Tale* is a play driving towards a conclusion quite different from the one it ultimately attains. The comic resolution that seems possible to the audience after Act Three requires only that Perdita be found and return to Sicilia. The reunion of father and daughter is primary because the oracle has declared that 'the King shall live without an heir if that which is lost be not found' (3.2.132–3). There is also a generic pull for Leontes to reconcile himself to Polixenes and Camillo, whom he has wronged, and for his past crimes to be buried with the marriage of Perdita and Florizel, to which Polixenes can only reasonably object while he remains ignorant of her birth. These issues are ready to be resolved in 5.1, when Leontes meets the young couple and then learns that Polixenes has arrived at Sicilia. In short, if Polixenes and Camillo are admitted to Leontes's court, and if the Shepherd's box is opened in the interim to reveal Perdita's bloodline, the play can end having resolved all that the audience can reasonably expect. But 5.1 ends with no such resolution, making it inevitable that spectators will anticipate these discoveries and Leontes's forgiveness in the following scene.

But 5.2 begins as a disappointment, not only because it does not deliver the reunion of the kings, but because it quickly informs us that they have already

---

[9] Booth, 'Speculations on Doubling', p. 146.

[10] Other pairings are possible for Antigonus. He and Autolycus, for example, both complain of injured shoulders, though pairing them cannot achieve effects comparable to those of the Leontes/Autolycus or Antigonus/Camillo pairings.

reunited … *offstage*. What is more, Perdita's identity has also been discovered, she has been reunited with her father, and Florizel has reconciled with Polixenes. The spectators have every right to expect that they would have been present for these revelations, which constitute the climax and resolution of the entire play. We seem to be left out of what concerned us most, and a play that was willing to represent anything imaginable suddenly fails to produce the most important things of all. To make matters worse, Paulina's steward ('Third Gentleman') invites further protest by assuring everyone that what we missed was indescribable:

> THIRD GENTLEMAN   Did you see the meeting of the two kings?
> SECOND GENTLEMAN No.
> THIRD GENTLEMAN   Then have you lost a sight that was to be seen, cannot be
> spoken of.   (5.2.37–41)

The audience will agree with the steward. But despite our urgent interest in this lost sight, we are left in the unfortunate position of Second Gentleman: unlikely to find comfort in a suggestion that amounts to, 'you should have been there'. The steward's arrival, four minutes into a scene that describes what 'cannot be spoken of' and what 'lames report to follow it and undoes description to do it', will not help appease the absent parties implicated, since some of what we expected to see seems to have occurred while we were here with the first two gentlemen (5.2.54–5). Still, as is typical for this play, the scene deprives the audience of something it eventually delivers in an unexpected way, only after it learns not to expect it anymore. Just as Mamillius, Antigonus, and Hermione can return to the play – not only as actors but, in a more profound way than we could expect, as themselves – so the expected but omitted resolution creates anxieties and suspense that make the unexpected resolution in 5.3 still more welcome and fascinating.

The play has repeatedly exploited tensions between the real and the unreal, the living and the dead, actors and characters – tensions that can be enhanced by doubling roles. In 5.2, the play deprives the audience of what it expects, while engaging in a full-scale assault on theatrical credibility. Second Gentleman says the news of the reunion 'is so like an old tale that the verity of it is in strong suspicion', and that even 'ballad-makers cannot be able to express it' (5.2.26–7; 5.5.23–4). Such lines remind spectators of the artifice of the 'winter's tale' they are witnessing, as improbable as the fantastical ballads described in Act Four. But while the play makes clear that ballads can express stories in which women become fish, the audience is left with the notion that this play, despite repeatedly proving capable of representing fantastic things, now cannot represent what seems comparatively easy: the reunion of the kings.

Adding to the scene's plays on representation, and the spectators' frustration at its unfulfilled promises, is the steward's description of the reunion in theatrical terms: 'The dignity of this act was worth the audience of kings and princes, for by such was it acted' (5.2.74–5). Leontes and Polixenes, as kings, have thus performed an 'act' worthy of a royal audience, an audience literally present in the persons of Florizel and Perdita. But the language of 'acting' partly undercuts these figures' royal character, even as the sentence asserts it. The steward then describes something that no audience could have seen: how Paulina had 'one eye declined for the loss of her husband, another elevated that the oracle was fulfilled' (5.2.69–71). Such a reception by Paulina is possible to imagine, but not to play. Though the spectators have longed to see the reunion, they were not likely to see any actor capable of this. Thus, the gentleman's suggestion that we have lost a sight that cannot be spoken of was misleading, since this particular sight can *only* be spoken of, and cannot be seen. The scene thus deprives the audience of the reunion, delays and builds suspense for a greater reunion we may not know is coming, then delivers something that even the reunion cannot have delivered – a conglomeration of effects like those achieved when Mamillius, Hermione, and Antigonus return to the play in new roles that help to advertise the presence of the old ones.

The gentlemen eventually leave the stage after disclosing what spectators may dimly suspect after learning they were shut out of the reunion: that the play has more in store, because the royal parties have gone to see a statue of the queen. The gentlemen depart intent on seeing Hermione's statue for themselves, with one declaring, 'Who would be thence that has the benefit of access?' (5.2.102–3). Well, of course, nobody would be thence; we would gladly be thither. So spectators may be again surprised that, when the characters go to see what everyone is talking about, they remain trapped in 5.2, alone with Autolycus. At this point, he reveals in soliloquy that we have missed even more than we thought, describing another scene that transpired while at sea. There, it seems, the princess's identity was almost discovered before 5.1 took place, which might have rendered most of the fifth act useless. Again, the spectators would like to have seen this for themselves.

In *The Winter's Tale*, these 'unscenes' are so interesting, and so difficult, because they resolve aspects of the plot that we are waiting to see resolved – and do so without us.[11] The result is informative, alienating, and powerful for allowing spectators to seem to transcend time and space. By this one, the play implicitly confirms simultaneous worlds of coherence, one real and one

---

[11] Marjorie Garber has used the term 'unscene' extensively to describe lengthy descriptions of offstage events.

imagined – each related to, yet capable of infringing upon, the other. The double character of the theatre, already augmented through doubling roles, gains additional depth from this invocation of a separate but concurrent imaginary world offstage. The gentlemen of 5.2 also simulate and describe what it is to see a play, both believing and not believing in people and events distinguished by dualities. Audiences familiar with the play will wait out the exposition – indeed, they tend to find it improbably exciting – but directors tend to pare it down, as if nervous that too much time is going by while the audience remains left out of what concerns it most.

The roles of the gentlemen are not easy. On the contrary, they are substantial, require prolonged enthusiasm and exposition despite no real action, and they stand in the way of a plot yet to attain an adequate sense of climax or conclusion. As I have suggested, it is unreasonable that actors thought sufficiently skilled to undertake such roles would first sit idle for two hours. In trying to determine who best to double with the gentlemen, we may remember that two other scenes in the play likewise describe sights the spectators may have wished to see for themselves. In 3.1, Cleomenes and Dion describe their visit to Delphos and a 'temple much surpassing / The common praise it bears' (3.1.2–3); in 3.3, the Clown describes both Antigonus being eaten by the bear and the deaths of the mariners at sea. The three 'unscenes' form a rhyme-like pattern, the Clown particularly anticipating the speeches by Paulina's steward when lamenting his father's inability to see what happened for himself: 'I would you did but see how it chafes, how it rages ...' (3.3.83). Each features enthusiastic accounts of what cannot be described, the earlier scenes seeming to anticipate the great unstaged revelations in 5.2, making the plot's most surprising turn seem natural. The relationship of these scenes can be underscored by having the same actors participate in each, a possibility that Shakespeare's plot allows since Cleomenes and Dion, the Clown and the Shepherd, and the gentlemen in 5.2 never meet onstage.

Doubling each pair of roles would allow the Clown and Shepherd to reprise the substance of their dialogue in 3.3 as the gentlemen, in the latter case learning the answers to all their initial questions about the backgrounds of Antigonus and Perdita. But the grounds for doubling the rustics with the gentlemen, a choice that would complement the king/beggar double by the lead actor, goes beyond the analogical relationship of scenes. And tracing out the dramaturgical bases for the choice can teach us something about the way Shakespeare plotted. Seven actors are required for 5.3. The play's structure anticipates the potential need to cast as few as ten actors for the whole. Three actors – the Clown, the Shepherd, and Autolycus – exit at the close of 5.2, one of whom (Autolycus) may need to make a quick change to return as Leontes. Autolycus, the Clown and Shepherd, and the gentlemen fail to appear in 5.3, though they all exit 5.2 intent on joining the others. We might excuse the rustics' absence in 5.3

because they remain onstage until the end of 5.2, but the gentlemen should
be there. That none of them arrives suggests that the actors were needed elsewhere, either doubling as characters who do appear in 5.3, or as characters who
participate in the latter part of 5.2. Both options are necessary to play with ten,
and both thematically improve *The Winter's Tale*. One of the three gentlemen
must appear in 5.3, likely as Polixenes or Camillo. But the play will make most
interesting use of the other two gentlemen by having them retire only long
enough for Autolycus to deliver his soliloquy, then returning as the Shepherd
and Clown.

Autolycus notes at their entrance: 'Here come those I have done good
to against my will, and already appearing in the blossoms of their fortune'
(5.2.116–17). These 'blossoms' of fortune should interest us. Autolycus point-
edly mentions the rich dress of the recently rustic pair, a topic the Clown
quickly takes up:

> See you these clothes? Say you see them not and think me still no gentleman born;
> you were best say these robes are not gentlemen born. Give me the lie, do; and try
> whether I am not now a gentleman born. (5.2.122–5)

It is odd for the Clown and Shepherd to have begun parading around in new
garments when the information that has gentled their condition is so fresh, and
given that Paulina has not yet led Perdita and Leontes to visit Hermione,
who is waiting to be revived in a chamber offstage. There can have been little time for them to change clothes, no sufficient reason to change, and no
reason to think that Leontes's priority before seeing the statue would have
been to hand out fancy robes. A reason that could account nicely for why they
appear in gentlemen's robes, so soon after several gentlemen have departed
the stage, is that they were those very gentlemen. In a moment of great daring,
Shakespeare may anticipate the rustics doubling as the gentlemen *without* a
change of garment, making the pair's appearance as actual gentlemen a bridge
to their first appearance as 'gentlemen born'. Of course, the change can be
indicated by posture and persona, and perhaps by hats or a shepherd's crook,
but the play could not better enhance the paradox involved in two shepherds
becoming 'gentlemen born' than by having them first appear as Courtiers
(possibly Cleomenes and Dion), then as rustics, then as real 'gentlemen',
and then as rustics in gentlemen's clothing. The scene in which they declare
themselves 'gentlemen born' gains interest because they still so clearly lack
sophistication after being declared gentle. Doubling allows them to be and
not be gentle, and much more. They reprise what they have been seconds
earlier and present a new version of their old reality in the same instant. Just
as Shakespeare manipulates the theatre into showing what cannot be shown,
here he makes it possible to double roles without doubling – at least, to do so
without a change of garment.

In this same scene, Paulina's steward talks about how distinguishing the play's characters can lead to confusion: 'There was casting up of eyes, holding up of hands, with countenance of such distraction that they were to be known by garment not by favor' (5.2.44–6). Shakespeare here obliquely acknowledges an unwritten rule of doubling: that an actor doubling roles must mark transitions between roles with changes of costume. In 5.2, Shakespeare may push past this rule, relying on his audience to register a change of character without a corresponding change of clothes. By bringing gentlemen onstage, who probably differ from commoners only in their clothes, before returning the play's chief commoners to the stage as gentlemen – *as those gentlemen* – we see an additional valence of truth in their supposed transformation, in the same moments that the theatre works to undermine all illusion by advertising the transformation. Shakespeare destabilizes his illusion *by* empowering the spectators, enabling them to experience the litheness of their own minds, conscious of their capacity to understand even in the absence of the logic that should make the changes understood.

Returning to the speculative doubling plan, the elegance and energy inherent in the play's structure is evident everywhere. The play allows Leontes and Autolycus to complement and comment upon one another; allows for the restoration of son as well as daughter; allows Paulina to regain her lost husband and a new partner in Camillo. Further, the plot enables the absurd 'gentlemen born' to be gentlemen indeed, both as Sicilian lords in the play's first half, and as the narrators of the unseen action in the second. Doubling Antigonus and Camillo allows the latter to remain loyal in Leontes' service even after betraying him, to die a true servant, and still to live in exile. Meanwhile, Dorcas and Mopsa can subtly corroborate Leontes's suspicions and allow Hermione a fleeting reconciliation with the Leontes actor in the person of Autolycus. Even Polixenes, whose actor is unusual in this play for featuring in both Sicilia and Bohemia and hence seeming unavailable for a sizable double role, is engaged in this play-wide dramaturgical pattern. Shakespeare disguises him alongside Camillo at the shearing feast, where he becomes as vile and threatening to Florizel and Perdita, his son and prospective daughter, as Leontes had been to his children. In this way Polixenes presents a kind of double of Leontes himself, something he acknowledges early when he describes the duo as 'twinned lambs', putting the audience in a position like that attributed to Hermione, of whom Leontes claims: 'You have mistook, my lady, / Polixenes for Leontes' (2.1.82–3).

Doubling even improves the play's ability to comment self-reflexively, as the steward's incidental observation about distinguishing people by their garments suggests, or when Leontes considers the possibility of remarriage shortly before Perdita's return:

> No more such wives, therefore, no wife. One worse
> And better used would make her sainted spirit

Again possess her corpse, and on this stage
Where we offenders now appear, soul vexed ...   (5.1.56–9)

Actors playing multiple roles make good case studies for those interested in
paranormal vexations of soul. Mamillius is living and dead. Hermione is dead
and living. When the audience finally discovers that Hermione's death was not
a death, Shakespeare undercuts the explanation of her preservation (which may
be literalized in Bohemia) by having Leontes make it clear that she was not,
technically, preserved: 'But yet, Paulina, / Hermione was not so much wrinkled,
nothing / So aged as this seems' (5.3.27–9). In a quest to have things both ways,
to augment the complexity of the stage figure by harmonizing other antonymic
qualities at the same point, Shakespeare allows us to conclude that Hermione
has aged *while* suspended in time. Thus, a play that thrives on impossible representations, from a 'bear' to time-travel to reanimation, enables a widow to
remarry her deceased; a husband to retrieve his wife from death by having a
conspicuously fleshly statue become 'real'; this couple to recover their dead son
in a living daughter; and that daughter to be a 'low-born' princess and a royal
sister to a rustic (though 'gentleman born') Clown. The play insists on having
everything both ways, which is nowhere better reflected than in how it manages
to seem wholly tragic before turning out wholly comic, a transformation far
more effective and more wondrous when doubled according to the hypothetical
plan I propose. When the characters exit at play's end, so that 'Each one (may)
demand and answer to his part / Performed in this wide gap of time' (5.3.153–4),
audiences are left with wholly coherent yet irreconcilable premises, along with
a reminder that this deeply engaging play was not worthy of belief, and continues to defy any attempts to credit it or its components.

The shearing feast, like the play at large, contains doubles and examples
of artifice too numerous to mention. To take just one more example, Florizel
christens himself 'Doricles' to conceal his royal birth, and he calls Perdita 'no
shepherdess, but Flora / Peering in April's front' (4.4.2–3), before citing divine
precedents for changing one's shape:

> The gods themselves,
> Humbling their deities to love, have taken
> The shapes of beast upon them: Jupiter
> Became a bull and bellowed; the green Neptune
> A ram, and bleated; and the fire-robed god,
> Golden Apollo, a poor humble swain,
> As I seem now.   (4.4.25–31)

Through it all, the Clown helps to prepare the feast, arranges entertainments,
and performs in them, showing versatility that recalls that of another rustic-
turned-gentleman, William Shakespeare. If he plays roles like Cleomones and

Third Gentlemen, the Clown will further resemble the *Johannes Factotum* that Greene saw in Shakespeare. As the Clown's life sounds echoes of Shakespeare's own, so the feast's rustic entertainments owe to Shakespeare's experience as a youth and add credit to the ongoing influence of his childhood in Stratford on his playmaking, even this late in his career.[12] Folk festivals were common, touring companies often stopped near Stratford, and Shakespeare likely saw some of them perform.[13] Such entertainments would have provided seeds for imagining future scenes like those at the shearing feast, but may have inspired, too, the rich shows of versatility and doubling that Shakespeare's play structure facilitates.

The Winter's Tale is based on Greene's *Pandosto*, though Shakespeare added the clown-turned-gentleman to the plot. That clown first enters the play flush with faerie gold but he soon concerns himself with accounts, attempting to determine his family's profit in the wool trade: 'Let me see. Every 'leven wether tods, every tod yields pound and odd shilling; fifteen hundred shorn, what comes the wool to? ... I cannot do't without counters' (4.3.32–6).[14] Like the sharers of Shakespeare's company, the clown is 'of all trades'. He tends sheep, shears, balances books, shops, prepares entertainments, dances and sings in them. He wants 'counters' to reckon his income precisely, and when shopping for the feast he displays a sharer's thrift, deciding what things can be done without, what things he can 'beg' rather than buy. If the Lord Chamberlain's/ King's Men were likewise economical, if they had learned from entertainments and travelling players like those who visit the shearing feast, and if they learned the tools of dramatic engineering that evolved throughout the sixteenth century, and understood the attraction of plays that expanded on and enhanced the duality of actors, then they should have taken up and refined the principles of dramatic economy that they inherited, relying on Shakespeare's experience and talent as an improver to double roles to greater theatrical and thematic ends than had been done previously.

But even if *The Winter's Tale* suggests that doubling remained an essential consideration when constructing and performing plays until the end of his

---

[12] The biographical parallels are extensive, though the key point here is that Shakespeare adapted what he saw and learned as a boy into subject matter for his plays, just as he likely adopted and refined theatrical conventions he attended to as a young man.

[13] As discussed in Chapter 2, the Queen's Men and Worcester's Men both performed in Stratford in 1569. In the 1570s Leicester's Men, Warwick's Men, and other companies also performed there or in the surrounding countryside. See McMillin and MacLean, *The Queen's Men*, and Halliday, *A Shakespeare Companion*.

[14] The lines are interesting when considering debates about authorship as well. Those who suppose Shakespeare could not to write speeches for kings and queens might wonder how courtiers could have written these.

career, questions remain. How many actors were necessary for Shakespeare's other plays? What does the historical record and the internal evidence suggest about the number of actors the company deemed necessary or desirable? And what are the arguments against Shakespeare's company having played with the minimum number possible, in line with so many precedents, if the economic and aesthetic benefits were obvious? These are questions I shall take up in the next chapter.

4   Dramaturgical Directives and Shakespeare's Cast Size

ഇൗൽ
'… and I hope here is a play fitted'.
~Peter Quince, *A Midsummer Night's Dream*, 1.2.54
ഇൗൽ

Conspicuous Absences

In *Romeo and Juliet*'s final scene Lord Montague enters the corpse-strewn churchyard and immediately learns of Romeo's death, only to respond with grim news of his own: 'Alas, my liege, my wife is dead tonight; / Grief of my son's exile hath stopped her breath' (5.3.210–11). The 99 lines that follow recount the story of the dead lovers and reconcile the households, but they never again mention Lady Montague. In fact, nobody even acknowledges that she dies. Since audiences are, of course, urgently concerned with the tragedy of the titular figures in a plot drawing rapidly to its close, the virtual silence on the matter of her death gets little notice.[1] Yet Lady Montague's quick dispatch and quicker oblivion is awkward, and it may provide a seam by which we can learn something about the work of the tailor.

Lady Montague's absence is awkward for several reasons. For one, it doesn't improve *Romeo and Juliet*. She is the least prominent among the lovers' parents, but having her learn of Romeo's marriage and lament its quick dissolution might contribute something to the mood at the play's end. Her death adds little matter and less art, occurring offstage and dismissed in two lines' time. Ophelia, Goneril, and Brutus's Portia also die offstage, late in their respective plays, each an intimate of an ill-fated protagonist.[2] Yet their deaths draw notice,

---

[1] The Nurse's absence is also conspicuous, given her intimacy with Juliet and her presumable interest in news of a resurrection. Meagher discusses her omission from the scene (and others) in 'Economy and Recognition', pp. 11–13.

[2] See *Hamlet* (5.1.162–82); *King Lear* (5.3.222–41); and *Julius Caesar* (4.2.146–57).

intensify the effects of onstage events, and thicken the atmosphere of tragedy. Lady Montague's death cannot be conceived to add weight to the losses of Juliet and Romeo. Nobody sheds additional tears because she too has died.

Shakespeare grants even minor characters like Iras and Titinius significant attention when their deaths are announced.[3] Their deaths do not appear to patch the play's fabric like Lady Montague's. Young Siward is a reasonable comparison, since his death likewise delays the ending of a play anxiously unconcerned with him.[4] Still, he furnishes Macbeth a step on which he momentarily rises again before his fall, adding an additional (though illusory) chance for the protagonist to overcome a long-assured fate. In *Romeo and Juliet*, Montague's report and its failure to interest anyone seem to excuse the character's absence rather than complement the tragedy. The omission feels forced, as if the actor had taken ill backstage. Whatever the reason, the playwright felt her presence too natural to omit without comment, but he did not integrate the death into his tragedy with customary elegance. Still, the greatest problem with Lady Montague's death is the stated cause: grief brought about by Romeo's exile. This seems doubtful by the play's own logic, when we consider that Juliet's mother has avoided a grief-induced demise despite the *deaths* of Juliet and Tybalt. Such grief should trump Lady Montague's complaint that Romeo now lives 20 miles away in Mantua. Lacking recourse to art, plot, or dramatic logic to explain a theatrically flimsy passing, we might fault Shakespeare for not thinking better and just sending the actor out for the last act. Unless, of course, he could not send her out.

I suspect that Romeo's mother dies not from grief but from theatrical necessity. She could not come out onstage, because she was already there. If the 12 actors on stage at the end of *Romeo and Juliet* were all that Shakespeare's company had available, or all it chose to employ, our understanding of the company's composition and distribution of labour may grow considerably. Further, discerning the casting patterns necessary to perform plays with 12 actors would add to our understanding of their construction and potential energies. Absences like Lady Montague's suggest that Shakespeare engineered plays with fixed casting limitations in mind, each constructed to be playable by a small, set number of players who would play multiple roles.

Of course, Lady Montague going early to the grave is hardly the kind of bedrock upon which to erect theories of Shakespearean playmaking, or to speculate on the extent to which his company doubled roles, since she speaks just three lines in her only scene. But her absence is material to us because

---

[3] See *Antony and Cleopatra* (5.2.283–94); and *Julius Caesar* (5.3.92–8).
[4] *Macbeth* (5.7.4–12).

Shakespeare felt compelled to answer for it while almost entirely preventing his play from caring. Her relative inconsequence makes it stranger that Shakespeare would not prevent the need to explain by sending her on with her husband. Still, if one stops to think about it (and generally one doesn't), characters routinely go missing from scenes in which the audience should reasonably expect them. Stephen Booth has noted Maria's conspicuous absence from the last scene of *Twelfth Night*, which Fabian excuses by means of some stunning news, 'Maria writ / The letter at Sir Toby's great importance, / In recompense whereof he hath married her' (5.1.350–2).[5] Though more welcome to audiences because of the comic revelation, the moment strikes many parallels with the news of Lady Montague's death. Each feels like an appended explanation that momentarily delays the plot's central concerns. Each explains the absence of a character by means of startling news that attracts no comment from those who ought to be interested. And each defies reason, since just moments before Toby had halted through the same scene, freshly beaten by Sebastian. By the plot's logic and implied timeline there was no opportunity, so Toby's marriage to Maria in the wings seems as unlikely as Lady Montague dying after Romeo relocated a full day's journey from his hometown.

Moreover, there is nothing in *Twelfth Night* to convince audiences that Toby feels remorse over his treatment of Malvolio, or that marrying Maria would atone for it. Unlike that of Lady Montague's death, this news contributes to the audience's satisfaction by adding a hyperbolic complement to other joyful unions and reunions in the scene, and by providing audiences eager for the betrothal of Viola and Orsino, a wedding that complements, and even surpasses in effect, the rapid coupling of Sebastian and Olivia. Nevertheless, the explanation for Maria's absence still seems to cover a structural deficiency. If not, Toby and Maria could come out to receive congratulations or share the story for themselves. Like the Fool's in *King Lear*, Maria's absence can reasonably be excused only if she is not absent at all. If the actor is onstage in another role, then the absence is born of necessity and may prove a theatrical virtue.

Similar examples are common. Cymbeline's queen suddenly dies offstage in the play's last act, as does Macbeth's. In *Much Ado About Nothing*, Ursula and Margaret attend Hero's second wedding after inexplicably missing the first. In *A Midsummer Night's Dream,* Egeus returns to Athens with the affianced couples but, at least in the Quarto text, goes missing at the pageant of Pyramus and Thisbe. And returning to *Romeo and Juliet* we see that the lovers, who attend the Capulets' ball for the expressed purpose of seeing their respective love interests, Rosaline and Paris, find that neither Rosaline nor Paris has bothered to show up. The creativity necessary to explain such

---

[5] Booth, 'Speculations on Doubling', p. 146.

omissions argues the probability that each results from the need to fit the play to the playing company. Cue Peter Quince – 'here is a play fitted' (1.2.54). There is no plausible explanation for suppressing Benvolio and then bringing in Balthasar to do Benvolio's job, unless the Benvolio actor was wanted in another capacity.[6]

Limiting Scenes

Most of these examples, what we might call conspicuous absences, occur in a play's 'limiting scene', David Bradley's term for the scene in which the largest number of speakers appear onstage simultaneously, thus determining a play's minimum casting requirements. *Romeo and Juliet* 1.5 and 5.3 – the scenes containing the Capulet ball and tomb, respectively – require 12 speakers to appear on stage simultaneously. They are limiting scenes for *Romeo and Juliet* and are among the largest ensemble scenes in Shakespeare. There is no play of Shakespeare's that cannot be performed uncut with just 12 speakers.[7] Playing with 12 means that no actor would be available to play Paris or Rosaline in 1.5, or Lady Montague in 5.3.

To be sure, when the company had surplus human and economic resources, nothing prevented it from using them. But the efficiency of Shakespeare's dramatic structures and the consistent number of actors necessary to populate them in full – from nine to 12 throughout the canon – suggest a playwright mindful of the possibility that no more than 12 actors might be available, or else that the company preferred using the restricted casts made possible by the plays Shakespeare produced. Whatever its actual or ideal practice, conspicuous absences are common in Shakespeare, and they – along with a consistent pattern of participation established by the limiting scenes – cannot be satisfactorily explained unless the company's pool of actors was limited, or unless it planned for the contingency of needing to play with a reduced cast. When a thirteenth speaker is wanted onstage, someone *always* goes missing. After all, as John Meagher points out, the Nurse doesn't make it to Juliet's second burial either.

---

[6] In *Romeo and Juliet* 5.1 Balthasar visits Romeo in Mantua to share the news of Juliet's death, despite Benvolio having been the likeliest candidate for such an office.

[7] While all Shakespeare's plays can be performed by 12 speakers, a handful of scenes seem to require more. *Romeo and Juliet* 5.3 appears to want 13 speakers, though if Romeo drags Paris offstage, as Paris requests, the actor can return as a new character later in the scene. At least three other scenes seem to call for 13 speakers – *Love's Labour's Lost* 5.2, *A Midsummer Night's Dream* 5.1, and *The Merry Wives of Windsor* 5.5 – but all ensure that someone departs so that the same actor might reappear in a new role. *Julius Caesar* 3.1 may be the largest ensemble scene in Shakespeare, with 14 named characters seemingly onstage simultaneously. Here, too, however, only 12 speakers are necessary. I discuss the scene in detail later in this chapter.

Table 4.1 *Number of actors necessary to perform Shakespeare's plays (c. 1592–1610)*

Plays (c. 1592–1610)	Limiting scenes	# speakers in limiting scenes[a]	# of speaking roles[b]	# necessary to perform[c]
The Taming of the Shrew (c. 1592)	5.2	12	34	12
Richard III (c. 1593)	5.3	12	64	12
The Comedy of Errors (c. 1593)	5.1	12	19	12
The Two Gentlemen of Verona (c. 1594)	5.4	9	19	8–10[d]
Romeo and Juliet (c. 1595)	1.1, 5.3	12	34	12
Richard II (c. 1595)	4.1	12	38	12
A Midsummer Night's Dream (c. 1595)	5.1	10	22	10–12[e]
Love's Labour's Lost (c. 1596)	5.2	12	19	12
King John (c. 1596)	2.1	12	28	12
The Merchant of Venice (c. 1596)	4.1, 5.1	9	23	11
Henry IV, Part 1 (c. 1597)	2.4	9	34	10
The Merry Wives of Windsor (c. 1597)	5.5	12	22	12
Henry IV, Part 2 (c. 1598)	3.2	12	50	12
Much Ado About Nothing (c. 1598)	2.1, 5.4	12	22	12
Henry V (1599)	5.2	12	47	12
Julius Caesar (c. 1599)	1.2, 3.1	12[f]	51	12
As You Like It (c. 1600)	5.4	12	27	12
Hamlet (c. 1600)	1.2, 5.2	9	32	9
Twelfth Night (c. 1601)	5.1	10	20	10
Troilus and Cressida (c. 1602)	4.5	12	30	12
Measure for Measure (c. 1603)	5.1	10	23	10[g]
Othello (c. 1604)	1.3	10	24	10
All's Well that Ends Well (c. 1605)	5.3	9	27	11
King Lear (c. 1605)	1.1	10	29	11
Macbeth (c. 1606)	4.1	12[h]	36	12
Antony and Cleopatra (c. 1606)	2.7	11	52	12
Timon of Athens (c. 1606)	1.2	12	45	12
Pericles, Prince of Tyre (c. 1607)	2.3	10	47	10
Coriolanus (c. 1608)	3.1	12	51	12
Cymbeline (c. 1609)	5.5	11	39	11
The Winter's Tale (c. 1610)	4.4	10	24	10
The Tempest (c. 1610)	5.1	11	18	11

[a] Includes simultaneously participating speakers and identified/acknowledged mutes (i.e. the number necessary to perfom the text without cuts, alterations, or conflations, though not necessarily inclusive of mutes who go unmentioned, and so can reasonably be dispensed with as necessary).

[b] Counts often vary based on how those counting combine messengers, lords, etc. These numbers correlate to those in the Appendix, where more detailed casting information is available for each role and play.

[c] The numbers 'necessary to perform' accounts for transitions between scenes, though quick changes are assumed to be possible. For instance, *Henry V* never requires more than eight speakers onstage simultaneously, but a ninth should be available, for instance, when Pistol exits 5.1 alone and eight others enter to begin 5.2.

[d] See Appendix for discussion of the play's casting requirements.

[e] Casting for ten actors is possible, as I discuss in Chapter 5.

[f] See discussion of *Julius Caesar*'s unusual limiting scene later in this chapter.

[g] I discuss a casting plot for nine in the Epilogue.

[h] Eight of these 12 are mutes – the pageant of Kings that appears before Macbeth. The scene is discussed later in this chapter.

Limiting scenes define the minimum casts necessary to perform, assuming two basic provisions: that two characters portrayed by the same actor cannot appear onstage simultaneously; and that a change of persona will be indicated by a change in costume.[8] In determining the largest scenes – or, more precisely, the moments at which the greatest number of speakers appears simultaneously – one also must account for actors departing at the end of prior scenes, and for those who must be ready to begin the ensuing ones, though quick (and even instantaneous) changes were common on Tudor and Elizabethan stages, as we have seen. Some grey area exists when determining the required number of mutes. Shakespeare deploys many nameless characters to fill speaking parts: servants and messengers, gentlemen, officers, sailors, watchmen. But there are also mute characters who fill out crowds, armies, retinues, or appear at feasts, typically in line with stage directions often inexact about the number in a given 'train' or group of 'others'. Twelve actors are always sufficient to perform all speaking parts, as well as all named or acknowledged mutes. Nevertheless, while I argue for Shakespeare's consistency and efficiency in plotting, I acknowledge that more people may have appeared onstage than were strictly necessary. Clearly, companies can increase or reduce the sizes of mute groups in accord with their resources. But the playwright would need to be precise about the actors on whom the plot's progress depends, and all of the plays were designed to be playable by 12 or fewer.[9]

In this context, Hamlet's desire to 'hear a play' might serve as a reminder that actors capable of speaking clearly, fluently, and audibly in a large playhouse require talent and training far beyond what would have been necessary for those whose primary duty was walking on and off stage without falling down. Tiffany Stern has written persuasively about the limited periods of rehearsal available to Elizabethan companies, but, however limited it was, those needing to speak on cue and interact with their fellows would surely need more preparation and context than the mutes in a lady's train. For this reason, I pay little attention to mutes beyond those directly referenced in the texts. Where plural attendants are called for, I assume that two were sufficient, even if more were used when more bodies were available.

---

[8] Of course, the technique of 'substitution', where a role is divided between two or more actors in a given performance, tests the rule here. Substitution was occasionally used, e.g. in Pickering's *Horestes* (1567), in Peele's *The Battle of Alcazar* (1594), and in Massinger's *Believe as You List* (c. 1653), examples that span Shakespeare's lifetime and beyond. Modern directors have occasionally substituted for parts, often to literalize a change in age (thus using a different Pericles) or to divide a substantial part (Richard III, Hamlet, Lear), or to facilitate a seemingly impossible double (Hermione/Perdita). I discuss substitution in the Epilogue.

[9] See Tiffany Stern, *Rehearsal from Shakespeare to Sheridan* (Oxford: Oxford University Press, 2008). There is debate whether and how plays were cut in the period, though there is no way to know. Cutting plays will generally increase possibilities for doubling. Regardless, the plays can be performed complete with only 12 actors.

The examples of absence noted thus far, and the consistent structural call for 12 or fewer speakers to participate across 38 plays and around a thousand scenes, suggest that Shakespeare anticipated his plays being performed by a company working at maximum efficiency, in line with historical precedents and economic considerations so far discussed. In addition, his structures reveal significant thematic and theatrical incentives for doubling roles, as my analyses of *Hamlet* and *The Winter's Tale* have demonstrated, as well as consistent patterns for using personnel, which are the focus of this chapter. I hope, hereby, to disrupt some assumptions about casting in Shakespeare's time and offer a fresh basis for projections about historical casting practices, with implications for scholars and practitioners alike.

It bears repeating that few definitive statements can be made about the number and nature of actors on Shakespeare's stages. We will likely never be certain how many actors participated, how roles were distributed among sharers, hired men, and apprentices, and how doubling was managed. While I argue that the efficiency and theatrical potential prefigured in the play structures is clear, consistent, and can be realized fully only by doubling roles – and thus should directly inform default assumptions about the practices of the Lord Chamberlain's/ King's Men – what really happened on the stages of The Theatre, The Curtain, The Globe, and The Blackfriars is not the focus of this book. Rather, it aims to describe the opportunities Shakespeare made available, for his own company and for all that followed, by designing the plays as he did. Since his plays experiment so extensively with ways to enhance or undermine the actor's duality, no company can realize their potential to do so, or their potential for thematic coherence and theatrical vitality, except by doubling roles in accord with patterns embedded in the structures. That said, similarities in these structures invite historical speculations that suggest a more reasonable theory of early modern casting than is current: namely, that the doubling practised by the company was more extensive and more imaginative than is commonly assumed, and that doubling was a constant and essential thematic component of the plays and their performance. If accidental, the consistency of the dramaturgical structures and the potential impact of the casting patterns across so many plays is miraculous. But the possibilities embedded in those structures are indisputable. Since the plays were designed, however knowingly, to be both more coherent and more complicated with ten or 12 actors than they can be with 20, common sense suggests that Shakespeare's company would have taken advantage of the fact by establishing and developing themes of the plot through what Ralph Berry has called 'conceptual' casting, thereby enriching their productions and their purses.[10]

Henry V famously makes the lack of human resources a subject of the fiction. Its Chorus asks the audience to 'Piece out our imperfections with your thoughts; /

---

[10] Ralph Berry, 'Hamlet's Doubles', *Shakespeare Quarterly* 37.2 (1986), p. 209.

Into a thousand parts divide one man / And make imaginary puissance'
(Prologue, 23–5). As we have seen, the productions before Shakespeare's time
consistently divided one man into many through doubling. And whatever his
company's exact historical practice, there is no question that it, too, doubled
roles. Nobody has argued that Shakespeare's company had 32 people on hand
to play *Hamlet*, or that casts of more than 50 were deployed for *Antony and
Cleopatra*, *Pericles*, and *Coriolanus*. In addition, evidence from the plays has
led scholars like Simon Palfrey and Tiffany Stern to conclude that 'so standard
was doubling by changing clothes there was a need for actors who changed
clothes without actually changing character to explain (often repeatedly) what
was happening, like Kent or Edgar in *Lear*, or Rosalind in *As You Like It*'.[11] In
determining how doubling was managed, we must look for structural patterns,
attending to who goes missing in a plot and who arrives late; who is absent
from a scene without reasonable cause; and where plays seem to strain to represent an abundance that they seem incapable of realizing.

Ellen Summers has compiled a list of structural cues for doubling in
Shakespeare. These include: early deaths or retirements (e.g. Mercutio); substantial roles limited to a few scenes (e.g. Leontes or Angelo); 'gratuitous references
to an absent character' (e.g. Lear's reference to Cordelia as 'my poor fool'); and
preliminary exits of individuals before a mass-exit (*'exeunt'*) at scene's end.[12]
Each is useful in thinking about how Shakespeare's dramaturgical strategies
facilitate doubling. The first two are variations on the ideas of suppression and
alternation discussed by Bevington. Shakespeare made frequent use of both, as
we have begun to see already. The third encompasses not only Lear's mention of
the Fool, but also things like the aforementioned references to Lady Montague
and Maria, at moments when they might be expected onstage. We can add to this
set of cues the conspicuous absences of characters like Rosaline and Paris from
the ball, despite those absences going unmentioned in the play.

While these three cues can help indicate roles that can be doubled to advantage, the fourth is little discussed but urgently relevant to the topic of limiting
scenes. There is a tendency among those who consider doubling roles and casting requirements to think in terms of *scenes* – as is evident in the Arden 3 'doubling plots', or in King's *Casting Shakespeare's Plays*. As a result, critics count
the total number of characters in a scene to determine its casting requirements.
Since most assume that characters cannot exit and return to the same scene as
other characters, and that a group exiting at scene's end cannot return early in the
following scene, they tend to come up with higher numbers than I do. However,
Shakespeare often facilitates a character's exit so that the actor can return to

---

[11] Palfrey and Stern, *Shakespeare in Parts*, p. 53.
[12] Ellen Summers, 'A Double Heuristic for Shakespeare's Doubling', in *Staging
Shakespeare: Essays in Honour of Alan C. Dessen*, ed. Lena Cowen Orlin and Miranda
Johnson-Haddad (Newark: Delaware University Press, 2007), pp. 60–75.

the scene in a new role, or else begin the following scene. Taking this idea to its extreme, it is possible for a messenger to be sent off to fetch someone and return *as* that someone, though most assume a new face is necessary. It is useful, then, to break large scenes down into several sections, as I do in the initial chart (for *Hamlet*) in the Appendix and to be mindful of all transitions between scenes. Every hypothetical doubling plan in this book was constructed based on a similar chart (two more appear on the Cambridge website as supplementary materials for this book). In constructing the charts, each scene is therefore divided into segments whenever there is a significant change in stage personnel – that is, any change that could affect the prospects for doubling. Summers's cues are accounted for in each chart, as are the conspicuous absences I have discussed. Cast size typically (though not always) accords with the largest scenes, and it always comes out at 12 or fewer. Creating the charts helps reflect the marvellous consistency in the necessary cast size, and in the size of the largest scenes in each play, while helping to demonstrate how doubling is facilitated by alternating plots and settings. In reading dramaturgical structures closely and producing the charts, I also consider what I call 'suggestive presences' and revisit internal evidence that speaks to the company's possible approach to casting.

But first, the scene that Lady Montague cannot attend is among the largest in Shakespeare, with 12 speakers on stage simultaneously, and it is the limiting scene for *Romeo and Juliet*. Yet determined thus, minimum casts – between nine and 12 throughout the Shakespearean canon – have mostly been rejected as a means to determine historical casting requirements. Baldwin, William Ringler, and more recently King, Meagher, David Bradley, and David Grote have all speculated about Shakespeare's casting requirements, each reaching a different – and excessive – conclusion, arguing that 13, or 16, or 20, or 26 actors were required to perform. Ringler has had the largest influence on critics who follow him, arguing that Shakespeare 'wrote for twelve men and four boys', with the implication that sharers played most adult male roles while female roles were taken up by 'boy' apprentices. King has also been influential, after conducting the most thorough study of casting requirements to date. King implies that doubling was something of a necessary evil, employed chiefly for minor roles and concealed when possible. He projects that a cast of 32 people would have been used for Q2 of *Romeo and Juliet*, based on assumptions that leads would not double minor roles; that those playing lords never doubled as ladies; and that employment must always be found for a sizable group of 'hired men'.[13] King concludes that while 15 actors could do about 90 per cent of the lines, most plays required 20 or more speakers and assorted mutes, and some more.[14]

---

[13] Ibid., p. 254.
[14] For King's information on casting requirements, see *Casting Shakespeare's Plays*, pp. 78–95, 254–5.

Contemporary directors show similar inclinations. Thumbing through pro-grammes suggests that an average professional production of Shakespeare employs about 18 actors, with women typically playing roles that Ringler and others single out for boys, and with larger budgets tending to correlate with larger casts. Of course, several acclaimed contemporary companies have restricted their acting pools and experimented with all-male or all-female casts, including Edward Hall's Propeller and Shakespeare's Globe. But if we take *Twelfth Night* as a model – a play whose dramatis personae is among the short-est of all Shakespeare's plays, and so should solicit from critics a near-mini-mum cast for any play – Meagher projects at least 13 actors; King, 15 speakers and various mutes; Ringler, 15 or 16; Baldwin, 16–18; and Bradley, 17–18.[15] David Grote suggests that minimums 'may not have been all that important to Elizabethans', and concludes that an average of 26 speakers were likely to have appeared in most of the original casts.[16]

Yet like *The Winter's Tale*, *Twelfth Night* is designed so that only ten actors are necessary, without a need for cutting, adaptation, or conflation of parts. And *Twelfth Night* has been performed with ten.[17] As the speculative doubling charts in the Appendix demonstrate, both the Q2 and Folio texts of *Hamlet* can be performed in their entirety with nine actors, as can *Measure for Measure*, while Q1 *Hamlet* and *The Two Gentlemen of Verona* are anomalies that can be performed complete with just eight. In this chapter, and extensively in the Appendix, I attend to the structures of plays like *Twelfth Night*, generating dou-bling plans governed by the only rules that seem to have bound Shakespeare's predecessors: the cast must be large enough to undertake the play's largest scenes; and none of the actors should be onstage in two roles at once.[18] To these I add only that, where possible, the choices should further the play's theatrical and thematic ends. Meanwhile, I will reconsider the bases upon which scholars have assumed the company employed more actors than were necessary.

Returning to Lady Montague, if she is re-billeted as one of the 12-member troupe anticipated by the structure of *Romeo and Juliet*, then the seemingly extraneous report of her death is logical, since the desire to have her present for the scene must be weighed against another character's loss. The same is true

[15] See especially John C. Meagher, *Shakespeare's Shakespeare: How the Plays were Made* (New York: Continuum, 2000); T.W. Baldwin, *The Organization and Personnel of the Shakespearean Company* (Princeton: Princeton University Press, 1927); Ringler, 'The Number of Actors'; Bradley, *From Text to Performance in the Elizabethan Theatre*; and King's *Casting Shakespeare's Plays*.

[16] David Grote, *The Best Actors in the World* (Westport: Greenwood Press, 2002), p. 219.

[17] The 'Shenandoah Shakespeare Express', the touring company that became the American Shakespeare Center, has produced most of Shakespeare's plays, including *Twelfth Night*, with 12 actors. I discuss an uncut production with ten actors in Chapter 7.

[18] Even these rules can be broken, and it may be that Shakespeare's plays occasionally anticipate their being broken. See my discussion of *The Fair Maid of the Exchange* in Chapter 2 and *Measure for Measure* in the Epilogue.

for Maria, who has good reason to participate in the finale of *Twelfth Night*. Because these are roles of disparate ages; because one is a bit and one a major part; because one is silenced early and one appears throughout the play, their parallel exclusions during the limiting scenes are more persuasive in helping to define limits Shakespeare bore in mind when writing. Since the pair suggests that resources were deployed in consistent ways, possibly with little regard to the actor's age, size, or stage time, it seems a good place to start in theorizing the mechanics of doubling in Shakespeare. If the company doubled roles to such an extent that actors were unavailable to come back as Maria and Lady Montague (or Benvolio, Cymbeline's queen, etc.), then some of our suppositions about who doubled and how extensively they did so may be mistaken. If so, prevailing assumptions about the roles of hired men or apprentice actors in the company must be re-examined, and our appreciation for the artistic coherence and efficiency of Shakespeare's structures may increase.

Rival Camps and Green Worlds

One reason to review assumptions about the importance of doubling in Shakespeare's artistry is his frequent use of familiar conventions like alternate plotting. Northrop Frye noticed how plays like *A Midsummer Night's Dream*, *The Winter's Tale*, *Merry Wives of Windsor*, and *Two Gentlemen of Verona* show 'the same rhythmic movement between normal world to green world and back again'.[19] The number of actors required to populate the alternate settings is often strikingly similar. *A Midsummer Night's Dream*, for example, separates the Athenian lords and ladies from their faerie counterparts, allowing the actors making up Theseus's court to reprise their roles in Oberon's. Ringler noticed not only chances for actors to perform secondary roles outside Athens, but also how Titania's faeries repeatedly enter soon after the 'rude mechanicals' depart. The play makes doubling a subject of the fiction when Bottom offers to play all the parts, heightening interest in (and providing a kind of sanction for) doubling roles within the green world and outside of it. *As You Like It* is strict about the lines between court and country, deploying only five characters (Orlando, Rosalind, Celia, Touchstone, and eventually Oliver) in both settings. The rest appear in only one place, allowing the Duke and his courtiers to play versions of themselves in the 'court' assembled in Arden forest. A sign that this was anticipated by the playwright becomes evident when Jacques de Bois (whose lone appearance occurs late in the final scene) explains that Duke Frederick, who had been leading an army into the forest to kill his brother, was prevented from coming due to a sudden religious conversion backstage. The Duke may as well have visited his brother and given over his worldly titles and

---

[19] Northrop Frye, *Anatomy of Criticism* (Princeton: Princeton University Press, 1973), p. 182.

property in person, unless he was onstage already, likely as the very brother he aimed to kill.

By genre, the 'green world' plays are comedies and romances, but many other plays establish distinct settings with few overlaps of characters, allowing actors to alternate in different roles. Most of *1 Henry IV* is set in three locations – Henry's court, Glendower's home in Wales, and the Tavern in Eastcheap – but only four rebels ever come into contact with Henry or those loyal to him. Northumberland and Glendower are central to the scenes in which they appear, but they go missing for long stretches, including the battle at Shrewsbury. Much of *Henry V* alternates between the English and French camps, with Montjoy the only character making appearances in both. Henry and the Dauphin rail against one another so frequently that we can overlook the fact that they never meet. Other plays that establish rival camps (or courts) include *Coriolanus, Julius Caesar, 1 Henry VI, Macbeth, Richard III*, and *Troilus and Cressida*. Since most of these feature wars between rival sides, the lack of interaction would be surprising if not for casting considerations. In *Troilus and Cressida*, Diomedes is the only Greek to visit Troy, and only the principal couple, Aeneas, and Ajax, also appear in both camps. Apart from these characters, Hector is the only Trojan who ever speaks to a Greek. Interactions are likewise severely restricted between the conspirators and the forces led by Antony and Octavius in *Julius Caesar*; between those defending and those besieging Macbeth's castle; and between the Romans and Volscians in *Coriolanus*.

Other plays use variations on the here/there structure. *Cymbeline* alternates the action between England and Italy, with only Posthumus and Iachimo appearing in both locations. In *Othello*, the central characters depart Venice at the end of Act One, leaving behind the Duke, Brabantio, and assorted senators who are then free to populate Cyprus. In *All's Well that Ends Well* the actors that fill out the French Court and Rousillon can return as Florentines, and in *The Taming of the Shrew* the actors who perform the Induction are available for the Shrew plot in Padua, and then for further duty at Petruchio's house. *The Two Gentlemen of Verona, Twelfth Night*, and *King Lear* also alternate between court settings, permitting only a handful of principals to appear in more than one place.

Some plays depend less heavily on settings to facilitate doubling, instead isolating characters within a subplot, so that actors from the main plot may be available to portray them. These plays include *Much Ado About Nothing* and *Measure for Measure*, each of which enables lead actors to perform key roles in the subplot. For instance, Dogberry and Verges never meet Benedick or Beatrice, creating at least the possibility that the main plot's primary comic duo can continue their mix of arguments and amity in the subplot. Meanwhile, plays more than usually focused on a lone protagonist – e.g. *Hamlet, Pericles*,

Timon of Athens – seem less dependent on oscillations between plots or settings, but create opportunities for doubling by phasing in consistently sized groups of secondary characters to interact with the central figure in a structure reminiscent of what we saw in *Mankinde*. In *Hamlet*, a play that requires only nine actors, a well-matched pair can enter and exit the play repeatedly in new roles, since Marcellus and Barnardo, Cornelius and Voltemand, Rosencrantz and Guildenstern, the Player King and Queen, the two Gravediggers, and the Sailors never meet onstage.[20] Such doubling would help to make stars of every actor and might also facilitate rehearsal, preparation, and performance because such pairs and small groups of actors would work together often, onstage and off.

Pericles may be the most interesting example of phased casting, since it introduces several pairs of characters that seem to echo pairs that the play has previously retired. Having the same actors play Antiochus and his daughter, Cleon and Dionyza, Simonides and Thaisa, the Bawd and his wife, can seem to intensify Pericles's struggle against fate, while underscoring otherwise momentary themes, like that of incest established by Antiochus's riddle in the first scene. Doubling roles like these can also create a sense of progress and redemption for malicious characters in keeping with the trajectory and genre of the romance. In addition, several trios in the play never meet onstage yet successively share the stage with Pericles (e.g. there are three lords in his court; three fishermen; three speaking knights; three pirates). If the same actors are deployed for each, they will underscore the play's structural coherence and make each trio more interesting and familiar to audiences. Depending on the resources and the effects sought, the same trio can begin the play as Antiochus/Daughter/Thaliard and return as Cleon/Dionyza/Leonine, or even the Bawd, his wife, and Boult – more prominent trios that are already thematically and behaviourally linked to the initial group of characters. Thirty of *Pericles*'s 52 roles are assigned ten lines or fewer. Yet the 52 roles are arranged so that ten actors can perform them all.

Of the 37 plays most commonly attributed to Shakespeare, only two have structures that suggest the redeployment of actors in secondary roles was not a clear priority: *The Merchant of Venice* and *The Tempest*. *The Tempest* is the only play other than *The Comedy of Errors* that seems to take interest in conventions that Shakespeare typically disregards, including the unities of time, place, and action. It may be that in creating *The Tempest* Shakespeare somewhat neglected traditional conventions like doubling, and took up others to

---

[20] Rosencrantz and Guildenstern are present – though mute – during the initial arrival of the players at Elsinore (2.2). They are conspicuously absent from the performance of *The Murder of Gonzago*, however. Note also that roles that are not paired, such as Fortinbras and Osric, are isolated within the play and may be candidates for the same actors as those who might double in the roles named here.

prove that he could.[21] Possibly confirming its exceptional status, Robert Henke has argued that the play shows a 'persistent impulse towards verisimilitude', one markedly different from his approach elsewhere.[22] *The Tempest* limits the dramatis personae to 15, not including the mariners in 1.1, and the trio of spirits that help make the masque in 4.1. Twelve actors can play it with minimal doubling, though there are still intriguing possibilities, if, for instance, Prospero and Caliban initiate their hierarchical relationship as the ship's Master and Boatswain.

Merchant is anomalous, too, because nearly all its principals interact, and, though the action is split between distinct settings (Venice and Belmont), many characters appear in both. Two things seem to explain the comparative lack of opportunities for doubling. First, it features more cross-dressing than any other play. Since three characters (Jessica, Portia, Nerissa) dress as males – a doctor of law, 'his' clerk, and a page – the play achieves doubling-like effects by alternate means. Portia and Nerissa's participation in the Venetian court initiates a micro-drama in which the two women may be found out, and even if they are successful in their performance, our reception of them and the victory they achieve is complicated by their illegitimacy (as doctor and clerk). The effects are therefore similar to those achieved through doubling, though the sense of discovery and illegitimacy perceptible in doubling roles occurs at the outer edge of the dramatic frame rather than within it.

Nevertheless, the play does present a few attractive opportunities for doubling, especially concerning Portia's suitors. The Bassanio actor is available to play Morocco and Aragon, a choice that would allow him to choose the wrong casket twice, making his choice of the lead casket seem even more inevitable. Doubling the roles seems well suited to the prodigal character we meet in the first act, helping to explain his otherwise rapid transition from the man who went after Portia as a 'golden fleece' to one who sees past the appearances of the gold and silver caskets. Having him play Morocco and Aragon creates a tacit moral education via the caskets, while simultaneously tainting a process of which the audience is already dimly suspicious, both because Portia offers to teach Bassanio 'how to choose right' and because, just before he selects the lead casket, she asks for a song in which all the end-rhymes are conspicuous for rhyming with 'lead' (3.2.63–72). Still, the most compelling result of the choice is the opportunity to see the two actors destined for each other on stage together more often, building suspense and greater investment in their eventual triumph. Shylock, too, is available to play one or both suitors, and the choice

---

[21] Philip Sidney had publicized some of Aristotle's dramatic theory, including the trio of unities in *The Defense of Poesy*.

[22] Robert Henke, 'Pastoral Tragicomedy and *The Tempest*', in *Revisiting the Tempest: The Capacity to Signify*, ed. Silvia Bigliazzi and Lisanna Calvi (London: Palgrave, 2014).

to have him play Morocco can seem to make him a victim to Portia's bigotry in Belmont, thus previewing his role opposite her at the trial, which would seem an inverse echo of the first meeting because Portia is now the one in disguise.

Suggestive Presences; The Mirror and the Monarchs

This chapter began by pointing out character omissions that seem to reflect the playwright's desire to fit the play to the playing company. Some of these absences are explained through surprise revelations or sudden deaths offstage; some characters vanish without explanation; others are displaced by someone unexpected. The deaths of characters like Caesar and Mercutio are clear and complete, while Flavius and Murellus (*Julius Caesar*), John of Gaunt (*Richard II*), Archidamus (*The Winter's Tale*), Northumberland (*1 Henry IV*), and Antiochus (*Pericles*) play prominent roles early in plays before retiring for good. Each structure appears to anticipate the use of these actors elsewhere. The best examples in this line may be Benvolio and Poins, whose absences from the latter halves of *Romeo and Juliet* and *1 Henry IV* are especially odd because the play doesn't yet seem finished with them. I have noted already that Balthasar seems to enter the play to do what should be Benvolio's job. The play creaks a bit when he does enter, because we have never met Balthasar, who is suddenly revealed as Romeo's close confidante, and because we already had a candidate for this kind of intimacy in Benvolio, who has inexplicably disappeared.

The same is true for Poins, who vanishes after 2.4, the playwright seeming to take Falstaff's advice to Hal – to 'banish Poins' – to heart. The trouble here is that the play still needs a trusted companion for Hal. Surprisingly, it finds one in Peto, one of the dupes at Gadshill, who suddenly takes Poins's place to joke with Hal about the contents of Falstaff's pockets. His presence doesn't make sense unless the Poins actor has left the stage (and the play) to prepare for a new role. Since the scene precedes 3.1, set at Glendower's home, the actor may have been wanted for Glendower, Mortimer, or even Hotspur.[23] It may be, too, that the actor was needed to double as Hal's brother, Prince John of Lancaster – in which case the two roles allow the actor to present fitting companions to both Hals: the soldier of the play's second half, and the profligate joker of the first.[24]

The unexpected appearances of Balthasar and Peto are like the absences of Lady Montague and Maria: suggestive moments at which the playwright either anticipates lacking sufficient men, or deems that a particular role arising within

---

[23] Summers suggests the possibility of doubling Poins and Glendower in 'A Double Heuristic', p. 62.

[24] Booth proposes the double in 'Speculations on Doubling', p. 141.

the plot is best served by the skills of an actor already elsewhere employed. As a result, the Benvolio role may close down to allow the actor to transition – likely to Friar Laurence – just as the Poins actor moves into a role such as Glendower, Lancaster, or Hotspur. When the need arises for someone intimate with Romeo to appear, an actor freed up in the interim does what Benvolio might have done, under a new name.

Advents like Balthasar's happen in other plays, too, perhaps nowhere as suggestively as in *Macbeth*. In 3.1, Macbeth charges two men to murder Banquo and, just 60 lines later, these two lie in ambush outside the castle, only to have a third man join them unexpectedly:

> FIRST MURDERER   But who did bid thee join with us?
> THIRD MURDERER   Macbeth.
> SECOND MURDERER He needs not our mistrust …   (3.3.1–2)

The addition of a Third Murderer feels like a rough edge, because the audience has seen Macbeth contract with *two* murderers only a few minutes prior. We have no more reason to expect a third than the murderers do, since Macbeth has not mentioned the possibility and has had little time to reconsider.[25] Banquo's assassination is consequently botched by the trio, which has inspired some directors to have one of the witches double as Third Murderer, the new arrival sometimes purposely thwarting the attempt to preserve 'the seed of Banquo' and thus enforce the fate the witches have foreseen. The play is fascinating for its unwillingness to resolve questions about the interplay of fate and human agency, and the witches – because of their uncertain status as both earthly seers and supernatural agents – seem to straddle the divide. All three are, therefore, attractive candidates to double as the trio of murderers. The conflation allows them to aid Macbeth's attempt to defy fate, while simultaneously fulfilling it through their failure to kill Fleance. Doubling the murderers and witches is another way to develop the central problem of distributing blame in the tragedy, while making sense of the Third Murderer's addition.[26] And if one of the witches has been doubling as Lady Macbeth – a choice made possible by Shakespeare's structure, and made appealing by its potential to enhance her manipulation of Macbeth while intensifying the tragedy's interplay of fate and free will – then Third Murderer's absence from 3.1, in which Lady Macbeth

---

[25] Compare, for example, the break in dramatic logic we experience when Hamlet, having entered Gertrude's chamber after leaving Claudius at prayer, suspects that the noise behind the arras comes from Claudius – the only character he can be sure is not there.

[26] Note also that the play begins with the witches discussing the prospect of meeting together 'In thunder, lightning, or in rain' (1.1.2), and the fact that 'rain' becomes topical here when Banquo observes 'It will be rain tonight', to which First Murderer responds, 'Let it come down' (3.3.18).

appears, is necessary, and his arrival in time for the main event would be as natural and familiar as it is surprising.[27]

Another scene in *Macbeth* may suggest further possibilities for doubling as well as the number of actors Shakespeare had in mind when composing the play. When he wrote *Macbeth* (c. 1606), the King's Men had received a patent for 12 players. As recently as 1603, there had been only nine sharers, and the plays written during the first few years of the century suggest that the company may have been working with an unusually limited number after some turnover of personnel.[28] *Hamlet, Twelfth Night, Measure for Measure*, and *Othello*, all written in the few years before *Macbeth*, feature atypically lean cast lists that require as few as nine actors and no more than ten. After 1604, the plays usually require 11 or 12, correlating more closely with the number of sharers established in the new patent issued under James I. *Macbeth* requires 12, but it seems to want more, at one point straining to present actors after its stock appears to have run out.

The scene in question is 4.1, in which Macbeth asks the weird sisters whether Banquo's issue will indeed reign in Scotland:

MACBETH	I will be satisfied. Deny me this,
	And an eternal curse fall on you! Let me know.
	[*The cauldron descends.*] *Hautboys*
	Why sinks that cauldron? And what noise is this?
FIRST WITCH	Show!
SECOND WITCH	Show!
THIRD WITCH	Show!
	Show his eyes, and grieve his heart;
	Come like shadows, so depart.
	A show of eight kings, and Banquo last; [the eighth king]
	with a glass in his hand.
MACBETH	Thou art too like the spirit of Banquo. Down!
	Thy crown does sear mine eyeballs! And thy heir,
	Thou other gold-bound brow, is like the first.
	A third is like the former. – Filthy hags,
	Why do you show me this? – A fourth? Start, eyes!
	What, will the line stretch out to th' crack of doom?
	Another yet? A seventh! I'll see no more.

---

[27] The choice strengthens the association between the unfinished murders in 3.3 (because Fleance lives and Banquo's ghost returns) and Lady Macbeth's aborted plan to kill Duncan: 'Had he not resembled / My father as he slept, I had done't' (2.3.12–13).

[28] There was significant turnover around 1599, when the Globe opened. George Bryan retired c. 1598, and Will Kempe left the company around 1600, along with Thomas Pope. See Gurr, *The Shakespeare Company*, pp. 227–46. Replacements were found, but the dip in cast size as predicted by the play structures – nine or ten for most plays written c. 1600–1603 – suggests that Shakespeare had possible departures or instability in mind when writing. The structures anticipate slightly larger casts and remain at 10–12 after 1604.

> And yet the eighth appears, who bears a glass
> Which shows me many more; and some I see
> That twofold balls and treble scepters carry.
> Horrible sight! Now I see 'tis true,
> For the blood-boltered Banquo smiles upon me,
> And points at them for his.   (4.1.103–23)

The 'show of eight kings', a number seldom mustered for productions, warrants attention. Why eight? Why not five or nine or the host of hired men reputed to have acted with the company? It is hard to see the advantage of an eight-man parade, and we must conclude that Shakespeare wanted merely to represent a long 'line of kings'. The scene lingers over the descriptions, allowing Macbeth to comment on each figure while growing fearful that the extended procession of kings indicates his end in near. But what is interesting here is not that the Folio stipulates eight exactly but that eight isn't enough. By having the last man in line bear 'a glass / Which shows [Macbeth] many more' (118–19), an indication that the line stretches beyond the eight on stage, the play reaches after an abundance that it does not – or cannot – embody. The play continues to emphasize the line's length, but it turns to reflections of the first eight kings rather than bringing on additional mutes. It is difficult to justify not using two more actors for kings nine and ten when Macbeth appears to comment on them in detail ('some I see [in the mirror] / That twofold balls and treble scepters carry' [119–20]) and when the play has already shown itself willing to employ so many human manifestations of the ghosts of Scotland future.[29] Shakespeare could surely have added two or three more bodies, provided that he always counted on his company having two or three more in store.

If the 12 liveried sharers of 1604 made up the entire cast, those remaining after accounting for Macbeth and the three witches will number exactly eight. The coincidence of the number – 12 in the limiting scene, 12 sharers, 12 in a scene that represents abundance with an abundance of men, then continues its attempt to represent abundance without them – might be explained by a playwright who assumed his company might have only 12 men to put on stage, or might at least desire the possibility of playing with 12. Much like the absences of Lady Montague, Maria, Poins, and Benvolio argue other employments for the actors, the eight kings and the mirror may suggest a limit to the company's resources in line with the play's limiting scene. In any case, the play is structured, once again, so that 12 can perform all speaking roles and identified mutes, whatever the company's actual or ideal practice.

Some may cry foul, however. Based on the foregoing stage directions from the Norton editor, it may seem that I have crushed the numbers a little.

---

[29] I have so far considered mainly the number of speakers and identified mutes necessary to produce the plays – in every case no more than 12. The mute kings are not all identified, but they are the clear subjects of Macbeth's attention, and of ours.

Though the bodies and reflections of the kings may suggest limited personnel available, Macbeth, three witches, eight kings, '*and Banquo*' appearing simultaneously makes *13*. But though most editors would probably guess that 13 are necessary here, the First Folio – the sole text for *Macbeth* – renders the stage direction, '*A shew of eight Kings, and Banquo last, with a glasse in his hand*'.[30] The line in the Folio tells a different story from that of most editors: here, Banquo carries the glass and is last among eight, rather than being set apart from the others. Macbeth makes this point obvious when he says 'And yet the eighth appears, which bears a glass'. Some editors assume either that because the first king looks 'too much like the spirit of Banquo' he must *be* Banquo or that, whether Banquo is first or last, he must be set apart from the line of eight kings. But, according to the playtext, the last king is the eighth, and the eighth is Banquo.

Alfred Harbage exemplifies what has become standard practice in his text for the Pelican Shakespeare, '*A show of eight Kings and Banquo, last [King] with a glass in his hand*'.[31] Harbage finds a minimally invasive way of altering the text to suit a bias, and many have followed his lead. But the Folio stipulates that Banquo is one of the kings; specifically, the one with the mirror. We may doubt the Folio's punctuation, but we must twist its sense to give the mirror to someone else. And Macbeth's description of the line supports the Folio's stage direction. He says the first king is 'like' Banquo, the second 'like the first', and the 'third is like the former'. In other words, the first is like Banquo, but so are the second and the third, and so on down the line. If the first king can be Banquo, so can the second or third. But it does not matter, since, when Macbeth sees Banquo, he knows him *as* Banquo – 'Horrible sight! Now I see 'tis true; / For the blood-boltered Banquo smiles upon me, / And points at them for his' (121–3). The temporal force of 'now' suggests that Banquo affirms his paternal role not only by raising a finger, but also by entering, last, in his own person. Macbeth does not notice the 'blood' on the kings that look 'like' Banquo, though he refers to it here, as he did during the banquet scene. That he notices blood only when the last of the line passes suggests that Banquo takes the place allotted to him by the Folio, confirming that 12 actors were sufficient to play the scene.

The distinction is significant because *Macbeth*, like *Romeo and Juliet, King Lear, Julius Caesar,* and several others, requires exactly 12 performers, and

---

[30] *The Norton Facsimile: The First Folio of William Shakespeare,* ed. Charlton Hinman (New York: W.W. Norton & Co., 1968), p. 144 (Folio). The Folio stage directions are often unreliable and can sometimes seem influenced more by a literary than theatrical sensibility; nevertheless, the detail here seems unusually precise.

[31] See 4.1.110–12 in *William Shakespeare: The Complete Works,* ed. Alfred Harbage (Baltimore: Penguin Books Inc., 1969).

because no complete text of Shakespeare's requires more than 12.[32] As I have suggested, the idea that Shakespeare could accidentally have written 37 or more plays consistently playable by 12 or fewer actors is absurd. If Shakespeare wrote the scene with 12 actors in mind, one might wonder about the potential advantages of playing it with 12. For one, if all actors other than those playing Macbeth or the witches are necessary for the line of kings, then Malcolm and Donalbain (likewise royal and likewise dispossessed) as well as Duncan (who may already have been resurrected within the play as his own avenger, Macduff) will add interest to the otherwise anonymous line of kings. The Fleance actor, who has retired from the play but not from the minds of audiences aware of his high destiny, complements a group of Macbeth's former and future rivals; as may Lennox, Ross, and Angus, nobles whom Macbeth deprives of both lands and families. In fact, when Malcolm is named King, he promotes these 'thanes and kinsmen' to 'Earls, the first that ever Scotland / In such an honour named' (5.7.92–4). So using the thanes in the line of future kings would anticipate the play's end, as though their final elevation in status were a literal, if extra-textual, fulfillment of the prophesied line of kings. Contemporary directors might be inspired to include Banquo's line of kings in productions more often, and audiences might appreciate the kings more when they do appear on stage, if the play's many dead and future kings were thus allowed to come face to face with Macbeth in 4.1, rather than being supplanted by unknown actors – or, as is supposed regarding Shakespeare's day, hired men or apprentice actors. Whatever the scene's status in contemporary production, it can be done with 12 actors, and makes possible for small casts of 12 things impossible for larger ones.

The Case for More Actors

As we have seen, the number of actors in limiting scenes correlates exactly with the number of actors necessary to perform every professional play before the 1590s for which we have casting information. As a result, we should be suspicious of assumptions that have led critics to project that Shakespeare's company used more actors than his play structures require. Those who project larger casts tend to do so based on assumptions about the number and participation of the 'hired men'; the role of specialization or 'acting lines';[33] the actors' capacity to memorize; the speed with which changes of costume (and persona) could be accomplished; the use of apprentices; the willingness

---

[32] Again, 12 actors can play all speaking roles and acknowledged mutes. A cast of 12 cannot always account for unreferenced (other than in stage directions) 'lords', 'attendants', 'others', etc. But if a company is willing to go without *additional* watchmen or soldiers, beyond those explicitly referenced in the text, or to use stagehands, apprentices, and the like to fill mute roles and crowd scenes, 12 actors are sufficient.

[33] Baldwin's theory of 'acting lines' is discussed later in the chapter.

of sharers to double or play minor roles; and the ages and employments of boy actors. Ideas about each of these have helped limit vision and expectations about the extent of doubling on Shakespeare's historical stages. In the following section, I briefly consider each of these aspects of Shakespeare's professional environment; present the research into these conventions that bears most directly on critical assumptions about cast sizes and casting options, and assess the validity of these assumptions in light of my claims respecting the economic, practical, and thematic incentives to double.

I. The 'Hired Men'

One reason to project larger casts than are necessary is the desire to account for the 'hired men' associated with Shakespeare's company. T.J. King has guessed that about 8–15 hired men would have been required in an average performance, presumably to play minor roles like Balthasar, the Apothecary, and Friar John, as well as assorted watchmen, messengers, and attendants.[34] Hired men may have played any roles left to them by the sharers, as well as those for which their appearances or talents were considered an especially good match. For example, John Sincler (Sincklo), a hired player known for being thin, might have been tapped for 'thin' characters such as Andrew Aguecheek or the Beadle in *2 Henry IV*.[35] If the company used 8–15 hired men for minor roles, it would dramatically decrease the need for doubling, establishing a one-to-one correlation between lead actors and major roles, thereby perhaps contributing to the coherence of the illusion rather than disrupting it. It would also make any doubling that did occur less noticeable, since an actor in one bit-part (e.g. Abraham or Potpan) could return inconspicuously in another (Balthasar or Friar John).

Many contemporary productions operate in this way, deploying an average of 18–20 actors and thus preventing the need for those with large roles to double, while allowing those in lesser roles to double unobtrusively. But while a cast of 20 is sufficient to perform most plays with little doubling, such plays as *Richard III*, *Pericles*, or *Antony and Cleopatra* would still require more than half the cast to perform three or more roles. Like King, Lawrence presumed healthy participation from hired players, rejecting the idea that sharers would consider impinging on the prerogative of the hired men by doubling minor roles.[36] Clearly, Lawrence expected the sharers had little in common with Bottom who asks to play both leads and several supporting roles. Based on the economic arguments so far advanced, it seems

---

[34] King, *Casting Shakespeare's Plays*, pp. 82–3.
[35] See Stanley Wells, *Shakespeare & Co.* (London: Penguin, 2006), p. 53.
[36] Lawrence, *Pre-Restoration Stage Studies*, pp. 71–2.

probable that Shakespeare's company used hired men when they were available and cost-efficient. But it likely employed hired men to reach the number necessary to play rather than paying a premium to give audiences worse acting and greater pretences to verisimilitude – neither of which appear to have been desirable. When the company had eight or nine sharers and needed 12 to play, it added the three or four necessary. If a sharer was ill, travelling, writing a new play, or the like, they could add hired men to cover the gaps. Certainly one or more, like Sincler, may have had desirable physical or emotional attributes, and so become valued and regular participants. The company could well have employed skilled apprentices or journeymen when one proved exceptional, and it could have used mutes or small parts to help train actors. But the plays Shakespeare produced were designed so they could be performed without significant outside help, designed to accommodate the personnel he knew would be on hand. I hope it is obvious that projecting large cast sizes because we imagine the company rigidly maintained principles prevented its sharers from doubling large roles, or because we assume the sharers were too generous or entitled to take small ones, is ridiculous. Lawrence and King imagine casting practices that hurt the company's bottom line while sapping the plays of theatrical vitality. And the reward would have been productions that were not only more expensive and less interesting, but also harder and more costly to rehearse, manage, and take on tour.

A major piece of evidence that suggests the King's Men used many hired actors is a 1624 licence granted to the company, which includes provision for 'twenty-one musicians and other necessary attendants'.[37] Obviously, the licence appears more than a decade after Shakespeare ceased writing for the company, long after those with whom he worked had retired or died, and after the First Folio had been published. These facts should limit the licence's value in projecting Shakespeare's casting assumptions or his company's dramatic practice, since he began writing plays more than 30 years prior. Nevertheless, if we wish to project so far back on its basis, we should note that it says little about *actors*. Instead, the licence prominently mentions 'musicians', who were numerous.[38] About six musicians are commonly thought to have been present at King's Men performances – excluding drums and trumpets. A contemporary observer noted in 1634 that the Blackfriars musicians were 'esteemed the best … common musicians in London'.[39] Such praise does not suggest a small band, but, whatever the exact number, it seems that about half of the 21 attendants would have been concerned primarily with music, though the musicians, like the sharers,

[37] Quoted in Halliday, *A Shakespeare Companion*, pp. 268, 391.
[38] On hired men and musicians, see Bentley, *The Profession of Player*, pp. 65–77.
[39] Bulstrode White, 1634, cited in Martin White's *Renaissance Drama in Action* (London: Routledge, 1998), p. 154.

may have performed other duties.[40] The other half (the 'attendants') had much to do besides acting. Men were needed as tiremen and prompters; to sew; to put up playbills; to operate traps and other machinery; to acquire plays, adapt them, and get them licensed; to copy out parts; and to help form the 'not less than twenty gatherers' and doorkeepers that W.W. Greg assumes must have worked daily at the Globe. Henslowe reports hiring a man and paying him '6s a week for buying of the clothing', and we can expect that men were needed at the Globe for such kinds of work.[41] As operators of two successful theatres in different parts of London, the King's Men stood in need of much help beyond acting, particularly when the sharers were available and best prepared to perform the roles onstage. Since less than a handful of hired men became liveried sharers during Shakespeare's writing life, and since most evidence for their participation comes from the late 1620s and 1630s, the notion that a dozen such men were regularly appearing in Shakespeare's plays during the 1590s has no logical or evidentiary basis. But even when we turn to evidence from that later period, which concerns productions of non-Shakespeare plays, Bentley notes that no production used more than *four* hired men in the same play.[42] So if the company was using just four or fewer hired men in 1626, why should we think they used more, or even so many, 20 or 30 years prior? Also, since no known licence or patent decreases the number of attendants, we must assume that the 1624 licence made provision for more attendants than the company had previously employed. And when we consider that the Blackfriars was not acquired until 1608, we must assume that the number was far smaller for most of Shakespeare's tenure, when the company was not running two theatres at once.

We know a lot about the number and identities of the sharers, since several patents exist documenting them. The company had at least seven but more likely eight sharers in 1595, remained at eight through the turn of century, then received patents for 10, 11 and finally 12 players between 1603 and 1604, remaining at 12 for the rest of its history.[43] No sharer entered the company unless another left, so that the retirements of George Bryan (c. 1597), Will Kempe (c. 1599), and Thomas Pope (c. 1600) were accounted for by additions of William Sly, Robert Armin, and Henry Condell. With 12 sharers, the King's Men was larger than most other playing companies in London, and the

---

[40] As I will discuss, these musicians may have come down to the stage to play musicians in some scenes, such as 4.4 of *Romeo and Juliet*, or 3.1 of *Othello*.

[41] Henslowe's costume purchases are discussed among other places in Ann Rosalind Jones and Peter Stallybrass's *Renaissance Clothing and Materials of Memory* (Cambridge: Cambridge University Press, 2000), pp. 184–6.

[42] Bentley, *The Profession of Player*, p. 69. Bentley also observes that the plot for *Frederick and Basilea* assigns some 'minor roles' to 'Attendants' and 'Gatherers', perhaps suggesting that hired men and apprentices were sometimes called on to fill small parts without any sense that acting was their primary duty in the company (p. 213).

[43] E.K. Chambers, *The Elizabethan Stage*, vol. I (Oxford: Oxford University Press, 1923).

only company likely capable of portraying all roles necessary to perform the plays written by its in-house playwright.[44] Given its unique economic success, and its plays' unusual number of female roles, roles that suggest a need for an extraordinarily capable and uniquely large stable of 'boy' actors, it may seem surprising that the company had more sharers than its competitors.

In fact, unless the sharers' participation was often restricted to minor roles in plays created expressly for them, or unless some played roles that scholarly tradition has allotted to boys, it is difficult to explain what many sharers did most of the time. In the case of *Twelfth Night*, if boys were employed for Viola, Olivia, and Maria, one of the principals would likely have had the glories of the Captain all to himself. Others, equal sharers in the company's profit and risk, may have pulled light duty in the form of Curio or Valentine, perhaps returning as an officer who arrests Antonio. Such critics as Marvin Rosenberg, John Meagher, Stephen Booth, and Stanley Cavell have wondered whether sharers may have doubled major and minor parts on Shakespeare's stages, typically balking only when it comes to female roles.[45] Others have resisted any such possibilities, such as David Grote who observes:

[I]t is not necessarily obvious that, because a play could be performed by a certain minimal number of actors, it was performed by a certain minimal number of actors. If there were twenty actors on the payroll it would be difficult to believe the company continued to pay some for doing nothing while others played three, four, or six roles.[46]

While it is correct to say that possibilities cannot stand for facts, the argument is built on shale. The idea that 'twenty actors' were on the payroll is fantasy. And, as I have pointed out, *not* doubling the 12 sharers would be likely to leave some idle, if hired men and boys were used to the extent commonly supposed. As a practitioner as well as a critic, Grote is probably aware that idle actors backstage can be a nuisance. Actors routinely complain about waiting out intervals, and the danger of them missing entrances increases the longer they remain uninvolved. The best way to keep them engaged is to keep them acting. Arranging plays for 12 players – 12 sharers perhaps – would have done just that. But such an argument also ignores Shakespeare's dramaturgical patterns and strategies entirely. The consistent sizes of the limiting scenes and the careful attention to keeping so many characters from ever meeting in scenes, along with the timely omissions of characters in favour of others

---

[44] This may not hold for all the plays the company bought or commissioned, though one such, *The Malcontent*, was adapted for their use and is playable by 12 men.

[45] See Marvin Rosenberg, 'Elizabethan Actors: Men or Marionettes?' in *The Seventeenth Century Stage*, ed. G.E. Bentley (Chicago and London: Chicago University Press, 1968); Booth, 'Speculations on Doubling', Meagher, *Shakespeare's Shakespeare*; Forse, *Art Imitates Business*; and Cavell, *Disowning Knowledge*. I discuss boy players briefly in this chapter, and at length in the next one.

[46] Grote, *Best Actors*, p. 219.

suddenly more necessary to a plot's progress, make it clear that the plays were designed to accommodate small casts. That such consistent dramaturgical patterns occurred 37 times in a row, suggests clear intent. The King's Men could have used 60 or more actors for *Pericles*, but it was incentivized, economically and aesthetically, to use ten. Anything more was superfluous, and that superfluity cannot have been lost on those whose livelihoods were at stake.

II. Acting 'Lines'

I have mentioned the commonplace notion that Shakespeare seldom acted or played only minor roles as his career progressed, a plausible speculation that has no evidentiary basis. The same is true for Lawrence's ideas that lead actors did not wish to play roles they considered 'beneath' them, or that they would not infringe upon the prerogative of hired players by taking their parts.[47] We have no reason to assume sharers resisted minor roles, particularly when the minor roles would have come *in addition* to the major ones. Third Fisherman is not an unattractive proposition when it is one of many things a skilled actor does in the play. At the risk of stating the obvious, actors like being on stage. Bottom's desire to play the lion and 'roar you as gently as any sucking dove', and his consequent brooding over having to settle for Pyramus alone may not be far off the mark when it comes to some actors. And, in the case of the King's Men, we must remember that any decision not to play secondary roles enabled by the structures would have cost them money.

One of the most influential arguments in determining larger casts than those dictated by the largest scenes was made by T.W. Baldwin, who wrote about Shakespeare's acting 'lines'.[48] Baldwin argues that specific character types (e.g. the young hero, the wise fool, the elder King, the ingénue, etc.) recur frequently across the plays, and he suggests that sharers would have taken such lines, perfected and performed them in play after play, meanwhile training apprentices eventually to take over those lines in the future. In the interim, those apprentices played female roles for the company and served as personal attendants. Polonius helps justify the theory when he mentions having once played 'Julius Caesar', often supposed an allusion to the performer's role in Shakespeare's *Julius Caesar*. Both characters are old, pompous, and verbose, yet in dignified positions, and so part of a single acting 'line'.

---

[47] Lawrence, *Pre-Restoration Stage Studies*, pp. 71–2.

[48] Baldwin argues for the theory througout *Organization and Personnel*. Though aspects of Baldwin's theory of typecasting linger into current ideas of historical practice, scholars such as Howard Skiles have shown that Baldwin's theory does not reflect the evidence. See 'A Reexamination of Baldwin's Theory of Acting Lines', *Theatre Survey* 26 (1985), pp. 1–20.

Baldwin argues that the kind of acting necessary for Caesar and Polonius – voice, mannerisms, gestures, and attitude – is similar, so actors adept at one such character were best prepared to present the same persona for the other, and for each similar character in subsequent plays. This casting practice would have facilitated rehearsal and made it easier to write for a standing company. The argument is attractive because it favours specialization and the increased quality that often attends focus within a narrow discipline, and because it suggests a sustainable model wherein particular skills are transferred to the next generation of actors. It is also attractive because some characters and relationships appear to be duplicated in successive plays, for instance, when Toby and Andrew's relationship in *Twelfth Night* seems to be reprised by Iago and Roderigo's in *Othello*, the two plays written within a three-year period.

The theory of acting lines is as pernicious as it is persuasive, though, because those who accept that the actor playing Julius Caesar returned as Polonius – quite possibly true – tend also to accept that the actor trained *only* for such characters, and so was essentially unfit for other 'types'. If this latter aspect of Baldwin's theory were true, it would dictate larger casts than the structures call for, since the actor skilled in one line should have limited experience and ability in another, and would struggle to do both within the same play.

But what then to make of the company's 'lead' actor, Richard Burbage, who appears to have played Hamlet, Othello, Lear, and Richard III? This list describes more of a constellation than a line. Those characters, among them a diffident student of 30, a Moorish general, a fiery and delusional King of four-score, and a hunchbacked tyrant, are as like one another as I to Hercules. Moreover, each role asks for great psychological complexity and range, in itself, since each character experiences sudden and significant transitions and shows wide ranging attitudes and behaviours. In fact, most of Shakespeare's memorable characters call for versatility. Hamlet is a prince and a clown; Lear is sentimental and rash; Olivia is a cool widow and a passionate lover; Cleopatra is marked by 'infinite variety'. Versatility is thus required within individual roles, as well as to play multiple characters in the same play. Baldwin's theory assumes that actors would have consented to the limits imposed by 'lines', but this too is doubtful. Today, we have actors known for playing particular kinds of parts. But I think it is safe to say that most of them would like to play Hamlet, too. And the idea that many actors fear being 'typecast' is widely understood today, even by those wholly uninvolved in theatre or film. The historical actors in question were co-owners of a company, had say in the matter, and likely wanted interesting things to do. Doing a range of small roles that showcased their versatility would likely have suited them.

In addition, Baldwin applies a kind of guild theory not to acting in general, but to acting a particular type. The stage had then, and has now, clowns and comics, and perhaps Kempe was such a talented clown that he was unlikely to play many straight parts. Critics have, in fact, observed how Shakespeare's clowns change with his departure and Armin's arrival. But an actor who only plays braggarts like Cloten is a bit like a pianist who only plays pieces in major keys. It is *range* – of voice and manner, across and within parts – that we value in good actors, and range is cultivated through attempts at various characterizations rather than repetitions of the same one. Macbeth has range all by himself, as does Hamlet, and Cleopatra. It is impossible to imagine becoming expert in the Cleopatra line. An actor who can do so has become expert in everything.

Things like physiognomy, physical shape and athleticism, age, depth of voice, and improvisational talent may well have dictated who would play the father and who the son, who the hero and who the villain, who the Queen and who her waiting woman. If we take the idea of guild training seriously, though, we see that playing various types will allow an actor to develop proficiency in the craft to a high level, whether or not that actor was trying to become expert in a given line. Baldwin's theory is dangerous because in agreeing that some character types recur from play to play, we may slip into assumptions that those actors embraced only those characters and rejected the versatility so clearly favoured by playwrights and audiences throughout the sixteenth century.

For a contemporary example of how talent and versatility tend to outweigh other considerations, we might look to Simon Russell Beale. Russell Beale is among the more celebrated performers of Shakespeare in recent years, having won praise for performances in the widest variety of roles: from Malvolio to Ariel, Macbeth to Iago, Benedick to Richard III. In the National Theatre's 2000 production (dir. John Caird), Beale gave one of the most acclaimed performances of Hamlet in the past three decades, a role for which, in the words of one reviewer, Beale was expected to be 'too old, too fat, too ugly and too gay'.[49] Despite these expectations, despite being almost 40 years old, and despite looking every inch a Malvolio, the performance felt definitive for some. In his review, Ben Brantley described it thus:

Mr. Russell Beale, who is shortish and stocky with a face whose seeming blandness belies its capacity for articulate expression, isn't conventionally youthful looking. Yet his Hamlet, when we first see him poised in resentment and wonder over his father's coffin, appears as inchoate and vulnerable as a newly hatched chick.[50]

---

[49] Lizzie Loveridge, 'A CurtainUp London Review; *Hamlet*', *CurtainUp: The Internet Theater Magazine of Reviews, Features, Annotated Listings*. www.curtainup.com. 5 September 2000.

[50] Ben Brantley, 'The Prince In Us All; Review of *Hamlet*'. Dir. John Caird. *New York Times*. 1 June 2001.

We can expect that vulnerability and trepidation were not the chief qualities with which he invested his Richard III or Iago. Brantley also reviewed the 1998 *Othello* wherein Russell Beale played Iago, calling him a 'soldier's soldier':

Mr. Russell Beale uses this perception of Iago as practicality incarnate to devastating advantage. Everything he says (to other people, that is) seems to smack of solid common sense, even when he reaches the point of telling Othello that it would be better to strangle his wife than to poison her. Similarly, in the famous speech where he tells Roderigo to 'put money in thy purse', he repeats the phrase like a folksy, adage-spouting uncle.[51]

Russell Beale attracts starkly different comments from the same reviewer because he brought different qualities to the roles. Yet he was acclaimed in each, and in several others, much as Burbage was in his time. I make a point that may be obvious because we sometimes too readily subscribe to the notion that things must have been different in Shakespeare's time. Like Russell Beale, Burbage played a wide range of parts, each demanding versatility. This alone would have prevented him from developing some special mimetic capability for one 'line' of characters that was inappropriate for other types. Baldwin may have been correct that some sharers had lines, but likely only insofar as they mean what they do today, when every acting company has those suited for romantic leads, bullies, stooges, pedants, soldiers, and the like, at least when compared to their colleagues. But good actors are versatile, or else Ian McKellen and Robert Downey Jr. would not be playing Marvel superheroes.

Adrian Lester, another contemporary star, played Hamlet, Rosalind, and Henry V within a year's time, leading Paul Taylor to ask, 'Who would have thought that a 6ft black male actor could create not just a convincing, but an utterly captivating Rosalind?'[52] Such shows of range by contemporary actors cannot prove that Shakespeare's actors worked similarly, but, given the versatility required within roles – the paradoxes, shifts of mood, and the psychological complexity that characterize Hamlet, Othello, Rosalind, or Cleopatra – it is not reasonable to imagine actors portraying these characters to think themselves incapable of doubling other kinds of roles. Such challenges as Hamlet's 'antic disposition' or Rosalind's attempt to counterfeit a persona that cannot quite counterfeit to swoon suggest the 'dauntless versatility' Bevington identifies as a prime characteristic of early English drama continued during Shakespeare's career in London.

---

[51] Ben Brantley, 'A Down-to-Earth Iago, Evil Made Ordinary; Review of *Othello*'. Dir. Sam Mendes. *New York Times*. 11 April 1998.

[52] Paul Taylor, 'Simon Russell Beale: A Performer at His Peak', *Independent*. 14 January 2005.

Boy Actors (Take One)

Shakespeare's plays required not only talented and versatile actors for female roles, but an extraordinary number of them. No other plays in the period contain so many female roles, such large female roles, or so many female characters participating simultaneously onstage. Consequently, the need for boy actors – actors typically thought incapable of doubling adult male roles – could have limited the potential of the historical company to use the small casts made possible by the play structures. In fact, the need to accommodate and uphold our theories of boy participation is a main reason that the casting possibilities suggested by Shakespeare's structures have never been examined thoroughly. The sixteenth-century plays offered for acting contained few female roles; those few could usually be performed by one or two actors. Shakespeare was unique in the period for requiring as many as five women to appear onstage simultaneously, and for writing multiple plays in which a female character has the largest role. It is surprising that he would have written so many female roles in the 1590s, considering the need to cast them. In 1595, around the time *A Midsummer Night's Dream* and *Love's Labour's Lost* were written, boy companies were not popular or well established, while John Lyly's company of St Paul's choristers had been inactive for about half a decade. Acquiring skilled boys would presumably have been more challenging than it was after the boys' companies rose to prominence around the turn of the century. We might reasonably wonder where his company found the five capable young boys to play the female roles in *Love's Labour's Lost*. And why would even the earliest Chamberlain's Men plays feature so many female roles, if it meant that the company would need to find, train, and provide for so many boys, and given the likely need to tour with so many boys after several recent playhouse closures due to plague? The company would have needed several reliable boys and to have been peculiarly quick in training and building trust in them, since, almost immediately after the company was formed, Shakespeare wrote several plays in which four or five women appear simultaneously.

Of course, the 'five-boy problem' of *Love's Labour's Lost* vanishes if adult members of the company could adopt some female roles. That idea is heresy to many, but it deserves more serious consideration. I have already cited evidence, from the printed plot for *The Fair Maid of the Exchange*, for actors playing adult male and female roles in the same play during Shakespeare's career. And I will discuss the status and participation of boy actors in detail in Chapter 6. For now, though, consider the exchange between Costard and the Princess of France:

> COSTARD Which is the greatest lady? The highest?
> PRINCESS The thickest and the tallest.
> COSTARD The thickest and the tallest! [I]t is so; truth is truth.

> An your waist, mistress, were as slender as my wit
> One o'these maids' girdles for your waist should be fit.
> Are not you the chief woman? You are the thickest here.   (4.1.46–51)

It was apparently not a given that the Princess of France was to be one of the 'slim-hipped' boys that Michael Shapiro has envisioned playing female roles for Shakespeare's company.[53] By the play's logic, the company has good reason to cast one of its comeliest actors as the Princess. But Costard's line suggests that the actor was tall and husky. Calling attention to the need for 'girdles for your waist' before doubling down on the insult by calling the Duke's love interest the 'thickest person here' may suggest that the actor wearing her dress was not one of the boys commonly imagined to have played Shakespeare's women. If the sharers of the Chamberlain's Men were literalizing Prynne's 'man-woman monsters' by assigning female roles to adult male actors (likely the youngest and smooth-faced among them, but still men capable of doubling young male roles), then it is easier to explain why the resident playwright anticipated having five different actors for major female roles.

This is not to suggest, of course, that no boys acted for the company, or that only men in their twenties and thirties played girls of 16. But – given the versatility prized in the period and demonstrated by the company; its apparent comfort with wide gaps between performers and characters; the precedents for having adult men play female roles; economic considerations; the number and size of Shakespeare's female roles; and the challenge of filling them with boy players – it is worth questioning the assumption that the company would have insisted on always filling such roles with boys, an established yet unproven theory based on critical projections about what constituted credible female impersonations in the period. Instead, it may be that those playing female roles – whether apprentices, hired men, or sharers – were also capable of playing young lords. In this light, we may recall that Rosalind is 'more than common tall', that Hippolyta is an Amazon whom Theseus must woo with his sword, that Titania is … well, named Titania. Elsewhere, *A Midsummer Night's Dream* asks three women to appear onstage alongside a chorus of faeries. But those faeries – who enter only after Bottom's companions have vacated the stage – are called 'Good Monsieurs'.

A crux of the argument about boy participation is whether their voices remained unbroken. Unbroken voices have often been thought ideal and even requisite for female impersonation, because of their greater pretensions to verisimilitude: the unbroken voice sounds more feminine, so it must be more convincing. It bears noting, though, that thin, undeveloped speaking voices are of doubtful use in a large outdoor theatre. Something similar may be true

---

[53] Michael Shapiro, *Gender in Play on the Shakespearean Stage: Boy Heroines and Female Pages* (Ann Arbor: University of Michigan Press, 1994).

of the boys' supposedly more 'feminine' bodies. In discussing boy players, Michael Shapiro reminds us of what should be obvious: boys do not look like women. They are beardless and high-voiced, but also 'slim-hipped and flat-chested'.[54] In other words, their presence still will not convince spectators that women stand before them. By basing casting requirements on what we imagine appropriate or credible limits of representation in the period, we may overlook actors – and characters – who surpass those limits. From the pageant of the 'nine worthies', to cross-dressed heroines, to the tempest in *The Tempest*, much in Shakespeare suggests a theatrical environment wherein players and spectators alike were comfortable 'minding true things by what their mockeries' were, wherein things were 'true' simply because they were asserted (e.g. Oberon's 'invisibility') and characters were known 'by garment, not by favor'.[55]

I will return to the subject of boy actors; here I only mean to suggest that most objections to determining casting requirements based on dramaturgical structure stem from biases about theatrical credibility, based on a notion that the theatre's success ultimately lies in its ability to represent people as they exist in nature. Lawrence typifies this bias with specific reference to doubling roles when he suggests the practice was a 'rural' phenomenon, but assumes that the 'illusion-marring expedients' necessary for wandering players would have been 'unfit for London', much as he dismissed the doubling plan for *The Fair Maid of the Exchange* as being designed for 'amateurs'.[56] But Shakespeare's plays seem to go out of their way to mar the illusion, frequently letting the world of the playhouse intrude upon that of the play. Of course, for a man to represent a woman is not much unlike a man representing *another* man, particularly when female representations – however they were accomplished – were conventional. Given precedents, and frequent cross-dressing for female impersonation (not to mention further cross-dressing so those 'females' could disguise themselves as males within fictions) doubling roles was no unique threat to credibility. Still, critics have tended to interpret descriptions of women on Shakespeare's stage (the 'maiden's organ' Orsino describes in Viola, the 'truly blent' beauty of Olivia's cheek) as though they are evidence of convincing representations of female beauty – most likely by prepubescent boys. Whether or not such boys played the roles, there was no authentic feminine beauty present. On the contrary, and as is well known, words created the reality. When Cesario describes Olivia's beauty, one young male actor gazes at another. The play, as we have seen, may be better for the gaps between the two actors and the women they play. Rather than adapting

---

[54] Cited by Orgel, in *Impersonations*, p. 70.
[55] *Henry V*, 4.0.53; *The Winter's Tale*, 5.2.46.
[56] Lawrence, *Pre-Restoration Stage Studies*, p. 61.

evidence to current biases, then, we might rather take in mind precedent, economics, aesthetics, internal evidence (and just common sense, given contemporary appreciation for cross-gender representation and impersonation) to project that Shakespeare wrote for a small, versatile company clever enough to optimize its resources.

Caliban, Hermione's statue, a bear, octogenarians and infants, ghosts and witches, an abundance of 'twins', cross-dressed pages: all speak to Shakespeare's comfort with the power of theatre to represent what it could not literally approximate. His theatre was grounded in representation rather than simulation, and it indicates a belief that spectators would piece out imperfections with their thoughts, rather than credit fictitious persons and events based on their literal approximations onstage. *Twelfth Night* supports this view, since writing a play with twins – indistinguishable to their closest friends, though one is a valiant swordsman and the other a woman scared of the least intimidating man in Illyria – merits the conclusion that holding 'the mirror up to nature' would not likely have shaped the company's casting policy.

For all their bumbling, Shakespeare's 'rude mechanicals' provide a useful analogue when thinking about Shakespeare's playwriting practice. Quince 'fits' his play to actors comfortable portraying supernatural (the Man in the Moon) and inanimate (a Wall) beings; they are adult males who play women, even when one has 'a beard coming'; they are keen to double, including minor roles ('let me play the lion too'); they are unconcerned by lacking a boy player; and they fret over how to represent everything necessary while hoping that the representations will not appear too life-like. The mechanicals don't worry about spectators seeing through the character to the actor; rather, they invite it.[57] That Shakespeare would allow this – would allow an audience at a play to watch an onstage audience in which the actors all admit that they are actors – favours a playwright for whom tacitly admitting the fiction and destabilizing the narrative frame through incongruous casting and frequent doubling would be an inviting, rather than a worrying, prospect. Conspicuously absent characters; suggestive presences; alternations of setting and personnel; suppression of characters; consistent limiting scenes – all suggest that the plays were built for 9–12 people to perform. Why would we, for lack of a document like those we have for *Cambyses*, *Like Will to Like*, or *Fair Maid of the Exchange*, assume that Shakespeare's company worked otherwise?

---

[57] The mechanicals want Snug to assure the ladies that he is not really a lion, and Bottom plans to state that he is 'not Pyramus but Bottom the weaver' (3.1.19).

5   Doubling in *A Midsummer Night's Dream* and *Romeo and Juliet*

ଓଔଔ
'Let me play the lion too.'
~Bottom, *A Midsummer Night's Dream*, 1.2.58
ଓଔଔ

Seeing Double in *A Midsummer Night's Dream*

In analysing Shakespeare's dramaturgical strategies and the ways his plots seem to facilitate doubling, I have thus far suggested that – whatever his company's actual casting practice – current projections about the number of actors that participated on his historical stages are unsound, and that closer attention to the evidence contained in the structures, as well as to the material record, can provide bases for a more persuasive casting theory. I now turn to *A Midsummer Night's Dream* and *Romeo and Juliet*, whose embedded casting patterns suggest that – quite early in the career – doubling was a central part of Shakespeare's theatrical vision and a superior means to deepen audience engagement. Having already considered how Shakespeare arranged the plots of *Hamlet* and *The Winter's Tale* to increase thematic interest and coherence through doubling, attention to these early plays may help demonstrate how sustained and essential the practice of doubling roles was throughout his writing life. The chapter aims to show the benefits of doubling for the individual plays, while strengthening the case that these benefits cannot have been wholly lost on Shakespeare and his company.

A Midsummer Night's Dream is one of three plays – with *Hamlet* and *King Lear* – at the centre of critical discussions about doubling in Shakespeare.[1] Some reasons for this are obvious: Brook's production; Bottom's desire to play all the parts; and the presence of a hierarchical structure in the 'green

---

[1] Ringler discusses the play in 'The Number of Actors', pp. 110–34, as does Booth in 'Speculations on Doubling', pp. 129–55. Both raise the possibility of doubling the mechanicals and faeries. Brook's production inspired frequent experiments with doubling by other directors, and its discussion by critics, ever since.

world' that mirrors the one in Athens.[2] But the play seems obsessed by doubles, since nearly every character and scene is involved in or concerned with some form of counterfeiting, replication, or transformation. The characters so frequently double for one another or transform into new versions of themselves that spectators cannot but join the mechanicals and their audience in giving conscious consideration to the artifice of the artefact before them. Double-casting can extend the play's other efforts to highlight the seams binding actor and characters together, and to expose the fragility of the illusion in which the characters participate.

As I have noted, the play prominently suggests its obsession with doubles by alternating the action between two similar settings. The Athenian court and the 'faerie kingdom' mirror one another, and the specific relationships between Theseus, Hippolyta, and Philostrate are repeated in Oberon, Titania, and Puck. Meanwhile, Lysander and Hermia, the central couple, are approximated by other pairs including Demetrius and Helena, the two royal couples, even Pyramus and Thisbe, whose story all three 'real' couples watch on their wedding night. The love triangle established in 1.1 – among Lysander, Hermia, and Demetrius – also finds echoes throughout the play. For instance, Oberon and Titania express jealousy over each other's romantic attachments (to Hippolyta and Theseus) and dispute the custody of a changeling boy. Titania also forms (or is forced into) a romantic attachment to Bottom (himself a kind of 'changeling' after being 'translated' to an ass), making Oberon the third in yet another trio. Demetrius and Lysander, who both love Hermia, eventually replicate and reverse the triad when they pursue Helena instead. Meanwhile, Egeus's efforts to prevent Hermia's marriage are complemented by Thisbe's father's attempt to keep Pyramus and Thisbe apart, the play within the play serving as a broad, parodic double of the main plot.

Several other examples of doubling and replication occur within the pageant of 'Pyramus and Thisbe'. And the mechanicals' subplot and court performance both duplicate aspects of the main plot, while adding layers to the inherent duality of the stage figures. The mechanicals are (actors playing) tradesmen who are effectively 'doubling' as actors – actors who play not only characters like Pyramus and Thisbe but also animals and inanimate objects. Still, the play takes all occasions to remind the audience that these men are not *really* actors – using their ineptness to reveal them as weavers, joiners, bellows-menders, etc. (which of course they are not). Yet these non-actors do little other than

---

[2] See the pageant of the 'Nine Worthies' in *Love's Labour's Lost*, where doubling is a primary concern in the pageant's rehearsal, performance, and reception. It is at least possible that Shakespeare was lampooning his own company and its lead actor when depicting Bottom and the others.

act, rehearse, and discuss theories of representation, and the acting that reveals them to be tradesmen also serves to conceal them as actors *playing* tradesmen – that is, each mimetic failure simultaneously confirms a mimetic success.

When they perform at court, their efforts at representation repeatedly break down, or suffer disruptions, and any remaining pretense to credibility is then undermined by their awkward script and staging. But the breakdowns engage rather than alienate spectators – at least those offstage. Spectators have no need for Bottom to 'tell them that I, Pyramus, am not Pyramus but Bottom the weaver', since the performance aggressively advertises the fact (3.1.18–19). But he is no more Bottom than he is Pyramus, so the play creates a double effect – reinforcing the legitimacy of one characterization while undermining the other. Failure and success in acting are thus synchronous, manifested by the same actor in the same moment. As a result, the play replicates – wholly within the fiction – the dual nature of the performers at its margins; that is, it is full of actor-characters, but by having actor-characters *play* actor-characters, they double their function, advertising the fragility of the fictional enterprise while affirming the truth of characters (Bottom, Flute, Snug) underneath the façades. Like all plays, this one is energized by figures participating concurrently in real and fictional worlds, but it goes further by undermining the nature of theatrical representation through unsuccessful playing, and by having characters appropriate the roles of fellow characters (e.g. Helena takes Hermia's place with the suitors, Bottom replaces Oberon in Titania's bower). Bottom's request to play all his friends' parts thus humorously expresses what is already somewhat manifest in the play. And, while he is permitted to portray neither Thisbe nor the lion, he does eventually land a second part when he is transformed into an ass-eared version of himself.

The play has other doubles in store. Spectators see a version of Hermia in Thisbe, but also in Helena, who describes the two as being 'like to a double cherry, seeming parted, / But yet an union in partition' (3.2.209–10). Helena even expresses a desire to be Hermia: 'Were the world mine, Demetrius being bated, / The rest I'd give to be to you translated' (1.1.190–1); and the play grants her wish when Demetrius and Lysander alter their affections in her favour. After attaining this end, Helena calls Hermia a 'puppet' and a 'counterfeit', though she has effectively counterfeited her friend's position in the suitors' eyes (3.2.288). Meanwhile, Demetrius and Lysander are often seen as copies of one another, such as when Lysander claims he is 'as well derived as [Demetrius] / As well possessed' (1.1.99–100), or when Puck mistakes Lysander for Demetrius because of their 'Athenian garments'. Puck further establishes the two as near-replicas when he impersonates both characters – mocking, challenging, and then eluding each by imitating the voice of the other. For his part, Puck answers to two names (Robin and Puck), takes turns playing both Lysander and Demetrius, desires roles as both 'auditor' and 'actor' at the

Table 5.1 *Hypothetical doubling plan for Shakespeare's* A Midsummer Night's Dream *(c. 1595)*

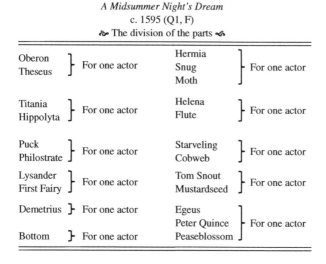

A Midsummer Night's Dream
c. 1595 (Q1, F)
❧ The division of the parts ☙

Oberon Theseus	} For one actor	Hermia Snug Moth	} For one actor
Titania Hippolyta	} For one actor	Helena Flute	} For one actor
Puck Philostrate	} For one actor	Starveling Cobweb	} For one actor
Lysander First Fairy	} For one actor	Tom Snout Mustardseed	} For one actor
Demetrius	} For one actor	Egeus Peter Quince Peaseblossom	} For one actor
Bottom	} For one actor		

mechanicals' rehearsal, and, at the play's end, freely reports his dual nature and that of his fellow characters, 'If we shadows have offended' (Epilogue, 1). Collectively, so many instances of duplicity and replication invite audiences, actors, and characters alike to see like Hermia, 'When everything seems double' (4.1.188).

The play's variations on doubles, role-playing, and replication outlast this catalogue, from Titania's 'double-tongued' snakes to Lysander's pretty riddling to Starveling's turn as the man in the moon. It is no surprise, then, that the play's structure enables actors to augment thematic interest in doubles by filling multiple roles. The casting plan in Table 5.1 is laid out for 11 actors, in accordance with 5.1, the limiting scene. Like some other plays of the mid-1590s, *A Midsummer Night's Dream* allows nine actors to play all major roles (and most minor ones), with two others doing relatively light work.[3] *Romeo and Juliet*, for example, requires 12 speakers, though nine can account for all but the citizens, musicians, and watchmen, parts with less need for rehearsal and that could have been filled by musicians, attendants, etc., if not by sharers or hired men.

William Ringler noted the play's structural partitions and patterns, seemingly designed to separate the two worlds, and to allow the actors playing

---

[3] Shakespeare may have experimented with two lines for apprentices or hired men early in his career, before the increased number of sharers, and greater efficiency in plotting, allowed the sharers the option to cover all roles from within their own number.

mechanicals to alternate as the faeries attending on Titania. He concluded that 15 men would have been necessary, assuming that the actors playing mechanicals doubled as faeries. Playing with fewer was impossible for Ringler to imagine due to quick changes and an abundance of female roles. King speculated that 24 actors were necessary for the Quarto text, including at least 20 speakers. The large cast owes to King's assumptions that major roles generally would not have been doubled, and that boy apprentices played all female roles (and were incapable of doubling any others). As a result, only one major character doubles according to King's plot (Hippolyta/First Fairy).

Booth does not suggest a cast size, but he argues that the company could have doubled the royal couples as well as the mechanicals and faeries, citing Brook's 'spectacularly workable' quick changes as evidence of the possibility in performance. He suggests that doubling the royal couples is sanctioned and enriched when one couple seems to refer to the other in lines 'designed to hold a maximum number and variety of examples of changes and confusions of persona'.[4] Just as Lear seems to reference both Cordelia and the Fool after Cordelia's death ('and my poor fool is hanged') so Oberon and Titania seem to refer to their relationship – *as* Theseus and Hippolyta – when he asks 'Am not I thy Lord?', to which she responds 'Then I must be thy lady'.[5] These terms had already been applied to Theseus and Hippolyta, so having the same actors revisit them in different personas can seem to invoke the absent couple without suspending the conversation of the one present, further extending the play's interest in identity and transformation.

Since doubling the royal couples occurs occasionally onstage, and has attracted significant critical comment, I will focus on other possibilities, as well as on timely omissions of characters that suggest how the structure may anticipate particular choices. Ringler noticed, too, that the play enabled Philostrate to double as Puck, another possibility Brook realized in production. Curiously, Philostrate appears only in the first and last (Quarto only) scenes, and then only briefly. But ten lines into the play, Theseus sends him away with a mission:

> Go, Philostrate,
> Stir up the Athenian youth to merriments,
> Awake the pert and nimble spirit of mirth,
> Turn melancholy forth to funerals;
> The pale companion is not for our pomp.   (1.1.11–15)

Though audiences can have no clear expectation about what role Philostrate will go on to play, it is remarkable that he is sent to do exactly what Puck does

---

[4] Booth, 'Speculations on Doubling', p. 132–3.
[5] *King Lear*, 5.3.304; *A Midsummer Night's Dream*, 2.1.63–4.

across the following three acts. When Puck enters the play, he immediately describes a series of jests he has undertaken as a 'merry wanderer of the night' (2.1.43); shortly thereafter, Oberon asks him to interfere in the affairs of an 'Athenian youth' in the forest. Again, it is not that the roles can be doubled; rather, the play improves as a result of the choice, here making retroactive sense of Theseus's otherwise inert command. If the roles are cast separately, Theseus dismisses an unknown character who either remains uninvolved until Act Five (Quarto), or vanishes altogether (Folio). In both cases, the exchange is needless and utterly forgotten by the play and its audience. But it sparkles if Philostrate exits to put on Puck's costume.

Moreover, Philostrate begins the play as Theseus's messenger – the role Puck initially performs for Oberon. And by meddling in the mechanicals' rehearsal, Puck becomes something of a master of the revels, the very role Philostrate fills in 5.1 (Quarto) when he provides Theseus a list of entertainments. Puck thus echoes Philostrate's first appearance and anticipates his second. Stumbling upon the mechanicals' rehearsal, Puck exclaims 'What a play toward! I'll be an auditor; / An actor too perhaps, if I see cause' (3.1.80–1). He thus proposes a double role for himself, one that he may otherwise achieve by returning as Philostrate to introduce the very play he has seen rehearsed. Philostrate later informs Theseus that the play is lacking: 'No, my noble lord, / It is not for you; I have heard it over / And it is nothing' (5.1.76–8). If the actor had played Puck, he would have a clear and theatrically vitalizing reason to know.

Puck further establishes himself as 'master of revels' by directing Lysander and Demetrius through the wood, and by arranging the affairs of the play's young couples:

> Captain of our fairy band,
> Helena is here at hand,
> And the youth mistook by me,
> Pleading for a lover's fee.
> Shall we their fond pageant see?
> Lord, what fools these mortals be! (3.2.110–15)

Here Puck orchestrates and watches a show every bit as ridiculous as the one Philostrate describes in 5.1: just the sort of 'fond pageant' Philostrate was asked to stir up in 1.1. Moreover, the chiasmic movement of the actor from Philostrate to Puck and back again is also played out among the romantic subjects that these lines concern. Both suitors transfer their affections away from and back to their intendeds, while the 'real' situation of Hermia and Lysander is at once an echo of fictional tales of the past ('the course of true love never did run smooth'); a source of present laughter for Puck and Oberon; and then once more a fictional subject (and source of laughter) in 'Pyramus and Thisbe'.

Like Philostrate, Egeus appears in only two scenes – three in the Folio text. The discrepancy between texts concerns whether Philostrate or Egeus is with

Theseus while he reviews the night's entertainment options, and some have taken the confusion as a sign that the roles may have been doubled.[6] Though possible, the play gains little by doubling Philostrate and Egeus, a choice that would still leave the actor idle through the middle acts. Egeus's absence from Act Five of the Quarto is unexpected, possibly arguing for his presence elsewhere in another role. The Quarto text has been preferred largely because his role in 5.1 of the Folio has so little in common with his role in 1.1. In 5.1 his presence is awkward because he does Philostrate's duty without mentioning the marriage or being overruled by Theseus, and he has no exchange with or moment of reconciliation to his daughter and Lysander. If we assume, then, that Philostrate is wanted here and Egeus is absent, we might expect to find him among the mechanicals, possibly doubling as Peter Quince. Quince writes, casts, and oversees the pageant, assigning roles and resisting Bottom's attempt to play them all. When Egeus and Quince are doubled, a faint echo of Egeus's struggle to dictate Hermia's choice is sounded, both in his choice of play and in his effort to dictate terms to the male lover. The link between the two is strengthened as the other parts are allotted:

> QUINCE Robin Starveling, you must play Thisbe's mother. – Tom Snout, the tinker.
> SNOUT Here, Peter Quince.
> QUINCE You, Pyramus' father: *myself, Thisbe's father*; Snug the joiner, you, the lion's part; And I hope here is a play fitted. (1.2.50–4, italics mine)

Here, Quince elects to play a father who bars his daughter from meeting her lover, a role that Egeus himself has played in denying Hermia her choice. Assigning both roles to one actor enriches both, preserving a spectre of Hermia's disapproving father in the wood outside Athens.

The Fairy that encounters Puck in 2.2 (the so-called 'First Fairy') is another good candidate for doubling. The role is notoriously difficult – to play and to cast – because it chiefly entails speaking sing-song rhymes about flitting about in the forest:

> Over hill, over dale,
> Thorough bush, thorough briar,
> Over park, over pale,
> Thorough flood, thorough fire,
> I do wander everywhere
> Swifter than the moon's sphere … (2.1.2–7)

---

[6] Barbara Hodgdon discusses variants between the Quarto and Folio texts, the latter altering the speech prefixes for Philostrate to retain Egeus in Act Five. See 'Gaining a Father: The Role of Egeus in the Quarto and the Folio', *The Review of English Studies* 37.148 (1986), pp. 534–42.

Many productions go limp after just a few such lines. Perhaps no casting choice can fix that, explaining why directors often make a spectacle of the scene or else marginalise it. But if Demetrius or Lysander returns briefly to do this turn – First Fairy makes only this one appearance – the later scene in which Puck leads the pair blindly through the wood will gain energy, particularly when Demetrius describes what he thinks of Lysander's sprite-like movement:

> Abide me, if thou dar'st; for well I wot
> Thou runn'st before me, shifting every place,
> And dar'st not stand nor look me in the face.
> Where art thou now?   (3.2.422–5)

The aesthetic incentive for doubling these roles is smaller than for some others, but there is no clear advantage to having an actor without prior or future connection to the play establish the wood as a faerie land. Several actors are available, any one of whom can do the faerie's duty while establishing rapport with Puck that may continue when the actor resumes his or her primary role.

Hermia and Helena, the faeries, and the mechanicals remain, and readers may have noticed that my chart suggests that Hermia and Helena can double as mechanicals who in turn double as faeries. Before discussing them, I should point out why doubling mechanicals and faeries is so compelling. For one, it complements the doubling of First Fairy by a major character. But the greater reason is the strikingly symmetrical pattern of the two groups' entrances and exits. The mechanicals first appear in 1.2, are displaced by faeries for much of Act Two, before returning in 3.1. The play's second half reverses the pattern by bringing the faeries on in 4.1, replacing them with mechanicals in 4.2 and during the first half of 5.1, only to call the faeries in again to sweep the stage at play's end. The chiasmic pattern (*abba*) established early is thus reversed late (*baab*), in accord with other patterns and reversals in the play and, through doubling, outside of it. Each of the eight group appearances requires four actors – who always work as a foursome. The pattern creates an opportunity for the same four actors to portray both groups, thus allowing the mechanicals (Quince, Flute, Starveling, and Snug) to be more closely aligned with their friend Bottom, transforming into faeries (as he does into an ass), and then continuing as his companions in Titania's bower.

The scenes work to establish ties between the tradesmen and their faerie counterparts, such as having a roll call for each group. Bottom badgers Quince to 'call [the actors] generally, man by man, according to the scrip' (1.2.2–3), repeating his request three times. After the faeries' entrance in 3.1, Titania calls them severally 'man by man', after which Bottom, again with more than necessary elaboration, calls each man forth to meet him, later reprising the ritual when he invites them to scratch his ears. The moments form a rhyme-like pattern even when the roles are not doubled. But the correspondences are deeper when underscored by doubling. The link between the foursomes is also strengthened by the fact that each is made up of three men who rarely stop talking and one that is almost entirely silent: Snug is 'slow of study' and incapable of remembering many lines; Moth is largely ignored in the conversations with Bottom.

The advantages of doubling the mechanicals and faeries seem even greater when Hermia and Helena also double as mechanicals. If they portray Snug the joiner and Flute the bellows-mender, they will not only augment a play in which many characters take secondary and tertiary roles – in and out of the fiction – but will also enact variations of their primary roles within the pageant of 'Pyramus and Thisbe'. Flute's Thisbe flees Snug's lion, just as Helena, whose 'legs are longer ... to run away' eludes the smaller Hermia (3.2.343). Doubling the roles underscores an already attractive relationship between the scenes, one that has further sanction because of the particular threat Hermia had posed to Helena:

> How low am I? I am not yet so low
> But that my nails can reach unto thine eyes.   (3.2.297–8)

In their discussion of how best to represent the lion the mechanicals attend repeatedly to the need for the actor to keep his nails long, striving to literalize one of the lion's features despite their intention to undermine the representation by having Snug announce himself as an actor. Bottom displays the inconsistency of their approach when giving the order, 'let not him that plays the lion pare his nails, for they shall hang out for the lion's claws' (4.2.35–6), shortly after suggesting that Snug inform the audience that he is not a lion at all: 'If you think I come hither as a lion, it were pity of my life. No, I am no such thing. I am a man, as other men are' (3.1.37–9). Given the focus on the lion's claws, the 'role' is directly linked to Hermia, who tries to chase down Helena and 'scratch out' her eyes. But the mechanicals' interest in revealing Snug beneath the lion's skin also helps sanction the possibility that an actor – one especially perceptible *as* an actor – might play the lion, because the lion's part, at least according to Bottom, seems to confess that very need. If Hermia doubles as Snug the joiner, her presence will valuably assert the artifice of the actor, and will complicate Snug's self-referential turn while playing the lion.

Of course, there is the sticking point that Hermia (and Helena too) should be found among the onstage audience during the mechanicals' performance. Curiously, the final scene in *A Midsummer Night's Dream* is dominated not by those in the play but by those watching it unfold, since the onstage audience has more lines than the actors in the pageant. Yet, despite this, Hermia and Helena never speak a word. Hippolyta is female and a new bride, yet she doesn't hesitate to join in evaluating the tradesmen's performance, so the silence of the other women is odd. We have already seen, in *The Fair Maid of the Exchange*, how a lengthy, unexpected silence could work to facilitate the actor's participation in another role. By making Hermia and Helena mutes, this play also makes it possible for them to absent themselves while the other mechanicals set up for their play, or, if they are already among the band of tradesmen, for two new 'women' to come out on Lysander's and Demetrius's arms, dressed as Hermia and Helena and wearing their wigs. Those two could sit with their backs to the audience and take in the performance, one in which Hermia and Helena fulfil their secondary obligations. The audience in such a case is much like Demetrius, for whom 'These things seem small and undistinguishable, / Like far-off mountains turnèd into clouds' (4.1.185–6).

Discussing the poet's ability to play upon his audience's imagination and expectations, Theseus confirms just how easily we can mistake what we see: 'Or in the night, imagining some fear, / How easy is a bush supposed a bear!' (5.1.21–2). The possible substitution of bodies in 5.1, Hermia and Helena seeming to appear as spectators at a performance in which they participate, would enrich Theseus's lines, making them a meta-commentary on the action in much the way the mechanicals' lines during the rehearsal may have proved to be. But his observation is equally applicable to spectators offstage watching actors double roles within the play, effortlessly supposing the mechanicals to be faeries; Theseus to be Oberon; Philostrate to be Puck; and so on. Doubling roles can enrich lines, moments, scenes, and characters that otherwise seem comparatively dull. Emphasizing how easily we can mistake what we see obliquely comments on the play's many substitutions and transformations, and on the audience's role in accepting the conventions whereby one body represents or replaces another. But the experience of audiences at productions that double roles as Brook did, and as Shakespeare's company may have done, is further enriched, because bodies displacing or standing in for other bodies then occurs in and out of the fiction, and because characters who otherwise seem independent become intimately associated. Spectators who suppose the lion is not a lion but a tradesman called 'Snug' are mistaken. But since Sung is no more Snug than he is a lion, can he not also be Hermia? And Moth, too? If the play merges these three characters in one body, it has a last laugh, since Bottom's comic request to play all the parts is realized literally in the fiction. After all, a play (and playwright) so devoted to stretching and upending the conventions of representation, that features a man playing a 'Wall' and another who is 'invisible' merely because he says so, would be unlikely to give up on a chance to have a hero – in this case, a heroine – 'play the lion too' (1.2.58).

Spontaneous Kinships, or Who Knew the Nurse and Tybalt were so Close?

In the last chapter I noted Lady Montague's peculiar absence from the close of *Romeo and Juliet*, a choice that seems to owe more to necessity than logic.

This begs the question of why she wasn't available backstage. While the actor may have gone on to play several others, Juliet seems a likely possibility, since the actor is available and presumably well suited to female roles. Having the actor double as Juliet also makes extra-textual sense of Montague's creaky explanation that 'Grief of my son's exile hath stopped her breath' since, if the Lady Montague actor is now lying dead as Juliet, then grief over Romeo really has stopped her breath (5.3.211). It seems preposterous for Lady Montague to die due to Romeo's banishment, but she might more reasonably have taken her life – as Juliet does – after finding her son (and husband) dead in the Capulet tomb. She is a minor character, but the choice explains her absence; allows 'her' to seem to attend on and grieve for her departed son; and allows a company to recycle an actor who would otherwise be idle for most of the play.

The speculative plan in Table 5.2 is arranged for 12 actors, the number of speakers appearing together in the latter half of 5.3, the play's limiting scene. *Romeo and Juliet* is a good place to see how too much dependence on traditional act and scene divisions can prevent us from determining exact

Table 5.2 *Hypothetical doubling plan for Shakespeare's* Romeo and Juliet *(c. 1595)*

Romeo and Juliet
c. 1595 (Q2, F)
ॐ The division of the parts ॐ

Chorus Prince Paris Mercutio	For one actor	Tybalt Nurse Friar John Chief Watchman	For one actor
Gregory Romeo	For one actor	Lady Montague Juliet	For one actor
Benvolio Friar Laurence	For one actor	Lady Capulet Apothecary	For one actor
Capulet	For one actor	Samson 1 Servingman 1 Musician 2 Watchman	For one actor
Abraham Peter Balthasar	For one actor		
Montague Old Man	For one actor	Montague's Man 2 Servingman Petruccio 2 Musician 3 Watchman	For one actor
Citizen 3 Musician Paris's Page	For one actor		

casting requirements, because more than 12 speakers appear in 5.3. Only if
we allow for exits and entrances within the scene, some of which are implicit
in dialogue, can we see that no more than 12 speakers need to be onstage at
any one time, and that the play always makes actors available in time to enter
in new roles.

Both King and Meagher have created doubling plans for the play, each
projecting a minimum necessary cast.[7] In line with his other projections,
King suggests that about 95 per cent of the lines can be delivered by
12 'principal' actors, distributing the remaining roles among nine hired men
and boys. He assigns the 12 principals one role apiece, leaving only the
hired men to double in roles such as the Chorus, the Apothecary, Balthasar,
and the watchmen. Meagher is rare among critics in trying to determine an
absolute minimum cast, which he fixes at 13. His analysis includes some
aesthetic implications of doubling across a small cast, and I follow several
of his leads here.

I want to pause to consider, though, why Meagher may misjudge the number of actors necessary, despite his very persuasive analysis regarding the
play's structure. If we add up the number of speakers in 5.3, we get 13. In
order of appearance, they are: Paris, Paris's Page, Romeo, Balthasar, Juliet,
Friar Laurence, three Watchmen, the Prince, Capulet, Lady Capulet, and
Montague. The stage directions indicate no departures, and the only character that leaves the stage – Paris's Page – returns and plays a significant role.
It is possible that one of the Watchmen could retire and return as Montague
after apprehending Lawrence or Balthasar, but it isn't necessary. For, as
Stephen Booth points out, one of the 13 speakers *asks* to be taken offstage.
When Romeo slays Paris before the Capels' monument, a curious exchange
ensues:

> PARIS   O, I am slain! If thou be merciful,
>   Open the tomb; lay me with Juliet.
>   *[He dies.]*
> ROMEO   In faith, I will.   (5.3.72–4)

Though the focus at this moment is on Romeo discovering Juliet's body, the
play takes time for Romeo to drag Paris into the tomb, which Romeo's ensuing

---

[7] King discusses a hypothetical plot for 18 speakers and some mutes (*Casting Shakespeare's
Plays*, p. 82). He offers few significant casting choices (e.g. doubling Tybalt and Balthasar), and
no clear rationale for them. The Mercutio actor in his plot retires altogether after 3.1. Meagher
analyses casting requirements for *Romeo and Juliet*, and their implications, in *Pursuing
Shakespeare's Dramaturgy: Some Contexts, Resources and Strategies in His Playmaking*
(Madison: Farleigh Dickinson Press, 2003), pp. 181–222.

speech affirms: 'Death, lie thou there, by a dead man interred' (5.3.87). In Shakespeare's time, the 'Capels' monument' was probably located in the discovery space, but whether Romeo drags the body there or down a trap, he potentially makes the actor available to return in another role. Paris's request, and Romeo's willingness to grant it, is not unreasonable in the way Maria's or Lady Montague's absence is, but it is curious that the play pauses over and comments on useless stage business – unless the business is not useless. Thirteen speakers also appear in 1.1, but if the play permits the Romeo actor to enter first in another role – one that helps to spark the ancient grudge's 'new mutiny', only to deplore it when he returns as Romeo – then, once more, 12 actors will suffice.

In these scenes, the play seems to reflect an awareness of its casting requirements. Whatever Shakespeare's intent or practice, his play carefully avoids the need for 13 speakers to share the stage at all times – as he does in every other play. When a scene with 12 speakers wants one more, something happens to excuse someone. These moments often seem to indicate the role for which the actor is being made available. When Romeo promises to help Paris lie with Juliet, for instance, he says something that is both rich and strange:

> In faith, I will. – Let me peruse this face.
> Mercutio's kinsman, noble County Paris!   (5.3.74–5)

Audiences anticipating the discovery of Juliet might easily overlook the striking news that Mercutio and Paris are kinsmen – a fact never before mentioned in the play. The two are related by blood but are also linked thematically: Mercutio is a friend of Romeo's who becomes an unexpected rival (when he exits the stage railing); Paris is a rival for Juliet's affection and an unexpected friend (Romeo praises him and complies with his wishes after the duel); both are hurt 'under [Romeo's] arm'.[8] The casual revelation of the two slain characters' relationship gains additional energy if the roles are doubled, a possibility that both Meagher and Booth advance.[9] Paris cannot be dragged offstage to return as the dead Mercutio, of course, but moments after his dragging off the Prince enters to see the carnage brought about by the feuding houses and, as if on cue, adds yet more news of relationships hitherto

---

[8] Though Romeo slays Paris, he does Paris's bidding after death and with sudden affection: 'O, give me thy hand, / One writ with me in sour misfortune's book. / I'll bury thee in a triumphant grave' (5.3.81–3). The fact that Romeo did not know who his rival was before acceding to the request to bury him along with Juliet suggests the decision owes more to dramaturgical than dramatic necessity.

[9] Meagher and Booth discuss the possibility, and Booth notes that the actor can also return as the Prince, thus combining three kinsmen in one. See Meagher, 'Economy and Recognition', p. 13; and Booth, 'Speculations on Doubling', p. 142.

unknown: 'And I, for winking at your discords, too / Have lost a brace of kinsmen' (5.3.294–5). Moments after we learn that Paris and Mercutio are kinsmen, the Prince reports that he is also a 'kinsman' to them both. This revelation will also gain interest, rendering the play more complete and coherent, when all three roles are assigned to one actor. The choice also makes the Prince's harsh words for the feuding houses a stronger echo of Mercutio's curse on both houses just before his death.

Sudden revelations of intimacy, like that between the Prince, Paris, and Mercutio, occur elsewhere in the play, also perhaps helping to justify relationships established by actors doubling roles. When Tybalt dies, the Capulet household goes into widespread mourning, but nobody takes the loss as hard as the Nurse, who responds to it with surprising news:

> O Tybalt, Tybalt, the best friend I had!
> O courteous Tybalt, honest gentleman,
> That ever I should live to see thee dead!   (3.2.61–3)

As she did in 2.4, Juliet waits for news of Romeo through several lengthy speeches, but when the Nurse finally reveals that Tybalt and not Romeo has been killed, she adds something the audience had no reason to expect: that Tybalt was her 'best friend'. The friendship seems unlikely, considering the behaviour of the two characters, and their differences of speech and social class. Moreover, Tybalt and the Nurse never meet onstage, and neither mentions the other until this moment. Also, 'courteous' may be the last adjective many would apply to Tybalt, so the Nurse's report does not seem to reconcile with what the audience has so far experienced.

The play also seems to take particular care to keep Tybalt and the Nurse from meeting. The other revelers remain onstage throughout Capulet's ball, but Tybalt leaves early – dismissed by Capulet about 20 lines before the Nurse appears to summon Juliet. The Nurse seems to have no desire to leave the party after delivering her message, so it is unclear why she was absent to this point. Again, one actor's disappearance and the subsequent arrival of another suggest the possibility of doubling the roles. If they are doubled, the Nurse's grief over her best friend's death becomes reasonable and aesthetically productive. The otherwise superfluous detail underscores roles that can be intimately associated with one another via the actor. Further in this line, though several actors are available to play Friar John, the Tybalt/Nurse actor can add something to John's otherwise isolated turn in 5.2, since he tries to carry news of Juliet to Romeo (as the Nurse has done), before indirectly helping to bring about Romeo's death (which Tybalt would have been motivated to see and help effect).

Sometimes a character's mere existence can help suggest the casting requirements and limitations presumed by the playwright. Balthasar, for instance, should alone convince us that Shakespeare's company anticipated the possibility of playing with 12 men, since he does not appear until Act Five; has never been spoken of; yet suddenly seems vital to Romeo, intimate with both him and the Friar. Act Five opens in Mantua with Romeo waking from pleasant dreams when 'his man' arrives with news of Juliet's death:

> Ah me, how sweet is love itself possessed
> When but love's shadows are so rich in joy!
> > *Enter* [BALTHASAR,] *Romeo's man.*
> News from Verona! How now, Balthasar?
> Dost thou not bring me letters from the friar?
> How doth my lady? Is my father well?
> How fares my Juliet? That I ask again,
> For nothing can be ill if she is well.   (5.1.10–16)

Romeo's unexpected exuberance may help excuse the strangeness of Balthasar's presence. But playgoers should reasonably wonder why he is the one trusted to bring news. If a servant, how does he have access to both households, and the freedom to travel between Friar Laurence and Mantua? If he is a friend, why he is doing Benvolio's job? In the first scene, the Montagues ask Benvolio about Romeo's whereabouts, trusting him to learn what is troubling their son. He is established as Romeo's confidante thereafter. Why does the play drop Benvolio, who never appears after 3.1, to bring in a similar character with a similar name?

Logic and precedent would suggest that the play needed one of its better actors in another role during the play's second half, and that freeing the Benvolio actor for the purpose was worth sacrificing the character. The most likely place to look for Benvolio, then, is in Friar Laurence's robe, a possibility that Meagher suggests.[10] Laurence doesn't enter the play until late in Act Two, becoming an increasingly dominant presence after Benvolio's departure in 3.1. Just after the scene at Juliet's window, we might expect Romeo to visit his friend to share the good news, but the Friar replaces Benvolio as the object of that visit. If Benvolio is wearing the Friar's habit, he will remain a friend and counsellor to Romeo, while also explaining Balthasar's appearance in 5.1. Considering this possibility, Montague's conversation with Benvolio in 1.1 is particularly interesting:

> BENVOLIO   See where he comes. So please you step aside;
> > I'll know his grievance or be much denied.
> MONTAGUE   I would thou wert so happy by thy stay
> > To hear true shrift. – Come, madam, let's away.   (1.1.151–4)

---

[10] Meagher also notes the speech prefix in the Folio that suggests the actor who played Peter returns to fill the role of Balthasar. See *Shakespeare's Shakespeare*, p. 113.

Much as the Nurse does in calling Tybalt her 'best friend', or as Romeo does in noting that Paris and Mercutio were kinsmen, Montague here casually establishes a link between Benvolio and the Friar by casting the former in the role of the latter. 'Shrift' is used four other times in the play, next by Friar Laurence, and thereafter with reference to him. In fact, Laurence uses the word in a phrase ('riddling confession finds but riddling shrift') that responds to Romeo's paradoxes about Juliet, somewhat reprising Romeo's riddling about Rosaline, which occurs when discussing his love for her with Benvolio. Both Benvolio and Laurence alternate between love advice and catechism, further suggesting their parallel functions.

An actor doubling Benvolio and the Friar must make two quick changes (2.2 to 2.3 and 2.5 to 3.1), but the changes are no more difficult to bring off than Cleanthes's disguises in Chapman's *Blind Beggar of Alexandria*, or what is necessary for the Athenian Lord and Lady to double their faerie counterparts in *A Midsummer Night's Dream*, two plays produced within a year or two of *Romeo and Juliet*. The Friar's robe would likely simplify changes in and out of character, as the Duke's revelation in *Measure for Measure* (effected by the removal of a hood) seems to confirm. Moreover, *Romeo and Juliet* includes details that support quick changes. One example coincides with the most difficult change (2.5 to 3.1), during which an actor speaks the final line in Act Two as Laurence and the first line in Act Three as Benvolio:

> Come; come with me, and we will make short work,
> For, by your leaves, you shall not stay alone
> Till Holy Church incorporate two in one.   (2.5.35–7)

Changes at a scene break could, of course, be covered with music or an interlude, but the Friar's final line could also be a guide and in-joke to the play's extra-theatrical potential through doubling. The prevailing sense of the lines – that the Friar will perform the marriage of Juliet and Romeo – is clear, though the lines potentially comment on a secondary incorporation of 'two into one'. The Friar entered the play in 2.3 expressing curiosity about the paradoxical qualities of many things found in nature (e.g. 'The earth that's nature's mother is her tomb'); here he acknowledges a similar potential for the players in the play. If the actor playing the Friar doubles as Benvolio, then his plan to make 'short work' so that the 'Holy Church' (here represented by the Friar himself) can 'incorporate two in one' informs and excuses his transformation back into Benvolio and any brief time it might require. If the character wanted good excuse to leave as one man and return immediately as another, without shifting attention from the plot or derailing its progress, this is it. That Benvolio immediately enters saying 'I pray thee, good Mercutio' adds to the connection through words casually pertinent to the religious context, a small sign that the holy church has incorporated two (roles) in one.

Several attractive possibilities for doubling remain among the minor roles. The Apothecary is among the most interesting, providing a chance for one of several characters – Tybalt, Mercutio, Capulet, or his Lady – to have a hand in Romeo's death, something that each might welcome. Any of these choices will add to the play's interests in justice, revenge, and fate. King assigns the role to Montague, with a negligible and somewhat confusing result, since spectators who perceive the actor across two small roles may see a vestige of the kind father helping to slay his son. But the plot will gain far more if, say, the actor playing Lady Capulet doubles the Apothecary. After all, when the Capulets arrive to find Tybalt dead in the street, it is Lady Capulet that insists on vengeance, while her husband remains silent.[11] Romeo's punishment does not satisfy her, since soon after it is handed down she tries to console Juliet with news of a plot:

> We will have vengeance for it, fear thou not.
> Then weep no more. I'll send to one in Mantua,
> Where that same banished runagate doth live,
> Shall give him such an unaccustomed dram
> That he shall soon keep Tybalt company.   (3.5.87–91)

Once again, the play establishes a surprising link between characters. Apparently, Lady Capulet happens to know someone in the poison business in Mantua. But her plan comes to fruition in a degree of detail that even she could not anticipate, when Romeo first goes to buy a 'dram' – he uses her word – and then takes it while inside the Capulet's tomb, thus literally 'keep[ing] Tybalt company'. Just as Laertes imagines that Hamlet's death will be sweeter for being the instrument of it, so Romeo's death can be more perfect if the 'caitiff wretch' that sells Romeo his death is Lady Capulet herself, then becoming an avenging instrument in her own plot.[12] It is common to assume that John Sincler played this role for Shakespeare's company, based on the speech prefix in *2 Henry IV* that indicates he played the Beadle who, like the Apothecary, is mocked for his thin frame. This could have been the case, but the deductive process that tell us that Sincler might have appeared here should likewise tell us that whoever appeared here, appeared elsewhere in the play.

Before turning away from *Romeo and Juliet*, it bears mention that the doubling plan I propose may underestimate the frequency of the doubling that took place in Shakespeare's day. Because the play's limiting scene anticipates 12 actors, I have distributed roles among 12. But no other play of Shakespeare's

---

[11] See 3.1.144–79.

[12] Tybalt could also double as the Apothecary with similar effects. Romeo would then keep 'company' with Tybalt sooner, and Tybalt would seem to have a hand in avenging his death. Meagher suggests doubling the Friar with the Apothecary based chiefly upon the Friar's interest in medicinal herbs.

gives three actors so little work as is allotted to the final three actors in this plan. For this reason, it may have been that Shakespeare's company arranged the plot for nine, in accordance with their number of sharers, possibly filling out the cast with three or more hired men or apprentices. The company could then assign the few roles the sharers could not cover to hired men or apprentices, or even to the real musicians that played for the company (note the presence of musicians as characters in 4.5). The democratic structure obvious in the Tudor plays is present here, but for nine rather than 12 actors, creating the possibility that three others were used minimally. This is pure speculation, invited only by the anomalous fact that little is available for three actors, and by the fact that several other plays before 1604 require only nine or ten actors to perform. It could be, too, that in 1595 Shakespeare was still refining his doubling structures, distributing work among 11 or 12 actors less evenly than he does in later years. It is certainly the case that other early plays, like *The Taming of the Shrew* and *Richard III*, are not as elegant in their dramaturgical patterning as those that came later.

At First Sight

In 1599, Thomas Platter of Basel visited the Globe for a production of *Julius Caesar*. He noted that the play was performed 'with a cast of some fifteen people; when the play was over, they danced very marvelously and gracefully together as is their wont, two dressed as men and two as women'.[13] Obviously, 'some fifteen' does not confirm the 12 that I expect spoke all the lines in *Julius Caesar*. Platter's phrase does not, however, discount what is true of *Julius Caesar*: that it is playable by 12, even if the company deployed additional actors as they were available. But it may be that only 12 spoke Shakespeare's text in the performance that Platter attended. The three additional actors Platter may have seen could have played music and/or been used for crowd scenes – to drum, fight, rattle thunder, and more – without taking roles in the dramatis personae. With the possible exceptions of *2 Henry VI* and *Coriolanus*, *Julius Caesar* demands more in the way of crowds and armies than any other play of Shakespeare's. A crowd of commoners celebrates Caesar's triumph in the streets; the people shout for Caesar; they lend their ears to Brutus and Marc Antony; a mob gathers to kill Cinna the poet. If Shakespeare's plays ever wanted extras, this was the time. And yet Platter only saw 'some fifteen', even after the company opened the Globe, when its access to resources was presumably greater than it had been previously. We should feel hard-pressed to conclude that the company ever needed or used more than 15 if they did not do so in this play, which contains not only crowds and armies but 51 speaking roles.

---

[13] *Thomas Platter's Travels in England, 1599*, trans. and ed. C. Williams (London: J. Cape, 1937), p. 199. Platter saw the performance on 21 September 1599.

In addition to being the play most dominated by crowds, *Julius Caesar* also features the *largest* 'limiting scene' in Shakespeare. I mean 3.1, the scene in which Caesar is assassinated. Though 12 speakers are sufficient for every scene in every play, 3.1 appears a clearer exception to that rule than any other, since 13 characters enter at the beginning and a fourteenth – Popilius Lena – speaks early in the scene despite not being introduced by the stage direction. When we add these 14 to Portia, who speaks the final line in Act Two, it is reasonable to think 15 really were necessary. But if we did admit that it needs 15, Platter's observation would still seem to confirm a cast working at maximum efficiency.

A cast that large, though, may prevent Caesar from returning to hold the sword upon which Brutus runs; it may also, tragically, employ a second actor for the second Cinna, a poet who tries and fails to distinguish himself from the first. Fifteen actors are not necessary, though, despite the seeming obstacles. For one thing, Portia can be recycled. The change of acts can mask a change of roles, but even this is unnecessary given that the start of 3.1 is notable for the commotion surrounding Caesar and his followers as he enters the Capitol. Portia can easily pull on a toga and become a senator. That brings us to 14. Next, the Soothsayer speaks the scene's second line – 'Ay Caesar, but not gone' – before vanishing from the play without a trace. He is immediately available to return to the scene, simply by removing a hood or cloak. The rush of petitioners at the start of 3.1 gives the actor ample occasion to renew his identity – possibly going on to play Cinna, Trebonius, or Popilius Lena, the latter a character that the Folio assigns a speech *without* mentioning his arrival onstage. The stage directions include no exit for the Soothsayer and no entrance for Lena, though one ceases participation and the other surprisingly takes part. Whether the Soothsayer disrobes onstage or ducks off to do so, he can reduce the required number to 13. And the reason a thirteenth actor is wanted owes only to Lepidus, who appears in the stage direction but never speaks. Whether or not this is a mistake or printing error, we are back at 12 speakers appearing simultaneously.[14] If Lepidus is to appear, the play only requires a mute or costumed stagehand here, but the fact that his presence goes wholly unmentioned by the conspirators (who methodically describe everyone else) suggests that, even if the stage direction is accurate, the playwright was prepared to do without him if necessary. Since Lepidus is as yet unknown to the audience and unmentioned in the scene, the audience could not identify him in any case, so there is not even a benefit in having the same mute actor play Lepidus when he enters the play in 4.1.

Thus, even the most populous scene in Shakespeare can be performed by 12 actors without cutting a line. And even if Shakespeare's company used 15, two or three of those could have been mutes, if the company preferred to allow its

---

[14] The scene recalls 5.3 of *Romeo and Juliet*, in which 12 actors are sufficient if Paris is dragged off in time to return as the Prince.

core group to do more acting. However accurate Platter was in his observation, he apparently did not see the 19 or 23 players projected by Bradley and King, respectively. If 15 or fewer were enough for *Caesar*, it is unreasonable to think more were used in other plays, given that no other scene in Shakespeare strains the cast's ability to represent characters and crowds like this one. And even with 15, the ratio of actors to parts was more than 3:1, suggesting that doubling roles was extensive and would have been essential to the play's construction and the audience's reception.

6   'What, are they children?'

Reconsidering Shakespeare's 'Boy' Actors

You should be women,
And yet your beards forbid me to interpret
That you are so.

~Macbeth, 1.3.46–8

ຕ

Though Shakespeare's recurrent efforts to advertise artifice in his plays suggest that realistic representation was neither necessary nor desirable for his playing company, the English stage does tend progressively towards verisimilitude across the Renaissance. At some point boy actors take over the majority of female roles on London stages, and, in 1660, the first English actresses displace them, suggesting that holding the mirror up to nature grew more appealing between the Digby *Mary Magdalene* and Etherege's *The Man of Mode*.[1] During the Restoration productions begin omitting overt references to acting and the theatre, such as Macbeth's 'a poor player / That struts and frets his hour upon the stage', suggesting that practitioners gradually sought to make their theatrical illusions seem more stable and more credible than those of their predecessors (5.5.24–5).[2] Since adult men had played female roles in the Tudor and early Elizabethan periods, and since printed doubling plans in the period counted on actors to play both male and female roles in the same play, the move by adult companies to cast boy actors in female roles represents a key step in English theatre's evolution towards realistic representation. But

---

[1] Actresses appear on English stages for the first time in 1660, though female impersonation by boys, young men (and not-so-young men) has persisted to the present day. The Digby *Mary Magdalene* was written c. 1515–1520; George Etherege's play appeared in 1676.

[2] Despite adding dialogue, songs, and spectacle to *Macbeth*, William Davenant tempers or elides several metadramatic references – a form, presumably, of 'civilizing' the stage. We can further trace the arc from barbarism to civility in Nahum Tate's *King Lear*, or in the later productions of *Macbeth*. John Philip Kemble's eighteenth-century production, for example, omits the ghost of Banquo entirely (see A.R. Braunmuller's 'Introduction' for his New Cambridge edition (Cambridge, 1997), p. 67).

156

precisely when and for whom boy apprentices begin playing those roles is uncertain, as are the ages of the boys themselves.

It is commonly supposed that Shakespeare's company was among those that used boy apprentices for female roles. This chapter will revisit the basis for that supposition. Whoever played these roles for the company would presumably have doubled in similar roles, and most of Shakespeare's plays enable one or two actors to specialize in female impersonation without expanding the necessary cast beyond what the play structures require. But if the company insisted that every female role be performed by a boy who could *only* portray women and children, then its options for doubling would be restricted, particularly for plays in which three or more women appear onstage simultaneously. I have argued that all Shakespeare's plays can be performed with 12 speakers, but this rule holds only if some actors can play both ladies and lords, as often happens in contemporary productions. Given that Shakespeare's play structures anticipate more extensive doubling than is generally assumed, and that scholarly opinion has held that those playing female roles did so exclusively, determining whether original productions could have used the small casts I propose depends on how old the company's boy apprentices were and the nature of their participation onstage. Thus far, my focus has been unearthing the intrinsic potential for doubling roles in Shakespeare plays. I have been less explicitly concerned to defend these potentials as actual, original performance practice. I now aim to show, however, that the doubling afforded by the play structures *should* inform scholarly assumptions about original casting practices and productions. I hope to expose some myths concerning the company's historical practice, while offering alternate casting possibilities more in line with Shakespeare's dramaturgy and the material record.

I use the term 'boy' as it most commonly has been understood when discussing the boy actors of Shakespeare's time: young males of about 13–17 years whose voices had not broken, who were not yet physically mature and had not grown facial hair, and who therefore can be supposed to have offered more convincing illusions of femininity than adult actors could. Since credibility is at stake for many critics, consistency in bias says that the immature voices and bodies that allowed these boys to represent women convincingly also prevented them from portraying adult men. Casting such boys (rather than having young adults use the high parts of their natural registers to mimic female voices) would have forced the company to deploy as many as five additional actors. Considering the boys' supposed lack of versatility, we can see why William Ringler projected that the company used four boys; why David Bradley estimated that most plays need six; and why Catherine Belsey thought *A Midsummer Night's Dream* 'would require at least eight'.[3] Though no play

---

[3] Ringler suggests that the company required 'twelve men and four boys'. Given prevailing notions about the use of teenaged boys, 16 seems a reasonable cast size for performing

requires so many boys as Bradley or Belsey suggest, if the company's idea of realistic representation prevented the Emilia or Paulina actor from returning as Florizel, and if Maria couldn't hear news of her wedding with the ears of Sebastian, then cast sizes must sometimes have exceeded what was necessary based on the play structures and the Tudor/early Elizabethan precedents.

Baldwin and Bentley thought Shakespeare's company began training boys at around age ten, sent them onstage two or three years later, and discharged them by the time they were 16 or 17.[4] Grote describes how the 'strike of puberty' would 'at any moment … make [the actor] unfit to play women', alleging that boys played female roles 'until no more than about seventeen'.[5] Richard Rastall has speculated that boys maintained unbroken voices longer in the early modern period, perhaps as late as 17.[6] If true, a boy apprenticed at age 12 might have trained for two or three years under a sharer while playing waiting maids and mutes, moving into major female roles like Viola or Desdemona at 14 or 15. If his voice held out, a career in those roles might last two or three years, perhaps including turns as Margaret or Cleopatra. But by 17, his voice would break, dashing the actor's pretence to credibility and forcing him to transition to adult male roles, or else retire from the stage.[7]

Andrew Gurr relates a version of this theory in *The Shakespearean Stage*:

> The boys apprenticed to the adults were bound for a period of several years' training before graduating to be hired men and eventually perhaps sharers in their company. They entered their bonds between the ages of ten and thirteen, usually playing the women's parts which their small stature and unbroken voices equipped them for.[8]

The theory has been so often rehearsed that we can forget it is only a theory. In the case of the Lord Chamberlain's/King's Men, at least while Shakespeare was the company's principal playwright (c. 1594–1610), it is not clear that any boy fits Gurr's narrative.

---

and helps explain the 16–20 actors King projects (four or five hired men filling bit parts). Bradley discusses the need for boys in *From Text to Performance*, pp. 230–43. Catherine Belsey addresses the question in 'Shakespeare's Little Boys', in *Rematerializing Shakespeare*, ed. Bryan Reynolds and William N. West (New York: Palgrave Macmillan, 2005), p. 56.

[4] See Baldwin, *Organization and Personnel*; Bentley, *The Profession of Player*, pp. 13–46. See also Michael Shapiro, 'Framing the Taming', *The Yearbook of English Studies* 23 (1993), pp. 143–66. There are reports of ten-year-old boys of being kidnapped to play in companies, but no evidence suggests such boys played alongside adult men rather than in children's companies.

[5] Grote, *Best Actors*, p. 12.

[6] Richard Rastall, 'Female Roles in All-Male Casts', *Medieval English Theatre* 7 (1985), pp. 25–50.

[7] Though we might expect that such an actor could begin playing young lords and heroes, it must be remembered that the sharers were not retiring every other year to make room for these Cleopatras, now past their salad days.

[8] Gurr, *The Shakespearean Stage*, p. 95. As an example of how critics have tended to take the theory as read, consider Jan Kott's assurance in beginning one essay: 'On the Elizabethan stage, the roles of young girls and even mature women were played by fourteen- or fifteen-year-old

The theory for boy participation leans heavily on scant biographies of a handful of actors, most of whom either are supposed to have played alongside future sharers of the Chamberlain's Men in the early 1590s, or else appear in records of company performances starting around 1610. These dates should raise questions. First of all, the company's operations were so different from those of its peers – e.g. the lack of a manager; the ownership of buildings; the large number of sharers; the comparatively large number and size of the female roles; consistent membership and success; a resident playwright – that we cannot casually assume that its casting practices or use of personnel can be determined by studying records of Pembroke's Men or the Admiral's Men. We also cannot reliably project its operations based on what the King's Men may have done in the 1620s (given that Shakespeare and his fellows had long been retired), or even after 1610, given Gurr's own observation that the 'long closure of the playhouses in London through 1608–10 seems to have led to a number of policy shifts'.[9] Considering its long hiatus from playing in London; Shakespeare's at least partial retirement; significant turnover in original sharers; and a decade during which boys' companies had risen to prominence, it is no marvel that the King's Men may have altered its casting and representational strategies around 1610, when the company resumed playing in London.[10] The appearance of boys in casting records of 1610–1611, that is, may be more indicative of decisive changes that had taken place in theatre practice than reflective of what had been done in the 15 years during which Shakespeare fitted plays to a relatively stable cast.

The main candidates to justify the theory described by critics like Gurr and Bentley are Nicholas Tooley, Alexander Cooke, Richard Robinson, and John Rice. All four became sharers in the King's Men and were listed among the 'Principall Actors' in the First Folio, and all four may have been apprenticed either to Burbage or Heminges.[11] However, no material evidence links any of them to a female role in one of Shakespeare's plays. In fact, three of the four lack known birthdates, so any argument that these are the young boy players so often imagined depends on, and may originate from, ignorance about their

---

boys, always, of course, before their voices broke.' See *The Gender of Rosalind: Interpretations: Shakespeare, Büchner, Gautier* (Evanston: Northwestern University Press, 1992), p. 11.

[9] Gurr, *The Shakespeare Company*, pp. 54–5.

[10] The writing of *The Tempest*, a play that famously abides by unities of time, place, and action, may be one sign of such a change. Remarkably, the play relies less on female impersonation than any other. Writing only one female role may suggest that Shakespeare anticipated a lack of available boys to travel with the company during plague times, though it may also be that the play's unusual attention to rules that Shakespeare typically ignored saw him likewise restrict doubling and adult impersonation of women that characterized performances of other plays.

[11] Heminges bound Cooke in 1597, and Rice in 1607. Tooley is thought to have been apprenticed to Burbage based on a reference in his will to 'my late M[aste]r Burbage', though this is uncertain. Kathman suggests that Robinson may have also been apprenticed to Burbage because he eventually married Burbage's widow. See 'Grocers, Goldsmiths, and Drapers', p. 21.

actual ages. Only Tooley's birth year is known (1582 or 1583).[12] He likely would have acted with the company before becoming a sharer in 1605, but whether he originated Juliet at 12 or began playing minor roles at 19 is unknown.

I shall return to these and other candidates for Shakespeare's boy players, but it is worth noting that others have suggested that adult actors could have played at least some female roles for the company. Marvin Rosenberg could not find 'a shred of evidence that a child played any of Shakespeare's great women', proposing instead that we might look for analogues to the mature male performers who took these roles in 'the cross-dressing theatres of our own day'.[13] Rosenberg singles out Cleopatra as a role that presumes training and experience unlikely to be found in teenaged boys; for him, Mark Rylance's celebrated portrayal at Shakespeare Globe (where he also played Olivia in *Twelfth Night*) suggests that a sharer could have enjoyed similar success during Shakespeare's time.[14] Rosenberg also cites Janet Suzman, whose turn as Cleopatra led her to suspect that the role, considering the extraordinary talent and versatility it demands, must have required a kind of Elizabethan Danny La Rue.[15]

While Rosenberg's argument about historical practice is based mainly on intuition and anecdote, James Forse offers economic and repertory-based arguments that adults may have played female roles for Shakespeare, suggesting that the company's practice may have been unique in this respect. Forse notes the irony with which scholars accept the premise 'that the Chamberlain's Men molded its *male* repertory to its existing partners, but shaped its female repertory to the prospect of cycling a boy into a partner-sized role every few days, and cycling a new boy into the company every couple of years'.[16] He observes that, like the male leads, the major female characters appear to age over the course of Shakespeare's career, casting doubt on the notion that those playing female roles would have entered and exited the company as frequently as the theory suggests. On this basis, Forse argues the possibility that 'Shakespeare wrote his great female roles for adult partners in the company', though he somewhat imperils the argument by proposing, as the resident master of female characterization, Shakespeare himself.

[12] David Kathman, '*The Seven Deadly Sins* and Theatrical Apprenticeship', *Early Theatre* 14.1 (2011), p. 129.
[13] Marvin Rosenberg, 'The Myth of Shakespeare's Squeaking Boy Actor – Or Who Played Cleopatra?' *Shakespeare Bulletin* 19.2 (2001), pp. 5–6. Carol Chillington Rutter also singled out Cleopatra's age and the actor's need to form a pair with Burbage to suggest that the role may have been intended for an adult actor. She cites Henslowe's expense in 1597 for a woman's costume ('bornes womanes gowne'), as a sign that some female roles may have been played by adult actors – considering that 'borne' (William Borne, or Bird) was an adult actor for the Admiral's Men. See *Documents of the Rose Playhouse* (Manchester: Manchester University Press, 1999), esp. pp. 124–6 and 224–5.
[14] Rylance played Cleopatra at the Globe in 1999 and Olivia in 2002, each to great acclaim. He won the 2003 Olivier Award for Best Actor for the performance of Olivia, ten years after he won the award playing Benedick for the RSC.
[15] Cited from Juliet Dusinberre, 'Squeaking Cleopatras: Gender and Performance in *Antony and Cleopatra*', in *Shakespeare, Theory, and Performance*, ed. James C. Bulman (New York: Routledge, 1996), p. 53.
[16] Forse, *Art Imitates Business*, p. 77.

Figure 6.1 Mark Rylance starring as Cleopatra opposite Paul Shelley's Antony at Shakespeare's Globe (1999, dir. by Giles Block). Rylance was 39 years old at the time. Photo © Sheila Burnett. Used by permission.

Ultimately, notions about what teenagers of the period could or could not do, or whether particular sharers were adept at female impersonation, must remain speculative. But Rosenberg and Forse raise interesting questions, and I hope to extend and strengthen their arguments, based on a more thorough study of material, circumstantial, and dramaturgical evidence. If adult males played at least some female roles, Shakespeare's company could have worked comfortably with the numbers anticipated by the play structures. And if the company trusted four adult sharers or hired men to play female roles they could have performed anything Shakespeare wrote, on tour or in London, without needing boy apprentices at all. Even if the company did prefer using adult sharers for all roles, boys and hired men may have made up the number necessary to play, covered the absence of a sharer, or been utilized for particular talents or physical features that the sharers lacked. But it would have been possible to perform each play with a cast of 12 or fewer.

Apprenticeship

According to critics such as Gurr, Bentley, and Grote, most female roles for Shakespeare's company are supposed to have been performed by males from

14 to 17 years old.[17] That range presupposes that boys were bound as young as ten and typically no later than 13, since the need for training would mean very short careers for older boys. Yet extant legal and other documentation from the period give strong grounds to believe that apprentices associated with theatre companies were of legal apprentice age and observed conventional apprenticeship contracts, commencing at 14–17 and lasting well into their twenties, by which point their passage into physical maturity was certain. The boys who acted for the company, therefore, may well have been young adults who could double in male roles.

Guilds and lawmakers followed a complex set of rules governing apprenticeship in the sixteenth century, which Elizabeth clarified and nationalized in the 'Statute of Artificers' of 1562.[18] It dictated that 14 was the minimum age for binding apprentices, that they should serve a term of at least seven years, and that one could not enter London's livery companies as a freeman until he was 24. Since apprentice contracts typically ran through the twenty-fourth birthday, they allow us to construe approximate ages for some apprentices. By barring young men the status of freeman or town citizen until completing apprenticeships, the law imposed a kind of boyhood on nearly every man under 24. If the King's Men operated according to the law, its sharers would have taken apprentices at 14 or older, kept them until age 24, and supervised their maintenance and training in a liveried profession other than acting.

Still, most apprentices were not bound until they were in their late teens. Steve Rappaport surveyed 1,317 records from the Carpenters' guild (from 1572 to 1594) and determined that the average age at which its apprentices began terms was '19.5 years', with an 'overwhelming majority' in their 'late teens or twenties'.[19] London was exceptional in that its young men were typically apprenticed earlier, but still at an average of '17.7 years'.[20] Rappaport also notes that, in 1572, the Drapers refused to allow Gilbert Lie to begin his apprenticeship because he was 'under the age of 16 years'; younger men serving apprenticeships was sufficiently exceptional that one young man drew special mention in 1604 for signing articles despite 'being but 17 years of age'.[21] According to Barbara Hanawalt, the average age at which apprentices were

---

[17] Kathman has found evidence showing 'boys' as old as 21 taking the stage. See, 'How Old Were Shakespeare's Boy Actors', *Shakespeare Survey* 58 (2005), pp. 220–46.

[18] O. Jocelyn Dunlop, 'Some Aspects of Early Apprenticeship', in *Transactions of the Royal Historical Society*, Third Series, Vol. 5 (1911), pp. 193–208.

[19] Steve Rappaport, *Worlds within Worlds: Structures of Life in Sixteenth-Century London* (Cambridge: Cambridge University Press, 1989), p. 295.

[20] Ibid.

[21] Ibid., p. 297.

bound during the first decade of the seventeenth century was 16 and climbing.[22] By 1700 the age had risen to about 18. Ilana Krausman Ben-Amos's study of nearly 2,000 apprentices in Bristol found that 90 percent of those completing apprenticeships were bound for between seven and nine years, numbers that suggest the average boy signed articles at 16 and was freed eight years later.[23] We should therefore expect most apprentices associated with Shakespeare's company, whether they acted or not, to have been between 14 and 24, if the company made even a pretence of abiding by the laws of the Guilds, which appear to have preferred older boys.[24] Nearly all such apprentices would have been capable of playing male and female roles, presuming they had undergone a couple of years of training before performing major roles alongside the sharers.[25]

Gurr claims that acting companies were above the law when it came to binding apprentices, that there 'there was no set pattern, and nothing like the seven-year apprenticeships that boys in the guilds went through before rising to the status of journeyman'.[26] If true, there was little incentive for the boys and their families to accept indentured servitude, without wages, and possibly without legitimate training for a profession. Gurr's assumption reflects a pattern in dealing with evidence concerning boy participation on Shakespeare's stage, wherein that which contradicts the theory is treated either as not applicable to the company, or being a rare exception to a supposed set of rules. In fact, most of those who became sharers in adult companies never served as apprentices to other sharers, and becoming a sharer required money and the departure of a current sharer, so the potential for apprentices to become sharers was extremely limited. Surveying about 1,000 records of boy players in London from the 1590s until the theatres closed, Bentley found fewer than ten boys who became sharers in major adult companies. Hired players were paid little, possibly explaining why so few continued to act. In all, only

---

[22] Barbara Hanawalt surveys apprenticeship practices in England before the Renaissance, noting that the average age for binding apprentices was 14 during the fourteenth century but increased to '15 or 16' by 1400, in *Growing Up in Medieval London: The Experience of Childhood in History* (New York and Oxford: Oxford University Press, 1993), p. 113.

[23] See Ilana Krausman Ben-Amos, 'Failure to become Freemen: Urban Apprentices in Early Modern England', *Social History* 16.2 (1991), pp. 155–72, esp. p. 166.

[24] Rappaport notes, for instance, that the Mercers 'refused to enroll youths under the age of sixteen years' in the early 1500s, and that, in 1557, the Drapers ordered that no apprentice could be bound for 'any less years than 9 (if he be under the years of 18 when he is bound)', suggesting that binding at or after 18 was usual and that some apprentices might be as old as 26. See *Worlds within Worlds*, p. 297.

[25] Curiously, few question the problems young boys may have faced when representing old women. If actors playing Hermia or Hero could not have played Lysander or Claudio why should they have been acceptable as Margaret or the Countess of Rousillon?

[26] Gurr, *The Shakespearean Stage*, p. 95.

about 35 boys apprenticed to members of playing companies went on to act as adults.[27]

E.K. Chambers thought that the boys were in the personal service of sharers, and 'the courts of the guilds would have a responsibility for seeing to it that the training was in their own craft'.[28] It does appear that the law mattered, since at least one apprentice sued a King's Men actor for not abiding by it. In his extensive research on the ages and participation of apprentices, David Kathman notes that William Trigge petitioned to end his apprenticeship to Heminges because he was 'only thirteen at the time, rather than the traditional minimum of fourteen'.[29] On one hand, Trigge's petition shows that in the 1620s some apprentices were being trained as actors rather than in trades, and that at least one was bound as young as 13. But Trigge's attempt to break his indenture on that basis suggests that both the apprentices and the company were aware that binding boys younger than 14 was illegal and would be sufficient cause to terminate a contract. As I will argue, the company seems to have made more extensive use of younger boys in the 1620s than they did 20 or 30 years prior. But even as late as the 1620s the laws governing apprentices were relevant to company practices.

For a butcher, grocer, or goldsmith turned sharer, acting could not have seemed a wholly reliable way to earn a living. London theatres were subject to frequent closures due to plague, politics, and weather. None of the sharers in Shakespeare's company had apprenticed as actors, none could formally take on acting apprentices, and most had other professions and maintained their liveried statuses in them. Over time the profession became somewhat more stable, and perhaps seemed a more viable option for apprentices seeking training, but this was after most of Shakespeare's plays had been written. The acquisition of the Blackfriars in 1608, along with the comparative plenitude of young actors trained by the boys' companies, may have influenced the King's Men to take on more apprentices expected to act; but this cannot reasonably have been the case in 1594, or even in 1604. It is more probable that sharers taught the few apprentices associated with the company the trades they had learned as boys. The most talented boys may have been also prepared for acting careers, but most would likely have learned other professions while appearing in small roles and as mutes, or while performing various offstage duties for the company. Kathman offers that since 'freemen were under no obligation to practice the trades of their company', apprentices would not necessarily have received training in such trades, making it 'theoretically possible for a boy to

[27] Gerald E. Bentley, *The Jacobean and Caroline Stage* (Oxford: Clarendon Press, 1941).
[28] E.K. Chambers, *William Shakespeare: A Study of Facts and Problems*, 2 vols (Oxford: Clarendon Press, 1930), 2:85.
[29] Kathman, 'Grocers, Goldsmiths, and Drapers', p. 11.

be apprenticed and freed as a Goldsmith, for example, without his ever having handled a piece of gold'.[30] But what would this mean for the 96 per cent of boy apprentices (according to Bentley's research) who did not go on to become actors after such training? It is possible to focus on the handful of apprentices who became sharers and forget that they are rare exceptions. Also, concerning the few who became successful adult actors, we may assume too readily that they, their parents, and the sharers knew from the start that the boy in question was destined for greatness, hence disregarding training in the trades in favour of full-time preparation for acting. More probably, all such boys would have trained as actors while learning a trade, and while some would excel on stage, others would disappoint. In short, the boys would be a risk, and all parties involved would have been mindful of the backup plan.

Like Gurr, Kathman assumes that the sharers of Shakespeare's company trained apprentices to act, stating that Chambers's notion that they were trained in liveried professions is 'directly contradicted by the evidence'.[31] It is worth revisiting the evidence on which Kathman bases this claim. Some of it comes from a Chancery lawsuit of 1655, in which a former actor, Ellis Worth, affirms that about 25 years prior, 'youthes & boyes' bound as apprentices 'vsually Acte & play partes' at the Fortune and other theatres, even though they were 'made free of such particular Trades as their severall Masters vsed besides playinge'.[32] Kathman also cites John Wright (bound to Andrew Cane in 1629), another former actor who confirms Worth's statement, saying that he was bound 'to Learne the trade of A Goldsmith, And hee sayeth that hee this Deponent Did vsually Acte & play partes in Comidyes & Tragedies in the tyme of his Apprenticshipp and was afterwards made free of the Trade of A Goldsmith which the said partie vsed'.[33] Clearly, these two men acted while serving as apprentices, yet Worth quite clearly states that the apprentices were made free of the trades their 'Masters vsed *besides* playinge' (italics mine). Wright acted during his apprenticeship, but he is named as a 'Goldsmith' in the deposition and appears to have maintained the profession, for which he would have required actual training. Although Caroline-era practices at the Fortune Theatre (or even at the Globe) naturally cannot predict how Shakespeare's company would have cast Titania or Queen Margaret some 30 years prior – it seems likely that even after the King's Men had begun using more and younger boys, those at the Fortune would have learned trades. But such evidence can in no way prove that Shakespeare's company was training boy apprentices exclusively as actors in the 1590s.

Since the theory espoused by Gurr and others suggests that the vast majority of boys would become unfit for playing female roles by the time they turned 18,

[30] Ibid., p. 3.
[31] Ibid.
[32] Ibid., p. 5.
[33] Ibid., p. 6.

the company would have had another problem in determining what to do with boys who were no longer useful. The sharers did not retire rapidly enough to offer shareholding positions to the relatively few boys who were capable, interested, and wealthy enough to consider purchasing company shares, let alone to all the boys who matured under their charge. Whatever the private agreements, the law required contracts that bound the boys for at least seven years and until they were 24. The company's sharers could not simultaneously have maintained 10–13-year-old apprentices in training, those acting for the company at 14–17, and those 18+ who had aged out of female roles, without confronting legal limitations on the number of apprentices each man could take. Such a scheme suggests numbers beyond what appear in the records Kathman compiles and certainly would have exceeded Alwin Thaler's estimate that 'the complement of apprentices, hirelings, and attendants attached to most of the companies (at the turn of the century) was generally about equal in number to the sharers'.[34] The sharers might have employed mature boys and young men as stagehands or in small adult roles, but if they discharged them before age 24 they would have risked not only legal but also recruiting repercussions.

In short, in considering theatrical apprenticeship in Elizabethan England, a series of questions arise almost immediately. Were the apprentices in Shakespeare's company older than we commonly imagine? Could they have served as personal attendants rather than as actors? Could one apprenticed to a barber have been taught barbering rather than, or at least in addition to, acting? Could those apprentices that did act have played messengers and mute stage attendants rather than female leads? Could older apprentices (i.e. 18–24) have played female roles, since they remained 'boys' according to the law? And what evidence supports the view that apprentices who appeared onstage played only female roles?

'… between boy and man'

In light of these questions, it is at least worth considering the possibility that the theory about the journey of the boy actor and his participation in Shakespeare's company is wrong. Instead, perhaps, there was a pattern for apprentices, who generally came into service to the sharers at an average age of between 14 and 16 and served until the age of 24; these apprentices would have been 'boys' insofar as they were not freemen, but they were unlikely to be recent graduates of a children's company, brought in to play challenging female leads. If Shakespeare's company operated under the law and was more like other guilds than Gurr expects, then the boys apprenticed to its members could have been

---

[34] Alwin Thaler, 'The Elizabethan Dramatic Companies', *PMLA* 35.1 (1920), p. 145.

young men. Company practices may have changed due to the acquisition of Blackfriars, the relative abundance of trained boys in London, the increased stability of the theatres after 1610, or merely to reflect changing taste; and it seems sure that the company made more extensive use of boys (and younger boys) in the 1620s and 1630s. But during Shakespeare's time with the company there were fewer apprentices than in later years, and fewer reasons to believe that they were originating major female roles, one of the most conspicuous being that Shakespeare's early plays tend to require more and larger female roles on average than those that came later.[35] In fact, Shakespeare's career suggests that the company needed the greatest number of trained boys when we have the least compelling reasons to think they would have been available to him in large numbers.

The apprentices of John Heminges are particularly important in the context of the present discussion.[36] Kathman notes that Heminges was a Grocer and took on ten apprentices between 1595 and 1628, and all ten are thought to have acted for the company. But Heminges binds just two apprentices (Thomas Belte and Alexander Cooke) between 1594 and 1607. The other eight are bound in the 20 years following. The increase suggests that the company had more need for apprentices in later years but comparatively little need (or capacity to train and manage them) during Shakespeare's time. The first three apprentices are bound for about eight years, increasing to ten years after 1611 and, by 1625, to 12 years. As a result, the boys bound before 1611 should have been about 16 years old, those bound after 1611 about 14, and those bound in the 1620s perhaps even younger, as Trigge's petition suggests. If in Shakespeare's time boys were bound at 15 or 16 and required two or three years to mature as actors, we cannot reasonably go on thinking that 15-year-olds appeared onstage in major female roles. Since contract terms typically would have run until the boy's twenty-fourth year, the gradual increases to the length under Heminges indicate that the company's apprentice actors got progressively younger after 1611. So the company seems not only to have used more apprentices after 1608 but also to have taken on younger boys. These changes make sense given the long closure of the theatres in 1608 and 1609, the acquisition of Blackfriars, and the policy changes that may have accompanied the retirements of Shakespeare and other sharers.

---

[35] Most of Shakespeare's plays require three performers of female roles, a fact often reflected in casting modern productions, though there are plays that need four or more. See Ida Prosky, *You Don't Need Four Women to Play Shakespeare: Bias in Contemporary American Theatre* (Jefferson: McFarland Press, 1992).

[36] The King's Men sharer and contemporary of Shakespeare's, John Heminges (c. 1556–1630) who published (with Henry Condell) the First Folio in 1623.

The Case for Shakespeare's Boys

Because the evidence concerning the age and participation of boy actors is spotty, any candidates fitting Gurr's description warrant close attention. Since prevailing casting assumptions disqualify most of the 'principal actors' listed in the Folio based on known age or their participation in adult male roles, candidates like Tooley, Cooke, and Thomas Belte become attractive because we can imagine them to have conformed to our casting assumptions and so 'justify' the theory. Of these three, Tooley alone has a known birthdate (1582 or 1583), and he may have served as an apprentice of Burbage's before becoming a King's Men sharer c. 1605.[37] He probably acted with the company before becoming a sharer, but we can only guess how early he began acting or which roles he played. The evidence that Tooley played female roles as a teenaged boy consists only of his relationship to Burbage and the possibility, argued by Karl P. Wentersdorf and Kathman, that he is the 'Nick' referred to in the plot of *The Seven Deadly Sins*.[38] Of unknown date and authorship, the *Sins* plot has commonly been associated with a performance by a mix of players from Pembroke's and Strange's men in 1590 or 1591.[39] Roslyn Knutson has noticed overlaps between its personnel and casting information from performances by Pembroke's Men in 1592–1593, seeming to confirm a date for *Sins* in the early 1590s.[40]

Kathman argues that *Sins* may have been a play for the Chamberlain's Men, though, dating it to 1597–1598, when Tooley was around 15. He cites similar overlaps between actors named in the plot and the sharers of the Chamberlain's Men, noting that 'Nick', 'Saunder', and 'T. Belt' in the plot may indicate Tooley, 'Alexander' Cooke, and Thomas Belte.[41] Belte was bound to Heminges in 1595, and he seems a near-certain match for 'T. Belt'.[42] Unfortunately, Belte is the only one of the three who is neither listed in the Folio nor present in the documentary record in any role. As for the others, their birthdates are unknown and, as Schoone-Jongen observes, the names are 'too common to inspire confidence'.[43] Another 'Sander', for instance, appears in the text of *Taming of a Shrew*, a play associated with Pembroke's Men (i.e. these very men) around 1592–1593.

---

[37] Kathman, 'How Old Were Shakespeare's Boy Actors?'.
[38] See Karl P. Wentersdorf, 'The Origin and Personnel of the Pembroke Company', *Theatre Research International* 5.1 (1979), p. 49.
[39] Greg first dated the play based on its personnel. See Chambers, *Elizabethan Stage*, vol. 3, pp. 496–7; Scott McMillin, 'Casting for Pembroke's Men: The Henry VI Quartos and *The Taming of A Shrew*', *Shakespeare Quarterly* 23.2 (1972), p. 411; and Knutson, *Playing Companies and Commerce in Shakespeare's Time*, pp. 24–6.
[40] Knutson, *Playing Companies and Commerce in Shakespeare's Time*.
[41] See David Kathman, 'Reconsidering *The Seven Deadly Sins*', *Early Theatre* 7.1 (2004), pp. 13–44.
[42] Kathman, 'Grocers, Goldsmiths, and Drapers', p. 8.
[43] Schoone-Jongen, *Shakespeare's Companies*, p. 125.

Assigning *Sins* to the Chamberlain's Men in 1597–1598 may be reasonable, though it hinges on several levels of uncertainty and may reflect a natural impulse to find work for apprentices that cannot otherwise be proven to have acted with the company. But even if we accept the argument, Shakespeare did not write the play, so its casting demands may not reflect those of his plays. And, in any case, the potential correspondence of the three names to apprentices associated with the company cannot confirm that boys with unbroken voices originated Shakespeare's female leads.

As noted, Belte has no recorded birthdate. His nine-year apprenticeship term suggests that he was likely 15 in 1595, making him 17 or 18 at the time Kathman thinks the play was performed. Had the company used only immature voices and bodies for its female representations, his career as a boy player should have been quickly drawing to a close. Tooley was about the same age (born c. 1582 or 1583). Cooke began an eight-year apprenticeship in 1597, suggesting that he may have joined the company at 16. Assuming any need for training at all, and biological constraints, Cooke's time to play female roles with an unbroken voice may have been just a year or two, and by 1600 or 1601, the Chamberlain's Men should have needed several replacements, which the material record does not suggest arrived.

If we return to Gurr's timeline, all of these boys, of similar ages, likely would have trained until 1597 or 1598. This would make it possible for them to perform in *Sins* given Kathman's date, but harder to maintain that they could have performed for the company in the mid-1590s. In 1595, for instance, who are the three women onstage simultaneously for *Romeo and Juliet*? Or *A Midsummer Night's Dream*? Who play the four women of *A Comedy of Errors*? Or the five who appear together in *Love's Labour's Lost*? Belte is not bound until November of 1595, and Cooke follows in January of 1597. By law, Tooley couldn't have become Burbage's apprentice until at least 1596, though there is no record of him being bound. All would have needed training. If these three primary candidates are thus excluded from originating Juliet, Hermia, Titania, and the Princess of France, then who did? And if there were boys trained and ready for those roles, who played Lady Capulet and the Nurse? Or Helena and Hippolyta, to whose height and military prowess the play refers?

In fact, among the 'principal actors' listed in the First Folio, none presents a sure candidate for a teenage actor of female roles. It is reasonable to expect the actors who originated Rosalind Desdemona, Juliet, and Cleopatra to appear on the list, though, so it's worth revisiting the other candidates. Two of Heminges's apprentices – Cooke and John Rice – are on the First Folio list, partly explaining why Edmund Malone suspected that Cooke played early female leads.[44]

---

[44] *The Plays and Poems of William Shakespeare*, vol. III, ed. Edmond Malone and James Boswell (London, 1821), p. 481.

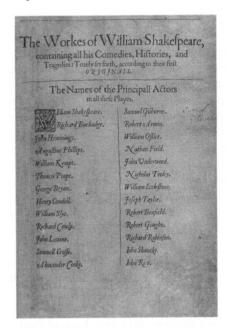

Figure 6.2 'The Names of the Principall Actors in all these Playes', from the First Folio (1623). Folger STC 22273.
Used by permission of the Folger Shakespeare Library under a Creative Commons Attribution-ShareAlike 4.0 International License.

While that suspicion may be true, he may have originated them while in his late teens, after his voice had broken, and when he was capable of doubling male roles. But since he doesn't become an apprentice until 1597 and his birthdate is unknown he cannot be expected to have originated parts earlier than 1598, if we assume any need for training.

Whatever Cooke's participation, the interval between his indenture in 1597 and John Rice's in 1607 is also hard to explain given the supposed need for boys to fill all the female roles. Rice presents similar problems as the earlier apprentices – we do not know his birthdate and cannot confirm his participation in one of Shakespeare's female roles during the playwright's tenure. He first appears in the documentary record as an actor in 1610. However, this was not for a King's Men play but a one-off pageant by Anthony Munday, in which Rice played 'Corinea, the beautiful Queene of Cornwall' opposite Burbage's 'Amphion'.[45] If he and Heminges followed the law, his turn as Corinea would

---

[45] Anthony Munday, *Londons Love, to the Royal Prince Henrie* (London: Printed by Edw. Allde for Nathaniell Fosbrooke, 1610), B4.

have come at 16 or 17. Since Rice does not become a sharer until 1620, we may guess that he played other roles in the interim, perhaps even female roles well into his twenties. But we cannot assume he acted much earlier than 1610, assuming any need for training and extended closures of the theatres in 1608 and 1609. Those who speculate that Rice originated Cleopatra can base it on little other than his appearance in Munday's sea pageant.

Another of the foremost candidates thought to justify Gurr's theory is Richard Robinson, who, like Rice, became a sharer and is listed among the principal actors in the Folio. Robinson is identified as 'The Lady' in a 1611 performance of Middleton's *The Second Maiden's Tragedy* (1611), and he appears in cast lists for three other plays including Jonson's *The Devil is an Ass* (1616).[46] In Jonson's play, Ingine and Meercraft discuss female impersonation and note Robinson's particular skill:

> INGINE   There's Dicke Robinson
> A very pretty fellow, and comes often
> To a Gentleman's chamber, a friend of mine. We had
> The merriest supper of it there, one night,
> The Gentleman's Landlady invited him
> To a Gossip's feast. Now, he Sir brought Dick Robinson,
> Dressed like a Lawyers wife, amongst 'hem all;
> (I lent him clothes) but, to see him behave it;
> And lay the law; and carve; and drink unto 'hem;
> And then talk bawdy: and send frolics! O!
> It would have burst your buttons, or not left you
> A seam.
> MEERCRAFT They say he's an ingenious youth!   (2.7.64–75)

Referring to Robinson as a 'pretty fellow' and an 'ingenious youth' in a play that describes him dressed up 'like a lawyer's wife' seems to make it clear that the company valued him for his ability to portray women, and it seems highly probable that Robinson would have played Shakespeare's women while with the company. Again, this may reflect a change in the company's taste after 1610. But it should also interest us that *The Devil is an Ass* comes *five years* after the first recorded appearance of Robinson in a female role. If Robinson could play females in a style the King's Men found acceptable across five or six years (1611–1616), then we are hard-pressed to imagine that his voice had not broken during that time. We don't know Robinson's birthdate but even a conservative estimate according to Gurr's model would have him joining the company at 12, training for two years before being cast in Middleton's play at 14 (in 1611), and then appearing in Jonson's play at 19, apparently still capable

---

[46] Chambers, *The Elizabethan Stage*, vol. 2, pp. 336–7.

of playing women to acclaim. If he was apprenticed at 14 or older he would have been in his early twenties in 1616.

It is also revealing that the play celebrating Robinson's ability to dissemble as a woman also features him as the 'young gallant' Wittipol. Robinson's skill at female impersonation seems to have been current, since Ingine proposes him as a candidate to impersonate 'an English widow', and Wittipol imitates one of the female characters, Frances Fitzdottrel, elsewhere. As a result, Robinson was apparently admired in 1616 for his ability to play *both* female and male roles. If that is true, the binary often imagined between acting male and female roles again seems not to have existed for the King's Men. Though by 1616 the company was involving more and younger boys, it may be that they continued to let boys of 18 and older play female roles. And since Robinson did not become a sharer in the King's Men until 1619, it is unlikely that Shakespeare wrote roles with him in mind.

We can deduce approximate ages for William Ostler and John Underwood, since both were members of the Children of the Chapel in 1600, when they should have been between ten and 12 years old (though such boys could be as old as 14).[47] This would put their ages at between 19 and 21 by the time they surface with the King's Men in 1609. If these two played female roles at such ages, they too would have been mature enough to double young lords. The arrivals of Rice, Robinson, Ostler, and Underwood seem to affirm both the interest and the greater availability of young actors after a decade in which the boys' companies had flourished, but all belong mainly to the period after the theatres reopened in 1610. Two other boys from the children's companies, Nathan Field and Joseph Taylor, do not join the King's Men until 1616 and 1619, when both were in their twenties.[48] Little is known of either Samuel Gilbourne or Samuel Crosse. Gilbourne was apparently an apprentice to Phillips, whom Chambers has argued may have been trained as a musician, based on his bequeathing musical instruments to Gilbourne.[49] If true, he may not have been an actor for the company, but this (like his birthdate) is unknown. Gurr notes that a 'Samuel Crosse' was born in 1568.[50] If this is the man named in the Folio, he would have been about 26 when the company formed, thus not a candidate for one of the teenaged actors.

William Ecclestone appears to have become a sharer in the King's Men around the time of Shakespeare's death, though he first acted with the company around 1610.[51] Like Robinson, Rice, Ostler, and Underwood, Ecclestone

[47] Lucy Munro, *Children of the Queen's Revels* (Cambridge: Cambridge University Press, 2005).
[48] Gurr, *The Shakespeare Company*, pp. 217–46.
[49] Chambers, *William Shakespeare*, p. 85.
[50] Gurr, *The Shakespeare Company*, p. 226.
[51] Ibid.

suggests the turnover and changes taking place around 1610. We don't know Eccleston's birthdate, but he was married in 1603, so assuming his marriage took place even as young as 15, he would have been at least 22 by the time he joined the company. Robert Benfield's and John Shank's birthdates are unknown, but both join the company in the second decade of the seventeenth century, having acted for other adult companies prior to their tenure with the King's Men.[52] Of Robert Gough little is known, though he appears to have joined the company after Shakespeare's retirement. His son Alexander was born in 1614, going on to act for the King's Men in the late 1620s, so Gough would have been an adult when he joined the company or soon after.[53]

These 15 men (14 appearing in the Folio list and Belte) are the major candidates for Shakespeare's boy players. Yet we can only reliably claim that five (Tooley, Crosse, Cooke, Gilbourne, and Belte) participated in Shakespeare's plays before the theatres closed in 1608, and, of these, it is not certain that any of them acted before their seventeenth birthdays. Some (like Robinson) appear, at 19 years or older, to have played female roles or been admired for their skill in female impersonation. But even if the five in question played major female roles during Shakespeare's tenure, they could not have originated roles in the mid-1590s, and they could not have combined to play all of the female roles in the early to mid-1600s unless the company was willing to let its 'boys' act female parts well into manhood. As I have noted, none is a reliable candidate to have acted at all before 1597, and there certainly are not five candidates available for *Love's Labour's Lost* around 1595. As a result, some men probably appeared onstage – as women. Moreover, since only five of the candidates for female roles could possibly have appeared in plays before 1609, while ten others are candidates thereafter, the desire for younger boys seems clearly to have increased around 1610, in conjunction with several policy changes by the company and the partial retirement of its chief playwright.

Post-Jacobean Players and Prologues

The early Caroline period provides more detail about who was playing female roles for the King's Men. John Honyman, for instance, played Domitilla in Massinger's *The Roman Actor* (1626) at the age of 13, and he is on the record playing additional female roles while still in his teens. It is plausible that he would have played female roles in performances of Shakespeare's plays at

---

[52] Ibid., pp. 220, 240.
[53] Ibid., p. 228.

that time. Honyman's career thus proves that the King's Men used teenage boys in female roles – but in 1626. By this date, the King's Men had aged two generations; built a theatre and watched it burn down; had seen the rise and fall of the boys' companies. We cannot assume that the King's Men in 1626, with Massinger as chief playwright, modelled the behaviour of the Lord Chamberlain's Men 30 years prior.

Significantly, though, Honyman also appears to have begun playing adult male roles by the age of 16.[54] And in 1631, at 18 years old, he played female roles but also a young adult male in *The Wild Goose Chase*.[55] The practice of having young men play both women and young adult males was not uncommon, since Robert Pallant played Cariola the *Duchess of Malfi*, but also doubled as the Doctor and a Court Official.[56] Though Kathman argues that Pallant would have been between 14 and 18 years old at the time, he seems to have been thought capable of representing an adult male.[57] The evidence suggests that voices may not have broken so late as Rastall has projected, or at least that their voices alone would not have dictated whether young adult actors could portray adult males. If a convincing male voice was possible at 16 or earlier, then the 'boys' considered thus far may have been more versatile than commonly imagined. William Trigge's biography seems to corroborate this point. Trigge describes training in 'l'arte d'une Stageplayer' while apprenticed to Heminges, and he played at least five female roles for the company between 1626 and 1632.[58] In 1632 Trigge was 20 years old, another example that argues against the possibility that the company considered unbroken voices essential for female impersonation. If as late as 1632 young adults were playing women onstage in London, surely it was happening decades earlier on Shakespeare's stage, especially when we consider that there were then fewer boys, more female roles, and clear precedents from the Medieval, Tudor, and Elizabethan periods.

Nevertheless, the Caroline period provides considerable insight into King's Men casting practices prior to the closing of the theatres. Though younger boys were used and less doubling is suggested – at least for non-Shakespearean plays – the evidence also indicates that the boys were older than they have commonly been imagined, and were considered capable of doubling adult male roles. Some interesting information about the period comes later, when the theatres reopen in the Restoration and comment on the Caroline theatre. The first play in England known to include an actress was a production of *Othello*,

[54] John Astington, *Actors and Acting in Shakespeare's Time: The Art of Stage Playing* (Cambridge: Cambridge University Press, 2010), p. 99.
[55] Lawrence, *Pre-Restoration Stage Studies*, p. 73.
[56] Chambers, *The Elizabethan Stage*, vol. 3, p. 510.
[57] Kathman, 'How Old Were Shakespeare's Boy Actors?', p. 234.
[58] Kathman, 'Grocers, Goldsmiths, and Drapers', p. 10.

produced by Thomas Killigrew and his company at the Red Bull Theatre. For its first performance on 8 December 1660, Thomas Jordan wrote a prologue in which one of the actors reveals something interesting about the cast:

> I Come, unknown to any of the rest
> To tell you news; I saw the Lady drest;
> The Woman playes to day; mistake me not,
> No Man in Gown, or Page in Petty-Coat ...   (ll. 1–4)[59]

Significantly, the company introduces the first English stage actress, not in the place of a 'boy' but a '*Man* in Gown, or Page in Petty-Coat' (italics mine). Like 'boy', the word 'Man' can simply denote a 'male' actor, but the fact that it is contrasted with 'Page' suggests an adult male. 'Boy in Gown' could have done just as well by the meter, especially if the candidates for playing females before the theatres closed in 1642 had been boys or adolescent pages.

The prologue then describes more explicitly those who played female roles before the restoration:

> ... in this reforming age
> We have intents to civilize the stage.
> Our women are defective, and so siz'd
> You'd think they were some of the guard disguis'd
> For, to speak truth, men act that are between
> Forty and fifty wenches of fifteen
> With bone so large and never so incompliant,
> When you call Desdemona, enter Giant.   (ll. 7–14)

The lines insinuate that the current production's move towards realistic representation is a move towards civilization, and that productions of Shakespeare's plays before the theatres closed were victims of a barbarous climate of crossdressing and age-inappropriate casting. According to Jordan and his company, the objectionable practices of the past included having grown men portray women. And for one of Shakespeare's plays, specifically, the practice appears to have continued much later than anyone has imagined. If we believe the theory that the King's Men circa 1604 had trained a handful of 13-year-olds so that one could play Desdemona at 15 or 16, to what is Jordan referring here? In order to maintain the theory we must dismiss this as hyperbole. The incidental phrases 'mistake me not' and 'to speak truth' caution against that, but it's remarkable that any exaggeration here concerns the advanced age ('forty to fifty') and large size ('Giant') of the adult male playing Desdemona, and not the fact that it was an adult male. The prologue seems to object not to adult men portraying women, but to the unusual sizes of some who did, since they

---

[59] Jordan, 'A Prologue to Introduce the First Woman', pp. 24–5.

Figure 6.3 Scene from John Madden's *Shakespeare in Love* (1998), starring Jim Carter as Juliet's Nurse.

were mistakable for 'guards'. Jordan and Killigrew had seen Shakespeare's plays produced before 1642. They apparently saw female roles filled by actors that they believed were inadmissibly old or large. They could not have seen *Othello* during Shakespeare's lifetime, so it follows that the barbaric practices most assume the company did not employ – like casting adult males in female roles – occurred even after he had died.[60]

Since Jordan speaks generally of 'the stage', his example of such a wide disparity between actor and character cannot have been isolated. And it isn't. In 1640, Robert Chamberlain takes one of his 'conceits' in *Jocabella* from an encounter with a stage player:

A Gentleman meeting a stage player in a sicknes time, who had formerly plaid womens parts; told him he was growne grave, and that he began to have a beard; the other answered, while the grasse growes the horse did starve; meaning, because there was then no playing, and therefore he did let his beard grow.[61]

If we do not disregard these accounts in favour of a prevailing theory, then some ideas about Elizabethan casting practices must be revisited. Like the prologue, Chamberlain's anecdote does not suggest that the actor who shaved to play women was exceptional. *Jocabella*'s subtitle is 'a cabinet of conceits'. The wit of this conceit is its novel use of the proverb, the actor being

---

[60] I stress that the prologue concerns a Shakespeare play because most evidence for the participation of teenaged boys does not, and because many practices of the Lord Chamberlain's/King's Men were distinct from those of other companies.

[61] Robert Chamberlain, *Jocabella, or a cabinet of conceits* (London: R. Hodgkinson for Daniel Frere, 1640), D5b–D6a.

depicted as poor amid excess (here, of hair). Chamberlain ignores any potential impropriety of an actor capable of growing beards playing women, as though it was not unusual or humorous.[62]

If Jordan's prologue and Chamberlain's player report what they saw, casting Flute as Thisbe (despite him having 'a beard coming') is not farfetched. The mechanicals' casting discussions are often dismissed as naive or parodic, but they may be more accurate than we expect, something John Madden intuited when casting the company's 'female' roles in *Shakespeare in Love*.[63] Several female characters in Shakespeare's plays (particularly early in his career) seem to suggest that the company planned to cast larger and more mature actors than the audience might expect. The exchange in *Love's Labour's Lost* between Costard and the Princess of France is one example:

> COSTARD   Which is the greatest lady? The highest?
> PRINCESS   The thickest and the tallest.
> COSTARD   The thickest and the tallest? it is so; truth is truth.
>   An your waist, mistress, were as slender as my wit
>   One o'these maids' girdles for your waist should be fit.
>   Are not you the chief woman? You are the thickest here.
>   (4.1.46–51)

As noted previously, the scene goes out of its way to advertise the stoutness of its leading lady. The exchange is comic, but the topic persists, ending with Costard's declaration that the Princess is 'the thickest' person onstage. When you say Princess of France, *enter Giant*. I have also noted that *Love's Labour's Lost* requires five women onstage simultaneously, a unique example in Shakespeare's plays that occurs before boys were apprenticed to company members. Costard's lines may thus contain a self-reflexive joke about the company's practice of using adult males in at least some female roles. What seem to be eyewitness accounts of adult men in female roles may help explain why Rosalind refers to herself as 'more than common tall', or why Hippolyta and Tamora are praised for their martial prowess, or why the weird sisters 'should be women' yet their 'beards' forbid Banquo 'to interpret that [they] are so' (1.3.46–8).

---

[62] Unlike Jordan's prologue, Chamberlain's player does not indicate King's Men's practice, but his turn of phrase does recall Hamlet's conversation with Rosencrantz after *The Murder of Gonzago*:

> HAMLET   Sir, I lack advancement.
> ROSENCRANTZ   How can that be when you have the voice of the King himself for your
>   succession in Denmark?
> HAMLET   Ay, sir, but while the grass grows – the proverb is something musty.
>   (3.2.315–18)

[63] Compare Polonius's list of all genres in which the 'tragedians of the city' are expert, which is in some sense more accurate in describing Shakespeare's generic combinations than the categories indicated in the First Folio.

What's in a 'Boy'?

Some may reject such examples as hyperbolic or ironic, as they may the descriptions in Jordan's prologue and *Jocabella*. But internal evidence has played a significant role in founding assumptions about the participation of the teenaged boys alongside Shakespeare's sharers. The notion that a short actor would have played Hermia and Celia alongside a taller Helena and Rosalind, for instance, has been widely accepted as a sign of the presence of two boys. And Cleopatra's famed (but supposed) self-reference to one who will 'boy' her 'greatness / I'th' posture of a whore' (5.2.19–20) is thought to confirm the presence of the boy delivering the lines, rather than being taken as a pejorative statement about the manner of representation. Such examples suggest that internal comments on physiognomy are admitted, but perhaps only when they conform to current assumptions. The preference for the prevailing theory explains why the males associated with Shakespeare's company without confirmed birthdates are assumed to be the very teenaged actors needed to justify it. Such 'evidence', along with our awareness that boys' companies were active in London; that the King's Men eventually hired some of those boys; and that some sharers took on apprentices, argues a supposedly clear case that Titania, Rosalind, Goneril, and Cleopatra were played by teenagers.

The case is far from clear, but the most troublesome thing about it is the strange currency and influence of the conjecture that these boys were pre-pubescent and maintained unbroken voices, an aesthetic preference that simply may not have been shared by the historical company or its audience. Critics have prized unbroken voices in female impersonation despite the fact that adult actors from so many cultures and periods have practised stage transvestism; despite the knowledge that using boys meant inexperience might offset any gains in likeness-to-life; and despite the manifestly impractical strategy of a company putting itself in a position to regularly, unpredictably lose its female leads.

The term 'boy' typically did not indicate 'pre-pubescence' in the Renaissance. Modern usage has pushed the meaning in that direction, but this use was rare for Shakespeare and his contemporaries. The *OED* gives the following definition:

boy, *n.*1 and *int.*

1. a. A male servant, slave, assistant, junior employee, etc.
   b. A male civilian informally attached to an encamped or travelling body of soldiers; a camp follower. *Obs.*
2. A male person of low birth or status; (as a general term of contempt or abuse) a worthless fellow, a knave, a rogue, a wretch. *Obs.*

3. A male child or youth. Also: a son, irrespective of age (chiefly as referred to by members of the immediate family). Sometimes restricted to male children below the age of puberty, or below the school-leaving age.[64]

In the period, the word 'boy' most commonly signified inferiority or a relationship of servitude, a meaning that persists today. Rank was more in question than years, and when the term did concern years they were more often relative than absolute. Jacques's description of 'second childishness' and Wordsworth's observation that 'the child is father of the man' speak to the comfort that English speakers possess for age-related paradoxes. As we have seen, apprentices were often considered boys into their twenties.

The boy in *Henry V* uses the term this way in his 3.2 monologue about Pistol, Bardolph, and Nym:

> As young as I am, I have observed these three swashers. I am boy to them all three. But they all three, though they would serve me, could not be man to me ... I must leave them, and seek some better service. (3.2.25–46)

'Boy' is here associated with servitude, correlating to 'man' as 'servant' does to 'master'. In the context, a boy could be as old as the man he served. Pistol's boy says he is 'young', but the word can accurately describe someone in his late teens or twenties, especially if he looks younger and is slighter of build than the other three. Shakespeare routinely uses 'boy' to signal social inferiority or contempt, as it does when applied to Edmund, Lear's Fool, Bolingbroke, Bertram, and many other adult male characters. If Shakespeare wrote Shylock, Othello, and Lear for Richard Burbage, a white, 30-something Englishman at the turn of the century, there is no reason he or his company should have balked at having a young adult take on Lucius, Rutland, Arthur, or even Mamillius. In fact, doing so would have been very much in line with their tendency to exaggerate the gaps between actor and character. If the sharers and any integral hired players had to exercise range and versatility for characters from Achilles to Aaron, Ariel to Caliban, on what basis would there have been concern about their ability to portray women?

Any sharers, hired men, or older apprentices that the company considered eligible to play female roles could also have made credible Hals, Claudios, or Bertrams. Jordan and Killigrew go further in their prologue for *Othello* – suggesting that men aged 'forty to fifty' played 'wenches of fifteen'. This may be hyperbole, but the lines invite consideration that even men of middle age may have played characters like Desdemona in a conventional transvestite theatre in which versatility reigned. Whether or not we accept that such men were

---

[64] 'boy, *n*.' *OED Online*. March 2013. Oxford University Press. 9 March 2013. http://dictionary. oed.com. The definitions have been cropped to focus on those most pertinent to Shakespeare's time. The numerical order is preserved.

over 40, the prologue's implications are clear: Shakespeare's company was comfortable with gaps in representation that were conspicuous and seemingly barbaric by the time Jordan and Killigrew staged *Othello* in 1660. Before that, relativity among available actors may have been the guiding principle of casting for the King's Men. As a result, a comparatively fair, small-boned, and clean-shaven adult actor might be found sufficiently credible in a female role when placed next to a larger, older, bearded one. And lack of teenaged performers with strong voices and sufficient experience (who would perhaps be no more credible as women than men in their twenties or thirties), should not have prevented the show from going on.[65]

Voice-Change and Puberty

Support for the theory that boys with unbroken voices played female roles in original productions likely outstrips the evidence because of a critical bias towards realism that initially brought boys, and then actual women, to English stages. Shakespeare presumably had lines he would not cross when it came to representation, but as Philip Sidney's critique in the *Defense of Poesy* suggests, Shakespeare was more willing to test limits or compromise audiences' ability to credit what appeared on stage than some others of his time. Recent scholarship has pushed back the ages of the 'boys' supposed to have played on some professional stages, providing grounds to imagine that Shakespeare's women, even if not played by the men of 'forty to fifty' described by Jordan, were played by 'boys' old enough to double in male roles. While Kathman writes that 'nearly' every female role was played by an actor aged 19 or younger, he has unearthed examples of female roles being portrayed for the King's Men by actors as old as 21.[66] There are too few records, though, to assume that any such examples are isolated exceptions to a rule. To accommodate what are supposed exceptions, Kathman guesses that some boys 'probably retained the ability to sing or speak in a treble voice until the age of twenty', allowing them to remain credible as women. Again, though, the notion that the voice must be 'retained' reflects critical presuppositions and not evidence drawn from the material record or the plays themselves.

Nevertheless, some have argued that voices of Renaissance-era boys broke later than they do today. Herbert Moller cites Benvenuto Cellini's biography, which mentions a '16-year-old boy dressed as a girl singing at a banquet' as an

---

[65] Kabuki; Harvard's Hasty Pudding Theatricals; wartime theatre in British and American military camps; Greek drama; and any number of other examples support the wide range of periods and peoples comfortable with extreme gaps between the figure represented and the one representing, including the representation of women by adult men. See Michael Dobson, *Shakespeare and Amateur Performance: A Cultural History* (Cambridge: Cambridge University Press, 2011).

[66] According to Kathman, Richard Sharpe appears to have played the Duchess in the *Duchess of Malfi* at the age of 21 for the King's Men. See 'How Old Were Shakespeare's Boy Actors?', pp. 220–46.

example of this delay.[67] More compelling is his review of S.F. Daw's study of boys' choirs in Leipzig from 1700 to 1745, wherein it appears that most voices in the eighteenth century began to break before age 18, but that the breaks could come as late as 25. Moller also suggests that musical compositions of the middle ages anticipate higher registers in both men and women than is common today, and that the 'bass' voice in men appears to be an innovation 'discovered' about 1450 in Flemish music.[68]

If Moller is right about the voice breaking later in the period, that too might present a chance for older boys or young men to play female roles, lending support to the notion that unbroken voices were key to their desirability in such roles. But, as we have seen, there are examples of actors as young as 16 playing adult males, and in the 1595 printing of *The Problemes of Aristotle*, the unknown author questions 'Why are boyes apt to change their voice about fourteen yeares of age?'[69] Bruce Smith argues on this basis that puberty was not much different then than it is now, when it came to voice breaks.[70] In *Children of the Queen's Revels*, Lucy Munro has researched the question in unprecedented detail, concluding that puberty occurred around age 14 in the period, much as it does now.[71] Munro argues that Rastall's sources are 'equivocal' about the age at which voices break, noting that the tendency for boys to exit children's companies by 14, along with period references in books to 14 signifying the end of childhood, confirm what is set forth in *The Problemes of Aristotle*.[72] The discrepancy may partly result from the fact that Moller and Daw focus chiefly on singers, the former making predictions about speaking voices based on musical studies. Since trained singers of any age often succeed in enlarging the range of notes they can sing, and increasing the power and clarity with which they can sing them, boy choristers likely acquired or preserved notes that became abnormal in natural speech. Though voice breaks may have been delayed when compared to the average today (per Moller, 13.9 years), the vocal chords of youth at that time must still have grown in length and thickness as those youth grew in size; and longer, thicker vocal chords without exception result in deeper speaking voices. Singers could maintain and even increase their range as they got older, but only a delay in growth of the voice box or vocal chords could delay the deepening of one's natural register. The presence of boys who had trained in the children's companies may have influenced the

---

[67] Moller, 'Voice Change in Human Biological Development', *Journal of Interdisciplinary History* 16.2 (1985), p. 245, fn. 10.

[68] Ibid., p. 248.

[69] Quoted in Bruce Smith, *The Acoustic World of Early Modern England* (Chicago: University of Chicago Press, 1999), p. 227.

[70] Ibid.

[71] Munro, *Children of the Queen's Revels*, pp. 39–40.

[72] Munro cites, for example, *The Office of Christian Parents* (1616), which states that childhood lasts until 14 for boys; and *The Academy of Armory* which describes the 'stripling or young boy' as a male between seven and 14, and the 'youth' as one between 14 and 21. Ibid.

kind of 'female' speaking that occurred onstage, given that some had trained as singers. But this would not have happened before nearly all of Shakespeare's plays had been written and performed.

If actors as old as 21 are documented as having played female roles for the King's Men, and if voices typically broke around 14, then we must reject the premise that boys were employed by the company *because* their voices were unbroken. In fact, even if we rely on Caroline practices by the King's Men, we have nearly as much evidence for 20-year-old apprentices performing as we do for 14- to 17-year-olds. Since young men of 21 (whose voices would have broken even according to Rastall and Moller) played female roles, what should have kept them from continuing to do so until a better option was found? And if the delay in voice breaks was more significant than we know – or if boys could 'retain' their ability to speak in 'a treble voice until the age of twenty', as Kathman suggests – then why could they not retain that ability into their mid-twenties, or later, as modern female impersonators have done?[73]

Beards and Beardlessness

Further illuminating the debate over the age of Shakespeare's female imper-sonators, Moller has offered persuasive evidence that some signs of puberty came later for boys of Shakespeare's time than it does today. He argues that diet and other factors contributed to delays in the onset of darkened beard growth in men, supplying biographical evidence that suggests the average Elizabethan man may not have grown darkened facial hair until 23 or 24 years of age.[74] In one example, Benvenuto Cellini fought a duel at the age of 23 (in 1523), after which he left Florence 'in the guise of a friar'; worried that he may not look the part, Cellini asked a friend to 'remove a few hairs from my chin, which were the first down of my manhood'.[75] In another, from 1556, a 20-year-old Thomas Platter worried that he might not receive a medical licence 'because he was still

---

[73] Several critics have written on the history and phenomenology of stage transvestism, includ-ing examples from modern culture. See Garber's *Vested Interests* (1997); Laurence Senelick, *The Changing Room: Sex, Drag, and Theatre* (New York: Routledge, 2000); and Roger Baker, *Drag: A History of Female Impersonation in the Performing Arts* (New York: New York University Press, 1995). Among other examples, Garber cites the frequency of cross-dressing in military entertainments, describing the 'Sea Queens' who played roles in drag for the British Navy (pp. 56–7). Senelick discusses stage transvestism beginning with the ancient Greeks, who did not use female actors, and continuing to the present day in musicals like *Hello Dolly*, or even in the frequent use of a male actor to play Lady Bracknell in *The Importance of Being Earnest* (p. 48). Baker describes female impersonation in Peking opera and Kabuki theatre, the latter calling adult males who play female roles 'onagata' (see Chapter 5).

[74] Herbert Moller, 'The Accelerated Development of Youth: Beard Growth as a Biological Marker', *Comparative Studies in Society and History* 29.4 (1987), p. 753.

[75] Ibid.

beardless and looked too youthful'.[76] Some men today do not grow facial hair until they are in their 20s, so Moller's examples could be anomalous. Still, if there was a delay in beard growth during the period, this is another reason that actors would not have become suddenly incapable of playing women by age 18.

Most interesting in Moller's argument is the implication that beard growth was necessary for one to be considered a 'man' during the period. In King John's description of the Dauphin as a 'beardless boy', and Cleopatra's contemptuous reference to the 'scarce-bearded Caesar', Moller sees confirmations of the late appearance of facial hair in the period, and the necessity of beard growth for one to be accounted a man. In his study of beards and masculinity in the Renaissance, Will Fisher makes a similar point, noting how 'early modern facial hair ... in some sense "made the man."'[77] According to Moller and Fisher, it is not age but beard growth that marked the line between boys and men. Like the apprentices whose social standing marked them as 'boys' until age 24 or older, beardlessness could preserve a marker of boyhood well into one's twenties. And since, as Fisher suggests, beards were malleable and prosthetic, actors could change from man to boy (and perhaps from man to woman) simply by shaving.

The documentary record favours just such transformations. In *Vexed and Troubled Englishmen 1590–1642*, Carl Bridenbaugh describes how a performance in Reading around 1600 was delayed because 'the queen was shaving'.[78] If Moller is right about beard growth, this 'queen' should have been at least 23. A shaving queen reminds us that removing a beard could remove manhood, making the age of the player somewhat irrelevant, and possibly making that player better suited than any boy to playing older female characters like Margaret (*Richard III*) or Paulina. If boys as young as 15 played queens for Shakespeare, we cannot imagine (given Moller's study of beard growth) that they were shaving regularly, nor can we presume that most young men of 20 grew beards of such thickness as to require removal for the stage. Like some other examples, the anecdote from Reading suggests it was not remarkable to see a grown man playing a woman onstage, since the player is singled out not for being too old, but too hairy. Together with Chamberlain's story of the actor of female parts who let his beard grow while the theatres were closed, the position that female roles were played exclusively by teenage boys in Shakespeare's time is simply untenable.

---

[76] Ibid.

[77] Will Fisher, 'The Renaissance Beard: Masculinity in Early Modern England', *Renaissance Quarterly* 54.1 (2001), p. 184. See also Eleanor Rycroft, 'Facial Hair and the Performance of Early Modern Masculinity on the Early Modern English Stage', in *Locating the Queen's Men, 1583–1603*, ed. Helen Ostovich, Holger Schott Syme, and Andrew Griffin (Burlington: Ashgate, 2009), pp. 217–28.

[78] Quoted in Forse, *Art Imitates Business*, pp. 91–3.

Shakespeare's plays support the notion that the beard made the man. In *Much Ado About Nothing*, Benedick insults Claudio by calling him 'lord Lackbeard', and Claudio is elsewhere described as having performed 'in the figure of a lamb, the feats of a lion' (1.1.12–13). Claudio is man enough to distinguish himself as a soldier, yet his masculinity is undercut in Benedick's view by his lack of a beard. Elsewhere, Beatrice evaluates potential marriage candidates based on facial hair:

> BEATRICE Just, if he send me no husband, for the which blessing I am at
> him upon my knees every morning and evening. Lord, I could not
> endure a husband with a beard on his face. I had rather lie in the
> woolen!
> LEONATO You may light on a husband that hath no beard.
> BEATRICE What should I do with him? Dress him in my apparel and make
> him my waiting-gentlewoman? He that hath a beard is more than a
> youth, and he that hath no beard is less than a man; and he that is
> more than a youth is not for me, and he that is less than a man, I am
> not for him. Therefore, I will even take sixpence in earnest of the
> bear-ward, and lead his apes into hell.   (2.1.23–34)

For Beatrice, a beard is a prerequisite for manhood, and a beardless man is a candidate to be dressed as a 'waiting gentlewoman'. In other words, a beardless man is a *boy* fit to impersonate a woman. Moller also cites a proverb from the townsmen of Cologne that expands the duration of boyhood still further: 'At 20 a youth, at 30 a man; and marriage without a beard is unseemly.'[79] Like Beatrice, the townsmen assume that a 'youth' was a male without a beard, even if he was nearly 30. Since beards seem to signify manhood in the Renaissance, we have more cause to reconsider who played female roles for Shakespeare's company, even if we admit the dubious condition that actors must retain some features of adolescence for the sake of credibility.

It is worth remembering that the text of *Hamlet* indicates that Hamlet has a beard, though he rarely does in modern productions. That a beard can have been ordinary for the character in the period, yet so unusual on stages today, may help us imagine just how feminizing a clean shave may have seemed to Shakespeare's actors and audiences. In Shakespeare's time, a shaved face automatically signified youth, possibly even femininity. Francis Flute's youth goes unmentioned. Rather, he says he cannot play Thisbe because he has 'a beard coming' (1.2.39–40). Quince takes the objection in stride, since Flute may 'play it in a mask' (1.2.41). Both statements imply that the beard is the problem. Flute does not say that he is too tall, too broad, or too old, and nobody

---

[79] Moller, 'Accelerated Development', pp. 752–3.

refs to him as a bellows-mender's 'apprentice'. Since cloaks, hats, and false beards were sufficient to signal identity changes on sixteenth-century stages, and since adult males typically wore beards, actors who were clean-shaven, of relatively slight build, and skilled at female impersonation could have played women well into their twenties.

Aeries of Squeaking Cleopatras

In *Hamlet* 2.2, Rosencrantz brings news that 'the tragedians of the city' are now out of fashion due to 'an eyrie of children, little eyases' (2.2.236).[80] The apparently topical reference to the growing popularity of professional boys' companies in London around the turn of the seventeenth century may provide a rare glimpse of Shakespeare's attitude about rival theatre offerings in London – specifically, about companies using young boys as principal actors.[81] In the context of my argument concerning the possibility that sharers and boys older than those commonly supposed likely played at least some of Shakespeare's female roles, the discussion within *Hamlet* of London's theatrical culture deserves scrutiny. Two major points stand out. First, that the increased availability of boy actors, an increase brought about by training and experience gained while acting for boys' companies, came too late to influence the company's practice significantly during much of the time in which Shakespeare was its principal playwright. And second, that Shakespeare's company may have resisted integrating teenaged boy players longer than other companies.

The first point concerns the timing of the boys' rise to prominence and their potential impact on Shakespeare's company. Siobhan Keenan observes that boys' companies were dormant throughout the 1590s until the Children of St. Paul's reformed in 1599.[82] It was not until 1600 that the Children of the Chapel formed, possibly the first such company to use boys who were not all choristers and to operate on a professional model.[83] Shakespeare had likely completed 22 of his plays before 1601. The boys' companies were on the rise through at least the first half of the decade (for instance, the Children of the Queen's Revels form in 1604), but their popularity seems clearly to have been declining by 1608.[84] The timeline suggests that such companies formed rapidly

[80] For the ease of readers using different versions of the text, the citations to the 'little eyases' passage refer to *The Norton Shakespeare*, 2nd edition.
[81] For the rise in popularity of boys' companies, see Munro, *Children of the Queen's Revels*, and Siobhan Keenan, *Acting Companies and their Plays in Shakespeare's London* (London: Arden, 2014).
[82] See Keenan's *Acting Companies*, pp. 12–13.
[83] Ibid., p. 14. Also see Astington's *Actors and Acting in Shakespeare's Time*.
[84] Ibid.

between 1600 and 1604, but that it would have been 1604 or later that enough of these boys had sufficient training and experience to join adult companies, if indeed they did so at all. Not until they aged out of the companies or saw the companies decline in popularity would many of these boys have cause to look for other work. Keenan notes that the age of the boy players increases during the decade's first half, suggesting that the boys were not expelled suddenly when they had reached an arbitrary age limit, implying that many were pleased (or bound) to continue with the children's companies, rather than join an adult troupe early in their careers. If the King's Men employed such boy players, then, it may not have done so until the decade's latter half, when all but a handful of Shakespeare's plays had been written and performed.

This speculative account tries to reflect what little we can learn from the material record about the increase in boy participation for the company around 1610. I have noted already that John Rice doesn't turn up in records associated with the King's Men until 1607, when he is bound apprentice to Heminges, and Richard Robinson does not appear until 1611, when he performs in the *Second Maiden's Tragedy*. William Ostler, John Underwood, and Nathan Field performed with the King's Men after having acted with the Children of the Chapel. But Field did not join the company until after Shakespeare had retired, while Ostler and Underwood could have joined the company as early as 1608, though their first known participation was in a production of *The Alchemist* in 1610.[85] It is not clear, then, that any member of a children's company played alongside the sharers of the King's Men until 1610, when the children were no longer children, when the company had acquired Blackfriars, and when Shakespeare was nearing retirement.

On the second point, while care must be taken not to read too much into the discussion of boy players in *Hamlet*, Hamlet and Rosencrantz take a rather cynical view of their success and theatrical practice. Rosencrantz reports that the children are a 'late innovation', whose public favour has come at the expense of the tragedians Hamlet admires:

> ROSENCRANTZ   But there is, sir, an eyrie of children, little eyases, that cry out on the top of question and are most tyrannically clapp'd for't. These are now the fashion, and so berattle the common stages – so they call them – that many wearing rapiers are afraid of goosequills and dare scarce come thither.
>
> HAMLET   What, are they children? Who maintains 'em? How are they escorted? Will they pursue the quality no longer than they can sing? Will they not say afterwards, if they should grow

---

[85] Gurr, *The Shakespeare Company*, pp. 227, 235, 245.

themselves to common players – as it is like most will, if their
means are no better – their writers do them wrong to make
them exclaim against their own succession?   (2.2.326–36)[86]

As Richard Dutton observes, 'there is a big difference between "novelty" being
the reason for drawing away audiences and "cry[ing] out on the top of the
question", making a scandalous noise like fledgling hawks'.[87] Rosencrantz's
description is full of criticism, for both the boy actors and the audiences that
appreciate them: the boys 'berattle the common stages' and are 'most tyranni-
cally clapp'd' for performances that seem to thrive on just what Hamlet fears
in his caution to the players: 'but if you mouth it, as many of our players do,
I had as leif the town-crier spoke my lines'.[88] For his part, Hamlet seems surprised by the boys' reception; compares their takeover of London's theatrical
scene to Claudius's theft of Old Hamlet's throne; and wonders about the boys'
maintenance and future prospects – questions that would have been urgent
for the King's Men if they employed many such boys. Given the arguments
so far advanced about the potential limits to or lack of participation by boys
on Shakespeare's stage, this scene implicitly raises questions worth considering: did the King's Men prefer boy actors to adult males for female roles? If so,
was their participation deemed worthy of expanding cast sizes, budgets, and
responsibilities for training, board, and their inevitable disposal? The passages
indicate clear opposition between adult and boy companies. Though reading
plays to get at Shakespeare's opinion cannot but prove inconclusive, the text
reminds us that the boys' companies then in 'fashion' were not to everyone's
taste. It seems relevant that the characters worry about the voice control of boy
players.[89] And Hamlet's evaluation of their acting hardly cries out that these
boys were just what the King's Men ought to seize on for its female leads.

   Alongside the 'little eyases', Cleopatra's shuddering prophecy of having her greatness 'boyed' in some distant land is probably the best-known
reference to boy actors in Shakespeare. But like Hamlet and Rosencrantz,
Cleopatra does not appear especially sanguine about the prospect of stage

---

[86] Again, the passage is cited from *The Norton Shakespeare*, 2nd edition.

[87] Richard Dutton, *Shakespeare, Court Dramatist* (Oxford: Oxford University Press, 2016),
p. 231.

[88] In 'Little Eyases', William Miller cites Edmund Bert's *An Approved Treatise of Hawkes and
Hawking* (1619), where Bert notes that many eyases 'will cry as loud to you as you speak to
them'. Shakespeare may have applied the epithet to child actors to suggest their ability to par-
rot voices but also their lack of self-directed subtlety and range. See *Shakespeare Quarterly*
28.1 (1977), pp. 86–8.

[89] For actors, developing vocal power, range, and control, to speak long verse speeches takes
time. Patsy Rodenberg doesn't begin training her Guildhall students to speak Shakespeare until
they have had at least a year of voice training because 'it is so difficult to attempt his texts if you
haven't got support or can't sustain an open sound'. See *Speaking Shakespeare* (New York: St.
Martin's Press, 2004), p. 66.

boys. Her line about being impersonated by one, 'I'th' posture of a whore', has been taken as something like conclusive evidence that teenaged boys appeared on stage in original productions (5.2.20). The potential for self-reflexive address here is indeed enticing, but since 'boy' often referred to men in their twenties during the period, we cannot assume Cleopatra means a pre-pubescent boy. Rosenberg has argued that the verb carries a negative connotation, so that Cleopatra's use of the word suggests a derivative or deficient style of representation. I have noted how the boy in the fictional playing troupe in *Sir Thomas More* could represent a deficiency rather than a desirable casting situation, considering that several actual Tudor troupes didn't use boys. It is reasonable that the boy in *Sir Thomas More* would play females and children, but his presence cannot attest to any natural superiority of the practice, without knowing anything about his individual talent, physical appearance, or experience. James Forse has proposed that Cleopatra's description may be a veiled attack on a contemporary revival of Samuel Daniel's play *Cleopatra* (1594), the phrase thus mocking the use of boy players in keeping with the attitude expressed in the 'little eyases' passage.[90] Whatever the case, Shakespeare's Cleopatra is clearly displeased at the prospect of being 'boyed' herself.

The short brunette and tall blonde characters that recur across several plays in the 1590s are also routinely taken as exemplifying the presence of teenaged boys on Shakespeare's stage. Attention within plays to the relative heights of Hermia and Helena, Beatrice and Hero, Portia and Nerissa, Celia and Rosalind argues the possibility that the same pair of actors was cast for all four pairs of characters, as several critics have argued.[91] Wigs may have accounted for hair colour, but if the references to their heights do indicate the reappearance of the same actors, then these actors would seem to have played major female roles for at least five years running – longer than two boys could expect to maintain unbroken voices by any theory thus far advanced.[92] And if those two actors were the same, what would have stopped them from playing Viola and Olivia, Cressida and Helen (*Troilus*), or Helena and Diana (*All's Well*)? If they paired up for plays that premiered between 1595 and 1600, and if Shakespeare

[90] Forse, *Art Imitates Business*, pp. 89–90.
[91] Roland Mushat Frye argues that between 1595 and 1600 all four pairs, along with Viola and Olivia from *Twelfth Night* would have been played by 'two extraordinarily competent boys', *Shakespeare: The Art of the Dramatist* (London: Routledge, 1982), p. 49. To Ackroyd, it 'seems likely that the same gifted pair of boys played all of these parts', *Shakespeare: The Biography*, p. 225. See also Richard David's *Shakespeare and the Players* (Oxford: Oxford University Press, 1961), pp. 155–6.
[92] *A Midsummer Night's Dream* is likely first performed in 1595 and *As You Like It* not until 1599 or 1600.

continued to utilize similar pairs of female characters thereafter, why would we assume the company dropped its most experienced female leads rather than having them continue by 'usurping' the voice of a woman?[93]

Portia's plan for herself and Nerissa to impersonate men and meet their husbands in Venice speaks further to the issue of producing an appropriate voice artificially:

> PORTIA   I'll hold thee any wager,
> When we are both accoutred like young men
> I'll prove the prettier fellow of the two,
> And wear my dagger with the braver grace,
> And speak between the change of man and boy
> With a reed voice, and turn two mincing steps
> Into a manly stride, and speak of frays
> Like a fine bragging youth ...
> NERISSA   Why, shall we turn to men?   (3.4.62–78)

Portia supposes that she can find middle ground between the voices of man and boy, as though she, like Dick Robinson, is capable of both. '[M]incing steps' and a 'manly stride' are likewise envisioned for the portrayal, Portia seeming thereby to literalize one of the 'man-woman monsters' deplored by Prynne. Portia and Nerissa refer to themselves as 'young men', 'youths', and 'men', and their speeches, here and elsewhere, suggest that the actors occupied a liminal space between man and boy, capable of portraying both.

At the play's end, when Bassanio and Gratiano are under fire for having given away their wives' rings, we hear like comfort with this liminality, along with a summary of the qualifications for boyhood now under consideration:

> NERISSA   Gave it a judge's clerk! No, God's my judge,
> The clerk will ne'er wear hair on's face that had it!
> GRATIANO He will, an if he live to be a man.
> NERISSA   Ay, if a woman live to be a man!
> GRATIANO Now, by this hand, I gave it to a youth –
> A kind of boy, a little scrubbed boy,
> No higher than thyself – the judge's clerk,
> A prating boy that begg'd it as a fee.
> I could not for my heart deny it him.
> ...
> My Lord Bassanio gave his ring away
> Unto the judge that begg'd it, and indeed
> Deserved it, too. And then the boy, his clerk,
> That took some pains in writing, he begg'd mine;

---

[93] In the framing scene of *The Taming of the Shrew*, the Lord expects the boy page to 'well *usurp* the grace, / Voice, gait, and actions of a gentlewoman' (Induction, 127–8, italics mine).

> And neither man nor master would take aught
> But the two rings.   (5.1.157–84)

My elision juxtaposes Gratiano's differing evaluations of the judge and the clerk. The boy clerk is 'a youth – / A kind of boy', much like Nerissa herself (5.1.161–2). Gratiano notes that the clerk will indeed 'wear hair on's face' provided that he live to be a man, confirming his youth and that facial hair is requisite for distinguishing men from boys. But he also fears this youth sleeping with his wife, suggesting that attributes of both boy and man were evident in the same figure. Soon after, Gratiano refers to the judge and his boy clerk as 'master' and 'man', suggesting the service relationship that occasions the paradox wherein 'man' and 'boy' can describe the same figure.

Yet another problem with the theory that young boys were necessary for convincing illusions of femininity is that, by this logic, those boys would struggle in the cross-dressed guises in which these heroines frequently appear. The theory cannot but prove inconsistent in its application, since it denies the ability of mature-voiced young males to convincingly portray women while expecting them to portray not only old women, but also characters such as the esteemed Doctor Bellario, who deploys a phony voice that convinces the onstage audience. Only critical bias can suggest that a beardless male actor in his twenties would invariably appear ridiculous as Portia. It is more plausible to suggest that a 14-year-old Portia, whose voice is naturally child-like, might appear ridiculous as a legal scholar. In short, every choice to cast a boy as a woman would need to be weighed against the need to have the actor present a credible version of masculinity in the male roles she goes on to assume. Julia, Rosalind, Portia and Nerissa, Viola and Imogen all must impersonate males, and the argument for verisimilitude undermines itself when young boys are employed in these roles.

As a final example of internal evidence, consider Hamlet, who greets the tragedians of the city by expressing hope that the voice of their specialist in female impersonation 'be not cracked within the ring' (2.2.353). This may be the surest evidence available to suggest that boys with unbroken voices participated in the plays. Certainly, some such boys could have done so, since nearly every play structure can accommodate one or two young actors who play female roles exclusively. Still, it is useful to consider this scene in the context of the Induction to *Shrew*; Portia's plot to play a man in *Merchant*; and Quince's directive that Flute 'speak as small as [he] will' (1.2.42) to be credible as Thisbe. Such examples suggest that actors simulated female voices – something that still would be necessary if teenage boys represented women.

The internal evidence, combined with the material record, suggests that the line between 'boy' and 'man' was fluid with respect to age. The very idea of such a line, though, may be detrimental when thinking about Shakespeare's heroines and those who portrayed them. As Stephen Orgel points out, the boy/man binary neglects or fails to define the *liminal* space between the two, which perhaps is inhabited by Claudio and cross-dressing heroines like Portia. This 'middle' age was one in which Shakespeare appears interested, and which resists definite expression in years. The plays contain several passages in which Shakespeare lingers over its definition, though among them Malvolio's attempt to describe the 'young fellow' at Olivia's door:

> OLIVIA   Of what personage and years is he?
> MALVOLIO Not yet old enough for a man, nor young enough for a boy; as a squash is before 'tis a peascod, or a codling when 'tis almost an apple. 'Tis with him in standing water between boy and man.   (1.5.145–9)

After their initial interview, Olivia repeatedly alternates between 'man' and 'youth' when referring to Cesario, a plausible confusion considering that Cesario is man enough that others can take him for Viola's valiant brother, Sebastian, yet young enough that Orsino thinks his features are all 'semblative a woman's part' (1.4.33). The play thus literally places Viola in 'standing water, between boy and man' and also between man and woman. Here Viola (and perhaps Sebastian) recalls the problem Beatrice described in trying to classify her marriage candidates, desiring those who are neither 'more than a youth' nor 'less than a man'.

Potentially self-reflexive moments invite cautious interpretation, since Shakespeare routinely uses language to inform his audiences of what is not: that 'the vasty fields of France' stretch out before them; that Macbeth sees a dagger before him; that Cesario is 'semblative a woman's part' despite having narrow hips and no breasts. Nevertheless, such moments may indicate that the actors playing female roles for Shakespeare's company were older than commonly supposed and capable of playing male roles too. Such actors would be candidates for Rosalind and Hero but also Orlando and Claudio. One of the 'young lords' whom the King of France calls on in *All's Well* could return as Diana. And, as suggested, the actors of short-lived roles such as Emilia and Mamillius could reverse their genders and return as Florizel and Perdita.

Contemporary Views

The work that Gurr and Kathman have done sifting through the documentary record for information on apprentices is extremely valuable, but the evidence for the participation of adult males in women's roles is more extensive than either critic suggests. Though Grote supposes that 'boys means precisely that – boys ... not young men ... in every instance they are referred to as boys', he and those who share the theory have it wrong: the appellation 'boy' applies comfortably to men in their twenties; and 'they' are not 'referred to as boys' in every instance. William Davenant, a contemporary of Killigrew, who also had seen performances before the theatres had closed in 1642, documented Charles II's decision in his patent application of 1662:

That whereas the women's parts in plays have hitherto been acted by men in the habits of women, at which some (audience) have taken offence, we do permit and give leave for the time to come, that all women's parts be acted by women.[94]

Davenant appears to confirm what Jordan and Killigrew had seen – something like the 'giant' who entered as Desdemona. The phrase 'men in women's habits', to state the obvious, provides a clear exception to Grote's rule. We can choose to understand the phrase to mean '15-year-olds in women's habits', but nothing prevented Davenant from using the word 'boy' here.

Contemporary attacks on the stage and its players level venom equally at 'boys' and 'men' who enact women. In *Playes Confuted in Five Actions* (1582), Gosson regrets how 'In Stage Playes … a boy (puts) on the attire, the gesture, the passions of a woman'. But John Rainolds in the *Th'overthrow of stage playes* (1599) asks his reader to 'condemne all stage-playes, wherein young men are trained to play such women's parts'. Prynne goes further in *Histrio-Mastix* (1633), citing 'Men-women actors' and 'our English Man-woman monsters'.[95] Prynne not only uses the word 'man', as Davenant, Jordan, and Rainolds do, but he criticizes the impersonations of females by men and by boys as *separate* acts of vice, once again suggesting that grown men were playing women on at least some stages. Since most critics acknowledge that Shakespeare demanded greater depth, range, stamina, and experience from those playing female roles in his plays than any of his contemporaries, shouldn't these 'Man-woman monsters' be supposed leading candidates for those roles?

Fortunately, some playgoers in Shakespeare's time documented their experiences of his plays, and their drawings and diaries can further help evaluate the claim for or against boy players. Take the familiar drawing of *Titus Andronicus*, attributed to Henry Peacham.[96] Peacham drew the scene with some care: armour, helmets, and spears are detailed; Tamora's dress shows elements of design and embroidery; Aaron's figure is darkened uniformly.

---

[94] Cited in Karl Mantzius, *A History of Theatrical Art in Ancient and Modern Times*, trans. Louise von Cossel, vol. II (London: Duckworth & Co., 1903), p. 280.

[95] The tracts are cited and briefly discussed in Chapter 2.

[96] Henry Peacham (c. 1567–1643). His drawing is most often dated 1595, though it's possible that it was made in the early seventeenth century. See Jonathan Bate's analysis of the drawing and its possible dating in his Arden edition of *Titus Andronicus* (London: Routledge, 1995), pp. 38–43.

Given the artist's skill and the details, it may be surprising to revisit it and find that the Tamora actor, though a 'woman' for lacking a beard and wearing a wig and women's dress, is *huge*. The figure is almost eye-to-eye with Titus, despite kneeling, and she is flanked by much smaller (adult) sons. The kneeling actor thus appears suited to one who rules the 'warlike Goths'. It is possible that Peacham drew the scene based on his imagination rather than his experience of a performance, but if the drawing does depict a scene onstage, and the figures are positioned as though they are, we have reason to suspect that the Tamora actor was an adult. In any case, Peacham had attended performances, and they would have informed his vision. What he drew suggests that Tamora was an imposing physical presence. The drawing gains interest if we consider Hippolyta, another early Shakespearean character. She too is a warlike queen, an Amazon, an internal detail that may excuse the large actor that Shakespeare expected to portray her. That idea is stronger for the fact that Hippolyta's counterpart, a role that can be doubled to advantage by the actor playing Hippolyta, is called Titania, a name advertising anything but a diminutive boy actor. The possibility that a large actor was expected here seems stronger still, given that Theseus had to woo Hippolyta 'with [his] sword'.

Several woodcuts and drawings from the period show no appreciable difference of height or girth between male and female characters on stage together. The 1632 drawing of a still from William Alabaster's *Roxana*, probably performed at The Cockpit, is one example. Differences in dress establish that two male characters and one female are on stage. One man is bearded; the woman is not. But the female character is as tall as either male. 'Her' dress and unshaven face are the actor's primary claims to womanhood. Given the actor's height, it is difficult to disqualify the 'woman' in the scene from adult male roles. Also revealing is the woodcut frontispiece for Middleton and Dekker's *The Roaring Girle, or Moll Cut-Purse* (1611), and the conceit of the play itself. The picture shows Mary 'Moll' Frith, the cross-dressing Virago who gives the play its name. The figure's theatrical pose and the wooden boards underfoot create the impression that the woodcut captures Moll as incarnated by an actor. And this actor is, we must believe, passable as a woman onstage in England in 1611, for 'she' at once presents the marriageable maid and that maid's martial front. The play depends on its audience to see Moll as a woman, even if she looks like the actor depicted. Whether the woodcut is meant to show Mary Frith, or the actor portraying her, we cannot but assume that the publisher thought the boy taking the part of Moll would not look like a boy at all – as 'her' well-muscled calves make evident.

The examples suggest that English audiences were attracted by tensions of ambiguous gendering, tensions that are likely to be dulled on stage when the actors representing men and women belong to wholly distinct age groups.

Figure 6.4 Panel from the frontispiece to William Alabaster's *Roxana* (1632). Folger STC 250.
Used by permission of the Folger Shakespeare Library under a Creative Commons Attribution-ShareAlike 4.0 International License.

The historical Moll attended a play at The Fortune around 1610, where it was reported that:

in man's apparel and in her boots and with a sword at her side she told the company then present that she thought many of them were of opinion that she was a man, but if any of them would come to her lodging they should finde she is a woman, and some other immodest and lascivious speeches she also used ...[97]

Theatre is energized for audiences when the gap between actor and character is wide, as it is to Moll's character and as it seems to have been for those who saw Mary Frith in person. The boys' companies experienced success using similarly aged actors of one gender to represent men and women, young and

---

[97] *Consistory of London Correction Book*, from Andrew Gurr's *The Culture of Playgoing in Shakespeare's London* (Cambridge: Cambridge University Press, 1996), p. 233.

old. Shakespeare's cast of sharers may have done the same thing with men in their twenties and thirties.

In 1617, Henry Fitzgeoffrey describes another androgynous figure making public appearances:

> Now Mars defend us! Seest thou who comes yonder?
> Monstrous! A Woman of the masculine Gender.
> Looke! Thou mayst well descry her by her groath,
> Out, point not man! Least wee be beaten both.
> Eye her a little, marke but where shee'l goe,
> Now (by this hand) into the Gallants Roe.[98]

Though the woman is considered perceptible by her 'groath', clearly not everyone saw through the façade. She capably passes for a male, since the author must 'descry' her by a sign. The excitement created by her duplicity, and the pleasure experienced by one seeing through it, may present an analogue for what Shakespeare's actors made available to audiences.

In 1654, Edmund Gayton writes about the theatre before the interregnum, how the players offered audiences a choice of plays, demonstrating the flexibility we see from players in *Hamlet* or *Sir Thomas More*.[99] Gayton reports that '*Tamerlane*', '*Jugurtha*', and '*The Jew of Malta*' were offered, but, 'none of the three taking, they were forced to undress and put off their tragick habits, and conclude the day with *The Merry Milkmaides*' to appease an exasperated crowd. Gayton here suggests that adult tragedians doffed their clothes so that the milkmaids could dance – that the *tragedians* became the maids. A company prepared to perform these Marlowe plays must have had a preponderance of adult males, but a dance of milkmaids asks for at least half the troupe to personate women. Such an anecdote, like the players not ready to perform because their 'queen' was shaving, means little in isolation. Collectively, however, the evidence speaks to the likelihood that at least some Elizabethan companies, and especially Shakespeare's, had at least some actors who played both male and female roles. This would have ensured that the Lord Chamberlain's/King's Men could work with casts of nine to 12 whenever they wished.

I have mentioned Thomas Platter's visit to the Globe for a production of *Julius Caesar* and his remark that 'when the play was over, they danced very marvelously and gracefully together as is their wont, two dressed as men and two as women'. The parallelism of 'two' and 'two' does not distinguish between actors in male dress and those dressed as women. He must have seen those known to history as Shakespeare's boy players, but if these actors were

---

[98] *Styres: and Satyricall Epigrams: with Certain Obserations at Blackfryers*, from Gurr, *The Culture of Playgoing*, p. 241.
[99] *Pleasant Notes upon Don Quixot* (London, 1654), p. 271.

different from the adult males onstage, Platter did not mention it. The sentence rather suggests that the 'boys' blended in seamlessly with other actors, allowing Platter to focus on the categories represented – *men* and *women* – without attention to differences in those doing the representing. In 1610, when Munday staged the sea pageant featuring Burbage and Rice atop a 'Whale' and a 'Dolphin', much is made of the difference in sizes between man and boy. If the talented adolescents and their maidenly voices were part of the production of *Julius Caesar*, Platter might have taken notice, particularly because he was a foreigner who would have seen other conventions of representation on the continent. The stage boy should have been a rare phenomenon to him, yet he is silent on the subject. This omission may occur, though, because the stage boys were not exceptional – because they were more like their fellow actors in age, body, and voice than has been supposed.

Another failure to notice the sensation of the boy actor is evident in the account of one who saw the King's Men's perform *Othello* in 1610 at Oxford, a tour brought on by the long closure of the London theatres and one for which the King's Men would presumably benefit by travelling with a lean cast. The playgoer records:

> They also had tragedies, well and effectively acted. In these they drew tears, not only by their speech, but also by their action. Indeed Desdemona, killed by her husband, in her death moved us especially when, as she lay in her bed, her face alone implored the pity of the audience.[100]

There is little to go on here, but we might reasonably expect that 'her' age would have stood out to the observer, as precocity was often singled out by those discussing boys' companies. The observer cannot have been fooled into thinking that the Desdemona actor was female. The illusion to which he subscribes would be no less complete if an adult man played the role.

Other eyewitness accounts of Shakespeare's plays are likewise notable for what fails to attract comment. In his first-hand account of 'Twelfth Night, or what you will' in 1602, John Manningham expresses delight at the scene in which Malvolio courts Olivia, but he makes no mention of the boy actor: 'A good practise in it to make the Steward believe his Lady widdowe was in Love with him.'[101] Simon Forman's accounts of plays at the Globe, while they rarely extend beyond plot summary, still fail to draw attention to the precocious boy actors in the roles of Lady Macbeth, Hermione, or Imogen. And Thomas Coryate, having returned from the continent, describes seeing actresses on stage, 'a thing that I never saw before – though I have heard that it hath been sometimes used in London –, and they performed it with as good a grace, action, gesture, and whatsoever convenient for a Player, as ever I saw any

---

[100] Translated from Latin by Rosenberg, in 'Elizabethan Actors', p. 98.
[101] John Manningham's *Diary*, cited by Gurr, *The Culture of Playgoing*, p. 111.

masculine Actor'.[102] Here again, Coryate neglects to compare these women to stage 'boys' or 'youths' of London. There were companies of boys, but Coryate's category – 'masculine actor(s)' – does not rule out adult men playing female roles in London.

(In-) Conclusion

My aim throughout this chapter has been to suggest that the category of boy actors can reasonably designate neither pre-pubescent boys nor late teenagers with a rare ability to leave their voices unbroken. Rather, the category more appropriately includes any relatively young actor or social inferior, very likely one who lacks a beard. When we refer to one of Shakespeare's boy actors, we have sufficient cause, evidence, and precedent to imagine a young adult in his twenties, possibly one of the adult sharers. Considering period anecdotes and Jordan's prologue, which suggest that adults appeared in female roles well after Shakespeare's time; the broad application of the term 'boy' in the period and in Shakespeare's plays; the ages of the apprentices as reflected by the law and the terms to which they were bound; the lack of evidence that any boy apprentice originated a female role for one of Shakespeare's plays; the lack of birthdates for those supposed to have done so; the probability that voice breaks were not delayed but that hair growth was; and the arguments of economy, versatility, and dramatic precedent advanced in previous chapters: all combine to support the claim that Shakespeare's heroines were likely played not by pre-pubescent boys, but by adult males. I suggest that the evidence reflects the high probability that adult sharers and hired men, most likely the relatively youthful or youthful-looking ones, were deployed to impersonate women; and that most apprentices who performed female roles would have been capable of doubling in male roles too, lest they become a liability to the company and the plays, and lest their tenure with the company be in violation of the law.

None of that is to say that teenaged boys did not participate or even originate some female roles during Shakespeare's tenure with the Lord Chamberlain's/ King's Men. As I have stated, nearly every play allows for one or two actors to specialize in female roles. But the company was not likely to have relied on teenaged boys exclusively for these roles when so many factors speak against it. While I cannot establish the precise age of Shakespeare's boys, and while it is possible that some teenaged apprentices played female roles for the company, the evidence within and around the plays clearly shows that references to adult male actors playing women in the period are not unusual, and that

---

[102] In Thomas Coryate, *Coryat's Crudities* (Glasgow: Macmillan and Co. Ltd., 1906), p. 386.

Shakespeare's company seems more likely than others to have engaged in the practice. Moreover, his dramaturgical structures reflect a call for versatility across small casts, and across the repertory, that is economic, sensible, and improving. In short, the 'gains' involved in engaging older rather than adolescent (or pre-adolescent) boys were substantial. Older boys might reasonably be regarded as more versatile; they could be more extensively trained; they were more experienced; and they had stronger voices, this last being crucial in open-air theatres. The prospective downsides of employing younger boys, meanwhile, were many: frequent, disruptive turnover of acting talent; continual need to recruit and train new apprentices; financial loss; legal peril for neglecting apprenticeship articles. To say nothing of Hamlet's own worries: 'What are they children? Who maintains 'em? How are they escorted? Will they pursue the quality no longer than they can sing?' (2.2.331–3).

Was there anything to be *gained* from employing young boys in such a setting? The answer would seem to be no. To imagine that the company stood at the mercy of such boys' biological development is to ignore the six-year run of the tall blonde and short dark actors, presumably both young men; to ignore the need of many of Shakespeare's female characters to believe that they can convincingly impersonate men – and then to impersonate men convincingly; to ignore the many 'boys' who impersonate women across five years or more, such as Dick Robinson and William Trigge; to ignore the influx of boys and former boys around 1610 and the gradual decrease in the ages of apprentices thereafter; to ignore the relative paucity of apprentices associated with the company before 1600; to dismiss as anomalous clear evidence that actors as old as 21 played female roles for the King's Men; and to ignore the insight available to anyone who, in reflecting on the casting of *Macbeth*'s witches, takes Banquo's observation at face value: 'You should be women, / Yet your beards forbid me to interpret / That you are so' (1.3.46–8).

7   Doubling in *Twelfth Night* and *Othello*

℘〇℘

And if these four Worthies in their first show thrive,
These four will change habits and present the other five!

~Love's Labour's Lost, 5.2.534–5

℘〇℘

Twelfth Night with Ten

In performance, the meeting of Sebastian and Viola in *Twelfth Night* is rare for its ability to excite both fascination and hilarity. On one hand, audiences are typically spellbound watching the twins' reunion, the suspense building as they work through a lengthy list of confirmations, repeatedly failing to acknowledge that they are brother and sister. On the other, some lines and interjections are sufficiently at odds with that tension as to surprise the audience and increase the scene's comic force, Olivia's 'Most wonderful' being the most famous such line. Because it intrudes upon the as-yet-unrealized reunion and follows hard upon a revelation that her new husband comes with a clone, the line typically carries sufficient overtones of sexual excess despite its seeming innocence to bring down the house. When I staged the play, Olivia had great success with 'most wonderful', but she got even more sustained laughter from a line that seems entirely unremarkable. It comes soon after Sebastian's entrance, when Olivia remembers that Malvolio may be just the person to help find Viola's missing frock:

> VIOLA The captain that did bring me first on shore
> Hath my maid's garments. He upon some action
> Is now in durance at Malvolio's suit,
> A gentleman and follower of my lady's.
> OLIVIA He shall enlarge him. [*to Attendant*] *Fetch Malvolio hither.*
>
> (5.1.264–8, italics mine)

I will not argue that 'Fetch Malvolio hither' is a great comic line. What made it one in this case was the necessity for a ten-member cast to send for Malvolio by means of an 'Officer' – an officer formerly known as 'Malvolio'. That is, the line was addressed to the Malvolio actor, the only person onstage capable of producing the character in question. Upon hearing the request, the officer simply nodded his head and walked off to get cross-gartered.

With striking consistency at each performance, audiences were surprised by the simultaneous rightness and wrongness of the circumstance: right because the actor playing the officer was the one person who must exit so that Malvolio could arrive; wrong because the person the officer went to find was already here. After a brief outburst, crowds tended to go nervously quiet, as if waiting for the actor playing Malvolio to notice what the production was up to. The actor did not break character as the officer, but he learned to slow down the exit, as if at the will of an audience waiting for acknowledgement that a kind of confidence game, concerning the artifice of the character and the play, had begun between itself and him.

Having Malvolio fetch himself is a gimmick, but it's a theatrically vital-izing one that complements the scene's central concerns. The choice makes a nondescript officer a site of fascination and pleasure without suspending the plot. In fact, the scene's momentary priority, Malvolio's arrival, becomes more interesting than it can be otherwise, because his arrival seems both more certain and more unlikely. Doubling roles always makes similar, though subtler, plays on each character's fluidity and essential unreality, advertising the actor's multiplicity *and* limitations in the same instant. The scene's major concern is the meeting of twins who test our ability to credit the illusion by claiming a likeness that cannot be in evidence (assuming the production doesn't cast identical twins); when the Malvolio–Officer double is utilized, the actor can achieve a parallel effect, presenting a kind of twin who cannot recognize himself. The audience becomes the uncertain partner of a bilateral anagnorisis, invited to recognize Malvolio even as it tries (and fails) to withstand the force of that recognition for the sake of the plot. While *Twelfth Night* can obviously succeed without asking Malvolio to exit in search of himself, I linger over the choice as an example of how doubling roles, even insignificant ones, can reveal latent sources of energy to further a play's aims.

The hypothetical doubling plan in Table 7.1 is arranged for ten. *Twelfth Night* resembles other plays written near the turn of the century (e.g. *Hamlet*, *Othello*) in that it has relatively few characters. Its 18 speaking roles can be distributed among ten actors, the number appearing in the limiting scene (5.1). Interestingly, the same lines that enable the Officer to fetch himself allow the same actor to augment the play's thematic coherence in another way.

Table 7.1 *Hypothetical doubling plan for Shakespeare's* Twelfth Night *(c. 1601)*

Twelfth Night
c. 1601 (F)
❧ The division of the parts ☙

Orsino 2 Officer	} For one actor	Viola	} For one actor
		Olivia	} For one actor
Curio Andrew Aguecheek	} For one actor	Maria Sebastian	} For one actor
Toby Belch	} For one actor	Sea Captain	
Valentine Antonio	} For one actor	Malvolio Officer	} For one actor
Sailor Fabian Servant	} For one actor	Sailor Feste Priest	} For one actor

Malvolio is wanted not for his presence alone but because he can produce the man necessary to help Cesario complete 'his' return to Viola:

> VIOLA The captain that did bring me first on shore
> Hath my maid's garments. He upon some action
> Is now in durance at Malvolio's suit,
> A gentleman and follower of my lady's. (5.1.264–7)

These lines can feel disorienting. The character we know to have been 'in durance' is not the Captain but Malvolio himself, whom Toby and Maria imprisoned after failing in his laughable suit to Olivia.[1] When or why the Captain has been imprisoned is unknown, and Malvolio is unlikely to have arranged his arrest, given that he has been locked up. But the Captain's otherwise inexplicable imprisonment makes sense, seems even fitting and necessary, when Malvolio doubles as the Captain. As Stephen Booth notes, the ambiguous potential of the word 'suit' establishes a link between the two characters.[2] In the present context 'suit' means 'petition', but if a production

---

[1] The officers have also arrested another sea captain in Antonio by this point in the play, who presumably has been 'in durance' before his appearance in 5.1.

[2] Stephen Booth first noticed the thematic parallels between the Captain and Malvolio and first suggested the Maria/Sebastian pairing. See 'Speculations on Doubling', pp. 147–8.

doubles the roles, the Captain has been confined, literally, in Malvolio's *suit*. That the Captain has been imprisoned upon some 'action' strengthens the link, because the need for the performer to 'act' Malvolio's part and wear his 'suit' explains his subsequent omission from the plot. The Captain is in durance because he has lost his own clothes, an idea the play exploits by indicating that he is the keeper of Viola's 'maiden's weeds' and thus critical to her ability to exchange one persona for another. Wherever Malvolio goes, the Captain goes as well – theatrically, if not in the plot – a possibility the lines support by suggesting that one is trapped by the other. Meanwhile, the choice to double the roles complements the effects initiated by the reunion of two others who look alike and wear matching suits – Viola and Sebastian.

After Malvolio storms off in the last act, Orsino commands 'Pursue him and entreat him to a peace. / He hath not told us of the captain yet' (5.1.366–7), again noting that Malvolio is key to finding the Captain. Such lines are reminiscent of Lear's 'my poor fool is hanged' in seeming to sanction and comment on a casting choice – indeed, to promote this choice as a position that best reflects the evidence. In other words, while the lines cannot prove how the King's Men cast *Twelfth Night*, they show what *Twelfth Night* was engineered to make possible, a choice that makes the play richer and more coherent. To assume that the Captain and Malvolio were played by two actors is, in some sense, tantamount to assuming that the fascinating potentials afforded by these plays were lost on Shakespeare's company, or else wilfully overlooked for the sake of involving more people in productions.

The Captain's only appearance comes early in *Twelfth Night* (1.2), but the thematic and linguistic apparatus for binding him to Malvolio is already developing. Viola asks the Captain for particulars about Olivia's household (about things Malvolio would know) in a dialogue punctuated by references to disguise and dress:

> CAPTAIN   That were hard to compass,
> Because she will admit no kind of suit,
> No, not the Duke's.
> VIOLA   There is a fair behavior in thee, Captain,
> And though that nature with a beauteous wall
> Doth oft close in pollution, yet of thee
> I will believe thou hast a mind that suits
> With this, thy fair and outward character.
> I pray thee (and I'll pay thee bounteously)
> Conceal me what I am, and be my aid
> For such disguise as haply shall become
> The form of my intent. I'll serve this duke.   (1.2.43–54)

The variations on the word 'suit' anticipate the suit Malvolio uses to confine the Captain later in the play, while creating a context germane to Viola's decision to disguise herself and serve Orsino. In context, 'suit' denotes 'petition' (1.44) and 'matches' (1.49); yet Viola's thoughts turn to disguise, and the resulting exchange implicates the Captain in a plot to conceal one person in the habit of another. None of this confirms that the Captain also changes into Malvolio's clothes, but it is doubtful that an actor playing a prominent role in the play's second scene would have sat idly backstage for the remaining acts.

Notably, Viola comments on the prospect that the Captain's exterior may not be consonant with his interior: 'nature with a beauteous wall / Doth oft close in pollution'. Having suggested that his true identity may be hidden, she then plans her own transformation, and the Captain agrees to keep her secret: 'Be you his eunuch, and your mute I'll be. / When my tongue blabs, then let mine eyes not see' (1.2.61–2). If the actor doubles as Malvolio, these exchanges gain considerable force. The actor playing both roles would for instance, as Malvolio, show how a well-looking 'wall' can 'close in pollution'. Malvolio is a puritan whom Toby describes as 'virtuous' but whose name means 'ill-willed', and he secretly harbours desires for Olivia along with petty grudges against others in her household. The actor will also complicate the Captain's promise to be secret, since one of his first duties in the play is to describe – at great length – Cesario's appearance – an appearance at odds with 'his' nature. Olivia questions the steward about Cesario's age and features, whose responses gradually betray the possibility that Cesario is not what he seems. So, in announcing Orsino's messenger, Malvolio's 'tongue blabs' concerning the very secrets the Captain had promised to keep.

When the roles are double-cast, the encounter between Malvolio and Cesario in 2.2, in which Malvolio 'returns' Olivia's ring, will inversely echo the exchange between the Captain and Viola, again using the language of disguise to comment on the 'poor monster' Cesario has become, and the no less paradoxical situation of the Malvolio actor. The initial plan is thus abandoned by both characters, the Captain no longer a mute just as Viola is no longer a eunuch. Meanwhile, Viola is a noblewoman who impersonates a servant, and who promises to pay the Captain bounteously, while Malvolio is a servant who impersonates a nobleman, then offers a ring to Cesario. Viola experiments with impersonation and crossing gender boundaries within the fiction; the actor playing the Captain and Malvolio can perform similar experiments at its margins, both the actor and the character of Captain then providing valuable analogues for Viola and complementing the dualities she manifests.

Companies leave a lot on the table when they choose not to double the roles, since prisons, language, disguise, clothing, and Viola's duplicity and confidences help bind the two together. Because the play is constructed so that ten actors can fill 18 roles, *somebody* must have doubled as the Captain. Forging so many links between him and Malvolio does not make sense unless the playwright is anticipating the possibility that one actor will take both roles. When viewed in the context of so many other roles linked by similar strategies (e.g. Tybalt being suddenly revealed as the Nurse's 'best friend') the links here cannot be supposed anomalous or accidental. Instead, the series of correspondences invites and seems to anticipate doubling.

Malvolio's 'suit' to confine the Captain echoes not only the exchanges between the Captain and Viola, but also the arrest of Antonio after he (mistakenly) comes to Viola's defence:

> FIRST OFFICER   This is the man; do thy office.
> SECOND OFFICER Antonio, I arrest thee at the suit of Count Orsino.
> ANTONIO   You do mistake me, sir.
> FIRST OFFICER   No sir, no jot. I know your favour well,
>   Though now you have no seacap on your head.
>   – Take him away. He knows I know him well.   (3.4.293–8)

Here the notion of a proxy, one character standing in for another, extends the theme of doubling and disguise at the heart of the play. The Second Officer arrests Antonio in Orsino's name. In my production, Orsino and Malvolio doubled as the two speaking officers, allowing Orsino to convey his own petition in the role of First Officer, and leaving Malvolio – who has apparently had a sea captain arrested already – to arrest Antonio at Orsino's 'suit'. If the Orsino actor calls for the arrest, or makes it himself, an otherwise ordinary moment gains interest. Malvolio's presence in Orsino's company, strange as it may seem, has some textual precedent, too, since Feste appears to freelance between the two households despite being in Olivia's charge. The officers' language when arresting Antonio reaffirms the idea that *clothes* are the primary means to identify people, the First Officer seeming proud to have spotted Antonio even without his 'seacap'.[3] Viola, Sebastian, and Feste (as Sir Topas) all rely on garment rather than favour to distinguish man from man. Antonio's impromptu defence relies on the possibility of mistaken identity, but, if Orsino doubles as the officer, the officer has reason to see through Antonio's 'disguise'.

Orsino's recognition of Antonio may generate more interest if Antonio, absent from the first two acts, had formerly been serving as a lord in Orsino's court, a choice likely required for a cast keeping within the limits imposed by the structure. He is a good candidate to fill the role of Valentine, who mentors Cesario when the latter comes into Orsino's service, much as Antonio looks

---

[3] See *The Winter's Tale*, 'they were to be known by garment not by favour' (5.2.43–4), Autolycus in his several manifestations, or Borachio and Margaret at Hero's chamber window in *Much Ado About Nothing*.

after Sebastian after their arrival in Illyria. The actor would thus perform twin functions for a pair of twins, while being an intimate (and enemy) of Orsino. Like the Captain, Valentine disappears from the play entirely before the first act is complete, freeing the actor for additional work.

Sebastian is one possibility for the Valentine actor, but there are more interesting candidates for Viola's twin brother. Just as the sudden announcement of the Captain's imprisonment at the hands of Malvolio may be a link between roles suited for doubling, so one of the most surprising moments in any play – the announcement of Toby and Maria's marriage – may reveal a playwright mapping out and incentivizing an opportunity for double-casting. I have discussed Maria's conspicuous absence from the finale of *Twelfth Night* already. But, oddly, the news of Maria and Toby's marriage, however improbable considering the circumstances, may be the least improbable part of Fabian's speech:

> Most freely I confess myself and Toby
> Set this device against Malvolio here,
> Upon some stubborn and uncourteous parts
> We had conceived against him. Maria writ
> The letter, at Sir Toby's great importance,
> In recompence whereof he hath married her. (5.1.347–52)

This all sounds reasonable, but – except for the wedding – it's pure fiction. Fabian had nothing to do with setting the 'device' against Malvolio; he hadn't entered the play when Maria and Toby conceived the plan. Feste was there, but there was not yet any indication that Fabian existed. Moreover, Toby did not ask Maria to write the letter. Rather, she concocted the plan alone and won praise from Toby for doing so.[4] As a result, what is shocking news – that Toby married Maria in the stolen moments between torturing Malvolio and earning himself a bloody coxcomb – seems the most credible thing on the list. The false narrative, though, may be a device of the playwright's, to help conceal or naturalize another, even more glaring improbability: just as Fabian now appears to have been present in a scene he didn't participate in, so Maria may be present in this scene without really being there.

Maria is the only major character absent from the final scene, raising the possibility that the playwright anticipated the actor might be needed elsewhere. If not, her absence is indefensible. The comedy ends with two improbable couplings. If Maria is backstage, why would she not enter and receive

---

[4] See 2.3.40–60.

congratulations for making up a third? The play takes incremental steps, though, to sanction the possibility that she is onstage – as Sebastian.[5] If Maria was played by a young man capable of female roles, it should be difficult to imagine a better candidate for Sebastian – the young lord who is often mistaken for his twin sister. Such a casting choice was seen elsewhere in the period, such as when the Bernard actor is asked to double Mistress Flower in *The Fair Maid of the Exchange*. Here, the choice allows the twin brother and sister to be twins to a degree otherwise impossible – each disguised by gender as well as dress, each thereby closer to discovery and reunion throughout the play (as Cesario and Maria), yet prevented by their outward personas from perceiving the sibling in the figure so nearby.

Doubling Sebastian and Maria has significant benefits for audiences already tracking the play's gender-based ambiguities and representational feats. The actor's transformation from one character to the other alternately resonates with and realizes Viola's own predicament as a 'poor monster', because she is both man and woman and also caught between a man and a woman (Orsino and Olivia). Sebastian seems to be pursued – perhaps romantically as well as physically – by both Antonio and Olivia, extending the parallelism of the two characters' situations. As Cesario, Viola is fit for neither Orsino nor Olivia; conversely, the actor playing Sebastian and Maria suits either Toby or Olivia (or Antonio) depending on his or her momentary chromosomal make-up.[6] Sebastian's dialogue helps suggest the character's potentially ambiguous gendering when he tells Antonio 'Fare ye well at once. My bosom is full of kindness, and I am yet so near the manners of my mother that upon the least occasion more mine eyes will tell tales of me' (2.1.33–6). The emphasis on Sebastian's feminine qualities links him more closely to the twin sister for whom he is mistaken, but it also may serve to highlight the gender reversals being carried out by an actor performing both male and female roles. Antonio's seemingly romantic desire for Sebastian ('I do adore thee so' 2.1.41) further emphasizes Sebastian's femininity, while the reference to Maria as a 'giant' in need of mollifying may suggest her masculine aspect, together making the actor another 'poor monster' to pair with Viola/Cesario.[7]

---

[5] Booth suggests the possibility in 'Speculations on Doubling', p. 146.

[6] Note, too, the inverse tenor of the relationship between the Captain and Viola in that of Malvolio and Cesario.

[7] See also the exchange between Viola and Orsino, wherein Viola describes one Orsino supposes is a mistress in terms applicable to Orsino himself, thereby somewhat feminizing Orsino,

> ORSINO What kind of woman is't?
> VIOLA   Of your complexion.
> ORSINO She is not worth thee then. What years, i'faith?
> VIOLA   About your years, my lord.   (2.4.24–6)

That Sebastian takes on an alternate identity – calling himself Roderigo – makes the prospect of doubling him still more advantageous by adding a layer of deception to an already layered deception. It lends casual sanction to casting the actor duplicitously, outside the fiction, much as he and Viola recast themselves within it. Sebastian subverts his identity further when revealing himself to Antonio:

> You must know of me then, Antonio, my name is Sebastian, which I called Roderigo. My father was that Sebastian of Messaline whom I know you have heard of. He left behind him myself and a sister, both born in an hour.   (2.1.13–17)

Here Sebastian, who is 'so near the manners of (his) mother' and whom Antonio adores, willingly adopts a split persona. Meanwhile, Sebastian is already a double in two senses: as Viola's twin, and as his father's namesake. The dualities that inform his character help suit him for double-casting – particularly with Maria who proves capable of 'putting down' men such as Andrew, with whom he later comes to blows. And since Viola calls Maria a 'good swabber', potentially a bit of seaman's banter between a brother and sister lost to one another in a shipwreck, the play works to create interest in the pairing.

As for Maria, she too displays an inclination for deceit and impersonation. Her plan to make a 'common recreation' of Malvolio, for instance, focuses intensely on ideas of replication and resemblance:

> I will drop in his way some obscure epistles of love, wherein by the colour of his beard, the shape of his leg, the manner of his gait, the expressure of his eye, forehead, and complexion he shall find himself most feelingly personated. I can write very like my lady, your niece. On a forgotten matter we can hardly make distinction of our hands.   (2.3.143–8)

Maria can mimic (double) the handwriting of Olivia, and she plans to use her skill to 'personate' Malvolio in the letter. In effect, she impersonates Olivia impersonating Malvolio in *writing* – itself a representation of thoughts or speech. Moreover, Maria casually posits Olivia's dual identity through apposition: 'my lady, your niece'. Such examples may seem incidental products of language, but they gain energy when the speaker plays multiple roles in a play obsessed with imitation and resemblance.

Andrew also exemplifies the play's interest in imitation. According to my chart he doubles as Curio, but more interesting is the way he 'doubles' Toby's speech and manner throughout the play. After Maria describes her plan to embarrass Malvolio, Toby expresses his delight: 'Excellent, I smell a device', which Andrew quickly seconds, 'I have't in my nose too' (2.3.149–50). The entire role can be summed up as variations on 'me too'. This 'me too' phenomenon is extended as characters repeatedly measure themselves against everyone in Illyria. Toby tells Maria that Andrew is 'as tall a man as any's in Illyria' (1.3.18); Andrew claims that he can dance as well 'As any man in Illyria' (1.3.104); Malvolio, imprisoned, tells Feste 'I am as well in my wits as any man in Illyria' (4.2.102). And so on.[8] Such comparisons based on one man being like any other help generate a context for the thematic doubles and disguises with which the play is concerned.

The antithesis inherent in doubling Sebastian and Maria finds parallels in other characters and actors. Much as Andrew mimics Toby's speech and behaviour to lesser effect, so Feste mimics those around him, perhaps nowhere so effectively as when he pretends to be a priest.[9] Feste takes it upon himself (at Maria's suggestion) to impersonate Sir Topas, alternating between two personas in his interview with Malvolio and thus offering the prisoner contradictory responses to his pleas for help. When Malvolio asks Sir Topas and Feste to 'go to my lady', Feste answers (as Sir Topas), 'Out, hyperbolical fiend, how vexest thou this man! Talkest thou nothing but of ladies?' (4.2.23–4), but then says in his own voice, 'I will help you to't. But tell me true, are you not mad indeed, or do you but counterfeit?' (4.2.107–8). The Fool thus alternates between roles while projecting his own deceit onto Malvolio, a character who is not deceitful save for impersonating a nobleman when at leisure – although, as we have seen, the actor may also take turns as officers and sea captains within the play. In addition, Sir Topas demands an extension of Malvolio's prison sentence and Feste facilitates his release, much as Sebastian and Maria alternate in wounding Toby and dressing his wound.

Peculiarly, Maria has Feste put on a disguise ('this gown and this beard') to play the priest, the clothes once again making the man. But Feste's disguise is pointless, since Malvolio cannot see him. Maria acknowledges that he might have carried out the deception just as well without the disguise, so the play appears to include a superfluous costume change merely to extend

---

[8] Perhaps the best example occurs in 2.5, when Toby sets to praising Maria for gulling Malvolio,

> SIR TOBY Wilt thou set thy foot o'my neck?
> ANDREW Or o'mine either?
> SIR TOBY Shall I play my freedom at tray-trip and become thy bondslave?
> ANDREW I'faith, or I either?   (2.5.163–7)

After the others exit, Andrew follows, saying 'I'll make one too' (2.5.81).

[9] Feste's interest in ambiguity is well known. His willful misunderstanding of Malvolio and Cesario and his exploitation of secondary and tertiary semantic senses of words and phrases also harmonize with the kinds of doubling, replication, and secondary signification on which I focus here. See, for example, 'A sentence is but a chev'rel glove to a good wit. How quickly the wrong side may be turned outward' (3.1.10–12).

the theme of people wearing other people's 'suits'. By dressing as Sir Topas, Feste also renews his play-long effort to merge secular and spiritual ideas. He offers to 'catechize' Olivia about her brother, calling her his 'mouse of virtue' (1.5.55–6), though when Viola later asks whether he is a churchman, Feste denies it: 'I do live by the church, for I do live at my house, and my house doth stand by the church' (3.1.5–6). And he reveals further internal complexity by assisting Malvolio and behaving reasonably towards him in his own person (a fool), though he is useless and cruel when disguised as the churchman.

Given the play's efforts to assign priestly language to the Fool, a company may be wise to cast the Feste actor as the *real* priest who enters to marry Olivia and the man she thinks is Cesario. After his turn as Sir Topas, Feste can be electrifying as the real priest merely by standing still, since the audience is familiar with him in the role and cannot but anticipate the kind of role-playing and hyperbole witnessed in the scene with Malvolio. However soberly this Priest fulfils his function, the presence of the same actor, likely in the same beard and gown, will retain a sense of possibility and dynamism that will energize an otherwise ordinary scene. The Priest is called to verify the marriage between Olivia and Cesario: a marriage that, fittingly, has not really taken place, since he and Olivia are unaware that Sebastian took his sister's place at the altar.[10] The moment is thus, paradoxically, comic and sincere, an effect enhanced when Feste appears (sincerely this time) in the Priest's robes. The play has long insisted that Feste is the character who best knows how to behave as a priest. So the choice surprises spectators with the thing they should perhaps have most expected. Again, doubling augments the play's central themes, in this case making a kind of religious version of the 'man-woman monster' that is Viola (and Maria/Sebastian). The Feste/Priest actor thus appears as a fool who co-opts a priest's language for comic ends; a fool mimicking a priest called Sir Topas; a fool denying all association with the church; and lastly, a real priest who is a dead ringer for the Fool.

As suggested, the repeated mistaking of Viola for Sebastian (and vice versa) can seem ridiculous, as can their inability to recognize one another in the final scene. But the mistakes may seem less ridiculous, even natural, if a production complements the mistakes and confusions through doubling. At the end, Orsino leads the cast offstage, telling Viola, 'Cesario, come – / For so you shall be while you are a man – / But when in other habits you are seen,

---

[10] 5.1.149–56.

/ Orsino's mistress, and his fancy's queen' (5.1.371–4). For Orsino, clothes determine Viola's name and gender, as other 'habits' have done throughout the play. Shakespeare here blurs boundaries of gender and identity at the end of a play which has done so throughout. Fabian confesses to a crime he didn't commit, and tells of a marriage that audiences can neither deny nor reasonably imagine – one that may seem truly impossible because 'Maria' is onstage as a newly married man. Meanwhile, the Fool is a false priest and a real one; Malvolio is in durance at Olivia's suit, has the Captain in durance at his, yet may be the officer who enforces the suits of others and even apprehends himself. All these potential pairings, impersonations, and copies surround a pair of twins (doubles) whose meeting Orsino describes in provocative terms: 'One face, one voice, one habit and two persons – / A natural perspective that is and is not' (5.1.206–7). The lines seem like a meta-commentary on the play's willingness to let each character's identity depend wholly on 'suits' and 'habits', the stuff doubling roles is made on. Given all this, a stage full of impostors, actors seen in many habits as many people, is ideally suited to *Twelfth Night*.

Trading 'Places' in *Othello*

The first known performance of *Othello* occurred in November of 1604. Shakespeare wrote the play during the same era that produced *Twelfth Night* and *Measure for Measure*, plays with which it has much in common, including a relatively short dramatis personae.[11] With only 23 speakers, and a vast majority of its action focused on just six – Othello, Iago, Cassio, Desdemona, Emilia, and Roderigo – one might expect limited potential for doubling, especially since some characters rarely leave the stage.[12] Nevertheless, *Othello* is rich with possibilities to further the play's thematic ends through double casting. T.J. King analyses the lean list of characters and concludes that the (longer) Folio text requires 'seven men (for) eleven principal male roles, and three boys (for) three principal female roles', though he anticipates an additional nine men and two boys were necessary to fill nine other speaking parts and several mutes.[13]

---

[11] This discussion draws principally on the Folio text, though the required number of actors and the possibilities for doubling apply to the Quarto of 1622 as well. For the date of first performance, see Chambers, *William Shakespeare*, vol. 2, p. 331.

[12] Iago, for example, appears in all but two scenes. One of these (2.2) consists only of the Herald's invitation to begin revelling, while the other (4.3) finds Desdemona singing 'willow' before bed. Cassio is absent only from these two and the first scene outside Brabantio's window. On the small number of characters, compare such plays as *Macbeth* (36 speakers) or *Antony and Cleopatra* (52).

[13] King, *Casting Shakespeare's Plays*, p. 91.

Like *Twelfth Night*, though, *Othello* can be performed uncut with just ten actors. Its largest scene (1.3) features 12 speakers, but the play is built to accommodate ten, provided that the Messengers who bring news about the Turkish fleet retire and re-emerge as members of Othello's retinue, and that the Officer dispatched with Iago to 'Fetch Desdemona hither' (1.3.121) can do his duty by putting on a dress offstage.[14] Ten is precisely the number of speakers necessary in 2.1, the second largest scene, and it allows for smooth transitions between all others, most notably when the six speakers who exit at the end of 1.2 give way to four others who initiate 1.3.

Table 7.2 presents a speculative doubling plan for *Othello* with ten actors. According to the plan nine actors speak over 100 lines across at least four acts, while the tenth has little work after Act Two.[15] As a result, it may be that the play wants only nine, which is possible if the Officer sent to Othello in 1.2 is redeployed as the one announcing the Messengers in 1.3, thus freeing the Emilia actor to play Second Senator.[16] Of course, it is also possible the play was intended for nine, with brief appearances of other characters being the lot of musicians (who are characters in the fiction), those in training, or those doing mainly offstage duties for the company.[17]

Whether the play best accommodates nine or ten, the chart shows how *Othello* facilitates extensive and thematically influential doubling. Its two-part structure transfers the action from one location to another, while leaving many characters behind for good. In the Duke, Brabantio, and the two Senators

---

[14] Neither F nor Q indicates exits for Sailor or Messenger. Though stage directions are often incomplete or erroneous, the Duke provides a verbal cue for the messenger's exit by commanding a follower to 'Write from us to him, post-post-haste. – Dispatch!' (1.3.46).

[15] Several of Shakespeare's plays written in the years 1601–1604 appear to feature a smaller dramatis personae and rely on fewer actors than earlier plays, perhaps in response to the significant turnover of personnel the company experienced in those years. Like other plans in the book, this one accounts for all identified mutes (though additional officers, musicians, torchbearers, and other attendants may have been used when available).

[16] Third Gentleman will also need to exit at 2.1.42 and return as Emilia at line 81. His lines do sanction an exit, since Montano's suggestion, 'Let's to the sea-side, ho!' elicits his eager compliance: 'Come, let's do so, / For every minute is expectancy / Of more arrivancy' (2.1.36–42). Cassio's arrival prevents the group from leaving, but Third Gentleman can depart after his speech. While no exit is indicated for him at that point, he is also left out of the later stage directions.

[17] Catherine Belsey has written about the possibility that Shakespeare's company used parts for pages and messengers to help train apprentices, noting that 'at least 20 of the plays include minor parts for pages and young boys', such as Fleance in *Macbeth*, the boy singer in *Measure for Measure*, and Benedick's boy in *Much Ado About Nothing* ('Shakespeare's Little Boys', p. 55). Apprentices may well have been used in small roles like these; the plays could then take advantage of the doubling patterns embedded within them while leaving such stray parts for actor training.

Table 7.2 *Hypothetical doubling plan for Shakespeare's* Othello *(c. 1604)*

Othello
c. 1604 (Q, F)
❧ The division of the parts ☙

Iago	⎬ For one actor	Duke	⎫
		Montano	⎬ For one actor
Othello	⎬ For one actor	1 Musician	⎭
Officer (1.2)	⎫	Brabantio	⎫
Desdemona	⎬ For one actor	3 Gentleman	⎬ For one actor
Bianca	⎭	Gratiano	⎭
Roderigo	⎫	1 Senator	⎫
Messenger (1.3)	⎬ For one actor	1 Gentleman	⎬ For one actor
Clown	⎭	Lodovico	⎭
Cassio	⎫ For one actor	2 Senator	⎫
Sailor	⎭	2 Gentleman	⎬
Officer (1.3)	⎫ For one actor	Herald	For one actor
Emilia	⎭	2 Musician (mute)	⎭

Shakespeare's company should have employed four verse-speakers of considerable ability, yet their night's work would end with Act One if they did not take on other roles. In the second act, the play moves to Cyprus, where its governor, Montano, and two 'gentlemen' await the landing of the Venetian ships. The scene presents a striking parallel to the newly abandoned court at Venice. The plot thus requires three similar people in three similar roles, and their subject of conversation – the impending Turkish wars and the arrival of Othello – are the very things previously discussed by the Duke and Senators. That each trio is made a foursome through a late arrival – Third Gentleman brings news and joins the conversation in 2.1, much as Brabantio arrives late to the Duke's council chamber – augments the parallelism, as does the fact that each scene's focus on the Turks is temporarily suspended by news of Desdemona, 'our great captain's captain' (2.1.74).

I venture that it is a more aggressive speculation to say that the roles were not written with doubling in mind than to say that they were, since the play so thoroughly correlates the scenes. These roles are further associated by the Duke's explanation for why Othello must leave for Cyprus: 'Othello, the fortitude of the place is best known to you, and, though *we have a substitute there of most allowed sufficiency, yet opinion ... throws a more safer voice on you*' (1.3.221–4, italics mine). *Othello* is often concerned with substitution. The word 'substitute' and its variants occur more frequently in this play than in any other, finding a rival only in *Measure for Measure*.[18] Here, the play goes out of its way to mention that someone – Montano – is already standing in for the Duke in Cyprus, and that the stand-in is a man 'of most allowed sufficiency'. This language of substitution contributes to a context of replacements that began with the play's first lines, in which Iago complains that Cassio has taken the 'place' that should have been his. That context is enhanced when the Duke appears in Cyprus *as* Montano, in his own place, and alongside his usual fellows. The Duke proposes that Othello replace Montano, who serves in the Duke's place, the result suggesting that the Moor is a potential substitute for both Montano and the Duke. In this case, doubling the Duke and Montano connects the dots, literalizing the relationship implied by Othello's perceived potential to stand for both. Much like the Prince's sudden revelation that Mercutio and Paris make up 'a brace of kinsmen', such language may link characters expected to be doubled in performance.

All four characters appear across Acts Two and Three, but only Montano continues into the fourth act. Unsurprisingly, the plot abandons the Gentlemen shortly before it needs to introduce Gratiano and Lodovico.[19] Like Brabantio and the first Senator in Act One, these Venetians speak a lot in their short time onstage. Since their entrances are delayed until Act Four, the actors should have been previously engaged. Again, we find some textual basis to assume that they would likely have played Brabantio and the Senator. Lodovico arrives in Cyprus bearing an 'especial commission' from 'the Duke and the senators of Venice', on whose behalf he greets Othello just before Othello strikes Desdemona in a rage. The Lodovico actor is thus suited to playing both a commissioner and the one commissioned, and it may add interest if he has played the senator who bade Othello a now prescient good-bye: 'Adieu, brave Moor; use Desdemona well' (1.3.288). The more interesting pair, though, is Brabantio and Gratiano, a possibility suggested by Meagher and one sometimes seen in productions. Gratiano is Desdemona's formerly unnamed uncle who goes on to inherit Othello's wealth at the play's close. Meagher argues the appropriateness of having Brabantio 'virtually and actively present' for Desdemona's death, and for using the Brabantio actor to relate the cause of Brabantio's death (Desdemona's 'unhappy match') while staring at his now lifeless daughter. Shakespeare's design thus allows Brabantio to see 'the tragic

---

[18] I discuss *Measure for Measure* and its plays on substitution of actors as well as characters in the Epilogue.

[19] Third Gentleman (or the third gentleman accompanying Montano in 2.3 and possibly Othello in 3.2) never speaks after Emilia enters the play, perhaps strengthening the argument for doubling these roles and using nine actors.

ruin of his beloved daughter through the match which he had so vehemently opposed'.[20]

The choice to double these roles has further textual sanction and value in performance. For instance, Gratiano enters 5.1 to find Iago and Roderigo crying aloud in the night. Cassio has been maimed while fighting with Roderigo, and Iago is yelling for everyone to awake and see the carnage that he has created. The scene thus rhymes with 1.1, wherein Iago and Roderigo raise a midnight clamour and wake Brabantio with news of his daughter's flight. Both Brabantio and Gratiano struggle to discern the sources of commotion, and both become easy targets for Iago's deceptions. If the historical company found its Gratiano elsewhere than in its Brabantio, it needlessly sacrificed a chance for the production to walk in step with the play. Moreover, having spectral vestiges of Brabantio linger in the person of Gratiano can only add to the audience's dawning and disturbing awareness of a 'truth' that makes the tragedy so difficult to endure: the possibility that Brabantio was right about the match of his daughter and the Moor, that he would use charms and magic before making her a victim of savagery.

The first act of *Othello* works much like a condensed version of *A Midsummer Night's Dream*, a play in which a curmudgeonly father resists his daughter's marriage to the handsome man of her choice. *Othello*'s audience initially takes comfort and pleasure from its sense of superiority to Brabantio and its awareness that Desdemona has made a good match, confident that Brabantio's accusations of witchcraft are unfounded. So when the story of the handkerchief unfolds ('That handkerchief / Did an Egyptian to my mother give: / ... There's magic in the web of it' [3.4.52–66]), the audience gradually finds itself faced with its own uncomfortable *anagnorisis*, one delegitimizing its claim to superiority or insight and suggesting that established facts are now in dispute. Brabantio's re-emergence in the person of Gratiano therefore deepens the tragedy itself, a tragedy that stems not only from the deaths of innocents, but also from the audience's newfound awareness that the least trusted (and perhaps even the least likeable) character had the most foresight, and that tragedy might have been averted had anyone onstage heeded him.

The potential for doubling to intensify tragedy is unusually great in *Othello*, nowhere more evident than in the prospect of doubling Desdemona and Bianca. Much like Gratiano and Lodovico, Bianca enters the plot late and yet becomes crucial to its resolution. Booth points out that she never appears in a scene with Desdemona, and that their similar names – 'Desdemona (Othello's innocent but falsely slandered white wife) and the urgently named Bianca (the white – the

---

[20] Meagher, *Pursuing Shakespeare's Dramaturgy*, p. 207.

hoar – whore)' – may signal that the playwright anticipated the roles being doubled.[21] For audiences, the ramifications of the choice are staggering. When Othello sees Bianca flirt with Cassio and pass the strawberry-spotted handkerchief to him, he wrongly concludes that Desdemona is a whore and has given away his handkerchief. Yet in a significant sense, he will be *right* if the actor playing Bianca has appeared first as Desdemona. In that case, albeit in a dimension outside the fiction, Desdemona does indeed give away Othello's handkerchief – to Cassio, her actual lover. The ocular proof that Othello seeks can thus be delivered – and not delivered – by the play; and Othello, a hero turned villain that elicits the audience's sympathy *and* condemnation, will in some sense seem reasonable saying 'This is a subtle whore, / A closet, lock, and key of villainous secrets' (4.2.20–1). Indeed, she may be precisely that, if the phrase simultaneously works to describe the 'whore' (Bianca) trapped in Desdemona's clothes.

Othello will continue to be wrong in the context of the fiction, of course, but the audience will better understand his situation, logically and even experientially, than they could have otherwise. Spectators can continue thinking that Desdemona is chaste, but not without the complicating factor of clear evidence that 'she' has been false with Cassio. As a result, spectators come closer than they usually do to the paradoxical position forced on Othello when Iago incites his jealousy:

> By the world,
> I think my wife be honest, and think she is not;
> I think that thou art just, and think thou art not. (3.3.380–2)

Like other tragedies, *Othello* depends for its energy on the audience's sympathy for his situation despite his mistakes and brutality.[22] But doubling Desdemona and Bianca will push the spectators much further in this direction by offering an implicit suggestion that Othello's horrifying actions are somehow justified. Though the justice pertains only to the actor's co-participation as a separable character, the secondary dimension forcibly intrudes upon our experience of the play. When the roles are doubled Desdemona can never wholly avoid carrying traces of Bianca, the more because the plot has so few major characters. Othello will attract some sympathy from spectators in any case, but the extra-dramatic fact of Desdemona's guilt complicates judgements about the guilt of both Othello and Iago and affects the degree and quality of sympathy that spectators feel for them. Most importantly,

---

[21] Booth, 'Speculations on Doubling', p. 151.

[22] Among Shakespeare's tragic leads, Othello may be the best example to justify Aristotle's notion of *hamartia* (see *Poetics* 13). Audiences seem susceptible even to the somewhat ridiculous statement that he loved Desdemona 'not wisely, but too well' (5.2.337).

perhaps, the double-casting puts the audience in a dramatic situation, forced to reconcile competing views about the same stage figure.

Brabantio's last words in the play are a warning: 'Look to her, Moor, if thou hast eyes to see: / She has deceived her father, and may thee' (1.3.289–90). I have suggested the role that this warning (and Brabantio's potential reappearance in the person of Gratiano) plays in deepening the audience's sense of tragedy. But a virginal Desdemona who doubles as a harlot realizes the prophecy in actual fact. Moreover, allowing the actor to play both madonna and whore adds interest to Desdemona's salacious banter with Iago on the shore at Cyprus, as well as to the scene wherein Emilia upbraids Bianca for whoring ('Oh, fie upon thee, strumpet!'[23] [5.2.119]), the latter occurring shortly after Desdemona says to Emilia that she could not imagine any woman would betray her husband, even if the whole world were her recompense.[24] Given that four centuries of audiences have testified to *Othello*'s merits despite almost no discussion or employment of this casting choice, one cannot claim that it is necessary. Still, the choice is made available and inviting by Shakespeare's play, and the roles are associated by name, dialogue, and incident. Its use can make *Othello* even more devastatingly effective.

A company can further the play's interests still more if it also thinks carefully about casting the Clown. Compared to Feste or Lear's Fool, the role seems dramatically and psychologically colourless, so it is frequently cut from productions.[25] But I suspect that if directors gave greater consideration to having one of the leads play the role, few would be inclined to cut it. The Clown makes two brief but prominent appearances, for which there are three candidates available for doubling: Roderigo, Brabantio, and Othello himself. It is significant that in a play concerned with Desdemona's supposed infidelity, the Clown appears twice in the position of a procurer or pander: first helping Cassio gain private access to Desdemona, then discussing with Desdemona where Cassio 'lies'. That Desdemona and Cassio seek out private meetings with one another subtly augments the circumstantial evidence for their supposed adultery. When their meetings occur in a production doubling Desdemona and Bianca, this evidence gains force, allowing yet more 'ocular proof' that Desdemona has been false with Cassio by seeking out his bedchamber.

---

[23] 'Strumpet' and 'whore' are also terms Othello applies to Desdemona several times (e.g. 4.2.81–9).

[24] Note that Emilia also reverses her position, first trying to persuade Desdemona that adultery is no very bad thing ('who would not make her husband a cuckold to make him a monarch? I should venture purgatory for't' [5.1.71–2]), then condemning Bianca in 5.1.

[25] In 26 productions, I have seen only three Clowns.

In this light, using a principal character as the pander between the two (or three) characters helps the play create the very confusions it is otherwise already pursuing. Roderigo is a plausible choice for being a comic in another context (a sort of Aguecheek to Iago's Toby) and being conspicuously freed by the plot, retiring at the end of 2.3 and not returning until 4.1, with the Clown's two appearances coming in the interim. Doubling Roderigo and the Clown gives a better actor more work and would allow Roderigo to seem to learn in the Clown's person why he should 'seek satisfaction' of Iago for not playing a proper pander between himself and Desdemona. Using the Brabantio actor in the role would allow him to seem to play a part in facilitating adultery, thus helping to break off the match Brabantio resisted in Venice and to see his daughter matched to a more agreeable prospect.

The most tempting choice, however, is Othello. The Clown enters the play as a proxy for Othello who orders the Musicians to stop playing on the general's behalf, and whose entrance to the unwanted music echoes Othello's entrance the night before to break up fighting and 'silence that dreadful bell' (2.3.168). In his scene with Desdemona, the Clown dwells on the subjects of honesty and lying, questioning Cassio's honesty in particular, and the place where he lies, subjects which concern Othello in scenes that alternate with those featuring the Clown. Othello several times refers to Iago's 'exceeding honesty',[26] and the conversations between the two take lying, in word or deed, for a central theme: 'Lie with her? Lie on her? We say "lie on her" when they belie her. Lie with her?' (4.1.33–4). Such lines closely link the Clown and Othello, irrespective of the prospect of doubling, which they invite and may be strengthened by. In addition, doubling the roles allows the Clown (or Othello-as-Clown) to see Desdemona pursuing Cassio and to see him pursuing her. The plot leans on Othello to make the swiftest of transitions from 'my life upon her faith' to 'Damn her, lewd minx'. Having the actor play a pander figure does not make the adultery convincing, but it adds to a pile of circumstantial evidence, allowing suspicion to inform a question whose answer is, nevertheless, never in doubt. Doubling the Clown and Othello is thus an ideal complement for doubling of Desdemona and Bianca, creating a dimension in which husband and wife double as pander and whore, haunting – without harming – the play's central truths and concerns. If both pairings are deployed in production, the audience

---

[26] The quote comes at 3.3.256. But references to Iago's honesty are everywhere, beginning in Act One, when Othello departs for Cyprus without his wife, 'Honest Iago, / My Desdemona must I leave to thee' (1.3.291–2).

sees clear occasions wherein Desdemona may have been false with Cassio, even though the prospect remains wholly inadmissible. The result raises the stakes of each couple's interactions across the late acts, and complicates the issues of blame and guilt that contribute to the audience's sense of tragedy.

Epilogue: Ragozine and Shakespearean Substitution

ಐಶೆ
'Like doth quit like'
~ Duke Vincentio, *Measure for Measure*, 5.1.414
ಐಶೆ

Throughout this book, I have argued for the doubling possibilities Shakespeare created for his company, mostly independent of the degree to which those possibilities were exploited on historical stages. I have also argued that the company would not have been prevented from realizing such possibilities fully in original productions. Biases towards verisimilitude have been projected onto Shakespeare's company, leading to widely held but largely unfounded assumptions: that sharers wouldn't double in minor roles; that the company would require significant time for actors to change clothes; that adult males never played female roles; that actors would not double multiple roles within the same scene. None of these rules govern modern companies and none can reasonably be imagined to have governed Shakespeare, whose plays reflect an unusual preoccupation with testing credibility and variously seek to advertise their artificiality.

If we forgo attachment to theories of Shakespeare's casting and staging that proceed from such rules, and if we concede that all the plays written for the company can be performed with 12 or fewer speakers, only two rules remain to restrict possibilities for doubling: first, that the characters doubled by a single actor cannot meet onstage; second, that a performance will indicate changes of person by changes of costume. Any other objections or obstacles can be overcome, and there is material evidence for all of them having been overcome in the period. These two rules seem indispensable. That said, there is reason to suspect that Shakespeare occasionally dispensed with them anyway. I have argued that 5.2 of *The Winter's Tale* seems to sanction doubling the Clown and Shepherd with two of the three 'Gentlemen' – without changing clothes. In fact, the scene improves, in comedy and coherence, if the Clown's immense pride in wearing 'robes' he believes confirm his status as a 'gentleman born' are the very robes the real 'gentleman' had worn earlier in the scene. When it comes to actors playing roles that encounter one another onstage, we have seen how the author of *The Fair Maid of the Exchange* creates opportunities for co-presence. But as he did with other supposed limits of representation, Shakespeare may have pushed further beyond these boundaries than anyone.

From around 1601–1604 Shakespeare's plays reflect a growing fascination with the idea of substitutions. In *Twelfth Night* a sister takes the place of her twin brother after his supposed death. In *Troilus and Cressida*, multiple characters' places are threatened by rivals: Troilus is displaced in Cressida's affection by Diomedes; Achilles's place as the foremost Greek is threatened by Ajax. *Othello* seems altogether obsessed with the idea of stand-ins. The tragedy hinges on Othello's belief that Cassio is filling his place with Desdemona. Iago begins the play displeased that Cassio has taken the 'place' he deserved, and he wonders whether 'twixt [his] sheets' Othello has 'done [his] office' (1.1.14–31 and 1.3.365–6). Othello is sent to replace the Duke's 'substitute' on Cyprus, effectively becoming a substitute for a substitute. And, late in the play, a commission arrives from the Duke 'deputing Cassio' in Othello's place.[1] Such examples find complements in the near-constant employment of variations on the words 'office' and 'officer', 'deputy', 'substitute', and 'place', the sum of which is greater in *Othello* than in all but one other play.

That one is *Measure for Measure*, likely written around 1604 and within a year of *Othello*.[2] In the opening scene, the Duke asks Escalus about Angelo's potential as a substitute:

> What figure of us, think you he will bear?
> For you must know we have with special soul
> Elected him our absence to supply:
> Lent him our terror, dressed him with our love,
> And given his deputation all the organs
> Of our own power.   (1.1.16–21)

The play takes all occasions to affirm Angelo's status as a stand-in, never settling for one reference when three will do. But almost every character and scene contributes to the theme. Early on, Claudio asks not that Lucio appeal to Isabella directly, but rather that he 'implore her, in my voice'; when she does approach Angelo on her brother's behalf, Isabella poses a hypothetical exchange of identity: 'I would to heaven I had your potency / And you were Isabel' (2.2.68–9). Language of substitution continues steadily throughout the play, with Lucio joking how Lord Angelo 'dukes it well' in Vincentio's absence; Escalus telling the disguised Duke that 'the duke's in us';

---

[1] See *Othello*, 1.3.222 and 4.1.223–4, and the discussion of its doubling possibilities in Chapter 7.
[2] Greenblatt discusses several instances of substitution in the play in *Shakespeare's Freedom* (Chicago: University of Chicago Press, 2010), pp. 11–15.

and the Duke responding to Lucio's slander with: 'You must, sir, change persons with me, ere you make that my report' (5.1.339–40).

Dramaturgical substitutions are also frequent and even more intriguing. Take, for instance, the inexplicable displacement of one friar by another. The Duke went into hiding in the first act with the help of Friar Thomas. These two are on intimate terms, the Duke telling Thomas, 'none better knows than you / How I have ever loved the life removed' (1.3.7–8). Yet when the time comes for a friar to help vindicate Isabella, the Duke has her seek out a hitherto unknown holy man:

> This letter then to Friar Peter give;
> 'Tis that he sent me of the duke's return.   (4.3.131–2)

Four acts into the play, the audience has never heard of Friar Peter, who enters the play to do just what Friar Thomas might have done.[3] Like Balthasar and Peto, Friar Peter is only explicable here if the Thomas actor wasn't available – unless, in this case, Shakespeare simply looked to pile up instances of someone doing the office of somebody else.

When Friar Peter arrives before the Duke, he is asked to take letters to the Duke's other friends in the city – Flavius, Valentinus, Rowland, and Crassus (not a Thomas among them) – but the Duke concludes by demanding, 'send me Flavius first'. Immediately, a new character enters and the Duke warmly greets him: 'I thank thee, Varrius, thou hast made good haste' (4.5.11). Varrius's main reason for being seems to owe to the fact that he is not Flavius, Thomas, or any of the friends just named. Odd moments like these complement the play's interest in deputation, but so does a character like Elbow, himself an 'officer' whose peppering malapropisms are yet further examples of substituting one thing for another:

> I respected with her before I was married to her? ... Prove this, thou
> wicked Hannibal, or I'll have mine action of battery on thee.
> ESCALUS If he took you a box o' th' ear, you might have your action of slander
> too.   (2.1.161–7)

Exhausting the play's examples of substitution would last out a night in Russia, but two more deserve mention. One is the most well-known substitution in the play, the bed-trick, by which Angelo is led to take one character for another when the Duke arranges for Mariana to 'stead up [Isabella's] appointment' with Angelo and 'go in her place' (3.1.240). The other is Ragozine.

Desiring proof that his order to kill Claudio has been carried out, Angelo sends for his severed head, to which request the Duke responds with a trick

---

[3] The substitution may reflect the need for the Friar Thomas actor in another role, as we have seen with Balthasar and Poins. But the substitution here carries additional interest given so many others throughout the play.

even more daring and improbable than the bed-trick just accomplished. He seizes first on the prisoner Barnardine, whose head he argues may be substituted for Claudio's on the pretense that 'death's a great disguiser' (4.2.166). Despite Angelo's familiarity with Claudio, the Duke assumes that one face may plausibly replace another. But when Barnardine cannot be persuaded to die, the Provost offers a variation on the Duke's plan:

> Here in the prison, father,
> There died this morning of a cruel fever
> One Ragozine, a most notorious pirate,
> A man of Claudio's years, his beard and head
> Just of his color. What if we do omit
> This reprobate till he were well inclined,
> And satisfy the deputy with the visage
> Of Ragozine, more like to Claudio?   (4.3.62–9)

The result is that the substitute head is substituted-for, based on the wonderfully timely death of one who happens to look a lot like the character for which we need a proxy. The Duke calls Ragozine's death an 'accident that heaven provides' (4.3.70). While his statement relates to the fictional world and builds thematically on other substitutions, it may be that this 'accident' also has dramaturgical and theatrical motives. In short, two characters are considered suitable surrogates for Claudio, since Ragozine – despite his great notoriety – can seamlessly replace Barnardine in the role of Claudio. The substitution works; Angelo is fooled by Ragozine's head. Combined with the bed-trick, the play here establishes a pattern: three times in quick succession, one body replaces another and succeeds in fooling the onstage audience. And each of these substitutions targets Angelo, who is repeatedly referred to as a 'deputy' or 'substitute'.

From its first scene *Measure for Measure* creates an atmosphere germane to the improbable substitutions upon which its conclusion depends. Yet it may be that the bed-trick; the substitutions of Barnardine and then Ragozine for Claudio; the malapropisms; Friar Thomas; Varrius; and the rest set the stage for something even more improbable, though uniquely suited to this play: a substitution of actors.[4] Though there is no reason to think that Shakespeare's

---

[4] Though most men of the period played many parts, companies typically allocated each part to only one man. Through 'substitution', wherein an actor takes over a role that another actor has vacated, plays like *Horestes* (1567) tested that rule. Some of Shakespeare's contemporaries and successors used substitution, e.g. George Peele, *The Battle of Alcazar* (published 1594) and Massinger, *Believe as You List* (c. 1631). Contemporary directors sometimes use substitutions to literalize a change in age (e.g. using an older actor for the latter half of *Pericles*). Others divide substantial roles for myriad practical/logistical reasons, among them, to make possible an otherwise impossible double. The RSC's 1969 *The Winter's Tale*, for instance, enabled Judi Dench to double the roles of Hermione and Perdita by having an actor unknown to the audience play Perdita in the final scene.

company regularly divided roles among two or more actors, *Measure for Measure* invites a substitution of actors that is vitalizing both thematically and theatrically, complementing the metaphoric replacements in the play by literally realizing, through the actor's body, the Duke's set of equations at the play's climax:

> The very mercy of the law cries out
> Most audible even from his proper tongue:
> 'An Angelo for Claudio, death for death.
> Haste still pays haste, and leisure answers leisure;
> Like doth quit like, and measure still for measure.' (5.1.410–14)

'Like doth quit like' epitomizes the play's chief concern – that one thing (character, word, body) may substitute for another. Though the Duke calls for Angelo to receive the same punishment as Claudio (or the punishment that most characters onstage think has been Claudio's) his lines equate the characters themselves, proposing that the deputy Angelo, already substituting for the Duke, should stand in for Claudio, too. In short, the lines seem to read as an advertisement for doubling the roles of the two men guilty of sleeping with women out of wedlock.

The Duke's speech complements an already well-established pattern of comparisons between Angelo and Claudio, characters who participate frequently in scenes and situations that echo one another, and who are constantly defined in relation to each other. Both contract marriages they cannot publicize for want of a dowry. Isabella visits both in private meetings that play out in similar ways, with her initial prayers on their behalves turning to curses, after each urges her to satisfy Angelo's lust. Isabella asks Angelo to look within himself to find something of Claudio's wrongs – 'ask your heart what it doth know / That's like my brother's fault' (2.2.138–9) – and she locates Angelo's lust *within* Claudio, asking 'Is't not a kind of incest to take life / From thine own sister's shame?' (3.1.140–1).[5] Isabella's comparisons morph into conflations and set pronouns to dizzying patterns while urging Angelo to pardon Claudio: 'If he had been as you, and you as he, / You would have slipt like him, but he like you, / Would not have been so stern' (2.2.65–7). And when she reveals to Claudio that no pardon is forthcoming, she takes up yet another variation on the language of proxy: 'Lord Angelo, having affairs to heaven, / Intends you for his swift ambassador' (3.1.56–7). The Duke likewise conflates the fates and faults of the two, telling the Provost that Claudio 'is no greater forfeit to the law than Angelo who hath sentenced him' (4.2.151–2). The play is relentless in

---

[5] Escalus, too, asks Angelo to look within himself to understand something about Claudio's crime (at 2.1.8–16).

associating the two characters who do not meet until the final scene, in which the Duke declares they can be substituted for one another.

Meanwhile, the play insists that the façades of the two characters do not correspond to what underlies them. Escalus calls Angelo an 'ungenitured agent' whose blood 'is very snow broth'; the Duke describes the extremes joined in Mariana's 'combinate husband, this well-seeming Angelo'; Isabella decries his 'false seeming' and concludes that 'this outward-sainted deputy ... is yet a devil.' Alternately, she strips Claudio of his own geniture, 'such a warpèd slip of wilderness / Ne'er issued from [her father's] blood' (3.1.142–3), while the Duke (himself in a friar's robe) counsels Claudio, 'Thou art not thyself / ... Thou art not certain, / For thy complexion shifts to strange effects / After the moon' (3.1.19–25). The idea that things are not what they seem is thus applied to two characters involved in a plot that makes casual reference to false seeming in every scene, from Lucio's Latin maxim before the disguised Duke, 'Cucullus non facit monachum. Honest in nothing but in his clothes', to Abhorson's explanation about how 'Every true man's apparel fits your thief' (5.1.269–70; 4.2.37).

Were it not for the play's final 63 lines, then, during which a 'muffled Claudio' enters a scene that counts Angelo among its participants, we would have more reasons to speculate about these two roles being doubled than any others in Shakespeare, with the possible exception of Posthumus and Cloten in *Cymbeline*.[6] In addition to literalizing the Duke's assertion at the climax ('An Angelo for Claudio'), doubling the roles would further the play's thematic concerns and extend the series of improbable substitutions at the play's core. The references are so explicit in asking audiences onstage and off to compare and conflate the two characters, that their appearance together onstage at the end is somehow strange for it. After all, Isabella pleads for Angelo's life alongside Mariana (as she formerly did for Claudio) and asks the Duke to look 'on this man condemned / As if my brother lived' (5.1.447–8). Doubling the roles would also help explain the near three-act disappearance of Angelo, who presumably would have been played by one of the company's best actors. Among other advantages, the choice to double would intensify Angelo's hypocrisy and add colour to the 'kind of incest' that Isabella perceives in Claudio when he asks her to assent to Angelo's lust, generating truths outside the fictional frame regarding the characters and situations within it. Each character can by this means become more attractive and repulsive to audiences, complicating reception by cultivating rooting interests for *and* against the outcome necessitated by the genre.

---

[6] Booth proposed doubling Posthumus and Cloten ('Speculations on Doubling', p. 148), which has been realized onstage, sometimes to spectacular success, in productions by Shakspeare's Globe (2001), Cheek by Jowl (2007), and Fiasco Theater (2011).

Though the roles are linked so thoroughly, prospects for doubling them apparently fade when Claudio enters the final scene. Nevertheless, through its emphasis on surrogacy and deputation, the play has suggested its own alternative to using two people in the two roles. By featuring so many substitutions of characters and language, the play prepares the ground for a final and more daring instance of substitution: for sending on a substitute actor, muffled, to play Claudio, while the Claudio actor is portraying Angelo. I will say more about how *Measure for Measure* is better able to achieve its thematic ends by means of that choice. First, though, consider the strange circumstances of Claudio's revelation, and the way the speeches related to it seem to perform dramaturgical work, though Claudio himself is entirely mute. His silence is strange, as are the descriptions of those who reveal and 'recognize' him. Rather than the dramatic unveiling the audience might expect, a precedent established when Lucio reveals the Duke under a friar's hood, the Provost introduces Claudio by name while he is still muffled:

> This is another prisoner that I saved,
> Who should have died when Claudio lost his head,
> As like almost to Claudio as himself. (5.1.491–3)

The language may be playfully elusive, but it is peculiar, both for spoiling the surprise and for suggesting that Claudio is a *substitute* for Claudio. The lines distinguish him from Claudio by suggesting how closely they resemble one another – the prisoner is 'almost' as like to Claudio, as *Claudio*. The next speaker is not Claudio but the Duke, who extends the Provost's strange theme, considering this Claudio quite 'like' the real one:

> If he be *like* your brother, for his sake
> Is he pardoned, and for your lovely sake
> Give me your hand, and say you will be mine,
> He is my brother too – but fitter time for that. (5.1.494–7, italics mine)

The Duke's sudden proposal has drawn significant commentary. Whatever other work it does, I suggest in this context that the proposal can serve additionally to distract us from the fact that the person Isabella embraces, one much 'like' Claudio and who is pardoned 'for his sake', but who is described as being always at one remove from Claudio, is *not* actually Isabella's brother. He may be another actor, standing in for Claudio while the Claudio actor plays Angelo. The situation allows, even invites, a new actor to substitute in the role of Claudio, just as the play has assured us can be done by others, including Barnardine and Ragozine. As a result, the strongly suggestive doubling of Angelo and Claudio is enabled and enriched. The new arrival to the cast may, like Ragozine, be of Claudio's years, his beard and hair of a colour much like Claudio's, yet he still may not be Claudio. And since the first Claudio wasn't really Claudio but rather an actor portraying him, the secondary representation is, essentially, no falser than the first. I suggest that such an exchange of persons is more in keeping with the thematic concerns of *Measure for Measure* than having two actors occupy the roles of Claudio and Angelo, whatever the historical practice of the King's Men. The choice will allow the two characters to suffer the same fate: condemned to and reclaimed from death for the same offences, each needing only to look within to find truths about the other, precisely as Isabella had foreseen.

At least two other aspects of the play invite and are improved by doubling Claudio and Angelo. One is the 'problem' of the play's ending. As is well known, *Measure for Measure* generates significant discomfort by setting the end appropriate to the genre, the marriage of the Duke and Isabella, at odds with the moral sympathies of most audiences. The Duke is so troubling because he has needlessly prolonged Isabella's suffering; allowed Mariana to be slandered in public; impersonated a friar and offered to confess men before their deaths – yet is credited at the play's end with solutions to the very problems he helped bring about. Beyond this, most audiences are vaguely familiar with the idea that friars (even false ones) ought not to marry nuns. The appropriate yet ill-seeming ending that results is enhanced in a production that doubles Angelo and Claudio. Those onstage might act as though this Claudio is indeed Claudio, just as the cast may rejoice at the prospect of Isabella being matched with the rich and powerful leading man. But for the audiences offstage both matches – of man and woman, and of man and man – ring hollow, potentially making us feel as though the play has won its generic ends on technicalities. Such a production would thus make a theme out of the play's simultaneous ability to please and displease its audience by the same means.

Another incentive to double is the added interest and uncertainty about the potential fate of Angelo. Spectators that have seen an actor doubling the roles will experience considerably greater anxiety as Angelo's death approaches, since Claudio's reappearance should require Angelo's departure. As Mariana and then Isabella kneel for clemency, the desire for Angelo to be preserved alive grows for an audience increasingly convinced that he cannot be saved if Claudio is to return. As a result, when the muffled bodies are brought onstage, the audience waits for what suddenly becomes a far less predictable, and therefore genuine, revelation. The audience, already aware of Claudio's presence in the person of Angelo, cannot know who or what is under the hood, even when the Provost begins to explain how like to Claudio the unknown figure is. Since the Claudio actor is present in Angelo, audiences must entertain the possibility that Claudio hasn't been saved after all – that something has gone wrong while attempting to preserve him from Angelo's judgement. This would accord well with the confusion over the orders and countermands already witnessed, and it would put the audience in a position much closer to Isabella's: in doubt about the life or death of Claudio. Only substituting an actor and doubling the roles can create so much suspense for the audience offstage, its experience then more in line with the characters' own. As a result, the audience enters its own dramatic role, suddenly uncertain about the facts and logic of the fiction. For Isabella, Claudio is likely to die, then dies indeed, then is found living. When the roles are doubled, the spectators first wonder if Angelo must die for Claudio to live. When the muffled actor arrives, they wonder whether Claudio had to die so that Angelo could continue. Confusion and doubt are both intensified and allayed by the revelation of one 'as like almost to Claudio as himself', but still one who may not actually be Claudio. Again, there is no ground to argue whether any of this occurred in 1604. However, considering Shakespeare's interest in substitution, doubling, and daring his audiences to disbelieve, I think it more likely than not that the play was built with the anticipation that the roles might be doubled, and doubled to advantage.

The doubling of Claudio and Angelo may be the most improbable and yet most compelling of potential pairings in Shakespeare. But the play's thematic concerns can be further developed through other casting choices. Like other plays of the early 1600s (e.g. *Twelfth Night, Othello*), *Measure for Measure* anticipates an unusually lean cast. Only nine actors are required, even if we do not admit the substitution. Table E.1 presents a speculative casting plot for nine.[7]

The Duke is one of the largest roles in Shakespeare, onstage so often that there is little secondary work that he can do. Of course, the character is disguised as a friar for much of the play, a kind of 'double' for the character rather than the actor. Still, a nine-member cast likely must turn to the Duke and Lucio to find actors for Froth and Justice, who appear in just one scene (2.1). Since Froth is brought before the Justice for frequenting a brothel, doubling the roles allows Lucio and the Duke to preview their Act Five encounter, in which the Duke sentences Lucio to marry the prostitute who has borne his child. Here, the Duke can punish Froth/Lucio as the Justice, or be punished by him, depending on who plays who. The scene carries meaning beyond its momentary significance, considering that it participates in a pattern of judgements meted out to Claudio (and later Angelo) for extra-marital liaisons, so doubling can enhance the pattern by involving the principal characters more thoroughly in them. If the Duke plays Froth, he eventually judges Lucio for a crime he himself has committed (albeit in another person), much as Angelo hypocritically judges Claudio.

---

[7] The chart does not the include the 'boy' who appears briefly with Mariana to sing a song at 4.1.1–6. He can be played by any available actor who can sing, though it may be that Shakespeare's company found him among its musicians, apprentices, etc.

Table E.1 *Hypothetical doubling plan for Shakespeare's* Measure for Measure *(c. 1603)*

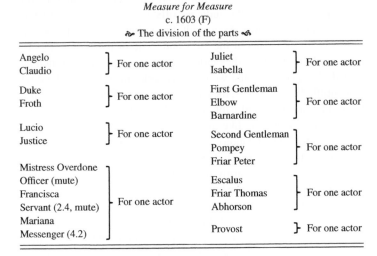

Measure for Measure
c. 1603 (F)
❧ The division of the parts ❧

Angelo Claudio	} For one actor	Juliet Isabella	} For one actor
Duke Froth	} For one actor	First Gentleman Elbow Barnardine	} For one actor
Lucio Justice	} For one actor	Second Gentleman Pompey Friar Peter	} For one actor
Mistress Overdone Officer (mute) Francisca Servant (2.4, mute) Mariana Messenger (4.2)	} For one actor	Escalus Friar Thomas Abhorson	} For one actor
		Provost	} For one actor

Doubling the roles also deepens the history between the Duke and Lucio, establishing the two actors in a pattern of justice and punishment that links them further to Angelo and Claudio. One effect of this is to make Lucio's defrocking of the supposed 'Friar' more relevant to Claudio's unmuffling by the Provost:

> LUCIO   Come, sir, come, sir, come, sir. Faugh, sir! Why, you bald-pated, lying rascal, you must be hooded, must you? Show your knave's visage, with a pox to you. Show your sheep-biting face, and be hanged an hour. Will't not off?
>
> [LUCIO *pulls off the Duke's hood*]
>
> DUKE   Thou art the first knave that e'er mad'st a duke.   (5.1.354–8)

The two moments are strikingly similar, in both the mechanics of the unveiling and the descriptions of transformation: after removing the Duke's hood, Lucio is credited with 'making' a duke. If the Provost makes 'a Claudio' through his language and delayed revelation – and because the actor under the hood is not Claudio – the two examples grow more intensely interrelated. The thematic parallel will be present in any case, but the doubling (Duke/Froth; Lucio/Justice) can more intimately associate the Duke and Lucio, making the pairing more relevant and analogous to that of Angelo and Claudio, while giving further sanction and interest to the arrival of a second 'Claudio'.

The play's extensive interest in hiding and revealing faces begins not with the Duke's disguise, but with Francisca, the nun who teaches Isabella the chopped logic of the priory:

> When you have vowed, you must not speak with men
> But in the presence of the prioress.
> Then, if you speak, you must not show your face,
> Or if you show your face, you must not speak.   (1.4.11–14)

The passage finds a complement in the last act, when the Duke bids the veiled Mariana, 'First, let her show her face, and after, speak' (5.1.173). Mariana's refusal to show her face under these circumstances, at least until 'my husband bid me', echoes Francisca's logic, creating a connection between them that can be strengthened through doubling. If the actor appears first as Francisca, she is a nun turned bride (nearly), setting a precedent for Isabella's like transformation at the play's end. Finally, Francisca's lines about not speaking when one's face is shown find an additional echo in the final scene when the typically verbose Claudio goes silent after his face is revealed. Significantly, both Francisca and Mariana make their entrances only after Mistress Overdone vanishes from the play. Though at opposite ends of a moral divide, Francisca and Mistress Overdone are quite like one another: elder-sister figures living cloistered lives devoted to the training-up of young women. Casting one actor in all three roles would link more intimately their livelihoods and living situations, while enhancing the theme of the 'outward sainted deputy' who has a devil within.

There are other cloistered women in the play, such as Isabella and Juliet, Claudio's unfortunate betrothed, whom Angelo sends into retirement to give birth. Though the Folio stage directions bring her back onstage in the final scene, she is conspicuously silent. Thus, neither Claudio nor Juliet speaks at their reunion; neither is addressed directly; and nobody so much as acknowledges Juliet's appearance, which should be striking either because she carries a newborn, or is still pregnant despite the Provost's report that she was 'groaning' and 'very near her hour' (2.2.16–17). Despite her pregnancy providing the basis for Claudio's imprisonment, and thus the whole plot, Juliet appears in just two scenes and is assigned only ten lines. Since there is no reference to the character at all in the last scene, a scene in which her reunion with her child's father should deserve at least slight attention, it may be that her inclusion in the Folio stage direction is a mistake.[8] But while the

---

[8] As noted, the Folio stage directions tend to be more elaborate than others, but they include several mute and unacknowledged characters in scenes, some of whom cannot possibly be present, and some of whom may be present for literary, rather than theatrical, ends.

King's Men could have allotted the small role to an attendant or apprentice, it may also have been filled by the 'female' playing Isabella. Considering the play's interest in substitution, and the possibility that its structure antici- pates the Claudio role being taken over by an unknown mute actor, it may be that Shakespeare prefigured a similar option for Juliet. This would allow the original Juliet actor to double Isabella or Mariana, an unknown actor eventu- ally entering in Juliet's dress and wig to stand beside the man impersonating her betrothed.

Whether Juliet is played by a substitute in the final scene or does not appear at all, there is good cause to double her with Mariana. Both have aborted mar- riages; both experience a shame-ridden aftermath and go into hiding. The roles of Francisca, Juliet, Mariana, and Mistress Overdone can all be played by one actor, building coherence across the line of housebound women who vari- ously conjoin virtue and vice: from nun to brothel-keeper, from one who was engaged to Angelo but must use a trick to sleep with him, to one who sleeps with Claudio but must forestall the engagement.

But the Juliet actor will also add thematic interest by doubling as Isabella. While talking to Lucio, Isabella makes casual reference to her intimate rela- tionship to Juliet:

> ISABELLA Someone with child by him? My cousin Juliet?
> LUCIO   Is she your cousin?
> ISABELLA Adoptedly, as school-maids change their names
>   By vain though apt affection.   (1.4.46–9)

I have noted already the 'kind of incest' Isabella perceives in Claudio's wish to take life from his 'own sister's shame'. These lines quietly prepare for the topic by suggesting that Isabella and Juliet are something like sisters. Doubling the roles would legitimize both the sisterhood and the incest. As a result, the trivial dismissals of Claudio's crime would be more troublesome, since however much the audience condones the decision to wait on a dowry while enjoying the fruits of a wife, it cannot easily forgive him when the wife is his sister – albeit in a purely theatrical dimension. The choice would present yet another strange sanction for the awkward potential engagement between Isabella and the Duke, whose offer of marriage would participate in a pattern of anxiety-inducing relationships. If an actor playing Claudio (and Angelo) would therefore argue that Isabella should give in to Angelo, he will promote not 'a kind' of incest but *the* kind. In addition, if the roles of Isabella and Juliet are doubled, the final reunion – otherwise odd for not allowing Juliet any attention – will allow for reunions of brother and sister, and of the affianced couple, Isabella's exuberance at seeing him then adding to the audience's sense of joyful reunion while simultaneously deepening its discomfort.

The speculative doubling plan accounts for three other actors, whose primary roles are Escalus, Pompey, and Elbow. Escalus, the loyal friend of the Duke, can continue to aid him in the person of Friar Thomas, a choice that will explain the strange disappearance of Friar Thomas (and the substitution of Friar Peter) later in the play, when Escalus is required. Escalus and Thomas are both offstage for most of Acts Three and Four, during which Abhorson appears twice. Convenience is the main reason to add this role to the others, though it is notable that Abhorson's verbal sparring and attempts to reform Pompey by teaching him an honest trade (4.2) recall Escalus's advice to Pompey when the latter appears before him for being a bawd (2.1). By the time Escalus returns late in Act Four, Pompey and Elbow have vanished, most likely because those actors are needed elsewhere. Otherwise, audiences have reason to expect Pompey would appear at the play's end, and possibly Elbow too. Pompey may make way so that Friar Peter can enter, while the Elbow actor could be present in Barnardine, a character that the play labors to suggest can stand-in for someone else. Since Barnardine's chance to play Claudio is taken by Ragozine, he may still possess a kind of double-favour by doubling as Elbow.

As the rest of this book makes evident, *Measure for Measure* is not alone in offering companies opportunities to better realize a play's thematic and theatrical potential through double-casting. But it is rare for its apparent invitation to use two actors in the same role. We have seen how disappearances of Benvolio and Poins, and the subsequent uses of Balthazar and Peto to fulfill duties previously reserved for the suppressed characters, suggest a kind of substitution. But in the case of Claudio (and possibly Juliet) the play maintains the role while still potentially freeing the actor to play another character. The evidence is not so compelling elsewhere for substitution taking place on Shakespeare's stage, but there are a few instances worth mentioning.

The most well known is Perdita/Hermione, a pairing that has been tried in several productions. It does not appear to have textual sanction like some others, though, since the characters are both focal points in the final scene, and they must speak to and embrace one another. That is not to say that the King's Men must have rejected the possibility, but I find the Perdita/Mamillius doubling more compelling given the play Shakespeare wrote, as I have argued. As noted, another possible substitution is suggested by the conspicuous silence of Hermia and Helena during the final scene of *A Midsummer Night's Dream*, when the couples gather to watch a play put on by the Athenian tradesmen. For Bottom, extreme examples of doubling roles (he wants to play both halves of the central couple and the lion too) are a matter of course, as is the audience's need to perceive the actor within the role. While he and the others perform their version of 'Pyramus and Thisbe', the conversation among the offstage audience is lively, but the silence of Hermia and Helena makes it possible for them to slip out and play mechanicals. Their exits are not accounted for, but neither is the (presumed) absence of the assembly that is to watch the plot of *The Taming of the Shrew* along with Christopher Sly. Many characters exit scenes where we have no indication of the exits in stage directions. As a result, Hermia and Helena may leave to play Snug and Flute, leaving the others to comment on the performance. And if the production, even the original production, had wanted them onstage, any two available men – musicians, apprentices, etc. – could have left the wings wearing the dresses and wigs that would signify Hermia and Helena, and sat silently through a 'tedious and brief' play that is at least as transparently artificial in its theories of representation as a play that would thus substitute for Hermia and Helena.

Yet another play that creates a possibility for substitution is *Twelfth Night*. I have mentioned that the plot appears to be laid out for ten actors. While that fact is not anomalous, its lack of a star male part is. Most plays of this period have a male role that runs close to 1,000 lines: such as Richards II and III, Hamlet, Iago, Macbeth, Lear, Henry V, and so on. Like *As You Like It*, though, *Twelfth Night* has no obvious star part for a male actor. But while *As You Like It* allows Duke Senior's court to reconstitute itself in the country, both plays restrict companies from combining other male roles by including them in the final scenes together. The comparative marginality of the male roles clearly owes something to the prowess of actors playing Viola, Olivia, Rosalind, and Celia, as well as to the stories themselves. Still, and though I think it unlikely to have been practised, it may be worth considering the possibility that Toby and Orsino might constitute a pairing that was either abandoned in the process of writing, or one that could have been used onstage by a company more comfortable with casting substitution than we know.

Much like Angelo and Claudio, Orsino and Toby meet only in the final scene. Unlike Angelo and Claudio, there are not a lot of advantages to doubling these two roles, other than the desire for efficiency and the chance to let Burbage have what may then be something more like a star part. If the roles were doubled, it would bring the necessary cast down to nine, the same number required for playing *Hamlet*, *Measure for Measure* (and, in a pinch, *Othello*). The lack of significant thematic advantages makes this feel more like an abandoned experiment, not unlike how Viola's plan to present herself as a 'eunuch' may be a vestige of an abandoned plot device. Still, the manner of Toby's arrival late in the fifth act, and his hurried departure and failure to reappear, may suggest otherwise.

Andrew enters first to announce that Sebastian, whom he takes to be Cesario, has given Toby 'a bloody coxcomb', and that both he and Toby need a surgeon. This would seem a remarkably useful device if the playwright was interested in obscuring the arrival of a new actor in a familiar role. The audience is well prepared to take the next stumbling drunk, a man with a bloody and possibly bandaged head and wearing Toby's clothes, for Toby, whether he is the original Toby actor or not. The Malvolio actor is available if the play is cast for nine. He could appear briefly in Toby's clothes, holding a handkerchief to his head, and half-drunkenly chide Andrew, before going to fetch Malvolio. This notion is wholly speculative, but – whether such a strategy was intended, aborted, or accidental – it may stimulate thinking about why two of the largest male roles are absent through so much of the play.

There are other near misses like this in the canon. Perhaps the most tantalizing is the potential to double Falstaff and Henry IV in *1 Henry IV*. But for one line ('Rebellion lay in his way and he found it' [5.1.28]) in one brief scene, Hal's two father figures never meet, and there are considerable thematic advantages for doubling them. Fortunately, even without stretching to cut such lines or to substitute a fresh actor for Toby, there are dozens of good options that Shakespeare made available to his company, and to all who produce the plays today. In the Appendix that follows, many such options appear in doubling charts for each play that Shakespeare wrote while serving as the company's resident playwright.

Appendix: Doubling Roles in Shakespeare's Plays

ഇന്ദ

'My jerkin is a doublet.'
~Thurio, *The Two Gentlemen of Verona*, 2.4.20
ഇന്ദ

The first table that follows outlines casting requirements and patterns for *Hamlet*, for which doubling is discussed in Chapter 1. The table divides 'scenes' according to any significant change to the personnel onstage. In short, any change that could have ramifications for casting becomes the impetus to create a new scene. The resulting scenes (what are sometimes called 'French scenes') are numbered sequentially (1.1a, 1.1b, 1.1c, etc.) so that one can follow along using nearly any text of the play with minimal difficulty. The casting charts that appear throughout this book have all been produced on the basis of tables like this one. Though space prevents including others here, readers may visit the Cambridge University Press website to consult additional charts for *Twelfth Night* and *The Winter's Tale*, two plays discussed in detail in the main text.

Following the *Hamlet* table are 32 hypothetical casting charts covering all the plays Shakespeare wrote for the Lord Chamberlain's/King's Men as its principal playwright (c. 1594–1610). The first is for *Hamlet*, paired with the initial table for convenience; the other charts are organized chronologically. The *Henry VI* plays, *Titus Andronicus*, *Henry VIII*, and *The Two Noble Kinsmen* are excluded, the first four written before the company's formation, the last two after significant changes to the company and Shakespeare's partial retirement. Nevertheless, those plays, too, follow the conventions of doubling described throughout this book (as Scott McMillin and Sally-Beth Maclean have persuasively argued concerning the *Henry VI* plays in their book on the Queen's Men). I include charts for *The Taming of the Shrew and Richard III*, despite these plays probably having been written before 1594, because of their popularity, and because they are less elegant structures (where doubling is concerned) than those that follow, and so may help suggest the refinements in dramaturgical structure that Shakespeare made as his career progressed. The charts are prepared for 8–12 actors, in each case the minimum number necessary to perform, and each should work for any texts (Q/F/Conflated) commonly considered authoritative. Identified or acknowledged mutes are accounted for, though I assume that two mute 'attendants', 'lords', etc. will suffice unless the text makes the presence of a greater number explicit. When an attendant is not specifically referenced, I allow for the possibility that a named character could be the person sent to see who knocks at the door, or to deliver a message.

Stage directions are followed strictly when they correspond to the text. When they do not, I privilege the needs suggested by language and dramaturgy over the needs of the stage directions. Specifically, I assume in a few instances that a character named in a stage direction that neither speaks nor draws notice from other characters, nor otherwise proves strictly necessary to the scene, may be employed elsewhere. Also, as is well known, the Folio stage directions are elaborate, and may sometimes suggest numbers that may not always have been available to Shakespeare's company. It may be that a literary sensibility helps account for their inclusion and detail, so that characters appear in stage directions where they reasonably should or could be present, even if the company omitted them from those scenes in performance.

The casting charts note one possible way to perform each play with a minimum cast. Where interest seems likely I include brief analysis and pose secondary options, as well as noting staging challenges and possible ways to overcome them when working with cast sizes predicted by the structures. Without doubt, there are many choices left unexplored, and each suggestion in the pages that follow – however successful it may be onstage – closes down options that could be even more generative in a particular production or better suited to the individual actors. When it comes to theatre production, my hope is less to define how a play should be cast, than to show the value of doubling, and to invite directors to be less random in the assignation of roles. Ideally, these charts would serve as guides that can inform productions and allow practitioners to make bold choices with a better understanding of what may be gained or sacrificed each time they send out an attendant, soldier, or messenger.

Hamlet, c. 1600 (Q2, F)

Key: x (speaker); m (mute); (x) concealed character

	Francisco	Barnardo	Marcellus	Horatio	Ghost	Claudius	Gertrude	Polonius	Laertes	Ophelia	Hamlet	Voltemand	Cornelius	Reynaldo	Rosencrantz	Guildenstern	1 Play.(King)	2 Pl. (Queen)	3 Pl. (ProlLuc)	Fortinbras	Captain	Others	1 Clown	2 Clown	Priest	Osric	Lord	Ambassador
1.1a	x	x																										
1.1b	x	x	x	x																								
1.1c		x	x	x																								
1.1d		x	x	x	x																							
1.1e		x	x	x																								
1.2a						x	x	x	x	x	x																	
1.2b						x	x	x	x	x	x	x	x									mm (Lords; Q: cum aliis)						
1.2c						x	x	x	x	x	x											mm						
1.2d											x																	
1.2e		x	x	x							x																	
1.2f											x																	
1.3a									x	x																		
1.3b								x	x	x																		
1.3c								x		x																		
1.4a			x	x							x																	
1.4b			x	x	x						x																	
1.4c			x	x																								
1.5a					x						x																	
1.5b											x																	
1.5c			x	x	(x)						x																	
2.1a								x						x														
2.1b								x		x																		
2.2a						x	x								x	x						mm ('cum aliis')						
2.2b						x	x	x																				
2.2c						x	x																					
2.2d						x	x	x				x	x															
2.2e						x	x	x																				
2.2f								x			x																	
2.2g								x			x				x	x												
2.2h								x			x				x	x												
2.2g								x			x				x	x	x					mmmm ('four or five players')						
2.2h											x																	
3.1a						x	x	x		x					x	x						mm ('Lords')						
3.1b						(x)		(x)		x	x																	
3.1c						x		x		x																		
3.2a											x						x					mm ('two or three players')						
3.2b								x			x				x	x												
3.2c				x							x																	
3.2d				m*		x	x	x		x	x																	
3.2e				m		x	x	x		x	x						x	x	x									
3.2f				x							x																	
3.2g				x							x				x	x												

*   Horatio is mute during 'The Mousetrap'. Given Hamlet's 'get you a place' (3.2.83–4), he may exit to become a performer.
^   Horatio's exit is unmentioned, but he is silent upon R&G's entrance and seems to exit sometime before Hamlet's closing soliloquy.
~   Q2 SD calls for another (mute) ambassador. The part is superfluous, though a nine-man troupe could fill it with the Lord retiring during the commotion onstage.
** These duties are at least partly filled by Osric and the Lord already participating in the scene. Two other actors in a nine-man cast will be available, provided that they retire in time to return as Fortinbras and the English Ambassador.

Hamlet, c. 1600 (Q2, F) *(continued)*

	Francisco	Barnardo	Marcellus	Horatio	Ghost	Claudius	Gertrude	Polonius	Laertes	Ophelia	Hamlet	Voltemand	Cornelius	Reynaldo	Rosencrantz	Guildenstern	1 Play.(King)	2 Pl. (Queen)	3 Pl. (Prol/Luc)	Fortinbras	Captain	Others	1 Clown	2 Clown	Priest	Osric	Lord	Ambassador
3.2h			m*^								x				x	x	m					x ('one with a recorder')						
3.2i			m					x			x				x	x												
3.2j											x																	
3.3a						x									x	x												
3.3b						x	x																					
3.3c						x																						
3.3d						x					x																	
3.4a							x	x																				
3.4b							x	x			x																	
3.4c					x		x	m (dead)			x																	
3.4d							x	m (dead)			x																	
4.1a						x	x								x(Q2)													
4.1b						x	x																					
4.2a											x				x	x												
4.3a						x																						
4.3b						x					x				x	x												
4.3c						x																						
4.4a																				x	x	'Armie'						
4.4b											x				x					x	x							
4.4c											x(Q2)																	
4.5a				x			x															x (Q2, 'Gentleman')						
4.5b				m			x			x																		
4.5c				m		x	x			x																		
4.5d						x	x																					
4.5e						x	x															x ('Messenger')						
4.5e						x	x															x ('Messenger')						
4.5f						x	x		x													xx (Laertes' 'followers')						
4.5g						x	x		x																			
4.5h						x	x		x	x																		
4.5i						x			x																			
4.6a				x																		x ('Servant')						
4.6b				x																		xm ('Sailors')						
4.7a						x			x																			
4.7b						x			x													x ('Messenger')						
4.7c						x	x		x																			
4.7d						x	x		x																			
5.1a																							x	x				
5.1b				x							x												x	x				
5.1c				x							x												x					
5.1d				x		x	x		x		x											mm ('lords')	x					
5.1e						x	m		x													mm			m			
5.2a				x							x																	
5.2b				x							x															x		
5.2c				x							x																	
5.2d				x							x																x (Q2)	
5.2e				x							x																	
5.2f				x		x	x		x		x											mm ('lords')				x	m*	
5.2g				x		x	x		x		x									x						m	m	x*~

Hamlet
c. 1600 (Q2, F)
෨ The division of the parts ෬

Ghost Claudius	} For one actor	Gertrude	} For one actor
Francisco Hamlet	} For one actor	Ophelia Servant (4.6) 2 Gravedigger Osric	} For one actor
Horatio	} For one actor	Marcellus Cornelius Rosencrantz Player Queen Sailor Priest English Ambassador	} For one actor
Laertes Reynaldo 1 Player/Player King Norwegian Captain	} For one actor		
Polonius Attendant (4.3, 5.2) Gentleman (4.5, Q2) Messenger (4.5) 1 Gravedigger Lord (5.2, Q2)	} For one actor	Barnardo Voltemand Guildenstern 2 Player (Prologue, Luc.) Fortinbras Sailor (mute)	} For one actor

Nine actors can play 32 speaking roles and one mute. Two play female roles, with Gertrude specializing and the Ophelia actor taking male roles after her permanent exit from the play. As celebrated as *Hamlet* is, it should be even more admired given the efficiency of its structure and the thematic enhancements it makes possible, for instance when Ophelia helps her father to dig her own grave, then returns as Osrick so that Hamlet can badger her again; or when Laertes goes to France, then goes there once more to spy on himself in the person of Reynaldo, only to return as a travelling player. The play also benefits by having the Rosencrantz and Guildenstern actors working often as a duo, first as Marcellus and Barnardo, then as Cornelius and Voltemand, then as members of the playing troupe, then as Sailors, and eventually as the English Ambassador and Fortinbras, who enter after the deaths of Rosencrantz and Guildenstern in England. I discuss other doubling possibilities and their effects in Chapter 1.

The Taming of the Shrew
c. 1592 (F)
❧ The division of the parts ❦

Lord Petruchio	} For one actor	Baptista Nathaniel Haberdasher	} For one actor
Hostess Katherine	} For one actor	2 Huntsman Grumio	} For one actor
1 Huntsman Hortensio Officer (5.1)	} For one actor	2 Servant Gremio Philip	} For one actor
1 Player Lucentio	} For one actor	3 Servant Biondello Peter	} For one actor
2 Player Tranio Curtis Tailor	} For one actor	1 Servant Messenger (3.1) Vincentio Joseph	} For one actor
Bartholomew Bianca	} For one actor	Sly Nicholas Merchant Widow	} For one actor

Twelve actors can play 34 speaking roles. One of these can specialize in female roles. Like other early plays (e.g. *Love's Labour's Lost, Two Gentlemen of Verona*) much of the 'doubling' takes place through disguise: Lucentio and Tranio exchange identities (by changing clothes); Lucentio disguises himself to become Bianca's tutor (as does Hortensio); a Merchant is found to impersonate Vincentio. The framing scene, however, allows almost everyone to double, which can be vitalizing in production. Playing with 12 requires that the performers of the Induction gradually leave their places to participate in the play. The Lord or Sly can go on to play Petruchio, with the hostess taking Katherina. The dizzying array of servants at the Lord's house seem appropriate given the Shrew plot's obsession with servants (e.g. Lucentio commands Tranio who orders Biondello about). Servants may speak a greater percentage of the text in this play than any other, and Petruchio's house teems with them, naming six in 4.1. These servants will be more interesting if they are cast from among the nobles and servants that Petruchio and Kate left behind in Padua.

Richard III
c. 1593 (Q1, F)
❧ The division of the parts ❦

Roles	For one actor	Roles	For one actor
Richard Priest (3.2)	For one actor	1 Carrier (1.2) Buckingham/Ghost 4 Messenger (4.4) Norfolk	For one actor
Clarence/Ghost Edward IV 3 Citizen (2.3) Lord Mayor Tyrrel	For one actor	Queen Margaret Catesby Ghost of Prince Edward	For one actor
Tressel (mute) Hastings/Ghost Archbishop of York Scrivener 3 Messenger (4.4) Blunt	For one actor	Queen Elizabeth Pursuivant Bishop of Ely Richmond	For one actor
Lady Anne/Ghost Edward Plantagenet Messenger (3.2) Thomas Lovell Christopher Urswick	For one actor	Duchess of York Vaughn/Ghost Sheriff of Wiltshire Messenger (5.3)	For one actor
Brakenbury Rivers/Ghost 1 Murderer 1 Citizen (2.3) 2 Messenger (4.4) Oxford	For one actor	Attendant (1.1, mute) 2 Carrier (1.2) Derby Messenger (2.4) Cardinal Bourchier Ghost of Henry VI	For one actor
Berkeley (mute) Dorset 2 Murderer 2 Citizen (2.3) Prince of Wales/Ghost Ratcliff	For one actor	Lord Grey/Ghost Margaret Plantagenet Duke of York/Ghost Page (4.2) 1 Messenger (4.4) Herbert	For one actor

Twelve actors can play 64 speaking roles (including ghosts) and 2 mutes. *Richard III* is Shakespeare's most complicated casting plot. It suggests that Shakespeare's art of dramaturgy was still developing in the early 1590s, though it also shows great ambition. Later plays like *Antony and Cleopatra* or *Pericles* allow for casting 50+ characters and moving through the changes necessary onstage with much greater ease. There are fewer aesthetic advantages to doubling in this play than in most others, though the plot allows

Richard to befriend and betray the same stage figures more than once, while also permitting most of those killed by Richard to have a hand in avenging their deaths. Like some other early plays, *Richard III* contains many parts for women and children, and at least four actors capable of playing female roles are required. Two of these (Margaret and Elizabeth in this chart) would also need to double adult male roles. In 3.7, most of the ensemble is available to play the citizens who 'shout' for Richard.

The Comedy of Errors

c. 1593 (F)

❧ The division of the parts ❧

Duke Balthazar } For one actor Officer		Adrianna } For one actor	
Egeon Pinch } For one actor		Luciana } For one actor	
		Luce Courtesan } For one actor	
Antipholus of Ephesus } For one actor		Angelo } For one actor	
Antipholus of Syracuse Headman (mute, 5.1) } For one actor		1 Merchant Messenger (5.1) } For one actor Abbess	
Dromio of Ephesus } For one actor			
Dromio of Syracuse Officer (5.1, mute) } For one actor		Jailer (1.1) 2 Merchant } For one actor	

Twelve actors can play 19 speaking roles and two mutes. Three actors can specialize in female roles, while the actor playing the Abbess would need to double at least one male role. Whereas *The Taming of the Shrew* achieves many 'doubling-' style effects through disguise, *The Comedy of Errors* does so by casting two sets of twins – twins who will presumably (and valuably) not look alike. Perhaps as a result, the plot reflects less interest in doubling roles than most that follow, though there are inviting possibilities, such as Egeon and Doctor Pinch. Egeon, the old Merchant of Syracuse whose 'bonds' – both figurative (to his lost sons) and literal (he is a prisoner awaiting death) – are the subject of the play, matches well with Pinch, given the latter's obsession with 'binding' Antipholus and Dromio and laying them 'in some dark room' (4.4.89, 108). Pinch rants about both master and man being 'possessed', and the comedy will be greater if he himself seems possessed, as he will if he appears initially as the comparatively sober Egeon.

Another attractive possibility is doubling the Courtesan and the Abbess. My plot does not include the choice because it requires an onstage transformation, but that transformation can be electric in production, since (like *Othello*) it seems to harmonize the madonna and the whore.[1] Such choices can seem to extend the play's interest in mistaken identity. Luc can be played by almost anyone in the cast, and is often a high point of productions. Her name may be an invitation to double her with Luciana or an excuse not to do it. In contemporary productions, the most popular doubling for the play is to ask one pair of actors to double both sets of twins, a choice that tends to excite audiences by displays of great virtuosity and ingenuity, though the misrecognition scenes can be somewhat diminished for it.

The Two Gentleman of Verona
c. 1594 (F)
❧ The division of the parts ❧

Proteus	}	For one actor	Antonio Host 1 Outlaw	}	For one actor
Valentine	}	For one actor			
Julia	}	For one actor	Panthino		
Lucetta Silvia	}	For one actor	Eglamour 2 Outlaw	}	For one actor
Speed	}	For one actor			
Thurio	}	For one actor	Launce		
Duke of Milan	}	For one actor	3 Outlaw	}	For one actor

Proteus	}	For one actor	Antonio Thurio 3 Outlaw	}	For one actor
Valentine	}	For one actor			
Julia Speed	}	For one actor	Panthino Duke of Milan Host	}	For one actor
Lucetta Silvia	}	For one actor			
Eglamour 2 Outlaw	}	For one actor	Launce 1 Outlaw	}	For one actor

[1] When I directed the play, the Courtesan exited at 5.1.281 to fetch the Abbess. When it came time for the Courtesan to speak her single line (5.1.393) the Abbess simply opened her robe to reveal the Courtesan's costume within while her expression changed to something sultry.

The first chart distributes 16 roles among ten actors. The second is arranged for eight, the smallest cast possible for any of Shakespeare's plays. The first chart allows two actors to specialize in female roles, while the second requires that the Julia actor double Speed, leaving only one actor who can play women exclusively. I include the second chart to show how it is often possible to play with fewer actors if minor concessions are made – though here a concession that still does not require any cutting or alterations to the text. The limiting scene (5.4) calls for nine actors onstage simultaneously, but if the company is willing to dispense with the third outlaw in 5.4 (the outlaws speak one line in the scene), and to cover a quick change so that the actor playing Julia can re-enter as Speed at the top of 2.2, eight is enough. Like other early plays, the doubling suggested by the structure is less elaborate and efficient than it is later in Shakespeare's career, though the outlaws, comic in any case, will always be more interesting when played by other comic characters, such as Launce and Thurio.

Romeo and Juliet
c. 1595 (Q2, F)
🙹 The division of the parts 🙸

Role(s)		Role(s)	
Chorus Prince Paris Mercutio	For one actor	Tybalt Nurse Friar John Chief Watchman	For one actor
Gregory Romeo	For one actor	Lady Montague Juliet	For one actor
Benvolio Friar Laurence	For one actor	Lady Capulet Apothecary	For one actor
Capulet	For one actor	Samson 1 Servingman 1 Musician 2 Watchman	For one actor
Abraham Peter Balthasar	For one actor		
Montague Old Man	For one actor	Montague's Man 2 Servingman	For one actor
Citizen 3 Musician Paris's Page	For one actor	Petruccio 2 Musician 3 Watchman	

Twelve actors can play 34 speaking roles. Based on the structure, two actors can play female roles exclusively, though only one does so in the chart because of the aesthetic incentives for having the actors playing the Nurse and Lady Capulet double Tybalt and the Apothecary. The doubling plan for Romeo and Juliet is discussed in detail in Chapter 5.

Richard II
c. 1595 (Q1)
❧ The division of the parts ❧

Richard Welsh Captain	For one actor	Bushy Bishop of Carlisle 1 Gardener's Man Exton's Servant (mute)	For one actor
Gaunt Northumberland Gardener	For one actor	Mowbray Attendant (2.1, mute) Harry Percy (Hotspur)	For one actor
Lord Marshall York	For one actor	Duchess of Gloucester Ross 1 Lady Surrey Duchess of York Keeper	For one actor
Bolingbroke Attendant (2.1, mute)	For one actor		
Aumerle Berkeley	For one actor	1 Herald (1.3) Queen Isabel Groom	For one actor
Bagot Salisbury Guard Exton's Servant	For one actor	2 Herald (1.3) Willoughby Servingman (2.2, 5.2) Fitzwater 2 Lady	For one actor
Green Sir Stephen Scroop 2 Gardener's Man Abbott of Westminster Exton	For one actor		

Twelve actors can play 38 speaking roles and three mutes. Three actors are required to play female roles, each needing to take on small male roles in order to play with 12. The plot shows increased elegance in design, when compared to Shakespeare's other early plays. Alan Armstrong has written persuasively about doubling in the play, observing that 'something like the fragments of a casting chart survive vestigially in the lines of the text' and attending to how frequently character entrances are 'marked by a prosaic, identifying line'.[2] As Armstrong notes, Gaunt and Mowbray are particularly attractive candidates for doubling, since both retire from the plot early after prominent turns. My speculative plot allows Mowbray to return as the equally impetuous Hotspur, while Gaunt returns first as Northumberland, and then as the Gardener, a role especially suited for him considering his long speech wherein he refers to England as 'This other Eden, demi-paradise', and 'This blessed plot' (2.1.42, 50). In addition, Northumberland is charged with

---

[2] Armstrong, ' "What is Become of Bushy?" ', p. 152.

seeing Bushy and Green executed. If he returns as the gardener, and 'Bushy' and 'Green' (whose names could not imaginably be better suited to the purpose) are his men, he will essentially see them digging their own graves. Meanwhile, Bushy and Green can return to Richard's side as the Bishop of Carlisle and Sir Stephen Scroop. The Duchess of Gloucester's return as Surrey lets her fight against Fitzwater, her husband's supposed killer (4.1), while the Queen's return as the Groom will make for a more interesting and emotional meeting of the two at Pomfret Castle (5.5).

A Midsummer Night's Dream
c. 1595 (Q1, F)
❧ The division of the parts ❦

Oberon Theseus	} For one actor	Hermia Snug Moth	} For one actor	
Titania Hippolyta	} For one actor	Helena Flute	} For one actor	
Puck Philostrate	} For one actor	Starveling Cobweb	} For one actor	
Lysander First Fairy	} For one actor	Tom Snout Mustardseed	} For one actor	
Demetrius	} For one actor	Egeus Peter Quince Peaseblossom	} For one actor	
Bottom	} For one actor			

Eleven actors can play 22 speaking roles. One of these can specialize in female roles. The plan calls on Hermia and Helena to double as mechanicals. I discuss the substitutions required and the thematic advantages of the other choices in Chapter 5.

Love's Labour's Lost
c. 1596 (Q, F)
❧ The division of the parts ❧

Navarre	} For one actor	Longaville Nathaniel	} For one actor
Biron	} For one actor	Dumaine Forester	} For one actor
Boyet Dull	} For one actor	Princess	} For one actor
Armado Lord (2.1, 4.1, mute)	} For one actor	Rosaline Jaquenetta	} For one actor
Holofernes Lord (2.1, 4.1) Marcade	} For one actor	Katharine	} For one actor
Costard Lord (2.1, mute)	} For one actor	Maria Moth	} For one actor

Twelve actors can play 18 speakers and two mutes. Three of the four actors playing female roles may do so exclusively, while Maria doubles as the diminutive Moth. 5.1 ends with Dull suggesting that he can't perform with his friends in the pageant of the worthies but will 'make one in a dance' (5.1.134). Yet he never turns up in 5.2, possibly because Shakespeare anticipated the actor would be needed elsewhere. While it is of course possible that the play was written with a cast of more than 12 in mind – this play, *The Taming of the Shrew*, *Titus Andronicus*, *Richard III*, and *Romeo and Juliet* all ask more ingenuity of a 12-man cast than any play written after 1595 – the structure calls for Longaville and Maria to go silent for the lengthy stretch of 5.2 during which the pageant is performed, thereby allowing them to double as two of the performers. In this respect, the scene is quite like 5.1 of *A Midsummer Night's Dream*, where Hermia and Helena are silent throughout the performance of 'Pyramus and Thisbe'. The pageant concludes with a song sung by 'Winter' and 'Spring', which can be represented by Holofernes and Costard, who are available to return after Nathaniel and Moth rejoin the other lovers.

Love's Labour's Lost makes doubling a prominent topic of the fiction when the onstage audience discusses how four men can present 'nine worthies' (5.2.530–41). Like other early plays, it is notable for including many disguises, that take the place of doubling as a central concern. Still, as Stephen Booth points out, in a play full of people mistaking one another for other characters, Rosaline and Jaquenetta are linked when Biron's letter to Rosaline is mistakenly delivered to Jaquenetta. According to Booth, doubling the roles would 'underscore the persistent, play-long comparison of Rosaline's suitor with Costard and Armado'.[3]

King John
c. 1596 (F)
❧ The division of the parts ❧

King John	} For one actor	Constance Peter of Pomfret	} For one actor	
Philip the Bastard	} For one actor	Messenger (5.5)		
Essex King Philip 1 Executioner Bigot	} For one actor	Arthur Prince Henry	} For one actor	
		Sheriff (mute) Citizen Hubert	} For one actor	
Chatillon French Herald* Pandulph	} For one actor	Robert Faulconbridge Dauphin	} For one actor	
Eleanor 2 Executioner (mute) Melun	} For one actor	Lady Faulconbridge Blanche Messenger (4.2, 5.3)	} For one actor	
Salisbury James Gurney English Herald	} For one actor	Pembroke Duke of Austria	} For one actor	

Twelve actors can play 28 speaking roles and two mutes. These numbers include unique roles for the two Heralds, whose functions can be filled by Chatillon and Salisbury without a change of character. Of course, musicians could have been brought on stage for flourishes, drums, etc. and so heralds may have been found among their ranks. In the chart, two actors play female roles as well as minor male roles, while one actor takes on both young princes, Arthur and Henry. To play with 12 requires that Pembroke not participate in 2.1, where he appears in a stage direction but is never involved or mentioned in the scene. His omission is reasonable considering that Salisbury is left out of the same stage direction but must be present in order to seek Constance at King John's command.

Like other early plays, the structure of *King John* is less efficient than most that follow, since it does not have attractive secondary prospects for the actors playing Austria, King Philip, Constance, Blanche, and Queen Eleanor, all of whom retire by the end of Act Three. Still, the Constance actor will make a more interesting Peter of Pomfret than a newly introduced actor, since it would

---

[3] Booth, 'Speculations on Doubling', p. 149.

permit her to return to court as the prophet who foretells John's (momentary) resignation of the crown. Chatillon is a good candidate for Pandulph, each playing an intermediary of sorts in his particular half of the play. Even a role as small as the 4.2 messenger can generate interest through double-casting. When he arrives to deliver bad news at court, John observes 'A fearful eye thou hast. Where is that blood / That I have seen inhabit in those cheeks?' (4.2.106–7). The description will seem strikingly appropriate if John addresses the actor formerly known as 'Blanche'.

The Merchant of Venice
c. 1596 (Q1, F)
❧ The division of the parts ❧

Antonio	} For one actor	Lorenzo Messenger (2.9) 1 Magnifico (mute)	}	For one actor
Bassanio Morocco Aragon	} For one actor			
Shylock Old Gobbo	} For one actor	Portia (Balthasar) Leonardo	}	For one actor
Salarino Salerio Balthasar	} For one actor	Nerissa (Clerk) Antonio's man (3.10)	}	For one actor
Solanio 2 Magnifico (mute) Stephano	} For one actor	Portia's Servingman (1.2, 2.9) Jessica	}	For one actor
Gratiano	} For one actor	Launcelot Tubal Jailer (mute) Duke	}	For one actor

Eleven actors can play 23 speaking roles and three mutes. At least two of the three actors playing female roles must double small male roles both in (as Bellario and the Clerk) and out of the fiction (here, as Leonardo and Antonio's man). The limiting scene is 4.1, wherein eight speakers appear simultaneously, though we can assume at least two 'magnificoes' should be available. In a pinch, a company could perform with ten by having both Jessica and Lorenzo become magnificoes, to some extent mirroring the disguised Portia and Nerissa at the trial. Salerio can respond to the Duke's commands in the scene, and, along with Gratiano and the magnificoes, help make up the 'three or four' that usher in Balthasar (Portia). Any musically inclined actor can play Stephano, as could one of the musicians. Salerio and Salarino are played by one actor according to the chart, and could be combined as one or played as two distinct roles. The confusion over their names may result from the same actor being needed where it seemed impossible for the *character* to be: that is, Salarino cannot reasonably speak with Shylock on the Rialto in Venice in (3.1), then appear in Belmont in the next scene (3.2), so a second role and slight variation on the name were introduced.

The doubling works fluidly for a cast of 11, and it creates interesting dynamics. Shylock, the play's arch-villain and human victim, can put his frailty and humanity on earlier display as Old Gobbo, whose role in helping Launcelot enter Bassanio's service is directly related to Shylock's own attempt to get rid of him. Launcelot, who enters the play trying to arbitrate between his 'conscience' and 'the fiend', can reprise the comic position in a serious setting as the Duke of Venice. The most interesting choice is probably the doubling of Portia's suitors. Shylock is available and attractive for Morocco, though my plot assigns both to the Bassanio actor, who then gets three attempts at choosing the right casket. I discuss the scene in Chapter 4.

Henry IV, Part 1
c. 1597 (Q1, F)
ଛ The division of the parts ঙ

King	} For one actor	Westmoreland	} For one actor	
Mortimer		Ostler		
Sherriff		Bardolph		
		Archbishop of York		
Prince Hal	} For one actor	2 Messenger (5.2)		
Falstaff	} For one actor	Lord (1.1, mute)	} For one actor	
Glendower		Carrier/Traveler		
		Kate		
Lancaster	} For one actor	Mistress Quickly		
Poins		Vernon		
Lady Mortimer				
Hotspur	} For one actor	Worcester	} For one actor	
2 Carrier/Traveler		Chamberlain		
Francis		Vintner		
		Sir Michael		
Blunt	} For one actor	Lord (1.1, 3.2, mute)	} For one actor	
Gadshill		Northumberland		
Servant (2.3)		Peto		
Messenger (4.1, 5.2)		Douglas		

Ten actors can play 32 speaking roles and two mutes. This number assumes that the carriers can speak the single line assigned to the travellers, whose party may be filled out by others in the cast. Two actors play female as well as male roles. Hotspur's servant may be combined with the messengers, though they are listed separately here. The play has several distinct settings – among them the court, the tavern, and Wales – creating potential for extensive doubling. Mistress Quickly and Francis, for instance, can transition to a domestic setting as Kate and Hotspur, while tavern regulars like Peto and Bardolph can take prominent ranks among the rebels as Douglas and the Archbishop of York.

Meanwhile, the actor playing Poins can become a literal brother to Hal by also playing Prince John, while Hal's surrogate father, Falstaff, can seem to extend that role by becoming a father-in-law to another prominent rebel, Mortimer, if he takes the role of Glendower. My plot offers Henry IV as a potential pairing with Mortimer, which further complicates both the characters' and the audience's ability to tell the traitors from the true men. While I suggest Poins (presumably a handsome, younger brother type) as a candidate for Lady Mortimer, she could be played by anyone capable of singing and at least pretending to speak Welsh. The most interesting choice may be Hal himself. If the actor playing Hal doubles as Lady Mortimer then Falstaff could seem to become his father indeed by doubling as Glendower. Moreover, Hal takes time to imagine domestic life among the rebels and even undertakes to impersonate both Hotspur and Lady Percy, afterwards proposing that Falstaff play Lady Percy to his Hotspur (2.4.91–102). This scene, along with the play's insistence on calling him the Prince of *Wales* (14 times) would lend some interest to his appearance in Wales as the Welsh woman.

The Merry Wives of Windsor
c. 1597 (Q, F)
☙ The division of the parts ❧

Falstaff	} For one actor	Slender	} For one actor
Simple	} For one actor	1 Servant (3.1, 4.2)	
Ford (Brook)		Sir Hugh Evans	} For one actor
Page	} For one actor	Pistol	} For one actor
Mistress Ford	} For one actor	Doctor Caius	
Mistress Page	} For one actor	Bardolph	} For one actor
Anne Page	} For one actor	Fenton	
Robin		Rugby	
William Page		Nym	} For one actor
2 Servant (3.1, 4.2)		Mistress Quickly	
Robert Shallow	} For one actor	Host of the Garter	

Twelve actors can play 22 speaking roles. Two actors can play female roles exclusively; two others must take male roles as well, though one of these can limit participation to pages and children. The play appears to anticipate young boys will be available for mute parts as faeries in 5.5, the limiting scene in which 12 speakers are required. The plot is not very efficient, leaving a few actors with little work for long stretches, and requiring two quick changes in 5.5. Like some other early plays, this one frequently uses disguise (including Ford as Master Brook and Falstaff as the 'fat woman of Brentford') which somewhat limits potential for doubling roles. Pistol and Doctor Caius make a good pairing, though, since both are quarrelers who are, in Mistress Quickly's terms, 'abusing … the King's English' (1.4.4–5). The Hostess can also double the Host of the Garter, allowing the actor to function similarly in separate venues. The most interesting candidate for doubling may be Fenton, who enters the plot late and marries Anne Page at play's end. Fenton can double any one of the otherwise disappointed suitors, or Bardolph who would thereby seem to be made amends after his dismissal by Falstaff.

Though the Q and F texts are quite different they are consistent in their need for personnel. For instance, Q includes Shallow in the final scene but not Pistol, while F does just the opposite. Both texts leave a character out of the final scene that might otherwise be expected there, seemingly in order to remain playable by a 12-man cast.

Henry IV, Part 2
c. 1598 (Q, F)
❧ The division of the parts ❧

Morton Lord Chief Justice King Henry IV	For one actor	Prince Hal Mouldy Coleville	For one actor
Falstaff Epilogue	For one actor	Lord Bardolph Bardolph Mowbray 1 Beadle	For one actor
Mistress Quickly Lady Northumberland Wart Clarence	For one actor	Northumberland Robert Shallow Westmoreland 2 Beadle (mute)	For one actor
Travers Poins King's Page (3.1, mute) Shadow Lancaster	For one actor	Rumour Fang Pistol Archbishop of York Warwick	For one actor
Lady Percy Doll Tearsheet Feeble Gloucester	For one actor	Porter Falstaff's Page 2 Drawer Messenger (4.1) Harcourt 2 Groom	For one actor
Hastings Gower 3 Drawer Peto Silence Blunt (mute) 3 Groom	For one actor	Servant (1.2) Snare Francis Bullcalf Officer (4.2, mute) Davy 1 Groom	For one actor

Twelve actors can play 50 speaking roles and four mutes. The limiting scene is 5.5, in which 12 speakers appear. Two actors are assigned two prominent female roles apiece, along with minor male roles. Like *1 Henry IV*, this play allows for doubling Poins and Prince John, and for tavern regulars like Pistol and Bardolph to double in the rebel camp. Doubling Hal and Coleville allows the Prince more time with Falstaff, and lets Falstaff seem to assert the upper hand ahead of the stinging reversal to come. King Henry can participate in a similar reversal if he doubles as the Lord Chief Justice. While Falstaff anticipates great things at Hal's hands but is disappointed, the Lord Chief Justice expects the worst but is greeted with honour. Rumour can be played by anyone in the cast, as can the epilogue. Booth assigns Rumour to Pistol, since the latter is 'all talk' and brings Falstaff news that mingles truth and falsehood.[4] The epilogue can seem to present a poignant commentary on the two *Henry IV* plays when delivered by Falstaff.

Much Ado About Nothing
c. 1598 (Q, F)
❧ The division of the parts ❧

Leonato Watchman (mute)	} For one actor	Hero 2 Watchman	} For one actor
Don Pedro	} For one actor	Margaret Boy Watchman (mute)	} For one actor
Don John Sexton	} For one actor		
Antonio Watchman (mute)	} For one actor	Ursula Messenger (1.1, 3.5, 5.1) Watchman (mute)	} For one actor
Benedick Dogberry	} For one actor	Borachio Friar Francis	} For one actor
Beatrice Verges	} For one actor		
Claudio 1 Watchman	} For one actor	Conrad Balthasar Lord (5.3)	} For one actor

Twelve actors can play 22 speaking roles (assuming only two watchmen speak). Four actors play female roles. The structure allows for at least three of these to do so exclusively, though I have included all four 'women' among the large group of watchmen. The play's limiting scene is 2.1, in which 12 speakers appear (though it is not clear they all participate in the masquerade simultaneously). The short dramatis personae does not encourage extensive doubling, but the Dogberry plot can be enhanced by having the nobles do extra duty there. Since the play is insistently concerned with mistaking and deception, the overt artifice involved in having Benedick and Beatrice double the subplot's central comic duo, Dogberry and Verges, will lend interest.[5] If Claudio and Hero play watchmen, this too will be thematically enhancing, considering Claudio's repeated inability to determine whether Hero is herself or an impostor (at the masquerade; on seeing Margaret with Borachio at her window; on seeing Hero veiled at the second wedding). The naivety that characterizes both, and their tendency to misunderstand what is before them, is

---

[4] Ibid., p. 141.
[5] Herbert Weil has discussed the prospects of doubling Beatrice and Benedick in the subplot. See ' "Be Vigilant, I beseech you": A Fantasia on Dogberry and Doubling in *Much Ado About Nothing*', *The Ben Jonson Journal* 6 (1999), pp. 307–17.

equally evident in Hugh Oatcake and George Seacoal. Borachio is an attractive candidate for Friar Francis, who is – like some other friars in Shakespeare – as comfortable with deception as he is truth or goodness. Since Borachio deceives Claudio and leads him to reject Hero, then attempts to make amends with his confession, the actor who doubles as Friar Francis can seem to repair Borachio's misdeeds by arranging a second deception that leads Claudio to repent and return to Hero.

Henry V
1599 (Q, F)
ও The division of the parts ৩

Chorus French Ambassador		Exeter MacMorris	For one actor
Montjoy Scroop Governor of Harfleur Huntingdon (mute)	For one actor	Westmoreland Fluellen Constable of France	For one actor
Henry V Lewis the Dauphin	For one actor	Warwick Nym Thomas Erpingham York	For one actor
Archbishop of Cant. Pistol Grandpre Burgundy	For one actor	Cambridge Berri (mute) Gower Rambures Court Salisbury Clarence (mute)	For one actor
Bishop of Ely Bardolph Bourbon Queen Isabel	For one actor		
Gloucester Grey Britaine Messenger (3.7, 4.2)	For one actor	Boy Messenger (2.4) Katherine Williams English Herald	For one actor
Bedford Charles VI Jamy Bates	For one actor	Hostess Alice Orleans Le Fer	For one actor

Twelve actors can play 47 speaking roles and two mutes. Three actors play female roles, two of these doubling minor male roles, while the actor playing Isabel (who does not appear until 5.2) is relied on for substantial male roles. Even among Shakespeare's plays, *Henry V* is notable for self-reflexivity, which invites assertions of artifice through double-casting. Both Q and F quietly make actors available just before introducing new characters, and the associations that the secondary and tertiary characters accrue can be powerful in performance. Tom Berger has written brilliantly about doubling in *Henry V*, posing a cast for 13, and I follow much of his lead here.[6] In my chart, notice that the Archbishop of Canterbury and the Bishop of Ely, who are wealthy as a result of upholding (and robbing) the church, can continue to pilfer churches in France as Pistol and Bardolph. Though more difficult, it would also be possible to have Bardolph, Nym, and Pistol – Henry V's former friends – be executed in the persons of Scroop, Cambridge, and Grey, a metafictional preview of Henry's decision to have Bardolph hanged for stealing. The chart also makes it possible for Henry to double as the Dauphin; for his chief courtiers to flank him in both the French and English camps; and for Alice and Katherine to take the battlefield: Alice (predictably) as two French-speaking lords, and Katherine as the soldier who debates with the King, a partial preview of the wooing scene in 5.2.

Julius Caesar
c. 1599 (F)
❧ The division of the parts ❧

Brutus	For one actor	Carpenter		
Cassius		Decius		
Ligarius	For one actor	1 Plebian	For one actor	
Antony	For one actor	Messala		
Caesar		Murellus		
Octavius	For one actor	Caesar's Servant (2.2)		
Caesar's Ghost		Artemidorus	For one actor	
Soothsayer		Octavius's Servant (3.1)		
Cinna		Lucilius		
Cinna the Poet		Flavius		
Pindarus	For one actor	Trebonius		
1 Soldier (5.4)		Antony's Servant (3.1)	For one actor	
Dardanius		1 Soldier (4.2)		
		Varrus		
Cicero		Calphurnia		
Publius		Lucius		
Lepidus		Popilius Lena		
Poet	For one actor	4 Plebian	For one actor	
Claudio		2 Soldier (4.2)		
2 Soldier (5.4)		Strato		
Clitus				
		Portia		
Cobbler		Metellus Cimber		
Casca		3 Plebian		
2 Plebian	For one actor	3 Soldier (4.2)	For one actor	
Titinius		Messenger (5.1)		
Volumnius		Young Cato		

---

[6] Berger, 'Casting Henry V', pp. 89–104.

Twelve actors can perform 51 speaking roles. There are only two female roles in the play, Calphurnia and Portia, both of whom exit permanently before Act Three, freeing the actors to take male roles thereafter. Portia declares herself to be Cato's daughter, so having the actor return as Young Cato will affirm a tacit link in the play while reuniting Brutus with his wife as his death approaches. As Strato, the Calphurnia actor can avenge her husband's death at Brutus's hands. Cinna the Poet, whom the mob cannot distinguish from Cinna the conspirator, will likewise gain interest by being assigned to the Cinna actor. Having the Casca actor return as Titinius continues his intimacy with Cassius, and adds poignancy to their twin suicides on the battlefield in 5.3, and to Brutus's impromptu elegy. The limiting scene requires ingenuity in staging for a cast of 12, which I discuss at the end of Chapter 4.

As You Like It
c. 1600 (F)
❧ The division of the parts ☙

Duke Frederick Duke Senior	For one actor	Adam Corin Jaques de Boys	For one actor
Rosalind Page (5.3)	For one actor	Dennis 1 Lord (2.1, 2.2, etc.) Silvius	For one actor
Orlando	For one actor		
Celia	For one actor	2 Lord (2.1, 2.2, etc.) Touchstone	For one actor
LeBeau Jaques	For one actor	Charles Amiens Hymen	For one actor
Oliver Oliver Martext William	For one actor		
Phebe Page (5.3)	For one actor	Lord (mute) Audrey	For one actor

Twelve actors can play 27 speaking roles and one mute. Four actors play female roles, three of whom must take roles for pages or mute lords. The actor for whom Phebe was written, however, may have been expected to do more speaking in the play's first half given her presumable talent and charm. She could, for instance, take the lord's role that is here assigned to Touchstone. As it stands, both the Phebe and Audrey actors have little to do beyond their primary parts. The plot alternates between scenes at court and in the forest of Arden, and the similar groups of personnel appearing in each location present attractive prospects for doubling, which may also be invited by the repetition of names (i.e. two Dukes, two Olivers, two Jacques). Duke Senior and Duke Frederick is a natural pair, underscored by the latter's failure to appear in the final scene. Jacques and LeBeau, two aloof Frenchmen, likewise seem well suited to one actor, and doubling the court entertainers, Charles and Amiens, can extend the theme. In Act Five, the play becomes focused on the rehabilitation of Oliver and Duke Frederick, which can seem to transpire in the countryside while the two appear in other roles. If Oliver plays the disappointed William, the latter will not be left out entirely from the rejoicing at play's end. 5.4 includes 13 speakers, so playing with 12 requires Amiens to exit and return as Hymen, a sensible role for him in light of his song at the wedding of the four couples. Meanwhile, Jaques de Boys' sudden introduction could, in a sense, restore the deceased Adam to the family he served.

Twelfth Night
c. 1601 (F)
❧ The division of the parts ❧

Orsino 2 Officer	} For one actor	Viola	} For one actor
		Olivia	} For one actor
Curio Andrew Aguecheek	} For one actor	Maria Sebastian	} For one actor
Sir Toby Belch	} For one actor	Sea Captain	
Valentine Antonio	} For one actor	Malvolio 1 Officer	} For one actor
Sailor Fabian Servant	} For one actor	Sailor Feste Priest	} For one actor

Ten actors can play 20 speaking roles. Two actors can play female roles exclusively, while one (Maria) also plays a male role. To play with ten, Malvolio will need to exit in search of himself in 5.1, and Curio (who appears in the stage direction but is never referenced in the scene) must be omitted from 5.1, or else he must exit as part of the group sent to summon Olivia, so that he can return as Andrew. I discuss the logistics and implications of the doubling plan in Chapter 7.

Troilus and Cressida
c. 1602 (Q, F)
❧ The division of the parts ❧

Chorus Pandarus Menelaus	} For one actor	Aeneas Patroclus Servant (3.1) Greek (5.6, mute)	} For one actor	
Cressida Andromache Servant (5.5)	} For one actor	Hector Calchas	} For one actor	
Troilus Trumpeter*	} For one actor	Ajax Antenor	} For one actor	
Troilus's Man (1.2, 3.2) Thersites Cassandra	} For one actor	Ulysses Deiphobus	} For one actor	
Alexander Diomedes Helen	} For one actor	Nestor Helenus	} For one actor	
Paris Achilles	} For one actor	Agamemnon Priam Margareton	} For one actor	

* May be a musician rather than a member of the ensemble.

Twelve actors can play 30 speakers and one mute. The Cressida actor can specialize in female roles (though she plays a servant here), while two actors play male as well as small female roles. Doubling is facilitated by confining several characters either within the walls of Troy or in the Greek camp. The largest scene is 4.5, in which 12 speakers appear. This scene presents an unusual challenge, since none of the 12 can double Thersites, who is not present. The problem can be solved, however, by having Patroclus retire with Cressida and Calchas in 4.5, since he does not participate in the remainder of the scene.

There are several inviting prospects for doubling. One of these concerns Pandarus, who can double not only the Chorus but also Thersites, who acts like something of an embittered chorus throughout the play's latter half. In the foregoing plot, I pair Pandarus with Menelaus, who thereby extends his position as one interested in and teased about the sex life of one otherwise intimate with him. Having him play the Chorus will also make his epilogue feel like a more inevitable and fitting conclusion for the play. Paris and Achilles also make a good pair, since Paris seems comparatively indifferent to the battle in which he, among the Trojans, should be most interested, while Achilles's reluctance to fight is a major topic of the play. Achilles also is accused of lazing about with Patroclus, as Paris is with Helen. A production that doubles these roles would gain additional energy by doubling Patroclus and Helen. However, doubling Helen with Diomedes is equally attractive, since the choice allows her (actor) to intervene in Cressida's relationship with Troilus and tempt her into a betrayal, thus reprising Paris's role in stealing her from Menelaus. Agamemnon is a natural match for Priam, and doubling the two roles can seem to manifest the audience's divided loyalties and ambivalences concerning those on both sides in the war. A similar effect is achieved by doubling Cassandra and Thersites, both of whom forecast doom and rail at their particular countrymen throughout the play.

Measure for Measure
c. 1603 (F)
❧ The division of the parts ⮞

Angelo / Claudio	For one actor	Juliet / Isabella	For one actor
Duke / Froth	For one actor	First Gentleman / Elbow / Barnardine	For one actor
Lucio / Justice	For one actor	Second Gentleman / Pompey / Friar Peter	For one actor
Mistress Overdone / Officer (mute) / Francisca / Servant (2.4, mute) / Mariana / Messenger (4.2)	For one actor	Escalus / Friar Thomas / Abhorson	For one actor
		Provost	For one actor

Nine actors can play 22 speaking roles and two mutes. At least two must play female roles, one of these taking minor male roles as well. The chart assumes that substitution, a central concern in the play, might also be undertaken in casting by literally substituting Angelo for Claudio, the latter appearing muffled and remaining silent during the final scene. If this choice is not made, ten actors can perform the full text. I discuss doubling possibilities for the play, as well as its seeming interest in actor substitutions, in the Epilogue.

Othello
c. 1604 (Q, F)
❧ The division of the parts ❧

Iago	} For one actor	Duke	} For one actor
Othello	} For one actor	Montano	
Officer (1.2)		Brabantio	
Desdemona	For one actor	3 Gentleman	For one actor
Bianca		Gratiano	
Roderigo		1 Senator	
Messenger (1.3)	For one actor	1 Gentleman	For one actor
Clown		Lodovico	
Cassio		2 Senator	
Sailor	For one actor	2 Gentleman	
Officer (1.3)		Herald	For one actor
Emilia	For one actor	Musician	

Ten actors can play 24 speaking roles. Two can specialize in female roles, though each is here assigned a role as an Officer. The play enables possibilities for doubling that are especially potent in reinforcing its themes and even the genre. I discuss these possibilities in Chapter 7.

All's Well That Ends Well
c. 1605 (F)
❧ The division of the parts ❧

Countess	For one actor	Rinaldo	
Mariana		1 Lord (2.3)	
Bertram	} For one actor	1 Lord Dumaine	For one actor
Lafew	For one actor	1 Gentleman	
Duke of Florence		2 Lord (2.3)	
Helena	} For one actor	2 Lord Dumaine	For one actor
Parolles	For one actor	2 Gentleman	
Attendant (5.3)		Page (1.1)	
King of France	For one actor	2 Lord (1.2, 2.1)	
2 Soldier		3 Lord (2.3)	For one actor
Lavatch		Diana Capilet	
1 Soldier (Interpreter)	For one actor	1 Lord (1.2, 2.1)	
Gentleman (5.1, 5.3)		4 Lord (2.3)	For one actor
		Widow Capilet	

Eleven actors can play 27 speaking roles. Two can specialize in female roles, while two others playing females also double as lords. The limiting scene is 5.3, in which 11 speakers appear simultaneously. The play's three distinct settings (Rousillon, the French court, and Florence) facilitate doubling, and the frequent references to 'young lords' in the French court may hint at the presence of the women who do not appear until late in Act Three. Either the King of France or Lafew is a good prospect to double the Duke of Florence, each a source of authority in France who stays behind when the others depart for the war. The Countess can keep looking in on Helena as Mariana, just as France and Lafew can observe their countrymen while playing Florentines. Lavatch can put his comic skill to further use as Interpreter, and his appearance as the Gentleman that Helena meets in France (5.1) can sparkle as a straight turn from the formerly comic actor. The Dumaine brothers are a challenge since they play discrete yet quite similar roles at home and abroad; an expectation that they would be doubled may explain the confusion about the lords' speech prefixes in the Folio text.

King Lear
c. 1605 (Q1, F)
❧ The division of the parts ❧

King Lear	} For one actor	Kent (Caius) Old Man	} For one actor
Goneril Servant (3.7)	} For one actor		
		Albany Gentleman (2.4, 3.1) Servant (3.7) Doctor	} For one actor
Regan Messenger (4.4)	} For one actor		
Cordelia Fool	} For one actor	Curan (2.1) Gentleman (4.3, 4.6, 4.7) Servant (3.7) Captain (5.3)	} For one actor
Burgundy Edmund	} For one actor		
France Edgar Gentleman (1.5)	} For one actor	Cornwall Knight (1.4) Gentleman (4.2, 5.3)	} For one actor
Gloucester Herald	} For one actor	Oswald Captain (5.3)	} For one actor

Twelve actors can play 29 speaking roles and acknowledged mutes. Three actors play female roles, two of whom need only to double a servant and a messenger, while Cordelia is assigned the Fool. The structure only demands 11 actors, since the roles here assigned to the tenth actor (Curan, etc.) can be given to other players. My sense, though, is that retaining this actor is preferable to playing with 11 because it creates a more coherent character for the 'Gentleman', who does a great deal of work across Act Four. Given the debates over the texts of *King Lear*, it is interesting that the casting chart works similarly for either Q2 or F (or a conflated text).

The Cordelia/Fool pairing is the most famous and possibly the most generative, while allowing Edmund and Edgar to vie with one another as Burgundy and France tacitly previews their interactions later in the play and Edgar's eventual triumph. Doubling Edmund requires his withdrawal in 1.1, made possible by Lear's entrance in state and Edmund's perfect silence once he does enter. If he does remain onstage he can be sent off to summon the Duke of Burgundy and then put on the gentleman's clothes. Gloucester makes an attractive herald, considering that he would then call together the contest between his sons; while Oswald is well suited to the Captain sent to execute Cordelia.

Macbeth
c. 1606 (F)
❧ The division of the parts ❧

1 Witch 1 Murderer Caithness	For one actor	Malcolm	For one actor
		Ross	For one actor
2 Witch Messenger (1.5, 2.1) 2 Murderer Menteith	For one actor	Angus English Doctor	For one actor
		Lennox Old Man	For one actor
3 Witch 3 Murderer Scottish Doctor	For one actor	Sergeant Lady Macbeth 2 Apparition Little Macduff Seyton	For one actor
Macbeth	For one actor		
Duncan Macduff 1 Apparition	For one actor	Donalbain Fleance 3 Apparition Lady Macduff Gentlewoman Messenger (5.3, 5.5) Young Siward	For one actor
Banquo (Ghost) Porter Hecate Siward	For one actor		

Twelve actors can play 36 speaking roles and acknowledged mutes. Two play female and male roles, excluding the 'bearded' and thus quite 'weird' sisters. The chart is constructed to accommodate the largest scenes and transitions, including the 'line of kings' discussed in Chapter 4.

The play structure yields excellent prospects for doubling. As noted already, having the witches double as murderers makes sense of the unexpected addition to the duo initially contracted for the purpose, as well as deepening the paradox wherein they foresee fate and help to achieve it. If they join the army fighting against Macbeth in Act Five, the theme is extended further. Duncan can become his own avenger if he plays Macduff; Fleance can become a more immediate heir to the throne by doubling with Donalbain; and Hecate will make an attractive pairing with the Porter, who imagines himself 'porter of hell gate' and talks incessantly of devils (2.3.1–16). The same actor is a good match for Banquo, who apparently has the key to hell gate, as evidenced by his return to the stage in 3.4 after being murdered. If Fleance goes on to play Lady Macduff and Young Siward, Macbeth will 'get his man' not once but twice, while still not getting Fleance: a play on the mysterious conflations of success and failure that are essential to the play. And if Lady Macbeth plays other roles like the apparition and Seyton, she can continue her occult leanings on one hand and her testy relationship with Macbeth on the other. This would also allow the Lady Macbeth actor, who we might expect was talented, to do more work. Hence, I assign her the 'bloody Sergeant' as well.

All this said, were I casting the play I would likely use fewer than 12 actors and go without some mutes. The reason is that Lady Macbeth would make an even better double for a witch, who thereby would become still more involved in manipulating Macbeth and 'unsexing' (or perhaps 'dual-sexing') herself. If a director is willing to dispense with some mutes and make quick changes, such as having Ross and Angus play witches alongside the Lady Macbeth actor, nine actors can perform the play without needing to cut a line.

Antony and Cleopatra
c. 1606 (F)
❞ The division of the parts ❞

Antony Egyptian Clown	For one actor	Enobarbus Decretas Seleucus	For one actor
Cleopatra 1 Servant (2.7)	For one actor	Alexas Messenger (1.4) Ventidius Eros Canidius Proculeius	For one actor
Charmian 2 Servant (2.7) Silius 1 Watchman (4.9)	For one actor		
Iras Octavia Boy (2.7) Messenger (4.6) 2 Watchman (4.9)	For one actor	Mardian Varrius Agrippa Servant (mute, 4.2) 4 Soldier (4.3)	For one actor
Philo Pompey Taurus Attendant (3.11, 3.13) 1 Soldier/Captain 　(3.7, 4.3, 4.4) 1 Guard (4.14, 5.2) Diomedes	For one actor	Messenger 　(1.1, 1.2, 2.5, 3.3, 3.7) Lepidus Attendant (3.11) Ambassador 2 Soldier (4.3, 4.4) 2 Guard (4.14) Gallus	For one actor
Demetrius Menecrates Maecenas Thidias Servant (mute, 4.2) 3 Soldier (4.2, 4.6) Sentry (4.9)	For one actor	Soothsayer Menas Scarus (3. Guard 4.14) Dolabella	For one actor
		2 Messenger (1.2) Octavius	For one actor

Twelve actors can play 52 speaking roles and two mutes. The discrepancy in roles in relation to other counts likely owes to conflations of messengers, attendants, and soldiers, as seen in the chart. Three actors play female roles and minor male roles. The largest scene is 2.7, in which 11 speakers appear simultaneously. Antony and Cleopatra is among Shakespeare's most complex plots and the possibilities for doubling seem inexhaustible. Key questions, though, concern the assignment of Octavia and the roles that Antony and Enobarbus assume after their deaths, since the structure demands nearly constant employment from all 12 actors. In the proposed chart, in which Iras plays Octavia, Cleopatra's former jealousy of Octavia can be rekindled when Iras dies by snakebite, leaving Cleopatra to worry that Iras will find Antony in the next world and receive the kisses that are due to her (5.2.292–4). Meanwhile, Antony doubles as the Egyptian who ventures to Caesar's camp to learn about Cleopatra's fate, then as the Clown who provides her with means of deliverance from Caesar in the form of a basket full of asps. Other good options for Antony are Proculeius, who can then seem to take revenge on Cleopatra, and whom Antony had told her to trust; and Dolabella, who comes (surprisingly) to Cleopatra's aid, thereby betraying Caesar's interests.

Timon of Athens
c. 1606 (F)
ও The division of the parts ৶

Timon	⎫ For one actor	Alcibiades	⎫ For one actor
		1 Stranger	⎭
Poet	⎫		
Servilius	⎬ For one actor	Lucius	⎫
Cupid		1 Senator	⎬ For one actor
Messenger (5.2)	⎭	2 Bandit	⎭
Painter	⎫	Messenger (1.1)	⎫
Flaminius	⎬ For one actor	3 Lady	⎬ For one actor
1 Lady		Varro's Servant	
Phrynia	⎭	Timandra	⎭
Jeweler	⎫	Lucullus	⎫
2 Lady		Isidore's Servant	
Caphis	⎬ For one actor	Philotus	⎬ For one actor
Varro's Servant 2		1 Bandit	
4 Senator (5.1, 5.2)	⎭	3 Senator	⎭
		Lucilius (incl. Servant 3.3)	⎫
Apemantus	⎫	Ventidius	⎬ For one actor
2 Stranger		Page	
Hortensius		Titus	⎭
Merchant	⎬ For one actor		
Flavius		Old Athenian	⎫
3 Stranger		Sempronius	⎬ For one actor
Soldier	⎭	2 Senator	
		3 Bandit	⎭

Eleven actors can play 45 speaking roles. Three play female roles, one taking only minor male roles, while two others play larger parts. The number of roles is smaller here than some other counts because several lords and servants are introduced anonymously but can take on assigned identities later in the play. I have consolidated these, though with no attempt to conflate discrete characters. The play's largest scene is 1.2, which requires 12 actors to participate simultaneously. As seen in the chart, this requires some ingenuity since the servants in Timon's household will need to present the ladies who dance with the lords. The chart allows some notably kind characters to double as loyal servants in Timon's household, and the stingy lords to continue stealing from him by doubling the bandits who come for the gold he unearths in the wilderness.

Pericles, Prince of Tyre
c. 1607 (Q)
ଇ The division of the parts ଵ

Gower Helicanus 2 Lord of Pentapolis	For one actor	Messenger (1.2) Dionyza Shipwrecked man (mute) Tyrian Sailor (5.1) Virgin (5.3, mute)	For one actor
Antiochus Simonides Philemon Cleon Lysimachus	For one actor	Escanes 3 Lord of Pentapolis Lychorida 1 Servant to Cerimon Marina	For one actor
Pericles Pander	For one actor		
Thaliard Marshall (1 Lord of Pent.) Cerimon Leonine Lord of Mytilene	For one actor	2 Lord of Tyre 2 Fisherman 2 Knight 2 Sailor (3.1) 2 Pirate 2 Gentleman (3.2, 4.5, 5.1 mute) Virgin (5.3, mute)	For one actor
Antiochus's Daughter Thaisa Bawd Diana	For one actor		
1 Lord of Tyre 1 Lord of Tarsus 1 Fisherman 1 Knight 1 Sailor (3.1) 1 Pirate 1 Gentleman (3.2, 4.5, 5.1) Virgin (5.3, mute)	For one actor	3 Lord of Tyre 3 Fisherman 3 Knight Messenger (3.0, mute) 2 Servant to Cerimon (mute) 3 Pirate Boult Mytilene Sailor (5.1)	For one actor

Ten actors can play 47 speaking roles and five mutes.[7] Three actors play female roles, one exclusively. The chart suggests that the two 'Gentlemen' in Mytilene preserve those roles across three separate scenes, though they can be differentiated by the same (or other) actors. It also conflates the Marshall for the tournament in Pentapolis with its 'First Lord'. Only the three speaking knights are included because three are sufficient. In 2.2 six mute knights pass over the stage, but their shields are the only means of differentiating them for Simonides and Thaisa, and new shields can be picked up before the second pass.

The most influential casting choices concern Antiochus and his Daughter, who dominate the play's opening scene and then disappear for good. Pericles can seem to achieve his goal of marrying the daughter if she doubles as Thaisa; or he can reunite with her as his grown daughter Marina, who again tells a riddle with an obvious yet unstated solution. Antiochus can go on to play other kings and lords, some likewise villainous (Cleon) and some good (Simonides, Lysimachus). If the actor doubles all these he may seem to have as great an odyssey as Pericles, and he, too, will eventually get his reward in the person of Marina, for whose hand he asks Pericles in a perfect inversion of the play's opening scene.

Pericles can also become a more complex moral figure by doubling as the Pander who buys Marina, though he seems the most benign figure in the brothel. Meanwhile, Gower can enter the fiction as Helicanus and help steer the course of his narrative at key points. Thaliard and Leonine are a natural match, each of whom fails to murder his victim, and the actor can subsequently seem to reform himself in the fiction by retrieving Thaisa from death, as Cerimon. Though all these are theatrically enlivening, perhaps the most pleasurable potential doubles are those implicit in the structure for the actors playing quite minor roles. The plot includes three Lords of Tyre; three fisherman; three knights; three pirates; and pairs of gentlemen, sailors, and servants, all of whom can seem increasingly integral to the play and highlight its interest in artifice and play-acting when portrayed by the same actors.

---

[7] The chart assumes the two 'Gentlemen' in Mytilene appear in three scenes, and conflates the Marshall for the tournament in Pentapolis with its 'First Lord'. These roles and the question of how many Knights appear in 2.2 accounts for discrepancies in counting the roles.

Coriolanus
c. 1608 (F)
❧ The division of the parts ❧

Coriolanus	} For one actor		2 Roman Senator*		
			2 Roman Soldier		
Menenius			Messenger (2.1, 4.6)	⎱ For one actor	
1 Volscian Senator	⎱ For one actor		7 Roman Cit. (2.3)		
1 Volscian Lord			2 Volscian Watchman		
Cominius			1 Roman Cit. (1.1, 2.3, 4.6)		
2 Volscian Senator	⎱ For one actor		Volumnia	⎱ For one actor	
2 Volscian Lord			1 Volscian Soldier		
			1 Servingman		
Titus Lartius					
Tullus Aufidius	⎱ For one actor		2 Roman Cit. (1.1, 2.3, 4.6)		
5 Roman Cit. (2.3)			Virgilia	⎱ For one actor	
			2 Servingman		
Sicinius					
Usher (mute)			3 Roman Cit. (1.1, 2.3, 4.6)		
3 Roman Soldier	⎱ For one actor		Messenger (1.1, 1.4, 5.4)		
Adrian			Gentlewoman		
2 Conspirator			Herald		
			2 Officer (2.2)	⎱ For one actor	
Brutus			2 Aedile (3.1, mute)		
Roman Lieutenant			Noble (3.2, mute)		
Nicanor	⎱ For one actor		Volscian Cit. (4.4)		
2 Messenger (5.4)			Young Martius		
3 Conspirator					
1 Roman Senator			4 Roman Cit. (1.1, 2.3)		
1 Roman Soldier			Valeria		
6 Roman Cit. (2.3)			2 Volscian Soldier (mute)		
2 Messenger (4.6)	⎱ For one actor		1 Officer (2.2)	⎱ For one actor	
Volscian Lieutenant			Aedile		
1 Volscian Watchman			Noble (3.2)		
1 Volscian Conspirator			3 Servingman		
			Attendant (5.6, mute)		

Twelve actors can play 51 speakers and five mutes. Three play female roles and minor male roles. 12 actors are necessary for the largest scene (3.1). Like *Pericles*, and other late plays, *Coriolanus* is notable for how easily its structure distributes its 56 roles among just 12 players. When the action shifts to Corioles, the Roman Patricians and Tribunes are freed to take new roles there; when they return the Volscians return with them in new guises and become Romans. Meanwhile, the citizens can double as women in Coriolanus's home, then again as domestics in Corioles. When the play requires 'seven or eight citizens' (2.3), it meticulously clears the stage of the Senators and Titus Lartius in time to produce them. Of course, the King's Men may well have produced such crowds with gatherers and other hired men, but it is striking that every one of these roles can be played by a cast of 12. The scarcity of major roles limits the potential for conceptual casting, though Titus Lartius and Aufidius make up an excellent pair. Lartius is Coriolanus's closest friend and Aufidius his most hated rival; yet, in the play's second half Coriolanus befriends Aufidius and turns on Rome. The last act also allows Sicinius and Brutus to play conspirators who kill Coriolanus, seeming to achieve their initial goal by proxy – and yet in person.

Cymbeline
c. 1609 (F)
⸮ The division of the parts ⸫

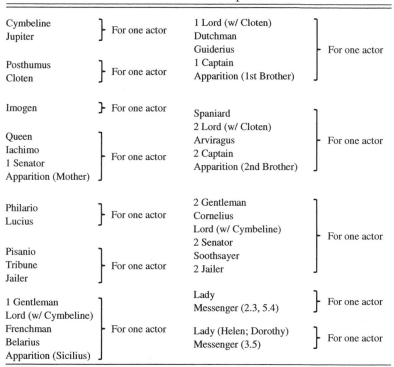

Twelve actors can play 39 speaking roles and various mutes. Three play female roles and messengers. The play can be performed by a cast of 11, provided that one lady appearing in 5.5 exits in time to return as Imogen. Nevertheless, it seems to have been designed for 12, though the result gives two actors unusually little to do. The two can play mute lords, jailers, attendants, etc. But there is no other plot so late in the career that limits two actors to speaking just 20–30 lines, suggesting that these may have been written for young apprentices training with the company. That is pure speculation, but it makes sense considering the potential for increased participation by boy players after the acquisition of Blackfriars in 1608 (see Chapter 6).

In any case, the play is full of inviting possibilities for the other ten actors to double roles. Posthumus/Cloten is the most prominent and exciting of these, and Booth has presented substantial evidence within the play that underscores the choice, including Cloten's desire to obtain and wear Posthumus's clothes; Imogen mistaking Cloten's dead body for Posthumus's; and their lack of meeting onstage, despite Cloten constantly talking about his wish to meet and fight with Posthumus.[8] The choice to double the roles can be complemented by having the Queen double as Iachimo, whose drive to sleep with Imogen thus extends the Queen's desire for Imogen to abandon Posthumus and embrace her son. That choice also could explain her offstage death in the final act, while Iachimo's efforts at reconciliation with Posthumus may seem partly to redeem her too. Additionally, Philario makes a natural pair with the Roman general Lucius, and the apparitions will be far more interesting if played by Posthumus' real though as-yet-unknown in-laws, Belarius, Guiderius, and Arviragus.

The Winter's Tale
c. 1610 (F)
❧ The division of the parts ❧

Leontes Autolycus	For one actor	Archidamus Jailer	
Polixenes 2 Servant (2.3) Officer 1 Gentleman	For one actor	Mariner Servant (4.4) Messenger (5.1)	For one actor
Camillo Antigonus	For one actor	Mamillius 1 Servant (2.3) Perdita	For one actor
Cleomenes / 1 Lord Shepherd 2 Gentleman	For one actor	Hermione Dorcas	For one actor
2 Lady Dion / 2 Lord Clown 3 Gentleman	For one actor	Paulina Mopsa	For one actor
		Emilia / 1 Lady Florizel	For one actor

[8] Booth, 'Speculations on Doubling', pp. 149–52.

Ten actors can play 24 speaking roles. Two can play female roles exclusively, while two others take one male role apiece. The structure is perhaps Shakespeare's richest, in terms of potential for doubling roles to impact the play and its reception. I discuss the chart and potential options in Chapter 3.

The Tempest

c. 1610 (F)

❧ The division of the parts ❧

Master Prospero	} For one actor	1 Mariner Adrian Stephano Juno	}	For one actor
Boatswain Caliban Iris	} For one actor			
Ferdinand }	For one actor	2 Mariner Francisco Trinculo	}	For one actor
Ariel Ceres	} For one actor	Antonio }		For one actor
		Gonzalo }		For one actor
Miranda }	For one actor	Sebastian }		For one actor
		Alonso }		For one actor

Eleven actors can perform 20 speaking roles. One actor plays Miranda only; three others play female 'spirits' as well as male roles. Unlike other plays of the period – *Cymbeline, Pericles, The Winter's Tale* – *The Tempest* does not seem to prioritize double-casting, though it makes interesting possibilities available in framing the play by means of a shipwreck, the Master and Boatswain ruling the ship much as Prospero and Caliban do the island.[9] The most interesting option beyond this concerns the masque, which will be livelier by far for starring Ariel, Caliban, and Stephano. The otherwise dry lords of Milan can add to the comedy if they undertake the nymphs and reapers that Ariel summons to participate in the show.

---

[9] Ibid., pp. 174–5.

Bibliography

Abrams, Richard. 'The Double Casting of Cordelia and Lear's Fool: A Theatrical View'. *Texas Studies in Language and Literature* 27 (1985): 354–68.

Ackroyd, Peter. *Shakespeare: The Biography*. New York: Vintage Books, 2006.

Archer, William. *Masks or Faces? A Study in the Psychology of Acting*. New York: Hill & Wang, 1957.

Armstrong, Alan. 'Doubling in *The Comedy of Errors*'. *Shaping Shakespeare for Performance: The Bear Stage*. Ed. Catherine Loomis and Sid Ray. Lanham: Fairleigh Dickinson University Press, 2016. 189–202.

' "What is Become of Bushy? Where is Green?": Metadramatic Reference to Doubling Actors in *Richard II*'. *Inside Shakespeare: Essays on the Blackfriars Stage*. Ed. Paul Menzer. Selinsgrove: Susquehanna University Press, 2006. 149–55.

Astington, John. *Actors and Acting in Shakespeare's Time: The Art of Stage Playing*. Cambridge: Cambridge University Press, 2010.

Baker, Roger. *Drag: A History of Female Impersonation in the Performing Arts*. New York: New York University Press, 1995.

Baker, Donald, Murphy, John L., and Hall, Louis B., Jr., eds. *The Late Medieval Religious Plays of Bodleian MSS Digby 133 and E Museo 160*. Oxford: Oxford University Press, 1982.

Bakhtin, M.M. *The Dialogic Imagination: Four Essays*. Ed. Michael Holquist. Trans. Caryl Emerson and Michael Holquist. Austin: University of Texas Press, 1981.

Baldwin, T.W. *The Organization and Personnel of the Shakespearean Company*. Princeton: Princeton University Press, 1927.

Barroll, Leeds. *Politics, Plague, and Shakespeare's Theater: The Stuart Years*. Ithaca: Cornell University Press, 1981.

Bearman, Robert. 'John Shakespeare: A Papist or Just Penniless'. *Shakespeare Quarterly* 56.4 (2005): 411–33.

Shakespeare's Money. Oxford: Oxford University Press, 2016.

Beckerman, Bernard. *Dynamics of Drama: Theory, Method and Analysis*. New York: Alfred A. Knopf, 1970.

Beckwith, Sarah. 'Stephen Greenblatt's *Hamlet* and the Forms of Oblivion'. *Journal of Medieval and Early Modern Studies* 33 (2003): 261–80.

Belsey, Catherine. 'Shakespeare's Little Boys'. *Rematerializing Shakespeare*. Ed. Bryan Reynolds and William N. West. New York: Palgrave Macmillan, 2005. 53–72.

Ben-Amos, Ilana Krausman. 'Failure to become Freemen: Urban Apprentices in Early Modern England'. *Social History* 16.2 (1991): 155–72.

Bentley, Eric. *The Life of the Drama*. New York: Atheneum, 1964.

Bentley, Gerald E. *The Jacobean and Caroline Stage*. Oxford: Clarendon Press, 1941.
The Profession of Dramatist in Shakespeare's Time, 1590–1642. Princeton: Princeton University Press, 1971.
The Profession of Player in Shakespeare's Time, 1590–1642. Princeton: Princeton University Press, 1984.
Berger, Thomas. 'Casting Henry V'. *Shakespeare Studies* 20 (1988): 89–104.
Berry, Ralph. 'Hamlet's Doubles'. *Shakespeare Quarterly* 37.2 (1986): 204–12.
Shakespeare in Performance: Castings and Metamorphoses. New York: St. Martin's Press, 1993.
Bevington, David M. *From Mankind to Marlowe: Growth of Structure in the Popular Drama of Tudor England*. Cambridge, MA: Harvard University Press, 1962.
Bloom, Gina. '"Thy Voice Squeaks": Listening for Masculinity on the Early Modern Stage'. *Renaissance Drama* n.s. 26 (1998): 39–71.
Bly, Mary. *Queer Virgins and Virgin Queans on the Early Modern Stage*. Oxford: Oxford University Press, 2000.
Bolton, J.T., ed. *A Philosophical Enquiry into the Origin of Our Ideas of the Beautiful and the Sublime*. Notre Dame: University of Notre Dame Press, 1968.
Booth, Stephen. *King Lear, Macbeth, Indefinition and Tragedy*. New Haven: Yale University Press, 1983.
'The Shakespearean Actor as Kamikaze Pilot'. *Shakespeare Quarterly* 36 (1985): 553–70.
Bradbrook, M.C. *The Rise of the Common Player: A Study of Actor and Society in Shakespeare's England*. London: Chatto & Windus, 1962.
'The Triple Bond: Audience, Actors, Author in the Elizabethan Playhouse'. *The Triple Bond: Plays, Mainly Shakespearean in Performance*. Ed. Joseph G. Price and Helen D. Willard. University Park and London: Pennsylvania State University Press, 1975.
Bradley, David. *From Text to Performance in the Elizabethan Theatre: Preparing the Play for the Stage*. Cambridge: Cambridge University Press, 1992.
Brailow, David G. '"'Tis here. 'Tis gone." The Ghost in the Text'. *Stage Directions in Hamlet: New Essays and New Directions*. Ed. Hardin L. Aasand. Cranbury: Associated University Presses, 2003. 101–14.
Brandl, Alois. *Shakspere*. Berlin: E. Hofmann & Co., 1894.
Brantley, Ben. 'A Down-to-Earth Iago, Evil Made Ordinary; Review of *Othello*'. Dir. Sam Mendes. *New York Times*. 11 April 1998.
'The Prince In Us All; Review of *Hamlet*'. Dir. John Caird. *New York Times*. 1 June 2001.
'Something Wicked This Way Comes; Review of *Macbeth*'. Dir. Rupert Goold. *New York Times*, 15 February 2008.
'Whips and Scorns of Time, Stinging All They Touch; Review of *Hamlet*'. Dir. Oskar Eustis. *New York Times*. 18 June 2008.
Bridenbaugh, Carl. *Vexed and Troubled Englishmen, 1590–1642*. New York and Oxford: Oxford University Press, 1976.
Brooke, Tucker. *The Tudor Drama*. Boston and New York: Houghton Mifflin Company, 1911.
Bulman, James C., ed. *Shakespeare, Theory and Performance*. London: Routledge, 1996.

Burke, Edmund. *A Philosophical Enquiry into the Origin of our Ideas of the Beautiful and the Sublime*. Ed. J.T. Bolton. Notre Dame: University of Notre Dame Press, 1968 [1757].

Butler, Judith. *Gender Trouble: Feminism and the Subversion of Identity*. New York: Routledge, 1990.

Calderwood, James L. *Shakespearean Metadrama*. Minneapolis: University of Minnesota Press, 1971.

To Be And Not to Be: Negation and Metadrama in Hamlet. New York: Columbia University Press, 1983.

Callaghan, Dympna. *Shakespeare without Women: Representing Gender and Race on the Renaissance Stage*. London and New York: Routledge, 2000.

Cartwright, Kent. *Shakespearean Tragedy and Its Double: The Rhythms of Audience Response*. University Park: Pennsylvania State University Press, 1991.

Cavell, Stanley. *Disowning Knowledge: In Seven Plays of Shakespeare*. New York: Cambridge University Press, 2003.

Cerasano, S.P. 'The Chamberlain's-King's Men'. *A Companion to Shakespeare*. Ed. David Scott Kastan. Malden, MA: Blackwell, 1999. 328–45.

Chamberlain, Robert. *Jocabella, or a Cabinet of Conceits*. London: R. Hodgkinson for Daniel Frere, 1640.

Chambers, E.K. *The Elizabethan Stage*. 4 Volumes. Oxford: Clarendon Press, 1923–1951.

William Shakespeare: A Study of Facts and Problems. 2 Volumes. Oxford: Clarendon Press, 1930.

Coldeway, John C., ed. 'The Digby Mary Magdalene'. *Early English Drama: An Anthology*. New York and London: Garland Publishing, 1993.

Collier, John Payne. *The History of English Dramatic Poetry to the Time of Shakespeare; and Annals of the Stage to the Restoration*. London: J. Murray, 1831.

Cook, Ann Jennalie. *The Privileged Playgoers of Shakespeare's London, 1576–1642*. Princeton: Princeton University Press, 1981.

Cooper, Helen. *Shakespeare and the Medieval World*. London: Bloomsbury Methuen, 2010.

Coryate, Thomas. *Coryat's Crudities*. Glasgow: J. MacLehose; New York: Macmillan, 1906 [1611].

Craik, T.W. 'I know when one is dead and when one lives'. British Academy Shakespeare Lecture, 1979, in the Academy's *Proceedings*, vol. lxv.

The Tudor Interlude: Stage, Costume, and Acting. Leicester: Leicester University Press, 1958.

Curry, John V. *Deception in Elizabethan Comedy*. Chicago: Loyola University Press, 1955.

David, Richard. *Shakespeare and the Players*. Oxford: Oxford University Press, 1961.

Davies, Robertson. *Shakespeare's Boy Actors*. New York: Russell & Russell, 1964.

Davison, Richard Allan. 'The Readiness Was All: Ian Charleson and Richard Eyre's Hamlet'. *Shakespeare, Text and Theater: Essays in Honor of Jay L. Halio*. Ed. Lois Potter and Arthur F. Kinney. Newark: University of Delaware Press, 1999. 170–82.

Dawson, Anthony. *The Culture of Playgoing in Shakespeare's England*. Cambridge: Cambridge University Press, 2005.

Dessen, Alan C. 'Conceptual Casting in the Age of Shakespeare: Evidence from Mucedorus'. *Shakespeare Quarterly* 43 (1992): 67–70.

Elizabethan Stage Conventions and Modern Interpreters. Cambridge: Cambridge University Press, 1984.

Recovering Shakespeare's Theatrical Vocabulary. Cambridge: Cambridge University Press, 1995.

'Two Falls and a Trap'. *English Literary Renaissance* 5 (1975): 291–307.

Dessen, Alan C., and Thomson, Leslie. *A Dictionary of Stage Directions in English Drama 1580–1642.* Cambridge: Cambridge University Press, 1999.

Diderot, Denis. *The Paradox of Acting.* Trans. Walter Herries Pollock. New York: Hill & Wang, 1957.

DiGangi, Mario. *The Homoerotics of Early Modern Drama.* Cambridge: Cambridge University Press, 1997.

Dobson, Michael. *Shakespeare and Amateur Performance: A Cultural History.* Cambridge: Cambridge University Press, 2011.

Donahue, Peter. Review of *Hamlet,* dir. Colette Rice. *Shakespeare Bulletin* 24.3 (2006): 89–92.

Downes, John. *Roscius Anglicanus (1708).* Introd. John Loftis. Los Angeles: University of California Press, 1969.

Dunlop, Olive J. *English Apprenticeship and Child Labor, a History.* London: T.F. Unwin, 1912.

'Some Aspects of Early Apprenticeship'. *Transactions of the Royal Historical Society* 5 (1911): 193–208.

Dusinberre, Juliet. 'Squeaking Cleopatras: Gender and Performance in *Antony and Cleopatra*'. *Shakespeare, Theory, and Performance.* Ed. James C. Bulman. New York: Routledge, 1996. 46–67.

Dutton, Richard. *Shakespeare, Court Dramatist.* Oxford: Oxford University Press, 2016.

Ellis, Henry, Sir. *Original Letters Illustrative of English History.* London: R. Bentley, 1846.

Encyclopaedia of Hindi Cinema. Ed. Govind Nihalani Gulzar and Saibal Chatterjee. Mumbai: Popular Prakashan, 2003.

Engle, Lars. *Shakespearean Pragmatism: Market of His Time.* Chicago: University of Chicago Press, 1993.

Fallow, David. 'His Father John Shakespeare'. *The Shakespeare Circle.* Ed. Paul Edmonson and Stanley Wells. Cambridge: Cambridge University Press, 2015. 26–39.

Farabee, Darlene. *Shakespeare's Staged Spaces and Playgoers' Perceptions.* London: Palgrave Macmillan, 2014.

Fineman, Joel. 'Fratricide and Cuckoldry: Shakespeare's Doubles'. *Representing Shakespeare: New Psychoanalytic Essays.* Ed. Coppelia Kahn and Murray M. Schwarz. Baltimore and London: Johns Hopkins University Press, 1980. 70–109.

Fisher, Will. 'The Renaissance Beard: Masculinity in Early Modern England'. *Renaissance Quarterly* 54.1 (2001): 155–87.

Flecknoe, Richard. *A Short Treatise of the English Stage.* London: Printed for Simon Neale, 1674.

Forman, Simon. *The Autobiography and Personal Diary of Dr. Simon Forman: the cele-brated astrologer, from A.D. 1552, to A.D. 1602, from the unpublished manuscripts in the Ashmolean Museum, Oxford.* Ed. J.O. Halliwell-Phillipps. London: For private circulation [Richards, printer], 1849.

Forse, James. *Art Imitates Business: Commercial and Political Influences in Elizabethan Theatre*. Bowling Green: Bowling Green University State Popular Press, 1993.

Fotheringham, Richard. 'The Doubling of Roles on the Jacobean Stage'. *Theatre Research International* 10 (1985): 18–33.

Frye, Northrop. *Anatomy of Criticism*. Princeton: Princeton University Press, 1973.

A Natural Perspective. New York: Columbia University Press, 1965.

Frye, Roland Mushat. *Shakespeare: The Art of the Dramatist*. London: Routledge, 1982.

Gadamer, Hans-Georg. *The Relevance of the Beautiful and Other Essays*. Cambridge: Cambridge University Press, 1986.

Gamboa, Brett. 'Letting Unpleasantness Lie: Counter-intuition and Character in *The Merchant of Venice*'. *Shakespeare's Sense of Character: On the Page and From the Stage*. Ed. Yu Jin Ko and Michael Shurgot. Aldershot: Ashgate, 2012.

Garber, Marjorie. *Quotation Marks*. New York: Routledge, 2002.

Vested Interests: Cross-Dressing and Cultural Anxiety. New York: Routledge, 1992.

Gaw, Allison. 'Actors' Names in Basic Shakespearean Texts, with Special Reference to *Romeo and Juliet* and *Much Ado*'. *PMLA* 40.3 (1925): 530–50.

Gayton, Edmund. *Pleasant Notes upon Don Quixot*. London: Printed by William Hunt, 1654.

Gibson, Gail M. *The Theatre of Devotion*. Chicago: University of Chicago Press, 1989.

Gibson, Joy Leslie. *Squeaking Cleopatras: The Elizabethan Boy Player*. Stroud: Sutton, 2000.

Gildon, Charles. *The Life of Mr. Thomas Betterton*. London: R. Gosling, 1710.

Girard, Rene. *A Theater of Envy: William Shakespeare*. New York and Oxford: Oxford University Press, 1991.

Goldman, Michael. *The Actor's Freedom: Toward a Theory of Drama*. New York: Viking Press, 1975.

Shakespeare and the Energies of the Drama. Princeton: Princeton University Press, 1972.

Gosson, Stephen. *Playes Confuted in Five Actions*. Ed. Arthur Freeman. New York: Garland, 1972 [1582].

Grantley, Darryl. 'Saints' Plays'. *The Cambridge Companion to Medieval English Theatre*. Ed. Richard Beadle. Cambridge: Cambridge University Press, 1994. 165–89.

Graves, R.E. *Lighting the Shakespearean Stage, 1567–1642*. Cambridge: Cambridge University Press, 1999.

Greenblatt, Stephen. *Hamlet in Purgatory*. Princeton: Princeton University Press, 2001.

Shakespeare's Freedom. Chicago: University of Chicago Press, 2010.

Shakespearean Negotiations. Berkeley: University of California Press, 1988.

Will in the World. New York: W.W. Norton & Co., 2004.

Greenblatt, Stephen, Cohen, Walter, Howard, Jean E., Eisaman Maus, Katharine, and McMullan, Gordon, eds. *The Norton Shakespeare*, 3rd edn. New York: W.W. Norton & Co., 2016.

Greene, Robert. *Greenes Groatsworth of Wit, Bought with a Million of Repentance*. London: John Haviland, for Henry Bell, 1629 [1592].

Greg, W.W. *Dramatic Documents from the Elizabethan Playhouses; Stage Plots: Actors' Parts: Prompt Books*. Oxford: Clarendon Press, 1931.

Two Elizabethan Stage Abridgements: The Battle of Alcazar & Orlando Furioso. Oxford: Clarendon Press, 1923.

Grote, David. *The Best Actors in the World.* Westport: Greenwood Press, 2002.

Gurr, Andrew. *The Culture of Playgoing in Shakespeare's London.* 2nd ed. Cambridge: Cambridge University Press, 1996.

The Shakespeare Company, 1594–1642. Cambridge: Cambridge University Press, 2004.

The Shakespearean Playing Companies. Oxford: Oxford University Press, 1996.

The Shakespearean Stage, 1574–1642. 4th ed. Cambridge: Cambridge University Press, 2009.

Halliday, F.E. *A Shakespeare Companion 1564–1964.* Baltimore: Penguin, 1964.

Hanawalt, Barbara. *Growing Up in Medieval London: The Experience of Childhood in History.* New York and Oxford: Oxford University Press, 1993.

Harbage, Alfred. *Annals of English Drama, 975–1700.* Philadelphia: University of Pennsylvania Press, 1964.

Shakespeare's Audience. New York: Columbia University Press, 1941.

ed. *William Shakespeare: The Complete Works.* Baltimore: Penguin, 1969.

Hartwig, Joan. *Shakespeare's Analogical Scene: Parody as Structural Syntax.* Lincoln: University of Nebraska Press, 1993.

Henke, Robert. 'Pastoral Tragicomedy and *The Tempest'. Revisiting the Tempest: The Capacity to Signify.* Ed. Silvia Bigliazzi and Lisanna Calvi. London: Palgrave Macmillan, 2014.

Henslowe, Philip. *Henslowe's Diary.* Ed. R.A. Foakes and R.T. Rickert. Cambridge: Cambridge University Press, 1961.

The Henslowe Papers. Ed. R.A. Foakes. London: Scholar Press, 1977.

Heywood, Thomas. *An Apology for Actors.* New York: Scholars' Facsimiles & Reprints, 1941 [1612].

Hillebrand, Harold Newcomb. *The Child Actors.* New York: Russell & Russell, 1964.

Hinman, Charlton, ed. *The Norton Facsimile: The First Folio of William Shakespeare.* New York: W.W. Norton & Co., 1968.

Hodgdon, Barbara. 'Gaining a Father: The Role of Egeus in the Quarto and the Folio'. *The Review of English Studies* 37.148 (1986): 534–42.

Hodges, C. Walter. *Enter the Whole Army: A Pictorial Study of Shakespearean Staging 1576–1616.* Cambridge: Cambridge University Press, 1999.

Holmes, Jonathan. *Merely Players? Actor's Accounts of Performing Shakespeare.* London: Routledge, 2004.

Honigmann, E.A.J. *Shakespeare: Seven Tragedies: The Dramatist's Manipulation of Response.* London: Macmillan, 1976.

Hornby, Richard. *Drama, Metadrama, and Perception.* Lewisburg: Bucknell University Press, 1986.

Howard, Jean E. *Shakespeare's Art of Orchestration: Stage Technique and Audience Response.* Urbana: University of Illinois Press, 1984.

The Stage and Social Struggle in Early Modern England. New York: Routledge, 1994.

Hudson, Katherine. *The Story of the Elizabethan Boy-Actors.* London: Oxford University Press, 1971.

Hyland, Peter. *Disguise on the Early Modern English Stage.* Farnham: Ashgate, 2011.

Ichikawa, Mariko. *Shakespearean Entrances.* New York: Palgrave, 2002.

Ingram, William. *The Business of Playing: The Beginnings of the Adult Professional Theater in Elizabethan London*. Cornell: Cornell University Press, 1992.

'The Economics of Playing'. *A Companion to Shakespeare*. Ed. David Scott Kastan. Oxford: Blackwell, 1999. 313–27.

Johnson, Samuel. *The Yale Edition of the Works of Samuel Johnson. Volume VII. Johnson on Shakespeare*. Ed. Arthur Sherbo. New Haven and London: Yale University Press, 1968.

Jones, Ann Rosalind, and Stallybrass, Peter. *Renaissance Clothing and Materials of Memory*. Cambridge: Cambridge University Press, 2000.

Jonson, Ben. *Poetaster*. Ed. Josiah Harmer Penniman. Boston and London: D.C. Heath and Company, 1913.

Jordan, Thomas. 'A Prologue, to introduce the first Woman that came to act on the Stage in the Tragedy call'd The Moor of Venice'. *A Royal Arbor of Loyal Poesie, Consisting of Poems and Songs*. London: Printed by R.W. for Eliz. Andrews, 1663. *Illustrations of Old English Literature*. Ed. John Payne Collier. London: Privately Printed, 1866. 24–5.

Joseph, B.L. *Elizabethan Acting*. London: Oxford University Press, 1964 [1951].

Kathman, David. 'Grocers, Goldsmiths, and Drapers: Freemen and Apprentices in the Elizabethan Theater'. *Shakespeare Quarterly* 55.1 (2004): 1–49.

'The Seven Deadly Sins and Theatrical Apprenticeship'. *Early Theatre* 14.1 (2011): 121–39.

'Reconsidering *The Seven Deadly Sins*'. *Early Theatre* 7.1 (2004): 13–44.

'How Old Were Shakespeare's Boy Actors?' *Shakespeare Survey* 58 (2005): 220–46.

Keenan, Siobhan. *Acting Companies and their Plays in Shakespeare's London*. London: Bloomsbury Arden, 2014.

King, T.J. *Casting Shakespeare's Plays: London Actors and Their Roles 1590–1642*. Cambridge: Cambridge University Press, 1992.

Kleist, Heinrich von. 'On the Puppet Theater'. *Selected Writings*. Ed. and trans. David Constantine. Indianapolis: Hackett Publishing, 2004.

Knutson, Roslyn. 'Falconer to the Little Eyases: A New Date and Commercial Agenda for the "Little Eyases" Passage in *Hamlet*'. *Shakespeare Quarterly* 46.1 (1995): 1–31.

Playing Companies and Commerce in Shakespeare's Time. Cambridge: Cambridge University Press, 2001.

Ko, Yu Jin. *Mutability and Division on Shakespeare's Stage*. Newark: University of Delaware Press, 2004.

Kott, Jan. *Shakespeare Our Contemporary*. Trans. Boleslaw Taborski. Garden City: Doubleday, 1964.

The Gender of Rosalind: Interpretations: Shakespeare, Büchner, Gautier. Evanston: Northwestern University Press, 1992.

Lawrence, W.J. *Pre-Restoration Stage Studies*. Cambridge, MA: Harvard University Press, 1927.

Letts, Quentin. 'Simon Russell Beale and Zoe Wanamaker Make Crumpled Lovers; Review of *Much Ado About Nothing*'. Dir. Nicholas Hytner. *Daily Mail*. 19 December 2007. Web.

Levine, Laura L. *Men in Women's Clothing: Anti-theatricality and Effeminization, 1579–1642*. Cambridge: Cambridge University Press, 1994.

Lomax, Marion. *Stage Images and Traditions: Shakespeare to Ford*. Cambridge: Cambridge University Press, 1987.

Lopez, Jeremy. 'Dream: The Performance History'. *A Midsummer Night's Dream: A Critical Guide*. Ed. Regina Buccola. London: Continuum, 2010. 44–73.

Theatrical Convention and Audience Response in Early Modern Drama. Cambridge: Cambridge University Press, 2003.

Loveridge, Lizzie. 'A CurtainUp London Review; *Hamlet*'. Dir. John Caird. *CurtainUp: The Internet Theater Magazine of Reviews, Features, Annotated Listings*. 5 September 2000. www.curtainup.com.

McGuire, Philip C. *Speechless Dialect: Shakespeare's Open Silences*. Berkeley: University of California Press, 1985.

Mack, Maynard. 'Engagement and Detachment in Shakespeare's Plays'. *Essays on Shakespeare and Elizabethan Drama in Honor of Hardin Craig*. Ed. Richard Hosley. Columbia: University of Missouri Press, 1962. 275–96.

'The Second Shepherd's Play: A Reconsideration'. *PMLA* 93.1 (1978): 78–85.

MacLean, Sally-Beth. 'Tour Routes: "Provincial wanderings" or Traditional Circuits?'. *Medieval and Renaissance Drama in England* 6 (1993): 1–14.

McMillin, Scott. 'Casting for Pembroke's Men: The Henry VI Quartos and *The Taming of A Shrew*'. *Shakespeare Quarterly* 23.2 (1972): 141–59.

McMillin, Scott, and MacLean, Sally-Beth. *The Queen's Men and Their Plays*. Cambridge: Cambridge University Press, 1998.

Malone, Edmund, and Boswell, James, eds. *The Plays and Poems of William Shakespeare*, Vol. III. London: Printed for F.C. and J. Rivington, 1821.

Mann, David. *The Elizabethan Player: Contemporary Stage Representation*. London: Routledge, 1991.

Mantzius, Karl. *A History of Theatrical Art in Ancient and Modern Times*, Vol. II. Trans. Louise von Cossel. London: Duckworth & Co., 1903.

Marks, Robert G. *Cordelia, King Lear and his Fool*. Sydney: House of Cordelia, 1995.

Matchett, William. 'Some Dramatic Techniques in *King Lear*'. *Shakespeare and the Theatrical Dimension*. Ed. Philip C. McGuire and David A. Samuelson. New York: AMS Press, 1979. 185–208.

Maus, Katharine. *Inwardness and Theater in the English Renaissance*. Chicago: University of Chicago Press, 1995.

Meagher, John C. 'Economy and Recognition: Thirteen Shakespearean Puzzles'. *Shakespeare Quarterly* 35.1 (1984): 7–21.

Pursuing Shakespeare's Dramaturgy: Some Contexts, Resources and Strategies in His Playmaking. Madison: Fairleigh Dickinson Press, 2003.

Shakespeare's Shakespeare: How the Plays were Made. New York: Continuum, 2000.

Melchiori, Giorgio. 'Peter, Balthasar, and Shakespeare's Art of Doubling'. *The Modern Language Review* 78 (1983): 777–92.

Mentz, Steve. 'Forming Green: Theorising the Early Modern Author in the *Groatsworth of Wit*'. *Writing Robert Greene: Essays on England's First Notorious Professional Writer*. Ed. Kirk Melnikoff and Edward Gieskes. Aldershot: Ashgate, 2008.

Miller, William. 'Little Eyases'. *Shakespeare Quarterly* 28.1 (1977): 86–8.

Moller, Herbert. 'The Accelerated Development of Youth: Beard Growth as a Biological Marker'. *Comparative Studies in Society and History* 29.4 (1987): 748–62.

'Voice Change in Human Biological Development'. *Journal of Interdisciplinary History* 16.2 (1985): 239–53.

Montrose, Louis. *Purpose of Playing: Shakespeare and the Cultural Politics of the Elizabethan Theatre*. Chicago: University of Chicago Press, 1996.

Munday, Anthony. *Londons Love, to the Royal Prince Henrie*. London: Printed by Edw. Allde for Nathaniell Fosbrooke, 1610.

Munro, Lucy. *Children of the Queen's Revels*. Cambridge: Cambridge University Press, 2005.

Normington, Katie. *Gender and Medieval Drama*. Cambridge: D.S. Brewer, 2004.

Nungezer, Edwin. *A Dictionary of Actors and of Other Persons Associated with the Public Representation of Plays in England before 1642*. New York: Greenwood Press, 1968 [1929].

Orgel, Stephen. *Imagining Shakespeare: A History of Texts and Visions*. New York: Palgrave, 2003.

Impersonations: The Performance of Gender in Shakespeare's England. Cambridge: Cambridge University Press, 1996.

'Nobody's Perfect: Or Why Did the English Stage Take Boys for Women?' *South Atlantic Quarterly* 88 (1989): 7–29.

Overbury, Thomas, Sir. 'An Excellent Actor'. *A Wife, now the Widdow of Sir Thomas Overburye. Being a most exquisite and singular Poem of the Choice of a Wife. Whereunto are added many witty Characters, and conceited Newes*. London: Lawrence Lisle, 1614. *The Miscellaneous Works in Prose and Verse of Sir Thomas Overbury, Knt. Now First Collected*. Ed. Edward F. Rimbault. London: John Russell Smith, 1856. 147–8.

Palfrey, Simon and Stern, Tiffany. *Shakespeare in Parts*. Oxford: Oxford University Press, 2007.

Peat, Derek. '"And that's true too": *King Lear* and the Tension of Uncertainty'. *Aspects of King Lear*. Ed. Kenneth Muir and Stanley Wells. Cambridge: Cambridge University Press, 1982. 43–54.

Pepys, Samuel. *The Diary of Samuel Pepys*. Ed. Richard Le Gallienne. New York: Modern Library, 2001.

Perrett, Wilfred. *The Story of King Lear*. Berlin: Mayer and Müller, 1904.

Platter, Thomas. *Thomas Platter's Travels in England, 1599 (rendered into English from the German, and with introductory matter by Clare Williams)*. London: J. Cape, 1937.

Pollard, Tanya, ed. *Shakespeare's Theater*. Oxford: Blackwell, 2004.

Potter, Lois. *The Life of William Shakespeare*. Chichester: Wiley-Blackwell, 2012.

'"Nobody's Perfect": Actor's Memories and Shakespeare's Plays of the 1590s'. *Shakespeare Survey* 1 (1990): 85–97.

Preston, Thomas. *Cambyses. Tudor Plays: An Anthology of Early English Drama*. Ed. Edmund Creeth. New York: Norton, 1966. 443–503.

Priestley, J.B. *The Art of the Dramatist*. London: Heinemann, 1957.

Prosky, Ida. *You Don't Need Four Women to Play Shakespeare: Bias in Contemporary American Theatre*. Jefferson: McFarland Press, 1992.

Prynne, William. *Histrio-mastix*. London: Printed by E. Allde, A. Mathewes, and W. Jones, 1633.

Rappaport, Steve. *Worlds within Worlds: Structures of Life in Sixteenth-Century London*. Cambridge: Cambridge University Press, 1989.

Rastall, R. 'Female Roles in All-Male Casts'. *Medieval English Theatre* 7 (1985): 25–50.

Rayner, Alice. 'Rude Mechanicals and the Specters of Marx'. *Theatre Journal* 54.4 (2002): 535–54.

Ridout, Nicholas. *Stage Fright, Animals and Other Theatrical Problems*. Cambridge: Cambridge University Press, 2006.

Ringler, William A., Jr. 'The Number of Actors in Shakespeare's Early Plays'. *The Seventeenth-Century Stage: A Collection of Critical Essays*. Ed. G.E. Bentley. Chicago and London: University of Chicago Press, 1968. 110–34.

Roach, Joseph. *The Player's Passion: Studies in the Science of Acting*. Newark: University of Delaware Press, 1985.

Robbins, Elizabeth. 'On Seeing Madame Bernhardt's Hamlet'. *North American Review* 171 (December 1900): 908.

Robinson, Marc. *The American Play 1787–2000*. New Haven: Yale University Press, 2009.

Rodenberg, Patsy. *Speaking Shakespeare*. New York: St. Martin's Press, 2004.

Rosenberg, Marvin. 'Elizabethan Actors: Men or Marionettes?' *The Seventeenth Century Stage*. Ed. G.E. Bentley. Chicago and London: University of Chicago Press, 1968. 94–109.

The Masks of Hamlet. Cranbury: Associated University Presses, 1992.

The Masks of King Lear. Berkeley: University of California Press, 1972.

'The Myth of Shakespeare's Squeaking Boy Actor – Or Who Played Cleopatra?' *Shakespeare Bulletin* 19.2 (2001): 5–6.

Rutter, Carol Chillington. *Documents of the Rose Playhouse*. Manchester: Manchester University Press, 1999.

Rycroft, Eleanor. 'Facial Hair and the Performance of Early Modern Masculinity on the Early Modern English Stage'. *Locating the Queen's Men, 1583–1603: Material Practices and Conditions of Playing*. Ed. Helen Ostovich, Holger Schott Syme, and Andrew Griffin. Burlington: Ashgate, 2009. 217–28.

Rye, William B. *England as seen by Foreigners*. London: J.R. Smith, 1865.

Schlueter, June. 'Tybalt in a Bloody Sheet, Paris in the Tomb: Speculations on Doubling and Staging in *Romeo and Juliet*'. *Shakespeare Yearbook* 2 (1991): 1–22.

Schneider, Rebecca. *Performing Remains: Art and War in Times of Theatrical Reenactment*. London: Routledge, 2011.

Schoone-Jongen, Terence G. *Shakespeare's Companies*. London: Ashgate, 2008.

Senelick, Lawrence. *The Changing Room: Sex, Drag, and Theatre*. New York: Routledge, 2000.

Shapiro, Michael. *Children of the Revels: The Boy Companies of Shakespeare's Time and Their Plays*. New York: Columbia University Press, 1977.

'Framing the Taming'. *The Yearbook of English Studies* 23 (1993): 143–66.

Gender in Play on the Shakespearean Stage: Boy Heroines and Female Pages. Ann Arbor: University of Michigan Press, 1994.

Sher, Anthony. 'Leontes in *The Winter's Tale* and *Macbeth*'. *Players of Shakespeare 5*. Ed. Robert Smallwood. Cambridge: Cambridge University Press, 2003. 91–112.

Shurgot, Michael W. *Stages of Play: Shakespeare's Theatrical Energies in Elizabethan Performance*. Newark: University of Delaware Press, 1998.

Sinfield, Alan. *Faultlines*. Berkeley: University of California Press, 1992.

Skiles, Howard. 'Attendant and Others in Shakespeare's Margins: Doubling in the Two Texts of *King Lear*'. *Theatre Survey* 32 (1991): 187–213.

'A Re-examination of Baldwin's Theory of Acting Lines'. *Theatre Survey* 26 (1985): 1–20.

Skura, Meredith. *Shakespeare the Actor and the Purposes of Playing*. Chicago: University of Chicago Press, 1993.

Slater, Ann Pasternak. *Shakespeare the Director*. Sussex: Harvester, 1982.

Smith, Bruce. *The Acoustic World of Early Modern England*. Chicago: University of Chicago Press, 1999.

Somerset, Alan. '"How Chances it they Travel?": Provincial Touring, Playing Places, and the King's Men'. *Shakespeare Survey* 47 (1994): 45–60.

Speaight, George. *The History of the English Puppet Theatre*. London: George G. Harrap & Co. Ltd., 1955.

Spencer, Charles. 'The Best Macbeth I Have Seen; Review of *Macbeth*'. Dir. Rupert Goold. *Telegraph*. 27 September 2007.

Sprague, A.C. *The Doubling of Parts in Shakespeare's Plays*. London: Society for Theatre Research, 1966.

Stern, Tiffany. *Making Shakespeare: From Stage to Page*. New York: Routledge, 2004.

Rehearsal from Shakespeare to Sheridan. Oxford: Oxford University Press, 2008.

Stroup, Thomas B. 'Cordelia and the Fool'. *Shakespeare Quarterly* 12.2 (1961): 127–32.

Stubbes, Philip. *The Anatomie of Abuses*. London: Richard Jones, 1583.

Summers, Ellen. 'A Double Heuristic for Shakespeare's Doubling'. *Staging Shakespeare: Essays in Honour of Alan C. Dessen*. Ed. Lena Cowen Orlin and Miranda Johnson-Haddad. Newark: Delaware University Press, 2007. 60–75.

Symonds, John A. *Shakespeare's Predecessors in the English Drama*. London: Smith Elder, 1903.

Taylor, Paul. 'Simon Russell Beale: A Performer at His Peak'. Theatre and Dance Feature. *Independent*. 14 January 2005.

Thaler, Alwin. 'The Elizabethan Dramatic Companies'. *PMLA* 35.1 (1920): 123–59.

Travis, Peter. *Dramatic Design in the Chester Cycle*. Chicago: University of Chicago Press, 1982.

Trilling, Lionel. *Sincerity and Authenticity*. Cambridge, MA: Harvard University Press, 1972.

Turner, Frederick. *Shakespeare's Twenty-First-Century Economics: The Morality of Love and Money*. Oxford: Oxford University Press, 1999.

van Es, Bart. '"Johannes fac Totum"? Shakespeare's First Contact with the Acting Companies'. *Shakespeare Quarterly* 61.4 (2010): 551–77.

Walter, Harriet. *Other People's Shoes: Thoughts on Acting*. London: Nick Hern Books Ltd., 2003.

Weil, Herbert. '"Be Vigilant, I beseech you": A Fantasia on Dogberry and Doubling in *Much Ado About Nothing*'. *The Ben Jonson Journal* 6 (1999): 307–17.

Weimann, Robert. *Author's Pen and Actor's Voice: Playing and Writing in Shakespeare's Theatre*. Ed. Helen Higbee and William West. Cambridge: Cambridge University Press, 2000.

'Representation and Performance: The Uses of Authority in Shakespeare's Theater'. *PMLA* 107.3 (1992): 497–510.

Wells, Stanley. *Shakespeare & Co*. London: Penguin, 2006.

Wentersdorf, Karl P. 'The Origin and Personnel of the Pembroke Company'. *Theatre Research International* 5.1 (1979): 45–68.

White, Martin. *Renaissance Drama in Action*. London: Routledge, 1998.

Wickham, Glynne. *Early English Stages, 1300–1660*. 3 Volumes. London: Routledge and Kegan Paul, 1959–1981.

Wickham, Glynne, Herbert Berry, and William Ingram, eds. *English Professional Theatre, 1530–1660*. Cambridge: Cambridge University Press, 2000.

Wiggins, Martin, in association with Catherine Richardson. *British Drama 1533–1642: A Catalogue. Volume II, III, and IV 1567–1589*. Oxford: Oxford University Press, 2012–2014.

Worthen, W.B. *The Idea of the Actor: Drama and the Ethics of Performance*. Princeton: Princeton University Press, 1984.

Shakespeare and the Authority of Performance. Cambridge: Cambridge University Press, 1997.

Index

actors, *see also* boy actors
  acting 'lines', 128–30
  characters as, 46
  direct address, 27
  as focus of drama, 40
  hired men, 18, 55, 83, 124–8, 153
  memory lapses (drying up), 11
  mutes, 1, 40, 154, 211n. 15
  paradox of the actor, 1, 40, 117
  physical vulnerability of, 5, 38–9
  playing dead, 35–41, 86
  representational gaps and
    failures of, 29–30, 34, 35, 39–40, 137–8,
    180n. 65
  versatility of, 130–1
Alabaster, William, 193
The Alchemist (Jonson), 186
All for Money (Lupton), 12, 58
All's Well that Ends Well, 28, 115, 179, 188
  doubling in, 191, 260–1
Alleyn, Edward, 54
Antony and Cleopatra, 15, 27, 105,
    111, 124, 129–31, 158, 160, 169, 178,
    183, 240
  'boy my greatness', 187–8
  doubling in, 264–5
apprenticeship, 123
  laws of, 162–4
  training, 163–5
Aristotle, 26
Armin, Robert, 126, 130
Armstrong, Alan, 18, 244
As You Like It, 3, 7, 27, 28, 60, 65, 93, 111,
    114, 131, 177, 178, 188, 190, 232
  doubling in, 256–7
audiences
  awareness of artifice, 2–3, 12
  engagement of, 2, 28
  'imaginative flexibility' of, 64
  as locus of reality, 5
  paradox of spectatorship, 5, 200

period accounts, 125–6, 153–5, 175–7,
    191–7
  as protagonist, 22–4, 26, 28, 45, 87

Bachchan, Amitabh, 9
Baker, Roger, 182n. 73
Baldwin, T.W., 16, 112, 113, 128–30, 158
Barroll, Leeds, 81
The Beatles, 89
Beckerman, Bernard, 25
Believe as You List (Massinger), 80
Belsey, Catherine, 157
Belte, Thomas, 167, 168, 169
Ben-Amos, Ilana Krausman, 163
Benfield, Robert, 173
Bentley, G.E., 57, 126, 158, 161, 165
Berger, Tom, 18, 255
Bernhardt, Sarah, 29–30
Berry, Halle, 10
Berry, Ralph, 18, 110
Bevington, David, 12, 16, 57, 64, 66, 67, 69,
    71, 111, 131
Billington, Michael, 23
The Blind Beggar of Alexandria (Chapman),
    69, 151
Bollywood, 10
Booth, Stephen, 17, 95, 106, 127, 140, 147,
    201, 246
boy actors, 14–15, 81, 124, 132–5, 156, 185,
    194
  ages of, 158–60, 161–3, 185–6
  opportunities to become sharers, 163–4
  physical characteristics of, 133–5
  puberty, 178–83
  retirements of, 165–6
  in Shakespeare's company, 166–73
  specializing in female roles, 74
  tall blonde and short brunette pairing, 188–9
  training, 125, 158, 211n. 17
  voices and voice breaks, 133, 157, 158, 174,
    178, 180–2

Bradley, David, 107, 112, 113, 155, 157
Brandl, Alois, 15, 111
Brantley, Ben, 23n. 2, 31, 31n. 21, 130–1
Bridenbaugh, Carl, 183
Brook, Peter, 9, 145
Bryan, George, 71, 120n. 28, 126
Bryant, Michael, 24
Burbage, James, 53, 71
Burbage, Richard, 29, 53, 129, 131, 159, 168,
    169, 170, 179, 196
Burke, Edmund, 22

Caird, John, 130
Calderwood, James, 27
Cambyses (Preston), 58, 69, 70, 77, 82, 135
    doubling in, 71–4
    female representation in, 74–5
    influence on Shakespeare, 71
Cane, Andrew, 165
cast size, 15, 19, 107–14, 115–16, 123–8
    according to play structures, 70–1
    actors required for Shakespeare's plays,
        108t. 4.1
    crowds and armies, 153
    impact of female specialization, 157
    impact of mutes on, 109, 235
    in contemporary performance, 113
    'limiting' scenes, 107–9
    Macbeth's 'line of kings', 120–3
    suggested by *Julius Caesar*, 153–5
    suggested by *Romeo and Juliet*, 147–8
casting
    in Caroline period, 80–2
    casting requirements for Shakespeare's
        plays, 108t. 4.1, 111–13, 123n. 32,
        139–40, 147–8
    credibility in, 133–5
    extras, 153
    plays with printed casting information, 59t. 2.1
    relativity in, 93, 179–80
    unusual demands for female
        representation, 132
Cavell, Stanley, 91n. 7, 127
Cellini, Benvenuto, 180, 182
Chamberlain, Robert, 176, 183
Chamberlain's Men, 15, 18, 20, 52, 56, 102,
    110, 132, 133, 158, 159, 168, 174, 195,
    197, 202, 234, *see also* King's Men;
    Shakespeare's Company
    economics, 57
    origins of, 71
Chambers, E.K., 126n. 43, 164, 164n. 28, 165
characters
    as actors, 62, 137–8
    'deaths' of, 11, 35–41, 86

hierarchies of legitimacy among, 46
    inconsistencies of, 6
    size of star parts, 232
    suppression of, 69, 118–19
    types, 128
    versatility required for, 128–30
Charles II, 192
childrens' companies
    Children of St. Paul's, 185
    Children of the Chapel, 172, 185, 186
    Children of the Queen's Revels, 185
    rise and popularity of, 82, 83, 185–6
    St. Paul's choristers, 132
Chopra, Priyanka, 9
Cleopatra (Daniel), 188
Cloud Atlas, 10
Cockpit, 10
The Comedy of Errors, 116, 169
    doubling in, 241–2
Coming to America, 10
Condell, Henry, 126
Cooke, Alexander, 159, 167, 168, 169
Coriolanus, 27, 111, 115, 153
    doubling in, 268–9
Coryate, Thomas, 196
costumes and clothing, 49, 67, 99, 123, 202,
    208
    quick changes, 66–8, 79–8, 151
    sumptuary laws, 49
Craik, T.J., 74
cross-dressing, 3, 8, 117, 134, 135, 182n. 73,
    see female representation; transvestism
    as source of theatrical power, 51
Crosse, Samuel, 172
Cymbeline, 40, 114, 115, 130, 190, 196
    absence of Queen, 106
    doubling in, 269–70

Dallas Buyer's Club, 10
Daniel, Samuel, 188
Davenant, William, 192
Daw, S.F., 180
Defense of Poesy, 180
Dekker, Thomas, 193
Dench, Judi, 87
Dessen, Alan, 43n. 34
The Devil is an Ass (Jonson), 171–2
Digby *Mary Magdalene*, 156
    casting and staging of, 59–60
disguise, 1, 13, 34, 50, 78, 85, 91, 100, 118,
    134, 151, 202, 203, 204, 206, 208, 220,
    224, 227, 239, 241, 246, 248, 251
    disguise plays, 8, 69
    in *The Fair Maid of the Exchange*, 78
    in *The Winter's Tale*, 51

Dobson, Michael, 180n. 65
doubling
    advantages when touring, 55
    aesthetic incentives for, 4, 32
    in *All's Well that Ends Well*, 260–1
    in *Antony and Cleopatra*, 264–5
    in *As You Like It*, 256–7
    character suppression for, 69
    in *The Comedy of Errors*, 241–2
    in *Coriolanus*, 268–9
    costume changes, 66–8, 204
    in *Cymbeline*, 269–70
    dramaturgical bases for, 98
    economic incentives for, 55
    in film, 11
    in *The Fair Maid of the Exchange*, 75–80
    in *Hamlet*, 116, 238
    in *Henry IV, Part 1*, 249–50
    in *Henry IV, Part 2*, 252–3
    in *Henry V*, 254–5
    as intensifier of tragedy, 41, 214–16
    in *Julius Caesar*, 154, 255–6
    in *King John*, 247–8
    in *King Lear*, 261–2
    limits on, 219–20
    in *Love's Labour's Lost*, 246–7
    in *Macbeth*, 119–23, 262–3
    in *Mankinde*, 61–2
    in *Measure for Measure*, 219–33, 259
    in medieval drama, 57–60
    in *The Merchant of Venice*, 117–18, 248–9
    in *The Merry Wives of Windsor*, 250–1
    in *A Midsummer Night's Dream*,
        136–45, 245
    in *Much Ado About Nothing*, 253–4
    in *Othello*, 210–18, 260
    in *Pericles*, 116, 266–7
    quick changes for, 79–8
    in *Richard II*, 244–5
    in *Richard III*, 240–1
    in *Romeo and Juliet*, 145–53, 243
    in *Second Shepherd's Play*, 62–4
    in *The Taming of the Shrew*, 239
    in *The Tempest*, 116–17, 271
    in *Timon of Athens*, 265–6
    as topic of fiction, 110–11, 114, 246
    in *Troilus and Cressida*, 258–9
    in *Twelfth Night*, 199–210, 257
    in *The Two Gentlemen of Verona*, 242–3
    in *The Winter's Tale*, 85–103, 270–1
    without costume changes, 98–9
    without exiting the stage, 242
Downey Jr., Robert, 131
dramaturgy
    alternate plotting, 89, 114–18, 137, 211

conspicuous absences, 104–7, 118–19
evolution across Shakespeare's career,
    153, 246
female specialization, 74, 132, 157, 197
'French scenes', 234
'green world' plays, 114–15
'limiting' scenes, 107–9, 123
phased casting, 61, 115–16
simultaneous participation, 77–8, 246
substitution, 144–5, 221–7, 231–3
suggestive presences, 118–22
Dromgoole, Dominic, 33
The Duchess of Malfi (Webster), 174
Dudley, Robert, 71
Dutton, Richard, 187

Ecclestone, William, 172–3
Elizabeth I, 49
Enough is as Good as a Feast, 69, 77
Eustis, Oskar, 22
Eyre, Richard, 23

Face/Off, 10
The Fair Maid of the Exchange (Heywood),
    59, 75–80, 76f. 2.3, 93, 132, 135, 144,
    206, 220
    disguise in, 78
    objections to printed doubling plot, 75–7
    simultaneous participation in, 77–8
Fallow, David, 53
female representation
    by adult males, 74–7, 132–5, 160, 173, 174,
        175–7, 179–80, 185–91
    beards and beardlessness, 182–5
    casting, 93
    by female actresses, 156
    in *The Merchant of Venice*, 189–90
    originators of Shakespeare's female
        leads, 173
    simulated voices in, 174
    unusual size and number of female roles in
        Shakespeare, 132
Field, Nathan, 172, 186
First Folio, 122, 125, 159, 169, 171
    stage directions, 235
Fisher, Will, 183
Fitzgeoffrey, Henry, 195
Forman, Simon, 196
Forse, James, 160, 188
Frith, Mary ('Moll'), 193
Frye, Northrop, 114
Fulwell, Ulpian, 67

Gadamer, Hans-Georg, 7
Ganymede, 3, 7

Garber, Marjorie, 3, 97n. 11, 182n. 73
Gayton, Edmund, 195
Gilbourne, Samuel, 172
Goldman, Michael, 25, 29, 30, 40, 50
Goold, Rupert, 31
Gosson, Stephen, 192
Gough, Alexander, 173
Gough, Robert, 173
Greenblatt, Stephen, 43
Greene, Robert, 56, 102
Greenes Groatsworth of Wit, 56
Greg, W.W., 126
Grote, David, 112, 113, 127, 158, 161, 191
Guinness, Alec, 10
Gurr, Andrew, 52n. 10, 53, 158, 159, 161, 163,
    165, 168, 169, 191

Hamilton, 64
Hamlet, 1, 2, 4, 12, 15, 26, 27, 57, 70, 86, 104,
    109–16, 120, 128–31, 136, 184, 195,
    198, 232
    artifice of, 41–6
    doubling in, 6, 7, 16, 19, 41, 42, 45–6,
        116, 238
    'little eyases', 185–7
    'The Murder of Gonzago', 32, 45, 46
    ontology and reception of Ghost, 41–4
    Ophelia's madness, 40
    Polonius's memory lapse, 21–4
    production (Oskar Eustis, 2008), 21–3
    table of actor participation, 234
Hanawalt, Barbara, 162
Hanks, Tom, 10
Harbage, Alfred, 122
Harvey, 64
Hello Dolly, 182n. 73
Heminges, John, 159, 164, 168, 174, 186
    apprentices of, 167
Henke, Robert, 117
Henry IV, Part 1, 27, 71, 82, 93, 118, 179,
    221, 252
    absence of Poins, 118
    alternate settings in, 115
    doubling in, 249–50
    substitution in, 233
Henry IV, Part 2, 17, 124, 152
    doubling in, 252–3
Henry V, 57, 110, 131, 179, 183, 191, 232
    alternate settings in, 115
    doubling in, 17, 254–5
Henry VI, Part 1, 115, 234
Henry VI, Part 2, 153, 234
Henry VI, Part 3, 179, 234
Henry VIII, 234
Henslowe, Philip, 52n. 11, 54, 126

Honeyman, John, 173–4
Horestes (Pickering), 58, 69, 75, 77
Hornby, Richard, 27
Howard, Jean, 50
Hyland, Peter, 66

Impatient Poverty, 67
The Importance of Being Earnest (Wilde), 22,
    182n. 73
In Wisdom Who is Christ, 67
Ingram, William, 52, 53
internal evidence, 14, 82–3, 177–8
    concerning female representation, 185–91

James I, 120
The Jew of Malta (Marlowe), 195
Jocabella, 176
Joe versus the Volcano, 10
Johnson, Samuel, 1, 3
Jonson, Ben, 53, 171, 253n. 5, 282
Jordan, Thomas, 14, 175–7, 179, 180
Jugurtha (Boyle), 195
Julius Caesar, 69, 104, 115, 118, 122, 128,
    129, 179, 195
    casting requirements, 153–5
    doubling in, 154, 255–6

Kathman, David, 164, 165, 166, 167, 168,
    169, 174, 180, 191
Keenan, Siobhan, 185
Kempe, Will, 18, 71, 126, 130
Kenilworth Castle, 71
Killigrew, Thomas, 175, 179, 192
Kind Hearts and Coronets, 10
King John, 39, 108, 179, 183, 247
    doubling in, 247–8
King Lear, 5, 69, 104, 111, 115, 122, 129,
    136, 140, 179, 216, 232
    death of Cordelia, 38
    doubling in, 15, 41, 261–2
    Dover cliff, 6, 11, 39
King, T.J., 18, 111, 112, 124, 125, 140, 147,
    155, 210
King's Men, 15, 54n. 18, 80, 82, 102, 110,
    120, 128, 158, 162, 173, 186, 195, 196,
    230, 231, 234, *see also* Chamberlain's
    Men; Shakespeare's Company
    Caroline period, 173–7
    casting practices, 171–2, 174–6
    changes after Shakespeare, 81–2, 159
    female representation, 180, 182
    hired men, 18, 55, 83, 124–8, 153
    impact of boys' companies on, 185–6
    musicians, 125–6, 153
    off-stage roles, 125–6

King's Men (*cont.*)
  repertory, 69, 170
  sharers, 126–8, 159, 168, 195
  size and expansion of, 83, 124–8, 164
Knutson, Roslyn, 168
Kott, Jan, 39
Kynaston, Edward, 14

La Rue, Danny, 160
Lawrence, W.J., 16, 65, 77, 124, 125,
    128, 134
Lennon, John, 89
Lester, Adrian, 29, 131
Letts, Quentin, 29
Levine, Laura, 50
Lie, Gilbert, 162
Like Will to Like (Fulwell), 67, 135
*The Longer thou Livest the more Fool thou
    Art*, 77
Love's Labour's Lost, 15, 34, 38, 132, 134,
    169, 173, 199, 239
  doubling in, 246–7
  female representation in, 132–3, 177
  five-boy problem, 132
  pageant of 'the Nine Worthies', 32–3
Lusty Juventus (Wever), 66
Lyly, John, 132

Macbeth, 4, 39, 40, 115, 130, 156, 177, 187,
    191, 196, 198, 232
  death of Young Siward, 105
  doubling in, 119–23, 262–3
  line of kings, 13
  production (Rupert Goold, 2007), 31
  sleepwalking scene, 40
  witches in, 44
Maclean, Sally-Beth, 234
MacLean, Sally-Beth, 18, 67
Madden, John, 177
malapropism, 221
Malini, Hema, 9
Malone, Edmund, 169
The Man of Mode (Etherege), 156
Mankinde, 60, 62, 89, 116
Manningham, John, 196
Marlowe, Christopher, 12, 195
The Marriage of Wit and Wisdom, 67, 77
masks, 8
Massinger, Philip, 80, 81, 173
McKellen, Ian, 131
McMillin, Scott, 18, 67, 234
Meagher, John C., 17, 112, 113, 113n. 15, 147
Measure for Measure, 4, 15, 62, 108, 111,
    113, 115, 120, 151, 210, 211n. 17, 213,
    213n. 18

  doubling in, 19, 219–33, 259
  ending of, 62
  number of actors required, 227, 232
  substitution in, 220–7
medieval and Tudor drama
  Christian origins of, 8
  Corpus Christi plays, 75
  influence on Shakespeare, 70, 82
  morality plays, 61, 70
  Mystery Cycle plays, 8
  versatility of actors in, 74
The Merchant of Venice, 116, 179, 188, 190,
    191
  cross-dressing and disguise in, 189–90
  doubling in, 117–18, 248–9
The Merry Milkmaides, 195
The Merry Wives of Windsor, 114
  doubling in, 250–1
  metadrama, 27–8, 32, 38
A Midsummer Night's Dream, 9, 14, 28, 60,
    86, 114, 128, 132, 134, 151, 165, 169,
    177, 178, 188, 190
  absence of Egeus, 106
  boy participation in, 157
  casting requirements, 139–40
  doubling in, 9, 11, 17, 136–45, 245
  female representation in, 65, 184
  obsession with doubles in, 137–8
  production (Peter Brook, 1970), 67,
    136, 140
  'Pyramus and Thisbe', 32, 33, 70,
    137–8, 246
  'rude mechanicals' in, 124, 135, 177
  size of Hippolyta, 193
  substitution in, 144–5, 231
  theory of representation, 65
Moller, Herbert, 180, 181, 182–3, 184
Mrs. Doubtfire, 10
Mucedorus, 69
Much Ado About Nothing, 14, 27, 115, 179,
    188, 191
  absence of Margaret, 106
  doubling in, 253–4
  female representation in, 184
Munday, Anthony, 65, 170, 196
Mundus et Infans, 12, 58
Munro, Lucy, 181
Murphy, Eddie, 10
musicians, 54, 89n. 3, 125–6, 126n. 40, 139,
    172, 211n. 15, 217, 227n. 7
  potential to play roles, 89n. 3, 153, 211,
    247, 248

Normington, Katie, 75
Nunn, Trevor, 87

Orgel, Stephen, 191
Ostler, William, 172, 186
Othello, 4, 14, 15, 70, 115, 120, 129–31, 158,
    169, 179, 192, 227, 232
    the Clown, 216–18
    death of Desdemona, 37, 39
    doubling in, 7, 18, 210–18, 260
    Othello's fit, 38
    production at Oxford (1610), 196
    in Restoration, 174–6
    substitution in, 212
    themes of substitution in, 220

Palfrey, Simon, 66, 111
Pallant, Robert, 174
Pandosto, 102
Peacham, Henry, 192
Pericles, 60, 69, 71, 111, 115, 118, 124, 128, 240
    doubling in, 266–7
Perrett, Wilfred, 15, 111
Platter, Thomas, 153, 182, 195
playhouses
    Blackfriars, 54, 81, 89, 126, 164, 167, 270
    closures, 55, 159
    The Cockpit, 193
    The Fortune, 165, 194
    The Globe, 54, 80, 81, 126, 153, 165,
        195, 196
    plague, 53, 81, 132, 159n. 10, 164
    Shakespeare's Globe, 33, 160
    'The Theatre', 54
plays within plays, 1, 8, 27, 32–4, 83
    'The Murder of Gonzago', 12, 45, 46
    pageant of 'The Nine Worthies', 70
    'Pyramus and Thisbe', 70, 137–8
Pope, Thomas, 71, 120n. 28, 126
Potter, Lois, 30n. 20. 56n. 27
Priestley, J.B., 3
The Problemes of Aristotle, 181
Prynne, William, 50, 133, 189, 192
puns, 1, 3

Quem Queritis, 7

Rainolds, John, 192
Rappaport, Steve, 162
Rastall, Richard, 158, 174, 181
Rayner, Alice, 30
Redgrave, Vanessa, 29
Rice, John, 159, 169–71, 186, 196
Richard II, 118, 124
    doubling in, 244–5
Richard III, 115, 129, 131, 158, 165, 183,
    232, 246
    doubling in, 240–1

Ridout, Nicholas, 25, 26n. 8, 30, 40, 281
Ringler, William, 17, 112, 113, 114, 139, 157
The Roaring Girl (Middleton and
    Dekker), 193
Robbins, Elizabeth, 29–30
Robinson, Marc, 5, 31
Robinson, Richard, 159, 171–2, 186, 198
Rodenberg, Patsy, 187n. 89
The Roman Actor (Massinger), 80, 173
Romeo and Juliet, 13, 14, 18, 35, 39, 69, 93,
    111, 118, 122, 124, 169, 221, 246
    absence of Benvolio, 118
    cast size suggested in, 147–8
    casting requirements, 112
    conspicuous absences in, 104–6, 113
    doubling in, 13, 19, 145–53, 243
Rosenberg, Marvin, 37n. 28, 43, 127, 160, 188
Roxana (Alabaster), 193
Russell Beale, Simon, 29, 130, 131
Rutter, Carol Chillington, 160n. 13
Rylance, Mark, 25, 29, 160

Schneider, Rebecca, 4, 6
Schoone-Jongen, Terence, 71, 168
The Second Maiden's Tragedy (Middleton),
    171, 186
Second Shepherd's Play, 60, 62–4
Senelick, Laurence, 182n. 73
The Seven Deadly Sins, 168
Shakespeare in Love, 177
Shakespeare, John, 48, 53
Shakespeare, William
    as actor, 56–7
    as businessman, 52–3
    retirement, 81
Shakespeare's company, 40, 83, 102, 161, 202,
    212, 219, *see also* Chamberlain's Men;
    King's Men
    backgrounds of sharers, 164
    boy apprentices of, 166–73
    female representation, 175–7, 184, 191, 198
    finances, 52–7
    participation of boy apprentices, 157–8,
        163–5, 166
    sharer model, 54–6
Shank, John, 173
Shapiro, Michael, 133, 134
Shearer, Norma, 29
Sher, Anthony, 89n. 4
Sidney, Philip, 180
Sincler, John, 124, 125, 152
Sinfield, Alan, 6
Sir Thomas More (Munday), 65, 66, 188, 195
Sly, William, 126
Smith, Bruce, 181

Smith, Maggie, 25
Spencer, Charles, 31
Sprague, A.C., 16
Stern, Tiffany, 66, 109, 111
Stewart, Patrick, 31
Streep, Meryl, 25
substitution, 109n. 8
    of actors, 144–5, 222–7
    in dramaturgy, 221–2
    as theme, 220–1
Summers, Ellen, 111, 112
Suzman, Janet, 160

Tamburlaine (Marlowe), 195
The Taming of a Shrew, 168
The Taming of the Shrew, 108, 115, 189n. 93,
    190, 232, 241, 246
    doubling in, 239
    Taylor, Paul, 131
The Tempest, 116, 130, 134, 135, 179
    doubling in, 116–17, 271
Tennant, David, 1
Thaler, Alwin, 16, 166
The Tide Tarrieth No Man (Wapull), 75
the Trinity
    as analogue for doubling, 7
The Two Gentlemen of Verona, 108, 113, 114,
    115, 190, 239
    Crab the dog, 6, 31
    doubling in, 242–3
The Two Noble Kinsmen, 234
The Wild Goose Chase (Fletcher), 174
The Winter's Tale, 13, 15, 27, 40, 60, 70, 83,
    110, 111, 113, 114, 118, 135, 158, 179,
    183, 196, 219
    assertions of artifice in, 47, 85–7, 96–8
    casting requirements, 89, 91–2
    disguise in, 51
    doubling in, 17, 19, 51–2, 85–103, 270–1
    false climax in, 95–7
    mutes in, 89
    relationship to Shakespeare's life,
        48–9, 102
    statue of Hermione, 6, 86–7
    substitution in, 87, 231
    table of actor participation, 234
    'unscenes' in, 97–8
theatre
    of ancient Greece, 8
    Bunraku, 8
    Commedia dell'arte, 8
    credibility of, 134–5
    instability of, 6, 11, 24–5, 28–9, 39, 41
    Kabuki, 182n. 73
    Noh, 8

Peking opera, 182n. 73
puppets, 8
Puritan objections to, 51
realism, 4–7
    as component of fiction, 26
recitation, 25, 26, 28
rehearsal, 55, 80, 109, 116, 125, 129, 139
stage 'death', 35–41, 86
stage directions, 67, 109, 121, 147, 154,
    229, 235
    mistakes in, 229
stage properties, 31, 39, 63
    false beards, 184–5
    in Restoration, 156
    role of verisimilitude in, 156–7
theatre companies, 81
    Admiral's Men, 18, 54, 159
    American Shakespeare Center, 9, 29, 113
    Cheek by Jowl, 9, 29, 93
    Leicester's Men, 71
    Pembroke's Men, 159, 168, 168n. 39, 279
    Propeller, 9, 29, 113
    Queen's Men, 18, 67, 234
    Shakespeare's Globe, 9, 29
    size of traveling troupes, 65
    Strange's Men, 168
    traveling troupes, 65
    visits to or near Stratford, 71
    war of the theatres, 81, 187
theatrical failure, 2, 5–6, 24–6
    in recitation, 27, 34–5
Three Laws (Bale), 58
Timon of Athens, 116
    doubling in, 265–6
Titus Andronicus, 40, 177, 179, 234, 246
    Peacham drawing, 192–3
Tooley, Nicholas, 159, 168, 169
Tootsie, 10
transvestism, 50, 178, 179, 182n. 73, see
    cross-dressing
Trigge, William, 164, 167, 174, 198
Troilus and Cressida, 108, 115, 179,
    188, 220
    doubling in, 258–9
Twelfth Night, 15, 25, 27, 33, 34, 50, 71, 113,
    115, 120, 124, 129, 130, 134, 135, 158,
    160, 188, 190, 196, 211, 216, 227
    absence of Maria, 5.1, 106, 114
    age and stature of Cesario, 191
    casting requirements for, 113
    cross-dressing in, 50
    doubling in, 199–210, 257
    production (1602), 196
    production (Brett Gamboa, 2003),
        199–200

sharer participation in, 127
substitution in, 232–3
table of actor participation, 234
twins, 40, 135, 199, 200, 205, 206, 210, 241

Underwood, John, 172, 186

van Es, Bart, 56
Victor Victoria, 10
voices and voice breaks, 133, 157, 158, 174,
    178, 180–2

Wakefield Poet, 64
Wanamaker, Zoe, 29
Washington, Denzel, 25
Waterston, Sam, 21–3, 26, 28, 42
Wentersdorf, Karl P., 168
What's Your Raashee?, 9
Wiggins, Martin, 77
Wordsworth, William, 179
Worth, Ellis, 165
Worthen, W.B., 5, 35
Wright, John, 165